To Richard
from
Vern & Connie
Madison
1 - 14 - 05

Living the Dream

Sailing the South Pacific and Southeast Asia

By

Vern and Connie Madison

authorHOUSE™

1663 LIBERTY DRIVE, SUITE 200
BLOOMINGTON, INDIANA 47403
(800) 839-8640
WWW.AUTHORHOUSE.COM

First published by AuthorHouse 08/04/05

ISBN: 1-4208-3818-0 (sc)

Printed in the United States of America
Bloomington, Indiana

This book is printed on acid-free paper.

TABLE OF CONTENTS

We are "dragged" into a village wedding
Three equator crossings going up a river in Borneo
Third try's the charm: we escape from Borneo
Illustrations

Gales, currents, and mechanical failures
Crossing the busy Singapore Strait
Christmas aboard *Tainui*
Playing the land-and-sea breeze in the Strait of Malacca
Exotic, but gruesome, religious festival in Malaysia

Fantasy Islands of Phang Nga Bay
Side trip to Lake Toba in Sumatra
Tainui's steel hull disaster
Eighteen months on the hard in Phuket, Thailand
Nostalgic return to Penang Island
Tainui is sold
Illustrations

The Scary night watches
A woman's life at sea
Boatyard blues
The joy of travel and adventure
Illustrations

INTRODUCTION

Our seven-year retirement cruise was the result of the combination of two major factors in our lives: our longtime interest in international travel and our 25 years of recreational sailing.

Our interest in other cultures led us to interrupt our careers—Connie as a schoolteacher and me as a minister—for four years while Vern served on the staff of the Peace Corps in Malaysia. This in-depth involvement in another culture fueled a desire in us to become full time travelers rather than occasional tourists when we retired. *Living the Dream* is the story of how we, as persons of ordinary means, used sailing to fulfill our retirement dream of becoming full-time travelers.

We soon discovered that we were not alone in that dream. Whenever we told people about our sailing, especially when we made our video presentations to groups afterward, "I had dreamed of doing that myself" was a surprisingly frequent response. It seemed as though a kind of Jungian archetype of sailing off into the sunset was imbedded in the collective human psyche. *Living the Dream* is our tell-it-like-it-is, unvarnished account of what is it <u>really</u> like for relatively "ordinary" people to live the dream of sailing a small yacht halfway around the world.

Although <u>Living the Dream</u> was written in Vern's voice for the sake of simplicity, it was very much a joint effort. The book was written from Connie's extensive day-to-day journal. With the exception of Connie's chapter, Vern did the actual writing, but we continually reviewed and edited the text together. The original artwork for the cover design was done by our son, Tom Madison, graphic artist and lecturer in the art department at Oregon State University, making the finished product a family effort.

Vern and Connie Madison

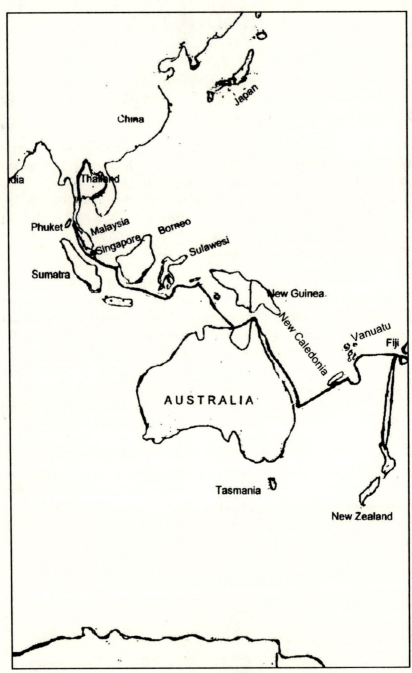

Voyage of *Tainui*

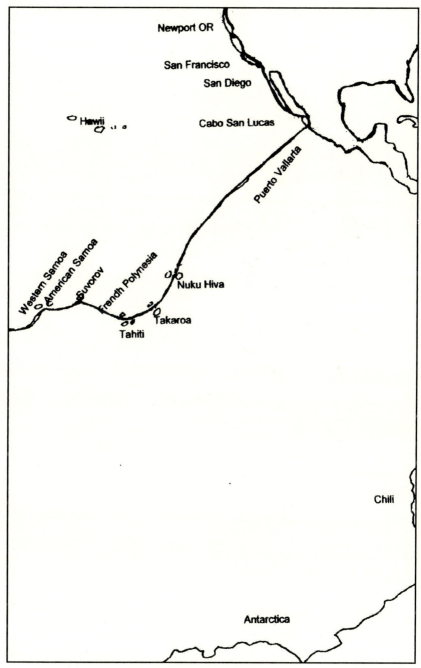

Voyage *of Tainui*

CHAPTER ONE

PREPARATION

The Satellite Navigation System beeped. I left Connie in the cockpit and ducked below to check our position. We were at 07:31:20 north and 128:25:15 west-halfway between Puerto Vallarta, Mexico, and Nuku Hiva, French Polynesia1,500 miles from land in any direction. We were approaching the equator and about to enter the Inter Continental Transition Zone, or doldrums—infamous for its lack of wind.

We had embarked on our retirement cruise—a seven-year sailing saga from Newport, Oregon, to Phuket, Thailand. I had no regrets about taking early retirement; this had been my lifelong dream. Growing up in Seattle, where my father worked on the waterfront, I'd watched the ships coming and going, read sailing books and magazines, and dreamed of sailing my own boat to faraway places. At age 16, I got a summer job on an Army Transport ship that sailed from Seattle to Hawaii, Guam, Okinawa, Yokohama, and San Francisco.

For Connie, it was another story. She had always regarded my dream of sailing away as a romantic fantasy—not even a potential reality. She grew up in the desert community of Coachella Valley, and although she loved to travel, she feared the water, largely due to a near-drowning experience when we were in college. Our early boating experiences also did not bode well for my dream. When I took her sailing on a lake in calm water, she panicked every time the boat tipped even a little a bit. My chances of persuading her to cross an ocean in a yacht had seemed slim—yet here she was years later, on our 35-foot cutter, *Tainui*, 1500 watery miles from land and showing no fear.

How did this come about? Well, it didn't happen overnight. We began sailing with a 10-foot car-top dinghy when our children were young. The kids and I loved it, and Connie would consent to go out on a calm lake in warm weather. Later, in Malaysia, where I was a Peace Corps officer, we sailed a 14-foot day sailor on the Straits of Malacca. Connie enjoyed sailing on calm days with the water temperature at 85 degrees.

Her fear returned back in the States when we began spending our family vacations in a 22-foot sailboat. We towed it behind our car to Anacortes, Washington, and sailed in the inland waters of Washington State and British Columbia. Our teenaged sons loved to sail with the rail in the water and the boat banging and splashing through the waves. Connie begged in vain for them to slow down, and once she even retired to the "V" berth in tears. Her worst scare was when our younger son fell overboard while leaning out to balance the boat on one of the boys' wild rides. We recovered him quickly, but "man overboard" remained her greatest sailing fear.

Her feelings began to change with our next boat, a very seaworthy 29-foot sloop. It was too big to put on a trailer, so to get from Newport, Oregon, to our favorite cruising grounds we had to sail offshore—up the Oregon and Washington coasts and in through the Straits of Juan de Fuca. Connie came along, provided we stopped every night, and I felt a faint flicker of hope that my sailing dreams might come true. When she eventually agreed to sail both day and night on the two-day downwind return trips, that flicker of hope grew brighter. Eventually, Connie became so comfortable on the ocean that her only condition for sailing away was that we buy a steel boat. She had read stories of wood and fiberglass boats hitting reefs, whales, or floating cargo containers and sinking. I was only too happy to meet that condition, which was how we came into the possession of *Tainui*.

We found *Tainui* lying in Richmond, a suburb of Vancouver, B.C. She was "salty"-looking, with a blue hull, a white house, and teak decks, trim, and steering wheel. *Tainui* had been named after one of the huge, double-hulled ocean-going canoes that originally brought the Maori tribes to New Zealand from somewhere in the South Pacific (their point of departure is not known) in A.D. 1300 or 1400. We don't know what plans her previous owner had when he chose the name, but we kept it because we liked the sound of it and because New Zealand was on our itinerary. *Tainui* was a 10-ton, steel-hulled, heavy-displacement full-keel cruiser. She was 35 feet long on deck, with a 3.5-foot bowsprit. Her beam was 10.5 feet, and she drew 4.5 feet of water. She was cutter-rigged with a single mast and two headsails: a jib from the top of her mast to the tip of her bowsprit and an inner staysail that stretched from two-thirds of the way up her mast to her true bow. Her auxiliary engine was a 25-horsepower two-cylinder diesel.

Although many used boats came fully equipped, we chose one with minimal gear and bought all new equipment. We installed it all ourselves so we would understand it when we needed to maintain it. With this in mind, we spent only a little over half of our budget on the boat itself and the rest for equipment and modifications. It takes a lot of work and expense to prepare a yacht for crossing oceans. Many sailors have made the mistake of spending so much on the purchase price that they didn't have enough money left to finish outfitting their boat.

When we bought *Tainui*, our scheduled retirement and departure were still two years away, which gave us ample time for outfitting her. Before we took her from Canada, where labor prices were good, we had a blue canvas dodger built to protect the companionway. We installed a VHF marine radio (a short-range ship-to-shore radio) and an EPIRB (Emergency Position Indicating Radio Beacon) in Seattle before sailing *Tainui* to our homeport of Newport, Oregon, where we continued the outfitting. On most weekends for the next two years we drove the 80 miles from our home in Salem to the Embarcadero Marina in Newport on Friday evening, worked on the boat, and returned home late Sunday night. Sometimes it was hard to get up and go to work on Monday morning.

We installed two autopilots: a wind-driven for when we were sailing and an electric one that steered by its compass when we were motoring. We would not have attempted to cross oceans without them. With no self-steering the two of us would have been stuck with the exhausting task of trading off hand-steering 24 hours a day.

The list of necessities grew and grew. We ordered a genoa jib and storm jib from Lee Sails of Hong Kong. We bought a 10-foot folding Portabote to go with *Tainui's* seven-foot wooden sailing dinghy and a 3.5-horsepower outboard, which could work on either of them. We also bought expensive binoculars, a 44-lb. Bruce anchor, a stereo system, and a brass clock and barometer. Our most expensive problem showed up on that first trip to Newport; the engine developed a serious oil-system problem. We pulled it out and hauled it to the dealer in Portland to be completely rebuilt, after which we reinstalled it ourselves.

There was also the matter of navigational aids and tools. At first, the price of satellite navigation was too high for us, so we bought a sextant with its attendant Nautical Almanac and Sight Reduction Tables, plus a couple of instruction books on celestial navigation. We acquired navigational charts, weather charts, and sailing directions for as far as Australia. I installed a radar, and after passing the exams for a General Class Ham License, a ham radio.

We did not trust *Tainui's* eight plastic portholes for serious offshore sailing so we replaced them with new bronze ones. *Tainui* did not come with the traditional double-berth in the bow; instead, a large head (marine toilet) and a child's bunk occupied that area. With the help of our skilled friend Glen Barton, we built in a diagonal double berth forward and installed a smaller head aft, at the foot of the companionway stairs—a more convenient place for wet gear when coming below in bad weather. We had a combination ice chest and chart table installed and a new galley table built from a beautiful piece of wood that had been in the family for years. These were the major projects, but we did many, many other tasks. Even after we sailed away, equipment changes and general maintenance were never-ending.

Our next problem was to get off the dock and get going. It was apparent that the list of "necessary" boat projects would never be completed. We had seen couples keep doing preparation forever and never leave the dock. Not wanting to be like them, we set the target date of July 10, 1988, for going—ready or not. When that day came, we threw our unfinished projects into the lazerette (the large locker under the stern deck), cast off the lines, and set sail—not south for Mexico and the South Pacific, but north for Puget Sound. Because the cyclone season in Mexico lasted into December, we were in no hurry to go there.

We spent the summer in the Puget Sound area, combining working on the boat and pleasure sailing with family and friends. A three-day cruise with my mother was the highlight of the summer. We picked her up in Anacortes and sailed her back to Seattle via the San Juan Islands. She particularly enjoyed our stops at the John Wayne Marina in Sequim, where we ate at the "True Grits" restaurant, and the quaint old seaport town of Port Townsend. Although she had never sailed before, she was not bothered by our rough crossing of the Straits of Juan de Fuca. In fact, she sat in the cockpit listening to a Seahawks game on the radio and barely noticed *Tainui's* rocking and rolling. She felt a lot better about our planned trip after experiencing how sturdy and seaworthy *Tainui* was.

Work tasks in Puget Sound included upgrading our icebox to a refrigeration system, replacing our diesel range with a propane cook stove, which would be much cooler in the tropics, and installing a six-person emergency life raft. We were able to add a Satellite Navigation System (Sat Nav) when the price dropped from $2,500 to $1,100. We felt much more secure with this system. Sextant navigation is complex, and celestial bodies are sometimes not visible for days in storms, which would be when we might need them the most. The sextant remained as our backup to the satellite system.

Our summer sailing in Puget Sound served as a kind of shakedown cruise and prepared us for the vicissitudes of full-time sailing. The starter fell off, the alternator strap broke, the engine overheated, and the batteries failed, all at the most inconvenient times. We could have called it our "shake apart" cruise!

The evening before our departure from Seattle, our son Larry came down to the dock to see us off. This would be our last contact before we headed off into the unknown. It was an emotional moment when he hugged us and said good-bye. Although all of our children supported our endeavor, they were still anxious about our safety. For the next seven years, Larry and his wife, Joyce, acted diligently as our agents, handling our finances, collecting and forwarding our mail, and rounding up and shipping parts to us in faraway places.

The next morning, September 12, 1988, we were off. It was a balmy day and we were helped up Puget Sound by a favorable tide. We arrived in Port Townsend early enough to enjoy a lazy, sunny fall afternoon of prowling the marinas and exploring the waterfront of this lovely historic town, with its Victorian captains' houses on the hill overlooking the harbor.

As we motored out the Straits of Juan de Fuca the next morning, a huge geyser of spray suddenly erupted a hundred feet into the air across the straits from us. A nuclear submarine had blown its ballast tanks and burst to the surface in an emergency ascent exercise. [Note: As we write this, a nuclear submarine making a similar ascent sank a Japanese fishing trawler off Hawaii with the loss of nine lives, a similar ascent].

We spent the night in Neah Bay, an Indian reservation at the mouth of the Straits of Juan de Fuca. Neah Bay is one of the few harbors on the coast that is not riverine. Without a river current, there is no dangerous bar, so the harbor can be entered safely at any state of the tide. It is 25 feet deep with good holding in mud throughout. We anchored near the narrow, low-lying sand spit that separated the bay from the ocean. Although the spit provided no shelter from the stiff wind blowing in off the sea, it was an excellent breakwater, creating a flat sea for a peaceful night's rest.

In the morning we set up our electric autopilot and motored out to Tatoosh Island, which marks the entrance to the Straits of Juan de Fuca. It had a tall lighthouse and diaphone foghorn whose low, mournful tone sounded intermittently in spite of the clear weather. A Honolulu-registered sailboat named *Columbine* followed us out and turned south with us when we cleared the island.

As we motored south under our electric autopilot, *Tainui* made big S curves, veering out to sea and then slowly turning all the way back toward shore. We experimented with various headings and found that she would steer accurately in any direction but south—rather unfortunate for a boat bound for Mexico! The wind vane steered us beautifully under sail, but when there was no wind, we had to hand-steer under motor.

With our limited self-steering, we decided to stop every night. Sitting at the wheel and staring at the dim glow of the red compass light through the long night watches would have been tedious. All instrument lights in the cockpit were red, because, unlike white light, red light did not require our eyes to adjust when we looked out into the darkness.

Our first refuge was La Push on Quileute Bay, 35 miles down the coast. We wound our way through a shallow inlet, bumped bottom twice, and tied up to a rickety abandoned dock with a sunken fishing boat alongside. La Push was on the Quileute Indian Reservation and had no visitor' facilities at that time, so we ate aboard *Tainui*.

Shortly after we arrived, *Columbine* came in and tied up alongside of us. Her captain, Werner Kraus, was attempting a solo circumnavigation. He spent the evening aboard *Tainui*. Werner was a tall handsome German in his 40s, who had immigrated to the United States when he was 16 years old. Being alone, Werner stopped every night to sleep, so we decided to buddy-boat down the coast. Werner and I studied the tide table and our charts and decided that we needed to leave at 5:00 the next morning to make the 90-mile run to Gray's Harbor in time to cross its bar in daylight. We would also get in before a predicted strong evening ebb tide, which could have made the Gray's Harbor bar rough or even impassible.

It was pitch black at 5:30 a.m. when we followed *Columbine* out of the shallow inlet. At first, a small island to the north provided protection, but as soon as we cleared it we were hit with heavy northwest swells that crested into steep, choppy seas. Each time *Tainui* crashed into a wave, she momentarily lost her forward motion. The wind and waves were pushing us toward a cluster of dangerous rocks to the south. We tried to find out how close they were with our powerful spotlight, but its beam rebounded off the mist and blinded us. Our radar signals bounced back off the big waves, filling its screen with bright green "sea clutter." With the big seas crashing into the rocks, *Tainui* would be pounded severely if she were driven onto them, and we would be lucky to get off safely. Hearts pounding and palms sweating, we fought our way north every time *Tainui* picked up some speed, and we prayed we would clear the rocks. The two hours before our depth sounder indicated that we were well past the rocks and could safely turn south seemed like an eternity. This narrow escape was a sobering lesson: crossing that rock-strewn bar in the dark into a rough sea was a bad decision.

We lost contact with Werner in our struggle in the dark, but found him in the early morning light waiting for us after his own ordeal in the dark. We regained our composure as we motored alongside *Columbine* all the way to Gray's Harbor on a sunny, windless day. With no electric autopilot, we traded off hand steering during the 12-hour run. We picked up the black-and-white "GH" entrance buoy at 5:00 p.m. and crossed the Gray's Harbor bar with no difficulty. Once inside the bay, we followed the channel markers around to the public docks in the town of Westport and berthed among the fishing boats. After dinner ashore with Werner, we took hot showers at the fishermen's dock. Warm, clean, and well fed, we turned in early and had a good night's rest.

The next leg of our journey would take us to the infamous Columbia River bar. With any sea running, all of the bars on the West Coast were dangerous on an ebb tide. The outgoing flow pushes up dangerous steep waves when it meets the incoming ocean swells. With the huge Columbia River pouring out of it, the Columbia River bar is one of the most dangerous in the world in adverse conditions. Full-sized ocean-going freighters have been sunk or driven ashore attempting to cross it in bad weather. Werner and I had listened to the evening weather report and concluded that conditions would be just right at our estimated time of arrival if we left in the morning. However, the tide tables showed that a small ebb tide would be running out of Gray's Harbor the next morning. We got up early and checked out the bar from a lookout tower. It didn't look too bad from there, so we motored out, but as is often the case, it turned out to be rougher up close than it had looked from a distance. There was no particular danger this time; there was no wind and there were no rocks to dodge. It was just wet and rough going as we crashed through the big steep waves created when big ocean rollers met the outgoing tide. We ploughed out to the sea buoy and turned south once again. This course put us in the troughs of the waves. With no wind to steady us, we rolled so heavily that we had to brace ourselves at the wheel to keep from sliding off our seats.

45 miles later at the Columbia bar, the seas calmed down as predicted. After we crossed the bar, we faced hundreds of the small boats participating in a salmon derby. We surfed in on smooth swells, dodging the fishing lines, sometimes with barely room to pass between

boats. We turned north and motored 11 miles up the narrow channel to the fishing village of Ilwaco on the Washington side of the river. We berthed at the public docks and Werner joined us aboard *Tainui* for a spaghetti dinner. Later that night a 45-knot wind blew up at sea without warning. On our marine radio we listened to accounts of the Coast Guard rescuing several small boats that wouldn't have gone out if their crews had known the gale was coming. It was disconcerting to realize that we could also have been caught out like that, even though we listened to marine weather broadcasts several times a day.

After recrossing a calm Columbia bar the next morning, we were back in Oregon waters motor-sailing toward Garibaldi, near Tillamook, on a beautiful warm day. Mist obscured the jetties as we approached the bar at dusk, but this time our radar worked brilliantly–the north and south jetties appeared on the screen as crisp green parallel dotted lines. The bar was calm as we entered Tillamook Bay at Barview and wended our way through the narrow dredged channel in the shallow muddy bay to the over-crowded fish docks at Garibaldi. The harbormaster had us raft up outside of two fishing boats tied to a high pier. To get up on the pier, we scrambled across the cluttered stern of the first boat and then climbed up onto the roof of the second. We got plenty of this exercise, because the Coast Guard closed the bar for the next three days.

Every morning Werner and I walked to the Coast Guard office to see if we could leave, with no success. In the meantime, we entertained ourselves by enjoying the antics of pelicans that perched on pilings and fished in the bay and watching the local fire department put out a house fire. On the fourth day, Werner and I took a good look at the bar from a hill and found it safely passable for our heavy-displacement cruising vessels—we had already survived much worse. We walked to the Coast Guard station and pled our case. The Coast Guard officer agreed with us, but explained that, if he opened the bar, the dozens of small open boats fishing for salmon near the mouth of the bay would go out where they would not be safe in existing conditions. Finally, he took pity on us and asked us when we could get our vessels to the bar. We told him that we could be there at 8:00 a.m., so he announced on the marine radio that the bar would be open that morning for one hour only, from 8:00 to 9:00 a.m. This gave us enough time to get out, but the smaller boats would not have time to go out and get back in before the bar closed. It worked like a charm.

Having escaped Tillamook Bay, another day of warm, comfortable motor-sailing brought us to our home port of Newport, Oregon, where we parted company with Werner and spent a week visiting with friends and family and doing some more work on the boat. I was especially anxious to solve the electric autopilot problem. I called the company, but its technician was not very helpful. When I told him that the autopilot would work in any direction but south, he asked, "When the boat is pointing south, is there any metal south of the autopilot that might attract the magnetic needle of its compass?" The autopilot was at the stern of the boat, so I replied, "Nothing but 10 tons of steel." He said that they had little experience with steel boats and didn't know what to recommend. The solution came to me when I remembered that the compass adjuster in Seattle had compensated *Tainui's* main compass by strategically placing small magnets around it. I bought some tiny magnets at a hardware store and put one on the back of the autopilot's compass housing. It worked! When *Tainui* was pointed south, the little magnet on the north side of the compass compensated for the big hunk of steel to the south of it. The autopilot continued to steer accurately in all other directions.

CHAPTER TWO

NEWPORT TO SAN DIEGO

We left Newport on September 28, 1988, for a leisurely, harbor-hopping trip down the coast. We had plenty of time because we needed to start south before the weather turned bad in the Northwest, but didn't want to leave San Diego for Mexico until January, in order to be well clear of the hurricane season.

Our first stop was to be Coos Bay, 90 miles to the south. We left Newport at 11:30 p.m. in order to arrive in daylight the next day. We had no trouble sailing out of our well-marked homeport in the dark, but the trip was an eventful one that taught us a few more lessons about ocean cruising. Out in the ocean there were big seas coming from the northwest with a following wind, so we let out the mainsail and ran downwind. The swells came across *Tainui's* stern at an angle, causing her to roll severely. The motion of the boat and the excitement of our first night out made it hard for us to sleep. While I was on watch, Connie tried sleeping in the V-berth and found that the bow was a wild and noisy place. It rolled and rose up like an elevator, then fell back with a thud and a splash on every wave. She wound up sleeping on some cushions on the cabin sole (floor). It had the least violent motion on the boat because it was close to *Tainui's* pivotal center.

During the day we rigged *Tainui* "wing-and-wing." I snapped one end of the heavy whisker pole to the mast and the other to the back corner of the big genoa jib and hoisted up the pole with the staysail halyard. Next I pulled the boom, which holds the mainsail, as far out as possible on the other side of the vessel and secured it with a line that ran forward to the bow. This line was called a "preventer" because it prevented the boom from getting back-winded, blowing across the stern, and crashing into the rigging on the opposite side. That could snap the boom in two or break the rigging and bring the mast down. It was also dangerous to a crewmember who forgot to duck—it is called the "boom"! Setting the sails up wing-and-wing was heavy work on a rolling deck, but once it was done, *Tainui* picked up speed. With her sails "winged-out" on each side, she rolled down the ocean like a giant bird.

We no sooner got this rig up than the Coast Guard tried to get us to take it down again. We knew by the big red diagonal stripe on its bow that the gray ship shadowing us on the horizon was a Coast Guard cutter. They launched a boarding party in a powerful inflatable craft called a Hurricane, which came flying across the swells toward us. On the radio they requested that we heave to so they could board us. I figured that they might not be able to force us to heave to if it placed us in any danger, so I replied that we would heave to if we had to, but that it could be dangerous for "a couple of old retired people" to handle our heavy whisker pole again under such rough conditions. Apparently I guessed right, because they dropped back, conferred with their "mother ship," then announced that we could continue on our course and they would attempt to board us under way, which switched all the risk back onto them.

Our next move was to inform them that we had a copy of the papers from a recent Coast Guard boarding in Newport. After another consultation, they came within reach and we handed the paper across to them. They dropped back, read and initialed it, powered up again and handed the form back to us across the waves, and let us go on our way. We were much relieved. I did not relish the task of pulling down the wing-and-wing rig and then setting it up again—even if, at age 57, I didn't feel like "an old retired person"!

We had a more exciting "lesson" as we approached Coos Bay. The winds had increased to 20 knots and bigger seas had built up. When it was time to enter the bar, Connie took the wheel and started the engine so that she could handle the boat when the sails came down. We were no longer sailing wing-and-wing, but under a reefed main and small jib, making six knots with our lee rail in the water. I cautiously crept up the wet slanting deck, trailing my safety-harness tether behind me. Whenever either of us left the cockpit at sea, we wore a harness with a tether that we shackled to the jack line that ran along the full length of the deck. When I reached the bow, the boat lurched and threw me against the lifelines on the low side of the boat. For a second I was suspended out over the side looking straight down at the water. Before I could recover, the upper lifeline broke and I toppled head over heels into the ocean. Man overboard! Connie's worst nightmare was suddenly a reality!

Initially, I went under the water. Fortunately I had hold of the lifeline and was also tethered to the boat. When I came up again, I was being towed across the surface at six knots. I waited for *Tainui* to roll toward me, and when the deck was within reach, I threw my leg over the rail, grabbed a lifeline stanchion, and rolled my waterlogged body onto the deck. The whole thing didn't take more than two minutes, but it seemed longer to me and like forever to Connie. She tried to stop the boat by turning off the engine, but the sails kept it going. When I was safely back aboard, I went forward again in spite of Connie's urging to the contrary, dropped the jib, furled the main, and got *Tainui* safely into the bay before I dried off and changed into warm clothes. Maybe because of the adrenalin rush, I didn't feel cold until I had completed these tasks.

Incidents like this provided valuable learning experiences for us. We had become captains of our own vessel without the years of apprenticeship that professional sailors have before becoming captains of commercial vessels. We had to learn as we went, by surviving and learning from our mistakes, gradually building up knowledge and experience, we hoped without running into something that we couldn't handle too soon. A short time before our overboard incident, a retired couple starting out on their maiden voyage in an expensive new yacht got in trouble in the Coos Bay bar. He fell overboard and swam to the jetty, but she lost control of the boat and it crashed into the jetty. It sank and she went down with the ship. Obviously he was not tethered to the boat.

The Coos Bay Coast Guard boarded and inspected our boat as soon as we tied up to the dock. We guessed that this was part of a deal worked out between headquarters and their ship when they decided not to board us at sea.

After we recovered our composure from our man-overboard experience, we debriefed to see what we could learn from it. We concluded that in similar situations, the person at the wheel should stop the boat by using the engine to turn the boat into the wind, and then keep it running in neutral so it could be used to maneuver the boat as needed to rescue the person overboard. This procedure is especially important because the boat will drift downwind from the victim, requiring the onboard crewmember to power the boat into the wind to get back to the person in the water. This incident reinforced our conviction to *never* go forward without a harness and tether. It would be embarrassing (to say the least) to fall overboard from a self-steering yacht and watch it sail over the horizon without you!

We continued to analyze our close calls and other people's near misses and disasters when we could get the details. By the time we finished our cruise, we personally knew eight boats that were lost in the South Pacific, mostly on reefs. Fortunately, there was a loss of life in only one case—the sinking of an old wooden boat in a storm with three men aboard. The reef incidents, all of which could have been prevented, were due to mistakes in navigation or errors in judgment by the crew. Their accidents became vicarious experiences that substantially added to our knowledge of seamanship and navigation.

After a short stay, we left Coos Bay at 4:00 p.m. for an overnight sail to Crescent City, California. The bar was rough as we went out. Once again we fought our way out to sea against the wind and the waves. *Tainui* stalled out to a dead stop when she bashed into an oncoming wave and slowly gained speed until she slammed into the next one. It took us three hours of this punishment to get six miles out to sea and turn south toward California. Once again *Tainui* rolled wildly as she sailed downwind in the troughs of the big waves. Exasperated, I centered the staysail by winching in both its sheets as tightly as possible. It acted as a kind of keel in the air, which dampened the roll somewhat. When the wind died during the night, we started the engine and set up the electric autopilot, which immediately blew its fuse. It was the only fuse in the electrical system that we did not have a spare for. We added spare autopilot fuses to our perpetual parts list and took turns hand-steering through the night. In the morning the wind and the rough seas returned, but we were relieved to set the sails and turn the steering over to the wind vane.

After a challenging day at sea, we radioed the Crescent City Coast Guard for a bar report and were happy to find that it was passable. It was a great relief to tie up to a quiet slip in the marina and relax. Although *Tainui* sat as still as a rock, we both had the sensation of motion for half the night. This is a common experience. People have even become "land sick" from this phantom sense of motion!

We were glad to have the time to harbor hop on our way to San Diego. We loved exploring small harbor towns and meeting people. In Crescent City we took a day off and walked around town, ate out, did laundry, and walked the docks to look at boats and meet fellow cruisers. We arranged to buddy-boat down the coast for a while with Bob and Carol McCann on *Sasaparilla*, who also were heading for Mexico.

The next morning we left Crescent City for a day sail to Eureka with Bob and Carol sailing alongside in *Sasaparilla*. As a result of our chance meeting on the dock, they buddy-boated with us all the way to San Diego, shared our experiences in Mexico, and have remained lifelong friends. The seas were so calm that day that Connie baked muffins, using her oven at sea for the first time. In the afternoon we saw what appeared to be a feeding frenzy of sea lions with dozens of gulls flying above. We sailed over to investigate, and some humpbacked whales surfaced close to us. We got some excellent videos of them diving with their giant flukes suspended in the air for a moment before they slipped below the surface of the water. The electric autopilot steered brilliantly all day after I put in a new fuse and changed to a larger compensating magnet.

Columbine was already at Eureka. Bob and Carol invited Werner and us for dinner on *Sasaparilla* to share a salmon they had caught under way. This spontaneous socializing was a regular part of the fun of cruising. A member of the Eureka Yacht Club stopped by all the visiting yachts and invited them to a club potluck the next night. *Columbine* went on, but *Tainui* and *Sasaparilla* stayed another day to participate. That evening Bob motored us across the river in *Sasaparilla* to "old town," where we put on our foul weather gear and went sightseeing in the rain. It was better than a rainy day at sea!

The next leg was an overnight trip to Fort Bragg. We had to pass Mendocino Head, which had a reputation for strong winds and heavy seas. Northbound ocean tugs had stood still at full power against those seas and winds! The wind tended to build in the afternoon, so *Tainui* and *Sasaparilla* made an early morning departure. We left in calm wind and moderate seas with visibility limited to three miles by fog. We rounded Mendocino Head just before the wind came up and had rough sailing in the afternoon. The wind decreased at sunset, and by midnight there was no wind at all, but big swells continued to roll in from the west and the fog was so dense that we had zero visibility. With no wind to stabilize us, *Tainui* rolled in the troughs and life aboard was so miserable that we wanted to find shelter.

Our cruising guide, <u>Charlie's Charts for the West Coast</u>, recommended an anchorage under the lee of Mendocino Head named Shelter Cove. It sounded good so we contacted *Sasaparilla*. They were not enjoying these conditions any more than we were, so we both decided to go in and anchor there. We were nervous as we felt our way in under radar in the dark, thick fog. There was no room for error because the buoy that marked the anchorage was only a quarter mile offshore. Our radar picked up the buoy from a half a mile away, and both boats anchored near it.

We tried to sleep but the name of the cove turned out to be a misnomer, at least that night with the seas rolling straight in from the west. Without any wind to keep her bow into the waves, *Tainui* drifted crossways to the seas and rolled mercilessly in the troughs. We both bedded down on the cabin sole—we couldn't fall to the floor if we were already there! Even that didn't work because the cove was so scary and noisy, we couldn't relax. The cove was surrounded by high rock cliffs. The waves crashing into them made a noise like muffled thunder that echoed around the cove. We were so close to shore that we kept an anchor watch on the radar. If we dragged our anchor, the waves would have us on the beach in a few minutes. We conferred with Bob and Carol again and all agreed to leave at first light. By then, the fog had lifted and we were shocked to see how close we were to the cliffs. We also saw the ominous sight of a sailboat lying on its side on the beach. We weighed anchor and gladly bid a not-so-fond-farewell to Shelter Cove, and "Thanks a lot!" to Charlie's Charts.

We motored on to Fort Bragg in lumpy seas with fair visibility. Fort Bragg had one of the narrowest entrances on the coast. It was so small that we could not make it out from the sea buoy, and we felt our way toward shore through the kelp fields on faith that we would find the entrance before we ran aground. It didn't open up to view until we were right on it, and it was so narrow we could practically spit on either side as we passed through; there was no way we could have passed a fishing boat coming out. The channel up to the marina was not much wider.

We had heard rumors that the harbor mistress at Fort Bragg was pompous and strictly required that yachts present their ship's papers— a common practice in foreign ports but unique at a local marina. She had the reputation of reprimanding sailors who did not comply with her strict rules. We were prepared and passed after a careful scrutiny of our official ship's papers. A story was circulating in the marina about Werner's check-in. His official Coast Guard ship's document had a number of blanks marked "information unavailable." The harbor mistress was incensed. How could she fill out her precious forms? Werner replied in a loud voice, "Oh, that's just the U.S. Coast Guard, not the *Harbor Mistress of Fort Bragg*!" Amused clerks were said to have snickered at her behind her back.

On our overnight passage from Fort Bragg to San Francisco, the weather was sunny but cool during the day, then clear, calm, and cold at night. We passed occasional whales migrating south, probably bound for their calving grounds in the Sea of Cortez. We were motoring close to shore, so we navigated by Loran rather than Sat Nav. The Loran gave continuous data from chains of radio stations onshore, whereas the Sat Nav gave fixes only when a satellite passed over and sometimes they were hours apart.

During the night, just when we needed it the most, the Loran quit. While we kept track of our distance offshore by radar and depth sounder, I studied the Loran owner's manual and found that Loran signals came from chains of radio stations and that we had passed out of the range of our original chain. After I reprogrammed the Loran to acquire the next chain, it went back to work for us. Years later GPS (Global Positioning System) brought incredibly accurate continuous satellite navigation, which rendered Loran obsolete.

The morning dawned crystal clear as we approached San Francisco Bay. We were thrilled at the sight of the huge red Golden Gate Bridge towering over us, with the sun rising above the city of San Francisco in the background. Sailing alongside *Sasaparilla,* we took turns taking pictures of each other's boats with the bridge and city in the background. Entering San Francisco Bay on this glorious morning was the high point of our trip so far.

Inside the bay, we turned north and anchored in a free anchorage at Sausalito. Layers of garments from the cold night came off as the sun rose on an unusually warm October morning in the Bay Area. We were anchored amid a mixed fleet of boats that ranged from luxury yachts to homemade derelicts. During our three days at Sausalito we had our first visits from friends. We ate dinner in Tiburon with Dr. Gordon and Jean Clappison from Independence, Oregon, and their daughter Patricia, a seminary student in the Bay Area. Connie and Jean had played the violin together in the Salem Pops Orchestra. Later Chuck Palmerlee, a seminary classmate of mine, and his wife, Joy, visited us aboard *Tainui.*

We needed dock facilities to work on our boat, so we sailed to the Marina Village in Alameda. The trip across San Francisco Bay on a sunny afternoon with picture postcard scenes all around us was exhilarating. We slipped past Alcatraz Island with the Golden Gate Bridge in the background, and when the afternoon wind reached 35 knots, we reefed down and raced past the San Francisco Yacht Club with our rail in the water and the city skyline in the background. The wind slackened as we passed under the Bay Bridge, with the Coit Tower and Telegraph Hill rising above us, and motored up the Alameda Channel close beside the runway of the Alameda Naval Air Station. We spent a week at the new Marina Village installing an automatic tuner and insulated backstay antenna for the ham radio and doing other tasks from our never-ending jobs list.

The marina's beautiful accommodations with free hot showers were a welcome luxury. Laurie Sinclair, daughter of our Salem friends Keith and Louise Putman, and her husband, Lowell, visited us at the marina. I had performed their wedding ceremony at the Pitman's' home in Salem and they were now living in the Bay Area. The day before we left the marina, we went sightseeing in San Francisco. We visited the waterfront, Ghirardelli Square, Pier 39, the Cannery, and the Maritime Museum. At 89 degrees, it was a record high for the date in San Francisco. We didn't see 89 degrees again until we reached Mexico.

On our way out we stopped for the night at Sausalito, then left early the next morning along with *Sasaparilla*. Under the Golden Gate Bridge we plunged into a blanket of fog so thick that we could barely see from one end of the boat to the other We were sailing in the separation zone between the incoming and outgoing shipping lanes and could hear the loud thump-thump of ships' engines on both sides of us. Being so close to these behemoths without seeing them gave us an eerie feeling. Fortunately, the big ships made excellent radar targets. We would not have braved the traffic in that fog without it.

When we had enough sea room, we turned south and threaded our way between the ships in the incoming traffic lane. After we cleared the traffic, we motored all the way to Half Moon Bay in patchy fog and rough seas. *Sasaparilla* went in and anchored first, and we came alongside and rafted up to them.

We all went ashore and took a hike around the little town of Princeton. We were surprised at the number of unfinished and abandoned do-it-yourself boat projects on the shore. Most of them were ferro-cement hulls. Our guess was that because these hulls were so cheap to build, some people started with hulls so big that they could not afford to finish them. The cost of the hull is usually only one-fifth the cost of the completed boat.

The next day we had an exhilarating sail to Monterey Bay. The sun was shining brightly in an azure blue sky with high wispy white clouds. The wind built to a steady 20 knots from the northwest, producing dark blue six-foot wind-whipped waves crested with white foam. *Tainui* fairly flew through the water. *Sasaparilla* raced alongside, spewing the froth from under her bow that sailors call "a bone in her teeth." I disengaged the self-steering and took the wheel to feel the thrill of handling *Tainui* at her best. We reveled in the feeling of the wind in our faces, the sight of the gleaming white rock-hard sails against the blue sky, the sound of the wind singing in the rigging, the gurgling white wake, and the snapping of the American flag on the backstay—a real sailor's high! We entered calm, beautiful Monterey Bay in the late afternoon, still in high spirits, and anchored alongside *Sasaparilla* off the town of Santa Cruz.

We all went ashore in *Sasaparilla*'s inflatable dinghy to explore the town. We had to land on the beach where there was a little surf running. We rode in on a wave, jumped out, and dragged the dinghy up the beach, but we weren't quick enough and got caught by the next wave. We felt a little self-conscious walking around town with our pants wet. We soon learned that it was a cruising sailor's cliché that you can tell the sailors in town by their wet backsides.

The next day we sailed across the bay to the city of Monterey. The bay teemed with life. Sea lions swam in the water, and gulls and pelicans flew overhead. A group of dolphins came up from behind us, swam within an inch of the bow, surfed off of our bow wave, and circled back and did it again. It was incredible that they could come so close without touching *Tainui*'s hull. We took turns standing out on the bowsprit where we could look straight down at them and see their wonderful streamlined bodies under the water. We were so close that we could have stepped on them when they surfaced beneath us. They appeared to be friendly, playful creatures.

We radioed ahead and managed to secure a slip in the popular and pricey Monterey Marina. At the entrance to the marina, pelicans blocked our way and refused to move until we practically pushed them aside with our bow. A group of sea lions under the pier greeted us with a loud, raucous chorus. As we approached our assigned marina slip, a mama sea otter and her baby surfaced right alongside our boat. She grabbed the baby by the back of its neck, submerged, and came up lying on her back with the baby on her chest. These cute creatures entertained us while we were their neighbors in the marina. It was a busy marina with a wide variety of fishing and recreational boats. We walked the dock and struck up interesting conversations with friendly sailors. Many of them were also on their way to Mexico.

Sightseeing in quaint and historic Monterey, we wandered through the John Steinback historical exhibits at Cannery Row and joined a guided tour of a house once occupied by Robert Louis Stevenson. (We later climbed a small mountain to his tomb in Western Samoa.)

After a good night's sleep and a lazy morning at the dock, we left in the afternoon on an overnight sail to Morro Bay. The ocean was glassy smooth, so we were treated to the noise and vibration of the diesel engine and the not-so-pleasant smell of its exhaust. The sky was obscured by a high thin overcast, but the moon must have been full because that night was unusually light with excellent visibility. The only thing notable about the trip was that everything worked perfectly.

The following noon, 15 miles out of Morro Bay, we turned in toward the high haystack-shaped rock that was a famous landmark for the entrance to the narrow channel leading to the town. We wound up-channel past the lumber mills whose tall red and white striped chimneys were also shown as landmarks on our nautical chart. The town sat on a river with a small island at midstream. We were tired from our night watch-keeping, which had required special diligence because we were sailing near shore and in a traffic area, so we anchored in the river and took a nap before we rowed ashore and explored the town.

The next morning we had breakfast ashore with Bob and Carol and new friends Les and Susan from the boat *Sunrise*. We all bought tickets to nearby Hearst Castle for the next day. Connie and I packed up our dirty clothes and spent the morning at a Laundromat—not our favorite chore.

The next day we got a lesson in the realities of life without an automobile. We learned that the bus would only take us to the town of Simeon Acres and we would have to walk the remaining three miles up a hill to Hearst Castle—in the rain! To our great relief, our bus driver took pity on us and graciously drove us all the way up to the castle.

Hearst Castle was filled with rare and beautiful artifacts from all over the world. William Randolph Hearst's guest list included celebrities from all walks of life. Our tour guide had his master's degree in history and brought the colorful past of the castle to life. He was also knowledgeable about the works of art and the architecture of the buildings.

By the time we finished our tour, the sun was out and we walked the three miles down the hill to Simeon Acres on a warm asphalt road, steaming from the recent rain. The road wound through the estate's wildlife menagerie. It was weird to see zebras grazing in the tall dry yellow-brown grass on these California hills.

The next day we made a short 20-mile hop to San Luis Bay. A long high pier that extended several hundred yards out was a sign of shallow water near shore, so we anchored well off the end of the pier. *Sasaparilla* came alongside us and we lashed the two boats together for the cocktail hour and a skippers' meeting to discuss our strategy for rounding Point Conception the next day. As was the case with Cape Mendocino, this point had a reputation for strong wind and heavy seas, which built during the day, becoming strongest in the afternoon. Once again, we planned a very early departure to try to get around the point before the strong afternoon wind built up.

We got our anchors up by 5:00 a.m. the next morning and motored around Point Conception on a flat calm sea. The wind didn't come up at all that afternoon. We didn't relish another day of motoring and we had been up early, so we decided to give <u>Charlie's Charts</u> another chance, and stop early at Charlie's recommended Coho Anchorage. We picked our way toward shore through thick kelp beds until we located the spot just off a highway drainage culvert where Charlie advised us to anchor.

We were glad we gave Charlie a second chance. We were anchored on an isolated part of the California coast in calm water near a shore that consisted of dry brown hills with no signs of life except a highway and a single set of railroad tracks. We spent a sunny afternoon relaxing aboard, followed by a peaceful night with nothing to disturb us but the sound of infrequent highway traffic and an occasional freight train rumbling along the shore. At night we could see the lights of the huge oil rigs that dotted the Santa Barbara Channel to the south of us.

At the Coho Anchorage we made a major change in our planned route to San Diego. The Santa Barbara Channel was full of traffic and oil platforms, and Santa Barbara, Ventura, Marina Del Mar, and Newport Beach all had busy and expensive marinas. After these ports, we would face the heavy ship traffic in San Pedro Bay, which served as the commercial harbor for Los Angeles and Long Beach. Our alternative was the beautiful Channel Islands 35 miles across the Santa Barbara Channel. They stretched southward to Catalina Island, which was just a 60-mile crossing from San Diego. Accordingly, we bypassed civilization and took the Channel Island route—a decision we did not regret.

We motored across the channel to Santa Cruz Island on a hot, windless day and explored several bays before we anchored in Pelican Bay along with five other yachts. In a radio chat we learned that all of us were bound for Mexico. We rafted to *Sasaparilla,* shared our evening meal, and stayed rafted up for the night—a tactic that works well only in calm water. When the anchorage turned rolly that night, it became noisy with the rubbing of the lines holding the two boats together and the boats themselves bumping and squeaking against the protective fenders inserted between them. We were not big fans of tying up with another boat at night. If conditions worsened, we would have to get up in the middle of the night, untie, and reanchor. Anchoring two boats on a single anchor also put a lot of strain on the one anchor chain. Both boats' anchors could not be deployed because the chains would twist around each other when the boats swung with the wind and tides, making it almost impossible to get the anchors up. We regretted our decision that night, but neither Bob nor I regretted it enough to get up and reanchor, so we all toughed it out.

During a routine engine check the next morning, I was shocked to discover that our bilge was nearly full of seawater. *Tainui* had a large open keel that ran nearly the full length of the vessel. Her bilge was a large open rectangular "hole" near the motor that went to the bottom of the hull and held about 75 gallons. Forward of the bilge, the keel was filled with ballast composed of concrete and iron punchings, and a 70-gallon diesel tank lay in the keel under the engine aft of the bilge. In the engine compartment I found a little stream of water pouring out of a hole in the exhaust elbow, which was an ordinary household lead pipefitting. The engine exhaust gases mixed with the hot saltwater from the cooling system and made a right angle turn downward in the exhaust elbow. Leaks caused by corrosion from hot saltwater and exhaust gases were common in this elbow, but, alas, it was another spare part we had not brought with us. (Of course, we bought two of them the next time we were near a hardware store.) I stopped the flow by shutting off the seacock on the engine cooling water intake, and the electric bilge pump quickly emptied the seawater from the bilge. I pondered how I could plug the hole so that we could use the engine. There turned out to be a good side to remaining rafted up to *Sasaparilla*. When Bob heard about my problem, he dug an oxyacetylene welding outfit out of one of his deep lockers. He passed me the two steel tanks, climbed aboard, lit his torch, and welded up the hole so quickly that we were under way by 10:00 a.m. You never know what a sailor might have in those lockers.

The next day was Halloween. We motored along the east shore of Santa Cruz Island with no wind and a hot sun. Late in the afternoon, we entered Smuggler's Cove in 20-knot gusts, which made it hard to anchor. After we got our boats safely anchored, we had a little Halloween entertainment. Carol made fudge, and they tried to share it with us. Bob and Carol got *Sasaparilla* under way and tried to bring it to us. It was too rough to bring her alongside, so they took *Sasaparilla* upwind from us and drifted some fudge toward us in a zip lock bag tied to an inflated garbage bag. It missed *Tainui* and Bob chased after it in *Sasaparilla*. Bob tried to recover it with his long-handled fish net. After several unsuccessful attempts, he gave up and let it drift away. However, the skipper of a large ketch anchored nearby observed the process and knew what was in the bag from overhearing our radio conversation, so he launched his inflatable dinghy, recovered the fudge, and delivered it to us. We, of course, invited him aboard and shared the fudge with him.

He was an experienced charter skipper out of San Diego and shared his local knowledge of our future stops at Santa Catalina and San Diego.

During the night we heard sea lions and elephant seals on the shore. The elephant seals' sounds were very different from the familiar bark of the sea lions, but it was too dark to get a look at them. Peering over the side of *Tainui*, however, we could see beautiful phosphorescent streaks in the water trailing behind the sea lions as they swam around our boat.

The next day, in the usual morning calm, we motored to Catalina Island in sloppy seas left over from the night winds. Catalina Island appeared to be burnt brown, barren and uninhabited until we approached the town of Avalon. Avalon was situated in a picturesque bay with a beautiful curved beach. We recognized the famous round casino building. During the summer, it was a very popular harbor due to its proximity to the southern California mainland, but it had few boats on this November afternoon. As soon as we entered, a harbor official came out and helped us moor very tightly between bow and stern buoys, which prevented us from turning or swinging. Tied to a single buoy, boats need swinging room to keep from hitting each other; using this system, during its high season Avalon lined up boats like cars in a parking lot.

The official came aboard *Tainui* and put a tablet in our head that would spread a bright yellow dye in the water if we flushed, whereupon we would be fined $200. Theoretically, we would have to go ashore to use the toilet, since we didn't have a holding tank. When he left, I smiled smugly and said to Connie, " Nice try, but he didn't make us *swallow a pill!*" Connie knew what I meant, but she preferred the "bucket and chuck it" system—with the "chuck it" part taking place when we were out to sea again. The marina charged us its off-season rate of $14, our highest fee to date—but that record was soon broken.

We walked around the town the next afternoon. Avalon was almost deserted on a cold and windy day under threatening gray skies. We decided it was not worth the high price of the moorage to spend another day there. Bob and Carol had us over for drinks; we ate dinner aboard and retired early in preparation for an early morning start. We hoped to make the entire 60-mile run to San Diego in daylight.

We were up at 3:30 a.m. and out of Avalon at 4:00. As soon as we left, a tugboat came toward us in the dark. After it passed we were about to turn behind it when we saw the single pale yellow lamp on the barge it was towing. If we had crossed behind the tug, we could have hung up on his tow cable until the barge hit us! If we had read the series of lights on its mast correctly, we would have known that the tug was towing— a potentially fatal lapse on our part. The captain radioed that *Tainui's*

23

navigation lights were so dim he couldn't see them until he was right on us. (In San Diego, we put in larger bulbs, but they melted the red and green lenses of our light fixtures. Ultimately, I installed a pair of big new navigation lights.)

The trip to San Diego was a lot slower than we planned. We motored all the way through choppy seas and fought an adverse current. The days were becoming shorter now that it was November, and we ran out of daylight well before we reached the coast. <u>Charlie's Charts</u> warned us that kelp fields extended two miles off the coast, so we approached Point Loma from three miles off and still found ourselves surrounded by kelp beds. Every few minutes the engine slowed down when kelp fouled the prop, and I unwound it by shifting the engine into reverse. The slow going and our inability to get out of the kelp in the pitch-black night frustrated us. Finally, we saw the lights of a boat coming toward us and hoped that it was a local boat that knew the way through the kelp. We fought our way through the thick kelp to the vessel, and to our dismay a floodlight on a large sign on the side of its house read "Kelp Cutting Research Vessel"! We had to laugh in spite of our disappointment.

When we finally extricated ourselves from the kelp, our challenge was to round Point Loma and find our way into San Diego Bay in the dark. We were not prepared for the confusing scene that confronted us when the city came into view. It was ablaze with all kinds of lights. We strained our eyes, with and without the binoculars, but we could not distinguish the red and green lights on the navigation buoys from the lights of the city. We would spot a green light that might be a buoy, only to see it turn yellow and then red.

This situation gave us some anxious moments. After our long day's sail and our frustrating experience in the kelp beds, we were fatigued and disoriented in the darkness. We were afraid that we were near some rocks that extended from Point Loma almost to the channel. We were sorry that we had broken our rule not to enter a strange harbor at night even if we had to heave to offshore until morning. We had reasoned that San Diego harbor was so big that it would be easy for us to find our way in.

Not knowing how to find the channel, we stopped *Tainui* so as not to get into any more trouble and tried to get our bearings. Our deliverance came from the U.S. Navy. We saw a big, well-lit Navy ship coming out of the harbor and figured it must be in the channel. We hustled *Tainui* over to its wake, swung her bow toward the city and saw, to our immense relief, the red and green channel buoys lined up like the lights on an airport runway.

On the way in we repeatedly radioed the harbor police for directions to a moorage, with no success. Finally an anonymous voice radioed back sarcastically "The San Diego harbor police are on permanent siesta." Another voice offered to guide us in to an empty slip next to their boat at the Sun Roads Marina. They turned on their masthead anchor light as a beacon, stayed up late, and talked us in on the radio. When we arrived, they took our dock lines, brought us aboard their warm cozy boat, and gave us mugs of hot coffee. This was an example of the helpfulness of cruising sailors that we experienced many times in the days ahead. Sun Roads turned out to be a very posh marina costing us a record $26 per night. Our benefactors were live-aboards who paid $900 per month for their slip.

We learned that the prospects of an inexpensive berth in the city were very poor, but that boats could anchor free for one week at Mission Bay about 10 miles up the coast. We took advantage of the free showers and laundry room at Sun Roads and left the marina before checkout time. This time we traversed the channel and cleared Point Loma in broad daylight, giving the kelp beds a wide berth. We motored up the coast and in through the narrow entrance to Mission Bay. The bay was small and round and surrounded by a park-like setting of lawn and trees. We enjoyed strolling through the touristy little seaside town of Mission Beach, which lies on a sandy strip between the bay and the ocean. Sea World Marine Park was nearby on the inland side.

We spent the next week exploring San Diego and looking for a place to leave *Tainui* while we went home for the holidays. The marina in Chula Vista advertised a one-month cruisers' special for $270 per month, which was by far the best deal we could find. We immediately took *Tainui* back around Point Loma and sailed through San Diego harbor on a bright sunny day with a lovely view of the city skyline. We passed under the gracefully curved bridge to Coronado Island with its lovely old Spanish-style resort with white adobe walls and red tile roofs, and proceeded up the channel to the new marina at Chula Vista.

After securing *Tainui* in the marina, we took the Amtrak home in time for Thanksgiving and Christmas with family and friends in Eugene, Salem, and Seattle.

In early January 1989, we returned to San Diego and spent the next three weeks preparing *Tainui* for the trip to Mexico. There were four or five big marine stores on Harbor Island in San Diego that were eager to outfit cruising boats. So eager in fact, that they threw fancy parties with free wine, beer, and snacks. "The way to a sailor's purse is?" They also supplied checklists of all the things we should have aboard for serious blue-water sailing, which, of course, they were eager to sell us. One of them even loaned us a pickup truck to transport a heavy barrel of 300 feet of new anchor chain to *Tainui* at Chula Vista.

Connie's brother, George Jeffery, who lived in the area, loaned us a car, which made it possible to commute from Chula Vista to the city and take care of all of the things we needed to do. When we were ready to leave, George and his wife, Roxie, and their son and daughter-in-law Vaughn and Judy threw a bon voyage party at Vaughn's home and presented us with a case of wine with a custom "*Tainui* Around the World" label. It was a thoughtful and much appreciated send-off.

The marina was kind enough to give us a second month at the cruisers' rate, but we still ran out of time. We moved back to the city and anchored temporarily at the police dock. While we were there, a sailor, who was also a doctor, was having trouble getting his new radio to work. It was a commercial long-distance radio, much like my ham radio. I went aboard his boat and got it working properly. In return, he helped us make a list of the drugs we needed for our medical kit and wrote prescriptions for the ones we couldn't get over the counter.

When we used up our three days at the police dock, we anchored in the channel off of Harbor Island in what sailors called the "rock and roll" anchorage, because of the wakes of passing ships, and completed our preparations for our departure for Mexico.

CHAPTER THREE

MEXICO

We left San Diego for Mexico at 3:00 p.m. January 26, 1989. We planned to sail down the coast of Baja California to Cabo San Lucas, with stops at Bahia Tortuga (Turtle Bay) and Bahia Magdalena ("Mag" Bay).

The first few days the winds were so fluky and variable that we alternately motored, motor-sailed, ran downwind, and beat back and forth against the wind. We changed sails and adjusted the self-steering night and day. The nights were so cold that we wore our "woolies" to keep warm on watch. Eventually we settled into a fast reach (wind straight from the beam), our favorite point of sail. We could hear the Baja ham net on our radio, but they could not hear us when we transmitted. This was disappointing; the radio had just come back from the shop in San Diego with a clean bill of health, and we were counting on it for emergency communication. Everything else worked well—the Sat Nav got regular fixes and the wind vane steered brilliantly. Connie was determined to cook, even though *Tainui* rolled in some big swells. She made pancakes for breakfast and spaghetti for dinner by cooking with one hand and holding on with the other. She kept things from sliding on the galley table by placing a towel on it. In heavier weather, a wet towel held even better. I enjoyed the hot meals, but worried about the risk she was taking.

Three days out, the ham radio began to transmit normally. Welcome to the world! We were now able to join the daily roll call on the Baja ham net—a group of volunteer ham radio operators who registered yachts on the way to Mexico and called us every morning to see if all was well aboard and record our position and weather conditions. The radio gave us access to the 24-hour a-day emergency frequency and allowed us to communicate with fellow cruisers and even our families back home. Our ham radio was a great source of security, information, entertainment, and communication. It was well worth the trouble of passing the license exam and installing the radio.

On long passages we towed a lure behind the boat on a strong high-test line with a steel trace connected to the lure. When we left it out at night, we sometimes found the steel trace cut in two and the lure gone, so we went to fishing only in the daytime. There must have been some big fish out there. We speculated that, after we hooked one fish, it became bait for a much bigger fish that swallowed the whole thing. Our first catch was a mackerel. When Connie cooked it for dinner, it had a strong fish-oil taste. Mackerel were plentiful and easy to catch, but not our favorite eating fish.

When we came near to Isla Cedros, we were tempted to anchor there for a good night's rest, but <u>Charlie's Charts</u> showed heavy surrounding kelp beds, so we pressed on toward Turtle Bay. That night a gale blew up. We wanted to heave to, but we were too close to the island. *Tainui* would drift downwind toward the island, which would be a lee shore. A lee shore is dangerous because the wind and the surf push a boat toward the beach, making it difficult to get offshore under sail, and even under motor in severe conditions. The coastlines of the world are dotted with the wrecks of old sailing ships and some newer vessels that were unable to claw their way off a lee shore. We headed out to sea under a double reefed main and the heavy-duty staysail close-hauled on an upwind beat until our Sat Nav put us 20 miles off the island, then hove to at about midnight. We hove *Tainui* to by taking down all sail but the mainsail and pointing her bow into the wind. The wind on the sail kept the back of the boat downwind and *Tainui* lay motionless in the water with her bow pointed about 45 degrees off the wind and waves. Heaving-to was a wonderful relief. Sailing to windward in the gale, the wind howled in the rigging, waves crashed into the boat, and *Tainui* slammed noisily into the oncoming seas; hove to, it became almost quiet. With no forward motion, *Tainui* gently bobbed up and down on the waves like a cork. We didn't realized how much tension we had been under until we felt that peace and quiet. We had a pleasant night below, in spite of the gale blowing outside.

The gale was still blowing in the morning, so we sailed off under shortened sails. While the engine was running to charge the batteries, its heat warning alarm went off. I had installed audible alarms to supplement the factory-installed warning lights on the ammeter and heat gauge. With automatic steering there were times when we were both below and would not see a warning light in time to keep the engine from overheating or an electrical short from starting a fire or draining the batteries. I went below and started working on the engine while Connie stood watch in the cockpit and *Tainui* steered herself. Suddenly, a big gust knocked *Tainui* over so far that her lee rail went well under water. Big waves broke over the high side of the boat, causing water to come rushing down the deck and pour into the cockpit. The pressure on the sails was so great that Connie could not free the sheets (lines holding the sails) to spill the wind from the overburdened sails. I had removed the companionway steps, which doubled as the engine cover, to get at the engine so I hoisted myself up through the companion way and into the cockpit like a gymnast. When I yanked on the mainsail sheet, my feet slipped on the wet, steeply slanted cockpit floor and I sat down hard. Bracing my feet against the side of the cockpit, which was now more like a floor, I managed to pull the mainsail sheet out of its cleat and release the sail. By that time Connie had freed the jib sheet and *Tainui* righted herself. There was chaos below. Everything that wasn't well secured was on the cabin sole or even in the bilge under the uncovered engine. We hove to again and restored order below, regained our composure, and I finished cleaning out the engine cooling system. It was not a good time to ask, "Are we having fun yet?"

The next day we were totally becalmed. As we were motoring along we heard the pitch of the motor change. I shifted into reverse in case something had wrapped around the prop, and the motor revved up to a high pitch. I shut the engine down as quickly as

Possible. This was the way an engine sounded when its prop fell off, but that would be impossible to confirm without pulling *Tainui* out of the water. I went below to see what I could learn from the inside. I found that the prop shaft had come loose from the engine. The engine was connected to the prop shaft by a hard rubber vibration-damping block, which had split in two. Fortunately we were becalmed. Forward motion would cause the prop to rotate and the free end of the shaft to swing about wildly. This action could have destroyed the rubber seal in the cutlass bearing (where the shaft leaves the hull) and let a lot of water into the boat. The repair took some ingenuity. It was imperative to secure the shaft from rotating so we could at least sail. I tied the two parts of the coupling device back together with a network of ropes and then secured it to a fixed point on the hull to keep it from rotating. I made the repair at night, lying on the engine and working with a flashlight. We could not use the engine for propulsion, but we could continue under sail and run the engine in neutral to operate the refrigerator compressor and charge the batteries. Our perishable food would be preserved and we would have power for the radio, lights, and navigation equipment.

Without an engine it would have been risky to negotiate the tricky entrances to Turtle Bay and Magdalena Bay with their tides and currents, so we decided to sail nonstop to Cabo San Lucas. The only problem with sailing was that there was no wind. We spent the entire day looking at Isla Cedros. The night was also windless. During her night watch, Connie awoke me to report that a freighter appeared to be heading directly toward us. We could see both her red and green running lights, which are on each side of the ship, which meant she was headed right at us! I hailed the ship on the VHF radio and explained that we were becalmed and engineless, and she quickly altered course and passed behind us. We were not sure whether or not they were aware of our presence before we called them. A number of yachts have been run down by ships that were lax about keeping watch.

Two sailors whom we had met in San Diego overheard our conversation with the freighter and called to ask if we needed assistance. We replied that our only problem might be a shortage of water, if our trip was extended due to lack of wind. One of the yachts was going into Turtle Bay and offered to bring us some water. The other was 30 miles ahead but offered to come back if we needed help. We thanked them, but opted to conserve water and go on unassisted.

The wind came up in the afternoon and stayed with us all the way to the tip of the Baja Peninsula. The rope securing the prop shaft held tight and we settled into a comfortable routine and enjoyed ocean sailing. One day we looked back and saw the wake of a large fish on our trailing line. I let *Tainui* tow it for a while to tire it out before I pulled it alongside. It was so heavy I could hardly get it aboard. Once aboard, a mighty struggle ensued between the four-foot yellow fin tuna and me. By the time I subdued it, there were blood and fish scales all over the cockpit and me. It had so much meat we kept just the best parts and tossed the rest overboard. The flesh was dark and tasted like beefsteak.

At first we took four-hour watches at night. These watches were long and boring, so we experimented with different watch schedules and ultimately settled on two hours on and two hours off twice each night. On watch, we read or listened to music on our Walkman in the cockpit. If we couldn't stay awake, we set a kitchen timer for fifteen minutes and dozed off. When the timer bell went off, we scanned the horizon for ships, checked the compass course and wind direction, and readjusted the wind vane and sails as necessary. These tasks completed, we set the timer and dozed off again. This made the watches tolerable.

We were thrilled with the wind vane steering mechanism. We called it "Otto" after the manufacturer's' name, Autohelm. We never needed to hand-steer at sea under any conditions. If Otto couldn't handle it, neither could we. Otto was a tireless crewmember who never complained, no matter how long the hours or how bad the weather. If he were more mobile, we would have taken him to lunch when we reached port!

We reported to the Baja ham net that we might need assistance entering Cabo San Lucas, and friends Bob and Carol on *Sasaparilla* called back and offered to help. They told us to call them on our VHF when we were closer and they would come out and tow us in.

We arrived becalmed off Cabo San Lucas on the evening of February 4, after nine and a half days at sea. We drifted for the night, keeping a careful watch because we were close to shore and in a traffic area. Bob and Carol answered our call and came out in the morning as planned. They came aboard for a happy reunion and a cup of coffee before Bob side-tied his inflatable dinghy to *Tainui* and ran us the three and a half miles around Cabo's famous "Los Rocos" and into the inner harbor. Our deep sense of satisfaction at arriving safely at our first foreign port was made even more wonderful by our warm welcome in the harbor. After we dropped our bow anchor, several sailors met us in their dinghies and pushed engineless *Tainui* stern-to toward a vacant spot on the crowded sea wall. Our new neighbors on either side stood by onshore and took our lines when we were close enough to throw them. We wound up with our stern tied to the sea wall and our bow held out by the anchor. This was our first attempt at what was called a Mediterranean mooring. It would have been tricky, even with an engine. We were immediately invited aboard *Sasaparilla* to meet several other friendly cruisers. In spite of the 'indignity' of being pushed into the harbor, it was a grand arrival.

Visiting Popi's Deli was another pleasant experience. Popi's was a well-known cruiser's hangout that we had read about in books and magazines. We perused their cruiser's log and found the names of friends who had arrived in Cabo before us, and Popi's Deli gave us the free hamburgers that they offered to all arriving cruisers. We were sleepy from our night watches, but we lingered and chatted with the friendly sailing couples gathered there. Although we still felt like neophytes, becoming part of the scene with these sailors made us feel more like real cruisers. Popi's also ran a daily local radio net that allowed yachts in the harbor to share important information with each other.

The next morning we formally checked in to Mexico. This process varied greatly from country to country. In some countries, we had to drop anchor and fly the yellow flag, which is the code flag representing the letter "Q" for quarantine, until we were cleared by the Health Officer. At that point it was often the case that only the "Captain" was allowed to go ashore until all other formalities were completed. We thought about sending Connie ashore as captain to see how the officials in some of the male-dominated societies would react, but decided that, as guests in their country, we felt that it would be better to be polite. In Mexico there was no restriction on going ashore and we had 24 hours to check in. We spent the whole day taking taxis to the Health, Immigration, Customs and Harbor Police offices, which were scattered all over town. We spent a lot of time waiting our turn, in non-air-conditioned offices. Hot and tired at the end of the day, we were officially in Mexico or, as it turned out, officially in Cabo San Lucas—we had to repeat this process at every Mexican port.

We spent 20 busy and happy days in Cabo San Lucas. Our replacement vibration dampener arrived and some friends helped me install it. We went on several outings by bus to nearby towns with fellow cruisers. Once a week we climbed the hill to the lovely Hotel Finestero to join our thirsty friends at their weekly happy hour on a deck overlooking the ocean where generous one-dollar margaritas were served from a bar hewn out of a solid rock cliff. We sipped our drinks and chatted with fellow sailors to the happy music of a mariachi band and the sight of whales spouting and rolling in the blue Pacific Ocean below the cliff. The trials and tribulations of our recent passage faded into insignificance in the warm glow of these moments.

We heard through the ham network that friends from Oregon, Gordon and Jean Clappison, were on their way by car and wanted to meet us in Mazatlan in about a week. We had not planned to go to Mazatlan because we had heard reports of stolen dinghies and yachts being broken into. There was no way we could contact the Clappisons again, and not much time, so we quickly did our last-minute shopping and secured our provisions and gear for the sea. A ham radio operator hailed us from the sea wall and gave us some radio parts to give to an American ham named Gus in Mazatlan. We were under way in the early afternoon of the same day.

We got off to a good start, sailing on a perfect beam reach on a sunny day along the southern tip of Baja California. The good weather stayed with us most of the way. We had light winds in the mornings, good sailing in the afternoons, and motored through windless nights.

Early on, we saw whales rolling their backs above the surface, spouting, and then diving with their huge flukes high in the air. We never lost the thrill of up-close encounters with these magnificent creatures. On another occasion, a school of hundreds of porpoises came leaping and diving past us. They seemed to be intent on their journey, with no time to stop and play with *Tainui's* bow wave. When we were out of sight of land, we filled our sun shower and heated it on deck under the noonday sun. When the water was warm, we pulled it up on the staysail halyard and had our first shower on the foredeck. It worked well on a relatively calm sea, but showering on a wet soapy deck in a rolling sea would be dangerous. We got a bit of a scare one night when a ship that wouldn't respond to our radio bore down upon us. Apparently they just wanted a closer look, for they circled close around our stern and went on their way.

The last morning of the trip turned out to be very frustrating. When we estimated we were about three hours out, the wind came up on our nose and blew harder and harder. The waves built up and once again *Tainui* was bucking into a steep chop. We spent a very rough six hours battling our way in against the wind and the waves. It was frustrating because the harbor looked so close, and yet it seemed as though we were never going to get there. Finally, we fought our way through the narrow entrance and motored into the shelter of the small boat harbor, dropped anchor and turned off the motor. *Tainui* lay quietly to her anchor in a pretty little harbor perfectly sheltered from wind and waves. We felt again that wonderful sense of peace and relaxation after the strain and tension of a wild ride at sea. No wonder whenever anyone asked Connie what was her favorite part of sailing, she answered, "Dropping anchor!"

We didn't go ashore because we were tired and we weren't sure it was safe to leave the boat unattended, or where we should land our dinghy. We contacted Gus by radio and he came right away to get his radio parts. We picked him up in our dinghy and brought him aboard for a visit and refreshments. When he left, he invited us to his home the next day. He was an American sailor who had married a Mexican woman and moved ashore. The one other American yacht in the harbor hailed us on the radio and invited us to come for a visit. They were a very friendly couple that anchored there several months each year while their parents occupied a condo ashore. They told us that the news of trouble in Mazatlan was old and that it now appeared to be reasonably safe there, but that we should have the people at the sport fishing dock watch our dinghy. There was still a chance that an outboard motor could disappear.

The next day we took the dinghy to the sport-fishing dock and asked a man to watch our dinghy while we went to visit Gus. When we mentioned Gus, he said in a loud voice, "Oh, you a friend of Gustavo! Don't worry, *senor*, we cannot let anything happen to the boat of friend of Gustavo!" We felt extra secure about our dinghy as we walked up the hill to Gus's house. It was an attractive big white adobe house with a great view of the bay, and was easily identified by a tall ham radio antenna on the roof. There was only one problem—no one was there! We never saw Gustavo again, but our dinghy was zealously guarded every time we went ashore in Mazatlan.

That afternoon we gathered up our passports and ship's documents and made the rounds of the checking-in offices. At the last office, we found the Clappisons, asking if we had checked in yet—a happy coincidence because we were not sure how we were to find each other. At the same time, we discovered that we had lost Connie's passport. The Clappisons helped us retrace our steps with their car, but we did not find it. A very understanding young U.S. Embassy official told us that it was highly unlikely that it would be turned in because U.S. passports were a valuable commodity on the black market in Mexico. Three days and $40 later, Connie had a replacement passport.

We were very glad we came to Mazatlan. The yacht harbor was just a short bus ride over cobblestone streets from the center of the old town, which was authentic Mexico with a minimum of tourism. It had a lovely park-like central plaza with a beautiful cathedral at one end. One Sunday we sat on a park bench and watched local families, dressed in their finest, promenading on the plaza, purchasing food from vendors with colorful carts and stalls, and picnicking on park benches. We also ate at some very good inexpensive restaurants in old town. We were entertained at one of them by a string quartet playing Mozart, while we were served by waiters in formal attire and dined off white linen and china.

Having friends with a car was a bonus for us. Gordon and Jean took us on a ride to the mountain village of Kapala, where we had lunch at a restaurant owned by an American with a Mexican wife. On the way back we stopped for dinner at the lovely El Mirador restaurant overlooking the harbor. In return, we took them on a sail up the coast to where we could view the beautiful beaches in front of the posh five-star resorts in the tourist area called the "Gold Coast."

On a local holiday we all hiked up the hill to the lighthouse overlooking the yacht harbor. We shared the trail with local families dressed in their Sunday best. *Senor* Antonio Villarreal Gonzales and his daughters struck up a conversation with us that resulted in an invitation to their home that evening. He was proud of the fact that he was the regional sales rep for the Coca Cola Bottling Co. This time someone was at home when we arrived—in fact the whole family of eight. When we entertained them on *Tainui* the next day, they insisted on bringing the food, which consisted of beer and pizza—so much for local cuisine!

After 10 days in Mazatlan, we prepared for departure to Isla Isabela, a kind of mini Galapagos off the coast between Mazatlan and Puerto Vallarta. It was the nesting ground for several species of birds and home to land turtles and monitor lizards. As in the Galapagos, the animals were so tame that visitors could observe them from close range.

When we turned on the key to start the engine, the warning buzzers sounded as usual but, when the engine started, they kept right on buzzing. I discovered that the electrical connectors had fallen off of both the alternator and engine heat-warning sensors. Maintaining the electrical system was a constant struggle—partly due to the warm, damp salt-air environment and partly because of the vibration of the diesel engine. I had two 12-volt marine electrical system manuals aboard and became very adept at troubleshooting that system. In this case, I simply cleaned the connectors and crimped them tightly in place.

Again, we had lovely sailing during the day and had to motor at night. About 3:00 the next morning, the engine slowed down and finally quit. This was getting old! Unable to motor, and with no wind, *Tainui* turned crossways to the waves and rolled and tossed in the troughs, making it difficult to sleep. After breakfast I tried the engine and it ran fairly well, slowing down and recovering from time to time until a light breeze came up and we were able to sail slowly into the bay at the south end of Isla Isabela and drop anchor. The anchor held, but as the boat swung around, the anchor chain made loud grinding noises as it dragged across the shale bottom. The noise seemed especially loud in the stillness of night when we were trying to sleep.

Fishermen's *palapas* (shacks) dotted the broad sandy beach on the gracefully curved shore of the little bay. Whole families occupied these temporary dwellings during the fishing season. Their scattered gear, household effects, and refuse gave what would otherwise have been a beautiful scene the look of a cluttered hobo encampment. The fisher people only replied begrudgingly when we spoke to them, which gave us the feeling that we were not welcome there.

There were no tours that day, but the ranger allowed us to go unaccompanied, provided we promised to stay on the trails. We got our video camera and set out on a shale trail that led up toward high cliffs that overlooked the ocean. At the base of the trail, we caught a glimpse of a monitor lizard and, as we climbed farther, we found many booby birds nesting on the ground alongside the trail. Most of them paid no attention to us even when we were within a few feet of them. The blue-footed boobies were the exception. They were very protective of their territory. The males charged out toward us making a very cross-sounding squawking noise. We got cute close-up shots of them looking right into the video camera, which also recorded their raucous scolding sounds. We walked past dozens of friendlier boobies, including some fluffy white fledglings trying out their wings. We also saw beautiful snow-white tropicbirds, with bright red beaks, nesting on the edge of the cliff. Looking down past their nests, we could see beautiful bright blue Pacific Ocean swells spewing sunlit white spray high in the air as they crashed into the base of the cliffs. On the way back down the trail, we could see hundreds of frigate birds in the trees in the valley below and dozens more soaring gracefully in the sky. The frigates were large black gull-winged, vulture like birds. Many of the males in the trees were displaying a large bright red sac below their beaks, which we assumed was part of their mating plumage. Frigates were thieves who survived by stealing fish in midair from the boobies, who were very adept dive-bombing fishermen. It seemed a bit unfair, but both species were obviously thriving.

Before we could leave Isla Isabela for Puerto Vallarta, I had to address our engine problem. I started by changing the fuel filter, which was "gunked up." Diesel was very susceptible to developing algae in the tropics, and a clogged filter could have caused the engine to die from fuel starvation. When I finished, I tried to prime the fuel system by bringing fuel up from the tank in the bilge with the engine's mechanical fuel pump. It turned out that the pump's diaphragm was worn out. The engine would not run without the fuel pump, so we had to leave for Puerto Vallarta without an engine. This time we would have to conserve electricity because we could not charge our batteries on the way. We estimated it to be about a two-day trip, providing we had wind. We would no doubt have to be towed into port for a second time in three passages.

Our immediate problem, however, was to get out of the bay safely under sail. There were waves breaking on the rocks at the entrance just downwind of us. When we first got off the anchor, we would have no speed for steerage, the bow would fall off downwind, and *Tainui* would drift toward the rocks until she picked up enough speed to turn. There was a good breeze that would be on our beam after we turned, so we could sail in the right direction once we got going, but there was a chance that we would not be able to turn in time. We wouldn't have risked it if the skipper of another yacht, who knew of our engine problem and sensed our predicament, had not voluntarily stood by in his inflatable, which had a powerful outboard motor. We hoisted the sails first, and then raised the anchor. *Tainui* swung down toward the rocks, and it became clear that we could not turn in time. Our "Good Samaritan" positioned his dinghy between *Tainui* and the rocks and pushed her bow away like a tugboat. He stayed with us until we sailed clear of the rocks. The necessity of relying on the kindness of strangers, though heartwarming, was becoming a bit embarrassing.

Tainui settled into a lovely beam reach and glided along with effortless ease through the afternoon and the first night. We enjoyed being under sail again and didn't miss the noise and worry of the engine. The next day and night we ghosted along with all possible sail up in light zephyrs and hand-steered much of the time to take advantage of every little shift of the breeze.

The next morning we were becalmed. We rigged a canvas shade as the sun grew higher and hotter, and *Tainui* drifted aimlessly on a sea turned to glass. We watched suspiciously as a small open local boat altered course and came in our direction. Piracy was rare, but there were isolated incidents where boats had been boarded and robbed, sometimes with violence. We were in an isolated area, dead in the water, and we felt particularly vulnerable. As the craft approached we could see it held two local fishermen, and when it came alongside, we saw that they had caught a sea turtle and an illegal porpoise, which did not vouch well for their character. They did not speak English, but one of them held up an empty bottle and requested *agua*. We knew that much Spanish and gladly filled his bottle with cool water from our refrigerator and gave it back to him saying, *"Agua fria!"* The man thanked us with a "Gracias," and to our great relief, they fired up their motor and sped away toward Puerto Vallarta.

The afternoon wind returned and we made good progress until the wind died in the evening. We drifted for the night on the calm sea only a few hours' sail from the harbor at Puerto Vallarta. *Sasaparilla* was already in Puerto Vallarta, so I contacted Bob on the ham radio. He and Carol would be away the next day, but he promised to arrange assistance for us. After a restful night's sleep, we sailed the rest of the way to the harbor entrance and called on the VHF. Bob had arranged for Merv and Bobbie on *Mallard*, whom we had met at Cabo San Lucas, to help us in. Like most sailors we hated to be towed into port, but we swallowed our pride once again and gratefully accepted their tow. They pulled us into the anchorage and came aboard for a great time of catching up on each other's news and gossip. Bob and Carol returned in the afternoon and we all ate dinner ashore at a restaurant on the Esplanade.

The next day we moved *Tainui* to a marina where we could charge the batteries, order a new fuel pump, and tackle some more of the tasks on our "boat work" list. It was scant comfort to learn that virtually every boat arrived in harbor with a similar list. We came to the realization that boat maintenance was going to be a half-time job, but at least we were working for ourselves and could leave it for a while when something fun came up. It was far better than working full-time for someone else and dreaming about cruising.

We enjoyed 40 days in Puerto Vallarta. Connie's sister, Lynn, and her husband, Ray, flew down and spent two weeks with us. This was fortunate timing because they were able to bring a new fuel pump with them. They took us touring into the countryside in a rental car one day, and on another occasion we got a free jeep for a day by listening to a time-share condo pitch. We saw rural Mexico by taking the jeep up dirt roads and even fording a stream. In return, we took them for a day sail to a quaint fishing village where we anchored off the pier and ate lunch aboard, watching local fishermen work on their nets ashore and booby birds dive for fish in the bay. Lynn and Ray were great company, and we missed them when they were gone.

We had now reached a crucial decision point. If we were really going to sail away, we needed to make a 3,000-mile crossing to Nuku Hiva in the Marquises in French Polynesia in April, to be in the southern hemisphere before the North Pacific cyclone season began in May. Some of our friends encouraged us to spend the winter with them at La Paz in the Sea of Cortez and cross the Pacific the next year. We considered this but felt that, if we put it off, we might never go. So we made preparations for the crossing as quickly as possible before there was time for either of us to change our minds.

Connie took charge of provisioning. It was a big responsibility. We estimated the trip would take 30 days, but provisioned for a minimum of three months to allow for contingencies such as becoming becalmed, engine failure, and navigation errors. We made many trips on foot to the nearby "modern" supermarket, returning with full backpacks and bags in each hand. Based on our extensive precruising reading, Connie made decisions about what to take. She bought a lot of dry goods, such as pasta and rice, and "tons" of canned goods, including cases of diet soda and juices. She packed a week's supply of fresh meat in our refrigerator.

For fresh produce, she chose potatoes, carrots, cabbages, lettuce, tomatoes, cucumbers, onions, apples' and oranges. Stowing all of this was a challenge. We hung fruits and vegetables in nets above the galley table and stored the sodas in the keel on top of the concrete ballast. Connie marked the contents of all the cans on them with a permanent marker before we stored them in lockers below the galley table seats. A couple had told us of a crossing during which their cans got wet and all the labels came off. At mealtimes they picked three cans and made a surprise meal out of whatever was in them; they had some unusual meals.

I secured five five-gallon jerry jugs of water and five more with extra diesel fuel on deck. This gave us 95 gallons of fuel and 80 gallons of water. *Tainui* sank a couple of inches deeper into the water when all provisions were aboard.

We made a last-minute trip to the health department to be checked for amoebas because so many of our friends had picked them up. The tests came back positive for one of the less virulent strains, but we were still given two types of strong medication to take for the first two weeks of our crossing. We formally cleared out of the country the day before our departure by getting our crucial *zarpe* from Mexican authorities. We needed it to prove at our next port of entry that we had left Mexico legally, leaving no unpaid bills, and were not escaping from the law. Every country we visited required a *zarpe* from our previous port of call.

Our trip so far had been close to shore, which was not much different from our summer coastal trips to the San Juan Islands and back. Sailing across the Pacific would be a much bigger challenge. It would be our longest crossing, even if we sailed all the way around the world. Our minds were full of questions. How would we react to being so far from land? What if we couldn't find Nuku Hiva? With her recent history of equipment failures, was *Tainui* up to the trip? What if one of us got sick aboard? What if we got into a great storm, etc.? We had butterflies in our stomach and did not sleep well that night.

The next day, April 23, 1989, after we had completed all the last-minute details, we took a deep breath, untied the dock lines, and turned *Tainui*'s bow toward the great unknown.

CHAPTER FOUR

THE BIG CROSSING
MEXICO TO NUKU HIVA

We motor-sailed 35 miles into a brisk headwind and steep five-foot waves in Banderas Bay on our way to the ocean. *Tainui* plunged and stalled and plunged again like a bucking horse, and spray swept across the house and deck into our faces. Conditions were better in the open ocean. The wind was the same, but the swells were farther apart and smoother. The ride was comfortable, but we both felt queasy and didn't eat much. This might have been caused by nervous tension, but we suspected the amoeba medicine, which kept our stomachs slightly upset for our first two weeks at sea.

Our check-in to the ham network cheered us up. Volunteer amateur radio operators maintained ham networks for yachts all over the world. We had signed up with the Pacific Maritime Net. Yachts initially registered their vital statistics: name of vessel, radio call sign, number of persons aboard, point of departure, destination, number of life rafts, and description of the boat as seen from the air, then responded to the daily roll call. In case of emergency or if yachts did not respond to the roll call, the net would contact rescue services and alert nearby yachts. The daily contacts provided us with a sense of safety and security. Even when we were far from any official rescue service, we knew that help was as close as the nearest yacht on the ham net.

As the newest enrollees, we were last on the list. We listened as the net controller called the 15 vessels before us, and we recorded weather information from their reports. Our check-in that night was typical of the many that followed. Our call sign was N7HVO. It went like this:

"November Seven Hotel Victor Oscar, this is Kilo Two Charlie Bravo Echo. Over." " K2CBE, this is N7HVO. How do you copy? Over." "N7HVO, you are loud and clear. Welcome to the net, Vern and Connie aboard *Tainui*. Go ahead with your report. Over." "K2CBE, all is well aboard *Tainui*. Our position is 26 degrees 2 minutes north and 103 degrees 50 minutes west. Our course is 232 degrees magnetic at a speed of 4.3 knots. The seas are from the west at 6 feet, the wind is northwest at 11 knots, the barometer is 30.1 and steady, and the skies are overcast. Over." "Roger that, N7HVO. Do you have any traffic? Over."

"Negative. This is N7HVO clear with K2CBE."

"This is K2CBE, is there any traffic for N7HVO? Over."

"N7HVO, this is Kilo Niner Papa Golf Quebec, Jerry, in Salem. Meet me up five megs (radio frequency megahertz). Over." "Roger, Jerry. N7HVO going up. Over."

I tuned up to the requested frequency and met Jerry. Jerry McCassland was our radio contact in Salem. Several of our sailing friends, who had been listening to the net, followed us up and wished us well on our trip. Jerry recorded our position on a wall chart, passed messages to and from our family members, and arranged weekly radiotelephone calls with our children. His services were a great comfort to us and to our family. The ham radio made us feel safer and connected us with family at home and friends on other vessels. Without the ham radio, the ocean would have been a lonely place.

With the wind on our nose, we made long tacks back and forth as close to the wind as we could sail, which made us travel a long way to make a little progress toward our goal. More sailing friends sent us greetings and well wishes following the ham net that evening. After the net the wind increased to 20 knots, so I reefed the mainsail and continued to fight for progress. Even though the seas calmed down around midnight, we couldn't relax. We had to maintain a vigilant watch and check our position frequently, because we were in the coastal shipping lanes and passing close to some outlying rocks and a small island. Connie saw two ships on her midnight to 4:00 a.m. watch, and I saw three more from 4:00 until 8:00 a.m.

By daylight we were tired after a sleepless night, but we had navigated safely past the obstructions and shipping lane. When I tried to hoist the staysail with its halyard I discovered that the shackle (fastener on the end of the halyard that attached it to the head of the sail) had come loose and gone up to a pulley three-quarters of the way up the mast. I had to get it down in order to hoist the sail. I waited until the wind quit to attempt my first ascent of the mast at sea. First, I took down the mainsail and in its place ran our portable mast steps up the back of the mast. The steps were a series of foot loops made of cargo webbing. Then I shackled a spare halyard to my safety harness as a backup, and Connie wrapped the other end of it around a winch and cranked out the slack as I climbed the steps. If the ladder broke or I fell off, I would be held up by the harness and she could lower me to the deck. As *Tainui* rolled in the waves the mast swung out over the ocean, back across the deck, and over the ocean on the other side—I tried not to look down. With one hand holding on to the mast, I pulled the halyard out a bit at a time with my free hand until it hung down to where Connie could reach it. I descended safely, pleased with my first experience of going aloft at sea.

As *Tainui* bobbed up and down on a glassy sea, we rigged a shade to protect us from the noonday sun and waited for the wind. A school of small dolphins shattered the surface as they leaped and splashed by. The wind picked up gradually in the afternoon, until *Tainui* moved along at an efficient five knots. Later, the wind increased to 25 knots, and I pulled down the big genoa jib, which is a light-air sail, and replaced it with the smaller, heavier working jib. Leaving the big sail up in strong winds could damage the sail or even lay *Tainui* over on her side. When to reduce sail is an important decision. A wise sailors' maxim advises: "If you are thinking about it, it's time to do it."

This occasion provides a typical example of reducing sails. Connie took the wheel, started the engine, and turned *Tainui* into the wind to stop the boat and take the pressure off the sails. *Tainui* was, however, still rolling heavily in the swells, and the sails were flapping in the wind—we only reduced the sails when the wind increased. I clipped the tether from my safety harness to the jack line and made my way forward along the side deck, between the lifelines and the cabin, until I reached the mast. There, I untied the jib halyard so that the genoa jib would be free to come down. Next, I crept across the wet, tossing foredeck to the bowsprit, which projected three and a half feet forward over the water. A narrow teakwood platform was attached to the top of the bowsprit, and a double stainless steel railing, called a bow pulpit, enclosed its sides. Netting was laced to the pulpit to keep the jib from going overboard when it was brought down. I worked on my knees in the bow pulpit to keep from falling as *Tainui*'s bow rose and fell in the waves. Sometimes I was suspended in air when the bow dropped suddenly, and then half submerged in seawater when it hit bottom. With *Tainui* turned into the wind, the genoa jib was whipping about, making a nerve-wracking noise like a flag in a hurricane. I reached up and pulled it down hand over hand as fast as I could, to quiet it down and keep it from flogging itself to shreds. My nerves relaxed a bit when the noise abated. I detached the big sail from the forestay—a steel cable that went from the bowsprit to the top of the mast—and I pulled the working jib out of its sail bag. I transferred the jib halyard to the top of the working jib and attached its 16 brass hanks (little piston clips that snapped on to the forestay). Then I transferred the jib sheets from the genoa jib to the working jib. The sheets were lines that ran from the back of the jib along each side of the deck to cockpit winches for controlling the tension on the jib. I completed my work in the bow pulpit by stuffing the genoa into its sail bag and lashing it down.

I crept back across the open foredeck, made my way to the mast, wound the jib halyard around the drum of a winch, and cranked the working jib up as tight as I could. The sail change completed, I returned to the cockpit. Connie killed the engine, let the bow fall off the wind, and put *Tainui* back on course. I adjusted the tension on the sails with the sheet winches and reengaged the self-steering vane, and we were under way again. The whole process took about 10 minutes. When the wind decreased, the process was reversed to get the bigger sail up again. In changing weather conditions, we made sail changes several times a day.

Tainui made good progress under a reefed main and the working jib. We hove to in the evening for the ham net and then sailed on. By midnight the wind moderated to a light breeze, but I left the small jib up and the reef in the mainsail to avoid having to make sail changes in darkness if the wind freshened. Running under reduced sails at night became our custom.

In the morning I took the reef out of the mainsail and pulled down the working jib and ran up the big genoa. *Tainui* glided along peacefully under full sail in a nice six-to-eight-knot breeze. Flying fish burst from the water, sailed across our bow, and skipped across the tops of the waves. We often found flying fish on deck in the morning. A sea turtle swam ponderously by, so close that we could see the barnacles on its back, and a booby bird landed on the starboard spreader (a cross arm far up on the mast). It struggled to keep its balance as *Tainui* rolled and soon gave up and flew off. It was a pleasant sailing morning, but our stomachs were still slightly queasy from the amoeba medicine.

The wind picked up to 25 knots in the mid-afternoon. *Tainui* picked up speed, and we heard a rattling noise in the back of the boat. One of the bolts on the struts that held the wind-steering mechanism onto the stern had worked loose. I needed to tighten it immediately in spite of the rough weather, because if the bolt fell out, our self-steering would be crippled. One of our biggest fears was that the self-steering system would fail and we would have to hand-steer day and night all the way across the ocean. I clipped the tether onto my safety harness and climbed up over the stern rail and down the wind vane struts. The loose bolt was so close to the waterline that it dipped in and out of the water as *Tainui* rose and fell on the swells. I couldn't tighten the bolt because I had to hold on with one hand and the job required two hands for two wrenches—one on the bolt and the other on the nut.

The solution was to go into the water behind the boat. We hove to and stopped *Tainui's* forward motion so I wouldn't trail behind her. Connie was nervous as I donned a life jacket, climbed down the wind vane struts, and eased myself into the water. She passed down the tether to my harness so I would stay with the ship as it drifted along. Then she tied strings to two wrenches and lowered them down to me so I couldn't drop them into the ocean. I could now use both hands on the bolt—if I could catch it. *Tainui* and I did not always go up and down together. Eventually I wrapped an arm around a strut and stuck a wrench on the nut. This held me in position and kept a wrench on the nut while I turned the bolt with my other hand. It was only our third day out, and I had been up the mast and down in the water. Oh, for the life of a sailor!

We beat into the wind in heavy weather the next three afternoons. It looked like we might not get favorable winds until we reached the northeast trade winds, which were a long way off. Fortunately the weather calmed down in the evenings, so we were able to enjoy dinner and radio time each night. We listened to news from the Voice of America and the British Broadcasting Corporation before our much-anticipated nightly ham net. By then, there were boats on the roll call behind us as well as ahead of us. The other sailors' voices were becoming familiar to us as we listened to their nightly reports. Connie marked their positions on a chart and plotted their daily progress; we looked forward to meeting them face-to-face at future ports of call.

Eventually the wind switched to a favorable 10 to12 knots from the east. We put up the big genoa jib and full main, and *Tainui* made great time right on course all the next day. Connie cooked the last of our fresh meat for dinner. Unless we caught a fish, it would be canned meat from then on. Conditions remained calm in the evening, and we spent a pleasant hour chatting with friends on other boats after the net. The ocean seemed like a friendly place when we started our night watches.

One day I "surfed" the ham radio frequencies and found a man in Seattle who connected me with our son, Larry, at his office. Larry told us of the birth of a daughter to his wife's sister. That evening, after the net, our transmitter quit while we were talking to our daughter, Kathleen. We could hear, but couldn't be heard. I checked all of the radio's connections with no success. In disgust, I smacked the top of the radio with my hand and it started transmitting again! I told the net operator about it the next night so he wouldn't be alarmed if we failed to respond to roll call and he quipped, "That's why I keep a rubber mallet by my radio, Vern!"

The wind was light, and we had smooth sailing most of the next day. I took advantage of *Tainui*'s relative lack of motion by taking sun sights with our sextant. When I compared my results with our satellite position, I was 12 miles off. Not a very good result—especially for a calm day. The average for small sailboats was about seven miles. Although we had electronic navigation, I practiced with the sextant in case our Sat Nav failed or we lost power. The calm weather also provided an opportunity for us to take showers on deck with the sun shower. It was a great feeling to get rid of the salt and grime and feel clean again. We were completely becalmed late in the day. We decided not to motor and enjoyed a peaceful evening. We ate dinner in the cockpit listening to jazz on our stereo and watched a pink and purple sunset. Our appetites were better now that we had finished one of the two amoeba medicines.

The wind came up again at our 4:00 a.m. change of watches, so we set sail. It was convenient that this happened at the change of watches when we were both up. Otherwise, the one on watch would have had to awaken the sleeping one. Even though either of us could change sails by ourselves, we never went forward to work the sails without both of us on deck. This was to provide help with the sails if needed or, perish the thought, in case of an accident.

The wind continued and we had another day of smooth, fast sailing on a beautiful blue ocean. We sighted many flying fish and sea birds, and Connie baked two loaves of bread that turned out well. I took a sextant sight using a system for getting both latitude and longitude from a single noon sight, and it came within three miles of our Sat Nav fix—an excellent result! This was the kind of day at sea we had dreamed about.

But there was another side to sailing. We never knew when a mechanical problem might occur, and one did occur then. When I ran the engine for that day's hour of refrigerator and battery charging, the gearshift's Morse cable stuck. The Morse cable was a small steel wire that slid inside an outer plastic sheath. I took it off, dripped oil into its outer casing, and worked it back and forth for two hours. This freed it up enough to get by, but I needed to replace it at our earliest opportunity, which would probably be Tahiti. If it stopped working, every time we needed to shift gears, one of us would have to go below, remove the clumsy combination engine housing and companionway-stairway, and manually operate the shift lever. So far, we had had only minor mechanical problems that were an inconvenience but not dangerous.

April went out on a dead calm. By midnight Connie got so tired of the noise of sails slatting and banging that she went forward and took them all down while I was sleeping. She didn't bother to wake me because we didn't need to take our usual precautions when *Tainui* was dead in the water. Even if someone fell overboard, *Tainui* would not sail off without him or her. A light northeast wind came up in the morning and pushed us along at two or three knots all day. We saw more flying fish and booby birds, and I got another three-mile sextant fix, which boosted my confidence in my ability to navigate with celestial navigation if necessary. The boat was going so slowly that I jumped over the side and tightened up all the bolts on the wind vane struts for preventive maintenance. Connie kept an eye out for sharks. Some of our friends actually swam off of their boats for recreation on slow days. Others called it "trolling for sharks."

We spent another night totally becalmed and began sailing in light air again in the morning. By noon the wind increased and our speed picked up to five knots. I began to teach Connie sextant navigation. We worked out the lines of position from sextant readings using the Nautical Almanac, Sight Reduction Tables, and an 18-step worksheet—a fairly complicated, but accurate procedure.

We needed to average 4.25 knots per hour to make our goal of 100 nautical miles in 24 hours, but so many nights without wind put us well behind that goal. We were nine days out and had covered only 633 miles. However, with the wind coming from behind us now, we rigged wing-and-wing for downwind sailing and made a healthy speed of five knots during the day and three to four knots at night. The next day was even better sailing. We made a pleasant four knots all day, and in the evening the wind increased and we surfaced down the face of the waves at seven knots all night and into the next morning. It was a wild ride, making it difficult to sleep, but we made 110 miles that day!

Seven knots must have been a good trolling speed, because I caught a four-foot Spanish mackerel, also called a "wahoo," in the morning. It was an even better fighter than the four-foot tuna I had caught off the coast of Mexico. I struggled to get it on board and wrestled it all over the deck, trying to get it to bleed in a bucket that was much too small for the job. Once again our lovely teak deck was covered with blood and scales—as was our captain. We kept about half of the fish and threw the rest overboard. The wahoo was a very good eating fish, with white-flaked flesh and no fish-oil taste. It was a treat to have fresh meat again.

The wind grew even stronger as the afternoon progressed, so I double-reefed the mainsail. Once again, Connie started the engine and steered the boat into the wind to take the pressure off of the sail. Before leaving the cockpit, I pulled the main sheet in as tight as possible, which centered the boom and reduced the swaying of the sail because the bottom of the mainsail was attached to the boom. I climbed up onto the cabin roof wearing my harness and tether. The steel roof was curved and wet, and *Tainui* was rolling in big waves. I steadied myself against the boom as I worked, but it still swayed back and forth about three or four feet. I untied the mainsail halyard, reached up, and pulled the sail down until the first row of reefing points reached the boom. The reefing points were a horizontal row of metal grommets; short pieces of line, called reefing lines, ran through them and hung down on each side of the sail. I slipped the first grommet onto a hook on the mast and then worked my way aft, tying the reefing lines under the boom with a quick-release reef knot. In order to double-reef the mainsail, I pulled more sail down until the second row of reefing points reached the boom and repeated the process with its reefing lines. Then I winched the top of the shortened mainsail back up the mast as far as it would go—about two-thirds of the way to the top. Finally, I climbed down off of the roof and returned to the cockpit. Connie shut down the engine and steered us back on course, and I let out the mainsail sheet. Double reefing reduced the mainsail to about half of its full size.

The wind died down in the night, but I left the reefs in until daylight. Then I went back up on the house, untied all the reef lines, and winched up the full the mainsail. We were then under full sail on a lovely beam reach. After breakfast, two brown boobies tried to roost on the bow pulpit, but one kept pushing the other one off. We named the bossy one "Lucy" and the victim "Charlie Brown." Poor Charlie tried again and again to gain a foothold, in vain. For over an hour he landed on the bow pulpit, Lucy pushed him off, and he flew around and tried again. Finally, he flew away in defeat and Lucy smugly stayed aboard. A squall came up in the afternoon, and I went up to the bow pulpit, took down the genoa, and put up the working jib. Lucy moved to the other side of pulpit and watched me suspiciously, but stayed on even though the sails flapped wildly and my hands came within inches of her. She was our guest for two days. By evening, we had made 145 miles in 24 hours—our best ever! The evening radio weatherman confirmed that we were in the northeast trade winds—good news!

We had more of the same the next day. In our eagerness to make up for lost time, we took a chance and left the full sails up at night. We should have kept with our routine. The wind became so violent at 1:00 a.m. that Connie couldn't control the boat under full sail and called me on deck from my cozy bunk below. The sail-reducing chores were much more difficult on a slippery deck in the dark, as *Tainui* heaved in wild seas and the wind shrieked in the rigging. This was an example of a bad decision leading to a dangerous situation. It was too much for Lucy; she flew away and never returned.

We were now entering the doldrums, an area of variable winds, calms and sudden squalls, which was officially called the Inter Continental Transition Zone, or ICTZ. Our strategy was to head due south to cross it as quickly as possible, and then turn west toward Nuku Hiva in the southeast trade winds. Fortunately, we were not becalmed for very long at any time, but for the first few days, the wind blew from the south. We therefore had to set a diagonal course, which would keep us in the ICTZ longer than planned.

We made our first attempt to catch rainwater off of the mainsail in the ICTZ where there were frequent heavy downpours. I slacked off on the mainsail halyard and pulled the sail down far enough to create a trough beside the boom. Next, I pulled up the back end of the boom with the topping lift (a line from the back of the boom to a pulley at the top of the mast). This sloped the trough down toward the gooseneck fitting that connected the boom to the mast. I waited until the rain rinsed the salt off the sail and then attached a bucket under the gooseneck. Rainwater ran down the trough and into the bucket. I poured six buckets of freshwater into our tanks from that rain shower. This gave us extra freshwater for showers and washing clothes. After the rain, the wind quit. We were becalmed and three booby birds perched on our bow pulpit. These boobies knew how to share. They preened themselves, tucked their heads under their wings, and took a nap before flying off. We spent the night rolling in sloppy seas with no wind to steady the ship.

About this time, we began noticing that our morning coffee had a funny taste. As time went by we identified the taste—our freshwater was becoming salty! This was a great puzzle to me. I examined and reexamined the deck fitting through which we filled the tanks. Everything was sealed tightly. The deck fitting was flush to the deck so we would not trip over it. Its flat plug was removed or tightened with a special tool that fit into two dimples in the top of it. I held the plug up to study it and noticed sunlight peeping through the bottoms of these dimples. Over time, seawater washing across the deck had dribbled enough saltwater into our tanks to make it taste salty. Our two water tanks were connected, so they were both contaminated. Fortunately, we had not used the five jerry jugs of freshwater that were secured on deck. They held enough water to get us to Nuku Hiva. I plugged the holes in the cap, and we continued to use the slightly salty water for cooking, showers, and washing dishes. (I had a replacement plug sent to us in Samoa, where I also installed a valve system that isolated the two tanks.)

One day in the ICTZ, I checked out a rainsquall on the horizon with our binoculars and sighted the tip of a mast just over the horizon. I called on the VHF but didn't expect a response, because most sailboats didn't run their radios when there were no other vessels around, in order to conserve their batteries. To my surprise, my call was returned by Jim Chandler on the sailing vessel *Nepenthe*. Jim was a single-hander out of Acapulco also bound for Nuku Hiva. We talked on the radio every day until we reached port. It broke the monotony and sense of isolation, and it gave us a sense of security that there was another vessel nearby that could lend a hand in an emergency—like coming back to pick us up if our boat was sinking!

By then we had become so impatient to "get there" that, once again, we kept the big genoa jib up day and night in light winds to maximize our daily runs. We got away with it for two days, but on the third night the wind blew up to 30 knots. I did another night reefing and stayed up the rest of the night managing *Tainui* in the gale.

The wind continued to blow from the south, so we were beating at a 45-degree angle into the wind, which caused the boat to heel over, making ordinary tasks difficult and tiring—even dangerous. We ate a lot of cold meals, because cooking on the slant was nearly impossible. In rough weather, Connie served food in half-filled bowls and cups to keep food and drinks from sloshing out. Sometimes, in desperation, she cooked "on the slant" by holding a pot on the stove with one hand while steadying herself with the other. I didn't like her to do it because I feared that the pot might spill and burn her.

In general, I was more concerned that one of us would have an accident such as a burn or a broken bone than that the boat would sink. I frequently warned Connie not to move about on the boat with both hands full. The boat could lurch or fall off a wave at any moment with serious results. Sailors have a saying for this: "One hand for yourself and one hand for the boat." One of our friends sustained a serious back injury when he fell against the corner of their galley table. His wife had to sail the boat on to port while he lay on his bunk, unable to move without severe pain.

Beating into the wind was hard on the equipment as well as the crew. The boat pounded into the waves; water crashed over the bow, ran down the deck and into the cockpit, and soaked exposed equipment in saltwater. One night the waves broke the genoa jib from its lashings on the bow pulpit, and washed it overboard. One end was secured to the boat, but the remainder was pulled under the bow. The drag slowed *Tainui* down to a crawl during the night. When I hauled it aboard in the morning, I discovered a giant tear. Connie spent much of the next three days sewing it up, using a leather sailor's palm to push the big needle through the thick Dacron material.

Jim soon reported that *Nepenthe*'s engine had quit. He worked on it, but had no success. It was not a serious problem; he went all the way under sail in the steady southeast trade winds and arrived in Nuku Hiva before we did. At about that same time, we discovered that our smaller battery bank was not charging properly. Even though the big bank was okay, from then on we conserved electricity as a precaution.

One day a Japanese freighter passed close by. We hailed it on the VHF radio. We couldn't see its name, but, since this type of radio has only a 20-mile range, those aboard would know that our call was for them. The radio operator was reluctant to speak at first, because of his broken English, but when he found out that we were able to understand him, he shouted, "Oh, you understand, you understand me!" and became excited and talkative. He told us that they were bound from Australia to the east coast of Canada via the Panama Canal. He asked a lot of questions about our boat and where we were headed. When he heard that *Tainui* was only 35 feet long, he said, "Very danger, very danger!"

The wind became variable for a while and then, on May 11, just as we reached the halfway point of our crossing, it shifted to the southeast and we were able to beat our way due south through the doldrums. We didn't think this wind could be the beginning of the southeast trades because we had not yet reached the equator, but we were hopeful that we would now escape the ICTZ more quickly. We celebrated the halfway point with a glass of wine and cheese and crackers. This was an exception to our long-standing family practice; we did not drink alcohol at sea because we wanted our full faculties at all times. An emergency could happen without warning. I could not bear the thought of losing the vessel or not being able to rescue a loved one because I was in any way impaired by alcohol.

That night was so bright with a myriad of stars and a half moon that I could see to work on deck without a flashlight. We were amazed at how much we could see at night once our eyes adjusted. While we were sitting in the cockpit enjoying the night, a brightly lit Scandinavian ship passed behind our stern and the skipper contacted us (we always turned our radio on when a ship was in sight). He was very polite and formal and asked in excellent English who we were, what port we were out of, and where we were bound. After we answered his questions, he reported that he was out of Peru bound for China and asked if we needed any assistance. We were moving so slowly, he might have thought we were broken down. We assured him that we were okay, and he wished us well and signed off. We appreciated his contact and willingness to help—it was a generous offer because it would have cost him considerable time and effort to stop his freighter and render assistance.

In the morning the wind built up again, so we reefed the mainsail and continued to beat our way due south. By evening the wind died down and the seas calmed enough that Connie was able to cook again. We had chicken and dumplings—canned chicken, of course, but the hot meal was a welcome change. We made 90 miles that day.

The wind vane steered *Tainui* the next day while we worked away below. Connie continued to sew away on the ripped genoa, and I worked on the engine. The steel alternator adjustment strap, which kept pressure on the alternator belt, had broken in two. We did not have a spare aboard, so I drilled holes in the two pieces, overlapped them, and bolted them together. This did the job, but as soon as I started the engine, the alternator belt broke. We had spares aboard for all our belts, but there were three belts coming off of the engine, and the alternator belt was, of course, the one closest to the engine, which meant I had to remove the other two in order to replace the broken one. I was busy at it for a long time, but we had a good sailing day and night, thanks to "Otto," our self-steering vane. Though we were working below, we made regular trips on deck to look out. We made 105 miles that day.

The following afternoon our Sat Nav fix put us at 01 degree (60 miles) north of the equator. During the afternoon, the engine overheated on its daily run. By then I had the process of flushing out its clogged water hoses down pat, so I had it running again in 30 minutes. In spite of these problems, the rebuilt diesel engine was very reliable. All of its difficulties were caused by peripheral equipment: the fuel pump, the water pump, the alternator strap, the gearshift cable, the cooling hoses, etc. The engine itself never faltered as long as it got fuel, air, and water.

We had an interesting time on the ham net that night. Jerry McCassland had taken his chart of our voyage to the coffee time after the worship service at our church, and he relayed greetings to us from many of our friends. Bob and Carol of *Sasaparilla* called in from Guatemala after the net, and we talked Jerry McCassland into calling my mother with our Mother's Day greetings. Because of my mom's hearing problem, we did not attempt to talk to her directly through the ham radio. Those contacts were often of poor quality and hard to follow even with good hearing.

At 4:00 a.m. on May 15, we crossed the equator. Later in the day, we held our little "line crossing" ceremony. We toasted the occasion with a gin and tonic and poured the obligatory libation into the sea for King Neptune. Unfortunately, we drank the good stuff and gave Neptune some cheap cognac that someone had given to us. The next four days were really rough sailing. I pride myself on not being superstitious, but my advice to other sailors is to give Neptune the good stuff!

That night on the ham net, Jerry reported that my mom was surprised and thrilled when a stranger called and wished her a happy Mother's Day from her gallivanting son and daughter-in-law. When I asked the net operator how far south the ICTZ extended, so we would know when we could alter course for Nuku Hiva, to my surprise he replied that the ICTZ had shifted to the north of the equator and we were already clear of it and in the southeast trade winds. Hooray!

The next four days were the roughest of the voyage (thanks to Neptune?). Turning downwind was a mixed blessing. Sailing into the wind, the relative wind speed is increased by the speed of the boat, making it noisy in the rigging, stronger on our faces, and more likely to blow things around on deck. But the wind pressure on the side of the sails holds the boat on a fairly steady slant. The reverse is true sailing downwind. The relative wind speed is reduced by the boat's speed, making sailing quieter and warmer, but with the wind from behind, there is nothing to stop the boat from rolling in the waves.

During this period, the winds fluctuated between calms and squalls. Connie and I put up all sails to make progress in light air, and we reduced sails, sometimes quickly, when the squalls hit. Several times we were hit so hard that *Tainui* was laid on her side. I would scramble onto the steeply sloping deck and release the sheets to free up the overburdened sails. *Tainui* would immediately right herself, with her loosened sails flapping wildly in the howling wind. These sail changes were done in the worst of conditions, with the boat rolling, the wind whipping things about, and often in torrential rain and the darkness of night. It was an exhausting time for both of us.

The nights were especially bad. It was too wild to sleep anywhere but on the cabin sole—if we could sleep at all. We spent many hours up at night with sail changes, wind vane adjustments, and minor emergencies on deck. We could only nap for short periods at a time, so sleep deprivation became a serious problem—affecting our mood and our judgment. A kind of lethargy came over me. I sat below groggily listening to conditions worsening outside and had great difficulty deciding what action I should take, and even more difficulty forcing myself to go out and do it. Our morale reached its lowest point at that time. We had expected easy sailing in the southeast trades and were frustrated by the rough days following our crossing of the equator. Even the fact that we were making more than 100 miles a day didn't cheer us up. One night in a 30-knot gale, we gave up trying to make progress, hove to, and went to sleep. We were out of all shipping lanes, so we set the timer for 30-minute intervals instead of our usual 15, and even slept through some of those. We hated to lose time toward our goal, but sleep had become a higher priority.

On the morning of May 20, following a wild and largely sleepless night, Connie baked biscuits for breakfast in the rolling seas. They tasted good, but she said it wasn't worth the effort. Finally, that afternoon the sky cleared up and the sea calmed down. As we sailed along in warm, pleasant conditions, Connie washed clothes on deck in a bucket using a plumber's helper as the agitator. We called it our "arm-strong" washing machine. I helped wring out the heavy things by wrapping them around a lifeline post and twisting them. That afternoon I took an old-fashioned bucket bath on deck. I tied a line to a bucket, tossed it forward into the water, watched it fill as it drifted back, hauled it up, and poured it over my head. I used a special saltwater soap that made a good lather if I used a lot of it. Connie hated to bathe in saltwater and insisted on rinsing in freshwater. However, I found that even though "air drying" left my skin tingling with salt, when I toweled off <u>immediately</u>, no salt remained on my skin. At 7:30 p.m. we had only 643 miles to go to Nuku Hiva. We should be there in five or six days. Now that we were clean and rested and sailing smoothly with the end in sight, our spirits rose.

The next two days were perfect. We were on a beam reach in 12-to-18-knot winds. We made 124 miles on the second day, leaving us only 468 miles to go, but at night we had slow sailing in fluky winds and a squall. On the net, our daughter, Kathleen, informed us that they had moved into their new house and that she was pregnant with their second child. The trip would have been emotionally difficult without this contact with our family.

When the wind shifted to the east, directly behind us, we again rigged wing-and-wing and the rolling returned. By afternoon the wind veered a bit, giving us a broad reach, which was more comfortable and was our fastest point of sail. We made another 124 miles that day and were then only 334 miles out. Our excitement was building with each day's run.

We were wing-and-wing downwind again the following morning. The swells built to12 feet and *Tainui* rolled worse than ever. I rigged the staysail in tight again to dampen the roll and that helped a little, but it was still impossible to cook. Connie's log entry reads, "Just cold canned food for dinner. Ugh!" We then tried tacking downwind in a series of alternating broad reaches, which proved to be much more comfortable. We had to travel a few more miles to make progress toward our goal, but we were sailing faster. That evening we had only 172 miles to go. We would get there in two days if the wind held. Our excitement continued to mount. We could hardly wait!

In the night the wind backed to the southeast, so we broad-reached on course without tacking. However, by evening we were back to running downwind again. This time we took down the jib and sailed under just the boomed-out mainsail and "center-lined" staysail. *Tainui* slanted that way and didn't rock back so far. It was our most comfortable downwind configuration so far. Finding strategies for handling such situations was a continuing trial-and-error process. We learned more seamanship sailing 24 hours a day on this 33-day passage than we had in our entire career of recreational sailing.

That night, I predicted that we should see Nuku Hiva's neighboring island of Ua Huka off the starboard bow at about 6:00 the next morning, providing the wind held and our navigation had been accurate. Connie had conscientiously marked our probable progress with little "xs", on a chart, but tomorrow would be the acid test. We were very excited, but I was a little apprehensive—I dreaded having to figure out what to do and what to tell Connie if we did not spot land.

Ua Huka, like the rest of the Marquises, was a high, lush green island visible from about 35 miles in normal conditions. I had the early morning watch, and at first light I climbed up on the cabin top, pointed the binoculars a little off the starboard bow, and searched the horizon. I did not see an island, but there was a pile of clouds where I thought the island should be. This was a good sign, because tropical islands often attracted their own cloud cap. As the sun rose higher and the day brightened, I saw the unmistakable shape of the tip of a blue-green "mountain" rising out of the sea—even without the binoculars. I woke up Connie, and we stood on the deck and hugged each other as we watched our first land after 33 days at sea slowly rising above the horizon, right where it was supposed to be. I cannot fully express how emotional that moment was for us. The sighting was a great relief. The tension and worries of the long passage melted away. We had made it! We also felt a sense of pride and accomplishment for having met the challenges of the voyage and satisfaction that our navigation was successful. Finally, we were excited in anticipation of our arrival in an exotic new world. The excitement of a landfall never got old, but this time, after our first and longest ocean passage, was our most exciting landfall.

We sailed under the south side of Ua Huka surrounded by birds and marveling at the velvety green hills. I looked for Nuku Hiva when we passed Ua Huka, but it was not there. Oops! Maybe I congratulated myself too soon! I consulted our charts and the last Sat Nav fix and found I was looking in the wrong direction. Reoriented, I made out Nuku Hiva, almost lost in the clouds. We crossed the channel between the two islands and coasted along the southern shoreline of Nuku Hiva, passing the Omoo valley, made famous by Melville's books <u>Omoo</u> and <u>Billy Budd</u>, and continued to the entrance of Taiahoae Bay. We turned in and passed between the red and green buoys that marked the harbor entrance. Ahead of us, a dozen or so yachts were anchored in the back of the bay. Connie started the engine, and I dropped the foresails and stuffed them into their bags to clear the bowsprit for anchoring. Then I pulled the mainsail down and lashed it to the boom. Connie steered us to an open spot in the bay, and I went forward and extricated the anchor from its storm lashings, which had held it securely through all that the seas had thrown at it. I signaled Connie to shift into neutral and, as the boat slowed, I released the brake on the anchor windlass and kicked the reluctant anchor free. The sound of the chain rattling out was sweet music after so long a time. When enough had run out, I locked the brake on the windlass and gave Connie a thumbs-up signal for full reverse to test the holding of the anchor. The chain stretched tight and then sank down again, pulling *Tainui* gently forward, and I knew the anchor had held. I gave Connie the cut signal, and she killed the engine. When the sound of the diesel died away, there was an immediate, incredible silence as *Tainui* sat absolutely motionless in the flat water. It felt as if the whole world gave a collective sigh of relief. We were there!

CHAPTER FIVE

FRENCH POLYNESIA

Soon after we anchored, Jim, the single-hander from *Nepenthe*, and two men from *Cornucopia* came over and welcomed us. We celebrated our arrival by sharing a bottle of our special "*Tainui* Around the World" wine, which had been given us at our bon voyage party in San Diego. I was startled when Jim asked me, "What happened to your beard?" I actually had shaved off my beard on the crossing, but Jim had never seen me. I wondered if Jim had some kind of ESP. It turned out to be an eerie coincidence; Jim had just formed a mental picture of me with a beard when we talked on the radio.

Tired as we were, we couldn't resist going ashore that evening to attend a local festival on the beach. We ate rice and barbecued meat "al fresco" and were entertained by Polynesian music and dancing. We regretted that we were too tired to stay and socialize with the many friendly cruising sailors at the festival. Back aboard *Tainui* at 9:00 p.m., we enjoyed our first full night of undisturbed sleep in more than a month. A good night's sleep was a simple thing that we took for granted at home, but it was an incredible luxury after keeping all of those night watches on the long crossing.

After a late breakfast the next morning, we went ashore to shop for food. We bought some chicken at an open-air meat market and a few baguettes at a small bakery. Prices were high and the selection was meager. A dusty box of corn flakes that was three years past its use date would have cost us US$5. The lack of fresh fruit in the market was our biggest disappointment—after a month of canned food, we had eagerly anticipated fresh tropical fruit.

After stowing our purchases aboard, we started to put *Tainui* back in shipshape, but we were still tired from the crossing and went back to bed. We were awakened in the late afternoon by friends knocking on *Tainui's* hull to invite us to go to the happy hour at the Keikahanui Inn—a celebrated yachtsmen's hangout run by an American couple. We obligingly aroused ourselves and accompanied them in their inflatable dinghy.

There was no dock near the inn, so we landed the dinghy on the beach. We surfed in on a small wave, and as soon as we hit the sand, we jumped out and pulled the dinghy up the beach, but not before the next wave got us wet to the waist! It was not as embarrassing on a tropical beach among fellow cruisers as it had been when it happened to us in Monterey Bay.

We walked up a steep bank to the inn, which was surrounded by tropical flowers, and looked down on the picture-perfect sky-blue bay, where *Tainui* lay at anchor among the other yachts. The boats riding at anchor were an international mix: two Swedish, one German, three English, one Scottish, two Canadian, two French, and five American. The lounge was crowded with experienced sailors. We met an octogenarian Scandinavian single-hander who was on his fourth solo circumnavigation and boating couples and families from all over the world. We soaked up the atmosphere and basked in the company of accomplished ocean-crossing sailors. It was a "pinch me!" moment; we had become part of a world that we had only read or dreamed about. We spent several more evenings at the inn during our stay in Nuku Hiva.

From that first happy hour up at the Keikahanui Inn, we went back to the final day of the festival on the beach for another evening of local food and entertainment. This time we were more rested and enjoyed conversations with many yachties and locals. Eric, a young French doctor from Papeete (pronounced pah-pay-**ay**-tay), who was on a short visit giving insurance physicals, was particularly friendly. He had hopes of cruising someday himself and asked us a lot of questions. We continued our conversation aboard *Tainui* the next day. He thanked us profusely for our hospitality and insisted we visit him when we got to Tahiti.

The group of yachts in the harbor was constantly changing, with new arrivals and departures almost daily. We monitored the ham net in the evenings to keep track of vessels under way that we had shared the net with on our way across. One of these was Pat Henry, a 49-year-old architect from San Francisco attempting a solo circumnavigation in her 31-foot yacht *Southern Cross*. She radioed in one evening that her engine fuel pump had failed. She still had a long way to go and needed her engine to charge the batteries for her radio, satellite navigation, and running lights. She solved the problem by siphoning fuel to the engine from jerry jugs on deck. She undoubtedly had the nasty taste of diesel fuel in her mouth. We found this solution to be typical of her spunk and ingenuity as we followed her progress around the world. If I had thought to do the same thing, I could have used my own engine to get out of the anchorage at Isla Isabela, instead of needing a push away from the rocks.

Sunday morning we went ashore to explore the town more thoroughly. It was a beautiful tropical morning, but we were already feeling the heat and humidity at 9:00. Taiohae Bay was a little town in a small valley surrounded by mountains on three sides and the bay on the other. The mountains were of volcanic origin, reached heights of 3,000 to 4,000 feet, and were covered with velvety emerald green foliage. The town of Taiohae consisted of four small grocery stores, a meat market, a bakery, a seven-room hotel, two restaurants, two banks, a post office, and some French administrative offices. All the shops were closed on Sunday. On our walk up the hill behind the town, we saw small houses peeking through the foliage and wisps of white smoke here and there from the roasting pits in which people were preparing their Sunday dinners—often a whole pig. Most of the people we saw were relaxing around their homes or visiting with neighbors. They gave us friendly smiles, but there was little communication; they did not speak English and we did not speak French.

As usual after a long crossing, we had a list of boat work to do. I discovered that a lot of paint had come off one side of the bow near the waterline. Because it was on the leeward side for most of the voyage, this side was submerged a great deal of the time. Still it was a bit of a surprise. One would not think that paint designed for boats would come off from being underwater. Working from the dinghy, I cleaned it off and painted it as well as I could with *Tainui* in the water. To deal with the saltwater contamination in our freshwater tanks, I pumped them as dry as I could and refilled them. Because water had to be ferried from shore in jugs by dinghy in Taiohae Bay, I hauled just enough to get by until we could get to neighboring Daniel's Bay, where freshwater from a mountain stream was made available to cruisers by means of a hose attached to a buoy in the bay.

One afternoon I donned my snorkeling gear and went overboard to check *Tainui*'s hull. As I suspected, she was covered with goose-necked barnacles hanging from the hull on "necks" two to four inches long. I spent a few hours free-diving under *Tainui* removing goose-necked barnacles with a wooden scraper. I enjoyed diving in the warm clear water surrounded by curious multi-colored tropical fish. Meanwhile, Connie polished the brass portholes and tidied up the galley.

After I finished diving, I couldn't warm up in spite of the tropical heat. Connie, *Tainui*'s official health and safety officer, took my temperature and discovered that it was 103 degrees! She thought it might be dengue fever, since we had often been bitten by mosquitoes and "no-see-ums," which spread that virus. Dengue fever is debilitating and can last as long as two weeks. I needed to see the local doctor, but he only spoke French. A Scottish woman from another yacht, who had studied at the Sorbonne, graciously came to my rescue as interpreter. The doctor decided it was just the flu and wanted to supply me with aspirin—which I am allergic to. He had never heard of Tylenol, and we would never have found the French equivalent without the help of our interpreter.

The fever went away in two days, but we delayed our departure for three more while I regained my strength. When I felt strong enough, I cranked up our heavy anchor and got *Tainui* under way for an afternoon run around the corner to Tai Oa Bay, nicknamed "Daniel's Bay" for the head of its celebrated (and only) resident family. The bay was spectacularly beautiful, in a deep inlet surrounded by high emerald hills and unspoiled by civilization. A right-angle turn after entering provided excellent protection from the ocean waves. There were eight boats in the anchorage, most of them friends from Taiohae Bay. Daniel was very accommodating to yachts, supplying water, inviting visiting sailors into his home, and sharing fruit from his trees and meat from goats that he hunted in the jungle-clad hills above his house.

In the morning we landed our dinghy on the white, palm-fringed beach and paid our respects to Daniel and his wife, Antoinette. He proudly showed us their home, nestled among the trees. It was a large house built off of the ground with a wraparound veranda. Nearby they had a large open-air kitchen shed with cooking utensils and stalks of bananas hanging from its rafters. He was especially proud of a bank of solar panels connected to car batteries, which powered their house lights, a radio, and the 12-volt refrigerator in which he stored his wild goat meat. Antoinette cut us a bunch of fresh bananas and Daniel invited us to fill our water tanks from the hose he had run from the mountain stream to a buoy in the bay.

After we finished watering at the buoy and reanchored, a French sailor rowed over and invited us to his yacht for drinks with his wife and five-year-old daughter. We were joined by a Dutch couple with a five-year-old boy and discussed international affairs. It was interesting to see how Europeans viewed Americans. It seemed to be combination of envy at our standard of living and resentment at the way we used our superior power in the world. All in all, it was an interesting day in paradise.

Before we left Daniel's Bay, we set out to find what we were told was an impressive 2,000-foot waterfall five miles back in the jungle. Geoff and Heather, a British couple from *Kanaka*, tackled the trek with us. It was hot, dark, and dank in the jungle, and our insect spray was only slightly effective against the swarms of gnats and mosquitoes. The trail was narrow and muddy in some places and rocky in others. Occasionally, we waded across streams on slippery stones. It was easier going on the ruins of an ancient stone highway cut straight through the jungle—evidence of a once-flourishing civilization. There were 60,000 Marquiseans living in these islands when Europeans first arrived during the "Age of Discovery" (a euphemism for "Age of Conquest"). Ignoring the rights of the indigenous people, the Europeans planted their respective flags, claimed the islands for their own countries, and subdued the natives. "White man's diseases" had decimated the population of the Marquesans to the point that there were a mere 5,000 of them by the time we arrived.

Rock cairns had been set out to mark the trail, but some were missing, and in one place they were deliberately misleading. After backtracking from the false lead, we found our way to the falls, where we were surrounded by 2,000-foot vertical cliffs. There was no vantage point from which we could see the entire drop, but we could see most of it. The water turned into a fine cooling mist by the time it reached the bottom of the falls. We sat on rocks and ate our lunches cooled by nature's air conditioner. On the way back we lost the trail and wound up pushing our way into Daniel's compound through waist-high grass. Fortunately there were no poisonous snakes on the island! It was a long hot day, but a welcome change from sailing.

Before we left Daniel's Bay, Connie had her hair cut by Lon, a professional hairdresser from the Dutch vessel *Janana* (this was the first of many haircuts from Lon, as our boats crossed paths in the future), and I put a final coat of paint on the hull and took on 30 more gallons of water. Daniel gave us a parting gift of a leg of a goat, and Antoinette gave us a tapioca root. Connie treated the goat like a pork roast and the tapioca root like potatoes, which resulted in a couple of fine evening meals.

There was a bit of excitement the day before we left. A shark attacked a couple of sailors who were fishing in their inflatable dinghy near the entrance to the bay. It bit off the end of one of their oars and repeatedly bumped the dinghy with its nose. If the shark had punctured their fabric craft, it would have put them both in the water. Fortunately, the shark didn't know how easy it would have been to have had them for dinner!

It was then mid-June, giving us time to make a couple of stops before arriving in Papeete for the Bastille Day celebrations in mid-July. We began with a short visit to the little island of Ua Pu, just 25 miles away. It was a rough ride into 15-to-20 knot headwinds, but we were able to beat our way across under a full main and a working jib before dark. The island, studded with weird pointed-rock outcroppings shaped like devils horns, looked like it had been designed by Dr. Seuss.

Our friends Bill and Kathy, on *Affaire d'Amour*, were already in the harbor. They contacted us by radio with the news that we could get ice cream if we got in on time. This motivated us to push *Tainui* a little faster. The bay at the town of Hakahau was rough, but we slipped in behind a stone jetty and anchored in calm water as the sun set. I quickly launched the dinghy, and we hurried to the store and bought our ice cream cones just before closing time. Ice cream was one of the first things sailors looked for after long periods away from civilization, especially in the tropics—we were no exception. We sat on the curb and savored every lick.

I went ashore at 6:30 the next morning and set out to find a house where I had been told I could get fresh baguettes—if I got there early enough! I found the baker operating out of a shed at the back of his white frame house and came back with four loaves. We went back to town later and bought provisions from the four small, expensive shops. Along the way we met a Swiss couple who told us how to order fresh tropical fruit from men who go out into the jungle and bring it back the next day. The Swiss sailors came aboard *Tainui* for drinks that evening, and we had strong European coffee and Swiss pastry aboard their boat the next morning—not a bad life! We made a quick trip ashore in the afternoon to pick up our fruit, fresh from the hills—bananas, papayas, and pamplemouss, (large grapefruits sometimes called pomelos). This was a real treat after our frustration at the lack of fruit in Nuku Hiva.

Before we embarked on the 600-mile passage to Takaroa in the Tuamotus, we took naps to rest up for the night watches. Back at sea, we were able to get on the roll call of the ham net and called our contact in Salem. We couldn't use the radio in port without a temporary license from the country we were in, and we couldn't get a French Polynesian license until we got to Papeete.

We received a rude reintroduction to ocean sailing. Changeable 25- to 30-knot tailwinds made for rough going and frequent sail changes. We headed for a small harbor on Ua Pu to take shelter for the night, but the wind and waves eventually calmed down and we altered course for the Tuamotus. We couldn't sleep while *Tainui* rolled in following seas. It was always hard to sleep the first night, especially in rough seas, but eventually we would get so tired that, when it was our turn to sleep, we would be out as soon as our head hit the pillow.

In the morning, we enjoyed our fresh fruit with breakfast as we rolled along peacefully in steady 10-to-15 knot trade winds on a beautiful broad reach (wind coming diagonally off the stern). These favorable trade winds stayed with us all the way to the Tuamotus, giving us a lovely passage. We made good time on this trip; *Tainui* was much faster without the crop of goose-necked barnacles on her bottom.

The days were sunny and clear and the breeze kept us cool at night. The moonless night sky was spectacular with no interference from the artificial lights of civilization. From *Tainui*'s deck, the horizon was only seven miles away, so the night sky was a huge bowl glistening with stars all the way down to the sea. A comet's tail of sparkling biophosphorescence churned up by *Tainui*'s wake added to the beauty of the night.

We took special care with our navigation approaching the Tuamotus. They were called "The Dangerous Islands" because they were low-lying atolls, only visible from within a distance of seven miles, and had surrounding reefs and unpredictable currents. Many boats had been wrecked on these reefs. We were thankful for our satellite navigation and radar. With only sextant navigation it would have been easy to miss our landfall and wind up on a reef. We were doubly cautious because we predicted a nighttime arrival at the atolls.

A few minutes before the sunset on our fifth day, we spotted the tops of a line of palm trees peeking above the horizon. Takaroa, like the rest of the Tuamotus, was an atoll—a circular string of low, flat islands called *motus* surrounding a central lagoon, with a fringing reef a few hundred yards offshore. The lagoon was entered through a gap in the reef followed by a narrow pass between two *motus*. Strong currents ran in and out as the tide filled and emptied the lagoon.

It would have been dangerous to enter in the dark. The radar showed the shore of the main island clearly, but did not show the reef at all. Our chart put the reef about a half-mile offshore. We hove to for the night about five miles off and kept a periodic radar watch to make sure the current was not drifting us toward the reef.

The atoll was a pretty sight in the morning. We could see the beach and the dark green palm trees. The ocean was light blue with a line of white breakers starting about two hundred yards off the reef. They crashed on the reef with showers of white spray. There were no navigational aids marking the entrance, but the pass showed clearly as a dark blue gap in the breakers.

We would need to enter the lagoon at slack tide. All lagoons have strong currents. Water cannot run through the narrow pass fast enough to keep up with a rising tide, creating a strong flood tide. On the falling tide, the reverse is true: the full lagoon must empty itself through the narrow gap, causing a strong out-flowing ebb tide.

A sad story in a book by a professional delivery skipper had taught me to make a straight-in approach from well off the reef. Approaching a similar atoll, he had seen a beautiful new yacht up on the reef near the pass being pounded by heavy surf. In the small hotel on the island, he met the broken-hearted retired couple who had sold their home and put the money into the yacht. They told him that they had approached the pass running just outside the line of breakers only to find that the breakers suddenly moved out beyond them and were pushing them toward the reef. They desperately fought their way toward the pass, but the breakers pushed them onto the reef near the entrance.

They were the victims of their ignorance regarding two important facts about atolls and reefs. First, the breaker line was unstable, moving out and in depending on the size of the waves; and second, the flood tide created a fierce current rushing into the lagoon near the pass. They were within a few yards of the entrance when they hit the reef. Once on the reef, each successive breaker pushed their boat farther up. Local people got the couple off, but there was no way to save the boat.

This is a good illustration of my belief that we amateur sailors need the luck to avoid facing a situation we can't handle while we are still learning from our mistakes. If this couple had been able to fight their way into the pass by the skin of their teeth, they would have been terrified but wiser. A few yards were the difference between a valuable learning experience and disaster. After hearing this story, I never took *Tainui* near any breakers, but I had to wonder what critical future situations might challenge my own relative inexperience!

My years of sailing on the Columbia River had taught me not to dock going downstream. The boat was harder to stop, because it had to be moving faster than the current in order to have steerage. If the lines were mishandled, the current would catch the stern and swing it out, creating an awkward situation. Coming in upstream, the opposite was true; we could come in as slowly as we wanted to and even stop, back up, or move sideways by adjusting our speed relative to the current. Our current tables for Takaroa predicted the current was flowing in, so we waited off the pass for the tide to change.

While we were waiting, three Tuamotuan men came out in an open boat to greet us. They wanted to know why we were not coming in. I had some difficulty explaining my theory about docking downstream, partly because of the language problem—they spoke broken English with a strong French accent. They seemed anxious to have us come in, arguing vociferously that it would be no problem at all and that they would be right there to help me. I couldn't figure out why they were in such a hurry, but against my better judgment, I followed them in, figuring that the current would not be very strong this late in the tide.

Entering our first pass through a reef was exciting. The gap was narrow and breakers were crashing onto the reef very close on each side of us with a loud ka-WHUMP! Inside the reef, the color of the water was a good indicator of its depth. Deep water in the pass was dark blue, and as the water got shallower, the color got lighter. The men led me toward a concrete wharf lying on our left side, parallel to the shore of the largest and most populous *motu*. The current was still running in at three knots, which meant an uncomfortably fast approach. I shifted *Tainui* into reverse as we neared the wharf and Connie stood by on the port side ready to throw a dock line. When we got close enough, she threw a stern line to a man on the dock. If he cleated it off, the stern would settle against the dock and the current would push *Tainui* alongside the pier with her bow pointed toward the lagoon until we could tie off the bow. But before he could cleat off the line, another man tried to stop us by grabbing the *Tainui*'s bow pulpit. When he pulled her bow in, her stern swung out into the current, spinning us around. I yelled at Connie to cast off the dock line and we were swept backwards into the lagoon. Coming back out against the current, I was able to stop *Tainui* alongside the wharf and hold her there against the current until the shorelines were securely tied. We were safely docked and no damage was done, but I wished I knew how to say "I told you so" in French.

A couple of five- or six-year-old children came aboard almost immediately. They spoke to us in French. Neither of us spoke French, but I had memorized about 500 French words. The word that stood out in their attempts to communicate was *bon bon*. That I understood. We were glad we had stocked up on candy, along with balloons, crayons, and coloring books, for just such an occasion. The father of one of the urchins stopped by and gave us some fresh fish that tasted like trout. We learned later that this was coral trout—an especially good eating fish in tropical waters.

Our candy must have been a success because several children came aboard at 6:00 a. m. the next morning. We let them hang out in the cockpit while we ate breakfast below. The children eventually wandered off and we went exploring. We walked across a bridge to a neighboring *motu* and followed the road to the beach on the inside of the lagoon. There we met a woman standing in the water cleaning fish and oysters. She greeted us in English and invited us into her home. Her name was Juanita and she introduced us to her husband, Sonny. They gave us some pretty shells, a pumpkinlike squash, some *poisson cru* (a dish of garnished raw fish "cooked" in lime juice), and some drinking coconuts. This kind of friendliness and generosity was characteristic of the Polynesian people. We appreciated it, but we were unsure what we should do for them in return.

Later in the day we walked to a cultured pearl farm. The manager took us through the whole process, from implanting the "seeds" in the shell to harvesting the finished pearls, and showed us some of their most beautiful specimens. Pearl farming was the biggest cash business on Takaroa. The owners and managers were all either Europeans or Japanese; the local people only held laboring positions. More Tuamotuans were involved in the copra (dried coconut) business, but the pay was at subsistence level.

When we returned to *Tainui*, we entertained Juanita and her baby on board. She requested our home mailing address, promised to send us a pearl, and asked us to send her some earrings in return. Typically, we never heard from Juanita again. This kind of request was common with villagers, but was seldom carried out.

The majority of the population lived on the largest motu. It had the only wharf, a small airport, and a little village with a few facilities. When I walked through the town to the house that served as a bakery, everything was hot and glaring white. The roads, houses, and yards were all the color of the white beach sand. I regretted leaving my sunglasses on the boat as I made my way along the road squinting in the brightness. A high-noon siesta-like stillness pervaded the village. The baker gave me three loaves of bread without charge, because he had burned them on the bottom that day.

Life at the copra wharf was interesting, but smelly and lacking in privacy. The drying copra had a pungent, offensive odor. We enjoyed watching men loading copra on small trading vessels or off-loading larger ships anchored outside the reef and carrying the loads in with lifeboats. Once a lifeboat came in carrying one enormous box about the size of a commercial freezer. It towered over the small boat and rocked back and forth precariously as it approached the pier. We doubted the men could get it safely up on the wharf; however, using ropes, skill, and lots of manpower they were successful. We never found out what was in the box.

The lack of privacy was mainly due to the children. They would never have left the boat if we didn't send them home at meal times, and there was no point in staying at the smelly wharf with a lovely lagoon beckoning.

We waited for slack tide the next morning and motored out into the lagoon. It was our first lagoon, and it was strikingly beautiful. We could see the bottom in such clear detail through the sparkling clear water that it appeared to be much shallower than it actually was. We could hardly believe our depth sounder! The white, sandy bottom made the water the translucent, light green color seen in travel posters of the Caribbean.

The lagoon was about five miles across and ringed with small *motus* with white beaches, backed by rows of coconut palm trees blowing in the trade winds. Connie stood up on the bow pulpit to watch for coral heads, which showed up as dark brown or purple areas in the water. I stood at the wheel, to take in the whole scene. Standing at the wheel with Connie on the bow pulpit holding onto the forestay with one hand and shading her eyes with the other as we sailed into this beautiful lagoon fulfilled my concept of the essence of cruising.

We motored for an hour across the lagoon, dodging coral heads, to a *motu* that had a small pearl culture operation on it. Three other yachts were anchored off its shore, including *Affaire d'Amour*, owned by our friends Bill and Kathy. We circled until we found a clear spot on the bottom where our anchor chain would not snag a coral head and anchored at a depth of 25 feet. This was the first time we could actually see *Tainui*'s anchor on the bottom. Bill had taken the once-a-week flight to Tahiti to pick up a boat part, leaving Kathy alone on *Affaire d'Amour* for a week or two.

The two families that ran the pearl business invited all of us sailors to an evening potluck on their dock. We were nervous watching their children, ages one and three, walking without life jackets on the dock and ramps. We all kept an eye on them, but they seemed to have adapted well to living above the water. After dinner we played a friendly dice game that they called "Quilcene." We ran into this game several times later in the South Pacific, called "5,000" and "Oh Hell."

We spent five days at the pearl farm anchorage. We took walks on the beach on the ocean side of the *motu* looking for shells. I fished off *Tainui* at anchor; there were lots of fish swimming around in her shadow, but the only ones big enough to eat were the parrotfish. Several of them bit, but I couldn't keep them on. Pilot fish, which are not good eating, kept taking my bait. They looked like miniature sharks with narrow oval suction cups on top of their flat heads. They stuck on to large fish, such as sharks and whales, which is how they got their name. Unhooking them, throwing them back, and baiting my hook again became such a nuisance that I gave up fishing. We also visited back and forth with Kathy on *Affaire d'Amour* and helped her with minor boat problems while Bill was away.

We delayed our departure from the anchorage for two days waiting out 30-knot winds and then became impatient and left in spite of the wind. All went well until we approached the main channel by the copra wharf. The lagoon was still emptying out, creating a strong current. I circled around to kill time until the current went slack. As I came back by the pass, I got too close to the opening and the current started to suck us in! I gunned the motor to get across the entrance, but soon saw that we were not going to clear the rocks on the far side of the channel. I had to either stop the boat or turn her around. With her full keel, *Tainui* needed lots of room to turn and her heavy displacement made her hard to stop. There was no time for indecision: I put the engine into reverse, gave her full throttle, and hoped she would stop in time. It seemed to take forever, but finally she ground to a stop with her bow inches from the rocks. I kept her in reverse and slowly backed her into the middle of the channel, and she was swept backwards all the way out into the ocean. We rigged our dock lines at sea and made a successful upstream docking at the copra wharf with the wind still gusting to 30knots.

The next day we went to the airport to see if Bill was coming in on the weekly flight. Airplane day was a big event in Takaroa. Everyone on the island seemed to be going to the airport. We had just started walking when we were given a ride in the back of a pickup truck. The entire population of Takaroa was probably not more than 200 or 300 people, so everyone knew everyone, and those with vehicles routinely offered rides.

The scene at the airport reminded me of a crowd waiting for a parade. When the small plane arrived, we found that very few of these people were actually meeting passengers, departing themselves, or seeing people off: airport day was an entertainment on an island with few other amusements! Bill was not on the plane, so it meant another week alone for Kathy.

Back in town, I got a strange gift for doing a favor. Sonny came by one day and asked me to go with him to fix a propane stove at the house of one of his friends. Parts were scarce on the atoll and I had brought a goodly supply for *Tainui*'s stove, but doubted that my parts would be compatible with his friend's stove. I felt obliged to help, so I made up a tool kit and a bag of parts and went along. The problem was simple and I soon had the stove going. Sonny's friend insisted on giving me the gift of a very large sea-turtle shell that was hanging on the wall of his hut, in return for my help. The shell was four feet long, three feet wide, and two feet deep. I didn't want it. It would be illegal to take it into the United States, and it would be an embarrassment aboard *Tainui*. However, I felt that culturally I had no option. I accepted it graciously, took it back to *Tainui*, and tied it to the stern pulpit. Our friends amused themselves by suggesting uses for it …. like maybe a bathtub …. or fitting it with oars for a spare dinghy.

It was still windy the next day as we continued to prepare for the trip to Tahiti. Sonny gave us three five-gallon jerry jugs of water from his cistern and a bag of limes. We shopped for food at the store (*magasin* in French) managed by Fred, an Australian man married to a Tuamotuan woman. His wares were limited. He had no butter, eggs, produce, or fresh meat—only canned goods. Fortunately we were only provisioning for a three-or four-day run. Fred gave us permission to fill three more water jugs from a cistern behind a Mormon church. This small atoll had three churches: a small Assembly of God church and churches for both branches of the Mormons: the Latter-Day Saints and the Reformed Latter-Day Saints. The LDS and the RLDS were worlds apart and had no intention of uniting; they were in fact a divisive issue on the island.

Back at the wharf, a French yacht was required to leave its space to make room for a copra boat. We gave them our space, cautiously maneuvered *Tainui* through the pass in the reef, and set our course for Papeete.

A light breeze moved us gently along under full sail throughout the first day, and by evening the usually brisk trade winds became lighter still. It was a relief to have calm weather the first day out. In rough-weather departures, I had to be very careful to avoid seasickness. I would stay in the cockpit and Connie, who *never* got seasick, handled navigation and the radio schedule below until I got my "sea legs." We continued to ghost along slowly for three days. I did not resort to motoring because I never really trusted the motor. I would get a sinking feeling in my stomach every time it slowed down or died. I didn't run it for long periods of time at sea for fear it would break down before we got to port. It was particularly important to have it working as we entered a harbor or a passed through a reef. My fear was not unfounded; we had already been towed into two ports in Mexico.

We also much preferred sailing to motoring. In place of the vibration, smell and worry of the engine, sailing in good conditions was an aesthetically pleasing experience. It was quiet and natural. The boat made progress by cooperating with nature, riding the wind and the waves rather than powering through them. I always felt a sense of relief when the motor went silent, and exhilaration when *Tainui* heeled over and strained forward, gathering speed as she was pulled silently along by the wind in her sails. Even though I understood the physics of how a boat could actually sail *toward* the wind, it still felt like magic to me when it happened.

Sailing so slowly in beautiful weather was relaxing. Without waves, the ocean turned the purest shade of blue that I had ever seen. We were going so slowly that multi-colored tropical fish congregated in the shade of *Tainui's* hull. We slid by a sunfish drifting near the surface. This strange creature appears to be nothing but a giant head five or six feet across. Normal activities could be carried out without the complications and dangers of rough-weather sailing. For example, Connie set up her portable typewriter on a folding table in the cockpit and typed some letters and an edition of our Travel Log, which we sent periodically to a list of friends and relatives. She was also inspired to cook more elaborate meals.

In the process of cooking, Connie discovered that holes had been chewed in boxes of flour and zip lock bags containing dry goods. We spent most of one day emptying the food lockers and inspecting them. We did not find any mouse or rat droppings, but did find some small black bugs. We cleaned and sprayed the lockers, threw away some old staples, double-bagged and replaced the rest, and hoped that we had solved the problem.

A sudden strong wind came up as we hove to off the pass into Papeete at 3:00 a.m. and waited for the sun to come up. When we entered the pass through the reef in the morning, a series of rainsqualls swept across us. I motored in with the sails furled, but still had difficulty keeping *Tainui* on course in the narrow pass with wind gusts pushing her bow around. Once inside the reef, we headed up the channel between the reef and the island toward a free anchorage. We immediately sailed into such a heavy tropical downpour that I could not see to steer. The wind came in straight from behind, soaking me and pouring down into the boat through the companionway hatch. The canvas dodger over the hatch was open to the stern and caught the following wind like a mini-spinnaker, making *Tainui* even harder to control. I made a quick U-turn in the middle of the channel, putting *Tainui*'s bow into the wind, and stopped the boat. Our dodger's windshield then served as my protection.

These early morning squalls were surprisingly cold for the tropics. When the rain relented, we came about and proceeded to the free anchorage just inside the reef and across the channel from the posh Maeva Beach Hotel and yacht moorage.

We arrived at the anchorage cold, wet, tired, and frustrated, but before I could get the anchor down, Jim from *Nepenthe* came over in his dinghy with a cheerful "Welcome to Tahiti!" As he helped me with the anchor the sun broke out from the clouds. Jim's act of kindness at just the right time and the feeling of the warm sun on our backs lifted our spirits.

The water in this anchorage was incredibly clear. I could see *Tainui*'s anchor in the sand at a depth of 20 feet and make out every detail of the bottom. Once, when we came back in our dinghy on a clear moonlit night, *Tainui* appeared to be floating in the air up above her moon shadow, tethered to the ground by her anchor chain. The water was so invisible that she looked more like a kite flying than a boat at anchor.

We gained access to the shore from this anchorage by rowing our dinghy across the channel to a small park, which turned out to be a popular spot for topless sunbathers—mostly Tahitian women. (Connie claims that I had never kept our binocular lenses so clean!) Due to the French influence, topless sunbathing was common on Tahiti's beaches. We were amused that Western missionaries had originally made the local women cover their bare breasts, but today's chic French women were leading them back to toplessness. This was true only in the French islands; throughout the rest of the South Pacific most local women still wore the colorful but formless "Mother Hubbard" dresses favored by the missionaries.

Our battle with the rat started on our first night in Tahiti. Lying in bed, we heard scratching behind the wooden lining right next to our heads. We had picked up a copra rat at the wharf in Takaroa. Connie was totally freaked. There was no way she would sleep anywhere inside the boat as long as a rat was aboard. It didn't help for me to argue that the rat was safely behind the wood lining. She hauled our cushions and bedding out into the cockpit. We slept on the deck with our heads under the dodger and tarps rigged to protect the rest of our bodies from the nightly rain showers. This kept us dry, but the water running along the deck soaked our cushions. I bought a trap in town, but it took us five days to catch the rat. We learned that French rats do not like peanut butter or even cheese (how un-French!). Bacon was the culprit's undoing. I was happy to get back into our dry double berth below. Sleeping in the fresh air on the deck sounds refreshing, but in the rainy tropics it left a lot to be desired. We found rat droppings and other evidence of the rat's mischief for days afterward.

About that time, harbor police ordered all yachts out of our lovely, quiet, free anchorage, and we were forced to take a mooring buoy at the ritzy Maeva Beach Hotel for US$3. a night. Many friends from former anchorages were there, and we made new friends. Once again there was lots of socializing between yachts and sharing adventures ashore with fellow sailors.

During the rat war, we explored the city of Papeete. We commuted the four miles to town on *le truck. Le trucks* had flatbeds with bench seats along the sides and a roof. They were usually open on the sides, but canvas curtains rolled down when it rained. Huge speakers blared out loud electronic music, either native Tahitian or American rock. We enjoyed meeting and talking to local people as we rode along. Many of them spoke only French, but there were always some who were eager to try out their English.

Papeete, the capital of French Polynesia, was a city of 65,000 people with lots of expensive shops and restaurants. The public fruit-and-vegetable market was the most immaculate (and costliest) of our entire trip. In spite of the high prices, we splurged a bit to enjoy some of the benefits of civilization. There was a major French presence in Papeete, including bureaucrats, military personnel, business people, expatriates, and tourists. Many French men had beautiful Tahitian wives and very attractive mixed-race children. The French had been in Tahiti long enough that many of the wives were also of mixed blood. We felt that the native Tahitian men and women were the handsomest race of people we met in our travels.

We attended the Bastille Day parade. The French portion was formal and military. Prototypically rugged men of the French Foreign Legion passed by, swinging their arms stiffly and wearing funny pillbox hats, which I thought were out of keeping with their macho image (mesh-covered combat helmets would have seemed more appropriate). The sergeant marching beside them chanted out his cadence with a loud "Gosh! Gosh! Gosh!" I knew *gauche* was French for "left," but I was amused at its double meaning. In contrast, the Tahitians in the parade were colorful, festive, and free-spirited. They wore flowery native costumes and sang and danced their way along the parade route. The women wore sarong skirts and black lacquered coconut-shell halves for a bras. The shells didn't look too comfortable, and with Tahiti's historical toplessness, they were not authentic traditional attire. We also found it ironic that these Tahitians were participating in the French Independence Day celebrations when they themselves were being denied independence by the French in spite of a strong Tahitian independence movement.

The parade route was on a broad park-like boulevard that ran along the sea wall where many visiting yachts were moored. After the parade, Connie and I made the rounds of parties of yachties picnicking on grassy areas under palm trees. We had happy reunions with old friends who plied us with goodies and drinks. Werner, our buddy-boating friend from the Washington and Oregon coasts, invited us aboard *Columbine*. *Columbine* was moored Mediterranean-style with her bow held off by an anchor and her stern tied to the sea wall. To get aboard, we got into his dinghy and pulled ourselves out along her stern lines. We caught up on past travels and had a lot of laughs, and a few more drinks. As we were leaving, Werner warned me to be careful stepping down into his round-bottomed wooden dinghy. I boasted, "Don't worry about me, Werner. I have had a rowboat since I was 11 years old—you can't tell me anything about getting into a dinghy." Of course, when I stepped off *Columbine* down into the dinghy, it immediately flipped over, dumping me into the water fully clad—a clear case of pride going before the fall.

After changing into dry clothes back on *Tainui*, we spent the evening watching the Tahitian version of hula dancing at the Maeva Beach hotel. It involved much more violent hip shaking than the Hawaiian style. I was amazed that these women could make such incredible gyrations with their lower bodies, while holding their heads so still they could have balanced a glass of water.

We exchanged visits with a Japanese couple from a yacht in our moorage. They came aboard *Tainui* bringing gifts, as was their custom. Friends who had sailed to Japan told us that reciprocating Japanese gift giving had been a big problem for them. On our return visit to their boat, we struggled to find an appropriate gift and settled on a photo of *Tainui*.

A few days after the initial exchange of visits, the Japanese skipper came back on board carrying a fishing tackle box, which contained an assortment of beautiful fishing lures. He explained that this was his hobby; he had made them himself: They were in the form of squid, with mother of pearl heads and colorful feather bodies. He selected an assortment of sizes and said, "These are for you." I suspected that I was being set up for something and wondered, "What on earth am I going to have to do in return?" Then he said, "I have *lequist*." I thought maybe *lequist* was another gift, maybe a kind of Japanese liquor. When I said, "I don't understand," he explained his "request." He said, "You have turtle. I promise my friend in Japan special gift from South Pacific. I like please to have turtle." Referring to his tackle box, he asked, "How many more you want for turtle?" I didn't ask for more, but he gave me several more lures and some other assorted tackle and took the "turtle." He had no idea how relieved I was to get the rid of that turtle shell.

On one of our trips to town, we visited the office of Eric, the doctor we had met at the festival in Nuku Hiva. He invited us to his home for dinner. He lived with his girlfriend in a lovely little house on a hill, surrounded by flowering vegetation. They fed us an elegant French dinner followed by passion fruit, which they obviously felt was a particularly exotic treat. As I recall, we scooped the contents out with a spoon and were not terribly impressed. However, as always, we were grateful for the opportunity to try something special that we might not come across again.

Eric generously loaned us his car for a day of sightseeing. We invited another cruising couple to join us and made a "circumnavigation" of the island of Tahiti. Several months later, the announcement of the birth of their first child came to us via our Seattle address.

Before we left Tahiti, we took *le truck* to the Gauguin Museum. It was set in a park with statues scattered about among its many bushes and trees, and it had its own lagoon where a few visiting yachts were anchored. The museum building was in a poor state of repair and contained many copies of Gauguin's paintings, but only one original. Originals had become so expensive that the museum could not afford to buy more.

As we prepared to leave for Moorea, we learned that our son Larry had sent a mail package to us at Tahiti. Instead of waiting for it, we arranged for Pat Henry, the solo circumnavigator on *Southern Cross*, to bring it to us at Moorea. Pat was supporting herself by selling her excellent watercolors in Papeete. She was moored beside us and did a lovely miniature of *Tainui* at Tahiti with the island of Moorea in the background.

Even though Moorea was only 10 miles away, we did extensive provisioning in Papeete because they were the last big grocery stores we would see until we got to Pago Pago (pronounced "Pango Pango"), American Samoa. Diesel fuel was so expensive that we purchased only enough to get us to American Samoa, where fuel prices were much lower.

Our route to Moorea took us through Tahiti's fringing reef by way of tiny Tapuna Pass. It was a little scary motoring through the small cut in the reef with heavy surf pounding it. Smaller breakers in the pass worried us, since our cruising guide warned us to watch out for shallow water. We proceeded cautiously, keeping a close watch on the depth sounder, and breathed a sigh of relief when *Tainui's* four-and-a-half-foot draft proved shallow enough to make it into deep water without bumping the bottom.

We had been casual in our preparations for the 10-mile trip to Moorea in fair weather. We hadn't secured all of our gear and were towing our dinghy behind us. All went well at first as we motored over soft smooth swells. Halfway across, however, the wind came up from the west, right on our nose, and blew hard. The seas built up quickly. I secured things on deck and checked on the dinghy. It was taking on water as it bucked and dove in the waves. I pulled the waterlogged dinghy alongside, attached its bowline to the mainsheet halyard, winched it up to spill the water out, and pulled it aboard. While I was tightening its lashings on the foredeck, Connie was hand steering. Two waves crashed together and hit *Tainui* alongside the cockpit, sending a column of water straight up in the air. The wind drifted it over Connie's head and it came straight down on her like a waterfall. Individually, the waves were not unusually big, but their collision made them much bigger. When this phenomenon occurs in a storm, it can produce a giant wave with a devastating impact on a yacht. Connie didn't appreciate the remarkable feat of timing it took to produce this unusual effect right over her head!

We motored around the north end of Moorea and proceeded to the pass into Cook's Bay, keeping well off the reef. The dark blue water in the gap was calm, protected by the wind shadow on the leeward side of the high island. We passed through uneventfully and anchored in the late afternoon among a dozen yachts in the back of the bay.

We ate dinner in the cockpit and enjoyed the view. Cook's Bay was the most beautiful anchorage of our entire voyage. It was a long and slender fjord surrounded by high craggy peaks. These lush green peaks were actually eroded crater rims ringed by needles of lava. Its white sandy beaches were backed by a row of palm trees, which, in turn, were backed by high hills covered with lush green jungle leading up to the volcanic peaks. We eagerly awaited the morning when we could explore this lovely island.

I got up in time to watch the sunrise. As it rose, the sun shone through a series of notches and passes in the mountains, illuminating different parts of the scene like a giant moving spotlight. I rowed my dinghy around the anchorage, exchanging greetings with some of the anchored vessels. A sailor from our home marina in Newport, Oregon, came along in his dinghy, and we held our boats together and had our first long conversation. Our paths didn't cross much at home; we were both busy working at our respective jobs and getting our boats ready. It took a chance meeting in a quiet anchorage in Polynesia thousands of miles from home for us to get acquainted.

I rowed to shore and bought fresh baguettes from a Chinese shop. We had breakfast in the cockpit, still in awe of the beauty of our surroundings. After breakfast we went ashore and explored the small town at the back of the bay. It consisted of four mini grocery stores, two hotels, two boutiques, and several restaurants. Along the way, we met Heather from *Kanaka*. She and her husband, Geoff, had been our companions on the jungle trek to the waterfalls at Daniel's Bay in Nuku Hiva. We walked half a mile down a narrow road to the Bali Hai Club. Multi-colored flowers were blooming in high banks all along the road. I recognized frangipani, which Polynesians call *tiara*, and hibiscus. It was like walking through a botanical garden.

The Bali Hai Club was a picturesque Polynesian-style resort. The guest rooms were cottages on stilts out over the bay. We indulged ourselves with the club's popular coconut ice cream. On the way back out to *Tainui*, one of the oarlocks broke, so we paddled with the oars like a Polynesian couple in a dugout canoe.

Our time in Cook's Bay was divided between working aboard *Tainui* on windy or rainy days and touring ashore in good weather. We attended a couple of late-afternoon happy hours at the Bali Hai Club and swam and snorkeled off their beach.

We went to church with a couple from California. She was a choir director and wanted to check out the local music. After church we attended a farewell potluck for their pastor, who was leaving to take another church. The meal was local cuisine, prepared by the women of the church. We were not sure what some of the foods were, but most dishes involved pork, bananas, and taro root, all cooked in coconut milk. Additional bottles of coconut milk, which the parishioners applied liberally as a condiment, were on the tables. There were no eating utensils; the Tahitians were all eating with their fingers. Thanks to our

Peace Corps experience in Malaysia, we had excellent "finger-eating-skills." During the meal, two dogs that had been scavenging under the tables got into a ferocious fight. Two big Polynesian men picked them up and threw them out an open window. That was the last we heard from the dogs. The people spoke very little English, so communication was difficult and the long speeches became boring, but once again we were grateful for the cultural experience.

The California couple later served us dinner in their Bali Hai Club thatched-roof hut above the water. Later, we had them aboard *Tainui*. They gave us a copy of Jack London's <u>Voyage of the Snark</u>, which chronicles his sailboat journey at the turn of the century along much of the same route that we were taking. It was interesting to see the difference between the South Pacific when he saw it and when we sailed through it.

We rented a car with a cruising couple we had known in Mexico and spent a wonderful day driving all the way around Moorea. Cresting a hill on the east side of the island, we looked down on an incredibly beautiful scene. The white sand of the beach extended under the water all the way out to the reef a mile away, making the water within the reef a translucent light green. It was dotted with coral heads and a few anchored yachts. The waves on the reef made a brilliant white line against the dark blue ocean, backed by majestic Tahiti across the channel.

We stopped at the beach and swam, snorkeled, and bodysurfed for the afternoon. We were amused when two large pigs came running down the beach, passing through the sunbathers and picnickers before disappearing into some bushes. A French family came down the beach on horseback and stopped and chatted briefly with a pair of topless sunbathers. On our way back, we stopped for dinner and a show at the Bali Hai Hotel (not the Club), which was started by four American GIs following World War II. We met the only one of them who was still there. He loved to tell how they made a pact to return after the war and start the hotel.

Judging by the crop of goose-necked barnacles I had scraped off at Nuku Hiva, *Tainui* was past due for a haul-out to renew her bottom paint—a toxic paint that prevents the growth of marine organisms. The boatyards in Tahiti would be expensive, so we decided to head for an affordable new facility on the island of Raiatea, a short distance to the northwest. The package from Larry had not yet arrived in Tahiti, and Pat Henry had already joined us at Moorea, so we made a similar arrangement by radio for another yacht to bring our mail to Raiatea.

We winched up the anchor, moved *Tainui* to the town dock, and prepared for the trip. I filled the water tanks, pulled the dinghy up on deck, and lashed it down, and Connie topped up our supplies of fresh bread and fruit. As we motored out through the reef, we sat in the cockpit and looked back to fix the beauty of Cook's Bay in our memories. Further offshore, we could see the entire island of Moorea rising above the sea behind us. Its hills and mountains jutted up out of the sea in picturesque shapes, and its valleys were dark shadows between the blue-green hills. As it faded into the distance it seemed to be floating in the mist above the horizon. We were told that Moorea was James Michener's inspiration for the island of Bali Hai in his book *South Pacific*. Other islands have also made that claim, but Moorea was a very convincing candidate as we sailed away.

The trade winds were silent that morning, so we motored for three hours in flat, calm seas to give the batteries a good charge; then we put up all of our sails to catch what little breeze there was and ghosted along at a peaceful two or three knots for the rest of the day and through the tropical night. A brisk north wind came up in the morning, putting us on a close beat to windward; but our progress was so slow that we motor-sailed the last 33 miles.

We arrived at the pass through the reef at Raiatea in fast-fading light at dusk. There is very little twilight in the tropics. The sun went straight down, and it was dark 15 minutes after sunset. There was not enough time to find the boatyard before dark, so we were planning to heave to for the night when I spotted the masts of two sailboats anchored in the shelter of a small islet just inside the reef. We went in, anchored beside them, and were relieved not to have to keep a watch at sea for another night. A little later we saw the red and green running lights of another yacht coming through in the dark. It steered toward our masthead anchor lights and turned on its deck floodlights, and the crew dropped their anchor beside us.

After a restful night, we motored up the inside channel past the town of Uturoa to the carenage (boatyard). It was Friday afternoon and there would be no workers to haul *Tainui* out until Monday, so the boatyard manager gave us the use of their mooring buoy for the weekend. A veteran cruising couple, Bob and Maria from *Countess Maria*, invited us aboard for a drink. Later, Dean, an old friend from our Mexico days, sailed in on *Sanity*. He hitched a ride to town with us and helped us celebrate our wedding anniversary at an excellent seafood restaurant called *Quay de Pecheur* (Fisherman's Wharf). A man at the restaurant told us that there was no public transportation at that time of night and graciously drove us the four miles back to the boatyard.

One sunny morning while we were waiting for *Tainui* to be hauled out, we took a leisurely walk to the town of Uturoa. It was a pleasant four-mile walk through flowers and fruit trees, interspersed with rustic village houses and farm plots. We were pleased to find that Uturoa, the second-largest city in French Polynesia, had good groceries and hardware stores and that we would be able to tie up at the town wharf for convenient provisioning when it was time to leave. We browsed the shops and Connie bought a pretty *pareu* at a small boutique. *Pareus* are colorful wraparound Polynesian sarongs.

We met Charlie, an American who had lived there for 14 years and was married to a Polynesian woman. He took us back to the boatyard one at a time on the back of his motorcycle. I enjoyed the ride and was surprised that Connie, who was usually nervous about such things, agreed to do it, and even enjoyed it. This may have played a part in her agreeing to rent a motorbike for our transportation in Thailand a few years later. When we returned, we got word on the radio that our wayward mail package had finally arrived in Papeete and was on its way to us.

Monday morning the yard hauled us out with a Travel Lift. *Tainui* was floated into a pen, which was a pit with cement walls dug into the shore. The tops of the walls served as tracks for the wheels of the Travel Lift. The lift itself was a huge machine about 15 feet high in the shape of a flat, horizontal U supported by four tall legs that rode on motorized wheels. The U was open to the front so it fit around our mast. Strong straps were run under *Tainui,* and four Polynesian men pulled her up by hand with chain hoists until she was lifted high enough to clear the ground. The Travel Lift then "walked" her to a place in the yard where she was set down on a wooden cradle.

We were pleased with the workers' careful handling of *Tainui* when they hauled her out. David, a very knowledgeable and conscientious boatyard manager, carefully supervised the process. It was important to place the straps under the boat carefully so that they did not damage the prop shaft, rudder, or other underwater equipment. David put divers in the water to monitor the placing of the straps and inserted wooden blocks under the straps near the deck to prevent *Tainui*'s teak trim from cracking—something a U.S. boatyard had failed to do and ended up making a costly repair at their expense. David took great pains to assure that *Tainui* was lifted out of the water vertically and set down carefully on a strong cradle. Not all boatyards were that careful—especially in the less developed countries.

A series of delays caused *Tainui* to be out of the water (sailors call it "on the hard") for a frustrating six weeks. Living aboard in a boatyard was the least favorite part of our cruising experience. Unfortunately, this was the first of many such experiences. It became the bane of Connie's existence—she could write a book about it (maybe she will). On the hard, the boat sat high off the ground and was entered and exited by a tall, skinny homemade ladder. The yard supplied power and water, and we had our own propane tanks for cooking, but the marine toilet could not be used on land. We had to climb down the ladder and cross a muddy yard that was cluttered with tools and equipment to use the boatyard's primitive facilities. This was especially galling in the middle of the night. Life in the boatyard was also boring for Connie. I did as much of the work as I could myself and supervised the rest, but Connie had little to do and an annoying lack of privacy. Whenever possible, we found other accommodations.

The work began with sandblasting the steel hull to prepare it for painting. We would have been miserable living aboard while this was going on, but an understanding couple came to our rescue and took us on a three-day cruise around the island of Raiatea on their steel yacht. We sailed mostly inside the fringing reef and anchored in a different bay each night. These waters were full of coral heads, which led to three groundings and some humorous situations. To reduce the risk of embarrassing these good people and salve my conscience for telling a funny story at their expense, I will call them Angus and Mary on the yacht *Penguin*. Angus, an older gentleman, was a captain of the old school. He sometimes treated the younger, free-spirited Mary more like a deck hand than a wife. He was quite embarrassed when he ran *Penguin* aground on his first attempt to anchor for the night and Mary used her command of French to secure a mooring buoy from a private company.

To make matters worse, on our second night I was awakened by the sound of steel grinding on coral. Our anchor had dragged, and *Penguin* had backed onto another coral head. I quickly dressed, knocked on the aft cabin, and shouted, "Angus, our anchor has dragged and we are aground!" A very sleepy-sounding Angus replied sheepishly, "Oh, I knew that! I was just getting up to attend to it." We were in a sheltered bay with no big waves, so there was no real danger to the vessel and we managed to motor off the reef.

Angus decided to leave the bay in the morning and get into deeper water, but the channel was full of coral heads. We needed the sun at our backs to see into the water, but the pass was directly into the sun. In spite of this, Angus sent Mary up the mast to watch for coral heads. We knew she could see nothing but the glare of the sun on the surface, but Angus stood at the wheel and yelled up to her, "Which way, Mary?" Mary, not knowing what to do, replied hesitantly, "Well, I wouldn't go left." Angus's face reddened and he remonstrated sarcastically, "For God's sake, Mary, *'I wouldn't go left"*! What kind of answer is that? 'Starboard,' 'Five degrees to port,' 'Full astern,' yes, but 'I wouldn't go left"?!

We felt sorry for Mary and wished she had just told Angus that she couldn't see anything with the sun glaring on the water. Immediately the inevitable happened: we went up on another coral head. There was a little open water on our starboard side, so Angus "kedged" us off by rowing an anchor out to starboard in his dinghy and winching *Penguin* off the coral. Angus asked me to take the wheel while he operated the winch. When *Penguin* slipped free, I could not see the coral head from my position at the wheel and didn't want to hit it again, so I asked Angus, who was looking down at it, "What do you want me to do, Angus?" He became flustered and shouted hysterically, "Miss it! Miss it!" I chuckled inwardly as I imagined myself replying, "For God's sake, Angus, *'Miss it! Miss it'*! What kind of answer is that? 'Slow ahead,' 'Full astern,' 'Hard to starboard,' yes, but 'Miss it! Miss it' "?! However, biting my tongue, I eased *Penguin* slowly to starboard and stopped her before she could hit anything else. Connie and I then got into a dinghy and led *Penguin* out the pass, peering over the side to spot the coral heads.

This little humor at their expense notwithstanding, they were lovely and gracious people, and we had a wonderful time with them.

The boatyard workers had sandblasted and painted the underwater part of the hull in our absence. I tackled the job of cleaning and sanding the "topsides"(that portion of the hull above the waterline). In the process, copious amounts of rust poured out from under the cap rail. The cap rail was a five-inch-wide teak trim attached to the top of the bulwark, which was a six-inch high steel border that ran all the way around the deck to keep things from falling off the boat. It had holes called "scuppers" to let water run off. I ripped the cap rail off and found that rust had eaten away so much of the steel that the bulwark was as thin as a knife blade in some places and completely eaten away in others. Welders repaired the damaged places and replaced the teak trim with a stainless-steel rod on top of the bulwark.

This was only the beginning of my education about the problems of wood on steel. We had been attracted to *Tainui* partly because her teak trim and decks gave her a "classic" yacht look. It turned out, however, that wood creates an acid environment, which accelerates rust. Wood on steel turned out to be a bad combination, and *Tainui* was dripping with teak. This became a more serious problem as time went on.

Halfway through the welding project we made another escape from the boatyard. This time Jean and John from *Arbaleste* invited us to spend some time with them on their yacht at Bora Bora. They were friends from our Mexico days and had shared our car trips around Tahiti and Moorea. We rode the 25 miles to Bora Bora on a ferry. I took advantage of the view from the top deck to survey the pass into Bora Bora, which was to be our next port of call.

Arbaleste was moored in front of the Oa Oa Hotel, an attractive Polynesian-style building nestled among the palm trees and fronted by a beautiful white sand beach. It was owned and operated by an American who had sailed to French Polynesia and settled down there. We snorkeled off the beach during the days and watched the sun go down over a drink with friends at outdoor tables in the evenings.

Bora Bora was a high, lush, green volcanic island. The brilliant turquoise water inside the reef was dotted with pretty *motus*. The airport was out on one of the larger *motus* because there wasn't enough flat land on the main island.

The four of us pedaled the 16 miles around Bora Bora on rented bicycles and enjoyed the views of the mountain and the lagoon. Frequent rain showers provided an unexpected opportunity to visit with local people, who invited us under their porches and carports and fed us fresh fruit. With their limited English, my 500-word French vocabulary, and some hand gestures, we were able to carry on simple conversations. The rain also caused Connie and me to take spills on the slippery, unpaved roads. We had "sticker shock" when we stopped for a dish of ice cream. The bill was a whopping US$5 a dish!

We heard on the radio that Joe, the skipper of the vessel *Champagne*, was suffering from a relapse of dengue fever. He was anxious to keep an appointment at the boatyard in Raiatea, but he did not feel up to operating his boat, and his wife, Kathy, was reluctant to make the crossing without help. We had never met them, but we introduced ourselves over the radio and offered to help sail *Champagne* to the boatyard instead of taking the ferry back. They checked us out with other sailors and accepted our offer. This turned out well for us, since our ferry was delayed three days due to bad weather. The crossing was a slow slog against the 30-to-35-knot winds that had discouraged the ferry captain. It took so long, in fact, that we couldn't make the 25 miles before dark. About dinnertime, we took refuge for the night at a resort called Marina

Iti (*Iti* means "little" in Polynesian) on the small island of Taha'a. We tied *Champagne* to one of their mooring buoys and went ashore for dinner. The mahi mahi was an easy choice, being the only item on the menu. Fortunately it was delicious. Back aboard, Joe was feeling better so we spent a fun evening playing games. We had many more contacts with Joe and Kathy on our trip and have kept in touch after we both quit cruising.

We were disappointed at the lack of progress on *Tainui* while we were gone and upset at some poor workmanship. Before we left, the welders were protecting *Tainui*'s teak decks from sparks with plywood sheets as they welded the stainless-steel rod along her portside bulwarks. After we were gone, however, they did the starboard side without any protection, leaving the teak deck pockmarked with dozens of burned spots. The manager was embarrassed. We could have forced him to replace that half of the teak deck, which would have been expensive and time-consuming, but we couldn't stay that long. Our visas would expire, and we needed to get *Tainui* to a safe place for the coming cyclone season. We settled for a US$500 discount on our yard bill, which was already US$4500. Connie rented a car with Joe and Kathy and toured Raiatea, while I stayed at the yard to personally supervise painting the topsides and cleaning and painting the bilge.

I became concerned about the workers' handling of toxic materials. They were using two-part epoxy paints, which were wonderfully strong, but the paint and its thinner were extremely toxic to the skin and the lungs. I was shocked to see the yard workers painting without shirts, masks, or even gloves. Worse yet, they cleaned paint off of their bodies and hands using epoxy thinner. The combination of inhaling the noxious vapors and absorbing the chemicals through their skin was guaranteed to destroy their livers and likely to cause leukemia and other cancers. I discussed my concern with the boatyard manager, who explained that he had held a two-hour meeting, read them all the warnings, emphasized the dangers, spelled out the required precautions, provided them with the necessary safety equipment, and pleaded with them to take all the precautions. Tragically, it all fell on deaf ears. It was heartbreaking to watch these friendly, fun-loving people destroying themselves in this way.

Finally, after five and a half weeks on the hard, the Travel Lift lowered *Tainui* into the water. When I started the engine to take her out to the mooring buoy, the alternator promptly died. After the yard workers and I spent two days trying in vain to fix it, I gave up and bought an overpriced replacement. We lost another day because they had lost the installation instructions for the new one.

The boatyard put on a barbecue for us the night before we left. Many yachting friends and all of the boatyard staff attended. It was a festive occasion. Everyone was so friendly and kind to us that our frustrations about the poor workmanship and delays melted away, and we left the boatyard the next morning with no hard feelings.

We provisioned for the next three legs of our journey at the town dock at Uturoa. Only limited supplies would be available at Bora Bora, and the only other stop before Samoa would be the almost deserted island of Suvorov. We shared the town dock with two young Swedish men on a pretty Swedish-built steel boat. We chatted about the pros and cons of steel boats and wished them well as they cast off for Hawaii. Later we heard that their boat had split in two at a seam and sunk! Fortunately, a passing ship had rescued them. A welder explained to us that a poorly welded seam could have air pockets in which seawater could collect and rust it out. This information shook Connie's sense of security, which was founded upon her trust in steel boats. She asked, "How do we know that our seams are safe?" There wasn't much I could say except that *Tainui* was built by a yard with a good reputation and that I had not heard of any of their hulls failing. This didn't stop Connie from worrying, but *Tainui*'s welded seams continued to take everything the sea threw at her as long as we owned her.

We accomplished the short trip to Bora Bora with one hour of sailing and four hours of motoring. It was uneventful with the exception that the motor intermittently lost revolutions. I became nervous every time it slowed down. I had no idea what caused the problem, and made no attempt to fix it at Bora Bora. Mysteriously, it did not recur.

We motored smoothly through the pass that I had scouted out from the ferry and took a mooring buoy in front of the Oa Oa Hotel. Mooring after motoring was practically effortless because we didn't have to pull the sails down and stuff them into their bags to clear the way for the anchor and chain. We had *hot* showers at the Oa Oa that night, which was a real luxury after months of cold showers. We enjoyed four pleasant days at the Oa Oa, using their laundry and shower facilities, taking occasional meals in the restaurant, and snorkeling off their beach. In the evenings we slipped back into the routine of sharing cool sundowners with friends at tables on the beach.

Unfortunately, the Oa Oa was for sale. It was a sad story. Greg, the owner, had begun the enterprise with great enthusiasm. He envisioned the Oa Oa as a haven for cruising sailors. A former cruising sailor himself, he spoke their language and enjoyed their company. He attracted yachts by installing mooring buoys in front of the hotel and offering free hot showers and affordable laundry facilities. He invited sailors to fill a page in his Cruisers' Scrapbook; on our page, I drew a picture of *Tainui* and Connie wrote about us. We enjoyed perusing pages by friends who had passed this way. Greg allowed cruisers to run a tab for their restaurant and bar bills. This was unusual; most businesses regarded us as gypsies who might sail away in the middle of the night, leaving unpaid bills in our wakes. But there was a reason for Greg's policy. We were required to put up a bond of US$800 per person at our port of entry into French Polynesia, which was returned to us at our port of departure. This was a lot of money—US$1600 per couple, and Bora Bora was the jumping-off place where the bond was returned for most of us. Many sailors owed most of it to Greg by the time they left.

The system worked well at first, when there were fewer cruisers and the relationships were more personal; but as yachting traffic increased, a few sailed away without paying. Greg took it personally; he became disillusioned and depressed. I don't think the issue was loss of money so much as disappointment that sailors, for whom he had established the Oa Oa, had cheated him. We were sad to see a place that we enjoyed so much end on a sour note, and we felt betrayed by the few unscrupulous sailors who had cheated Greg. This was a case in which the irresponsible actions of a few hurt the entire cruising community.

We were disappointed to find the name of one of our friends on Greg's deadbeat list. This person was wealthy and usually generous with his money (and liquor). The amount of the bill would have meant little to him. His problem may have been negligence, forgetfulness, or a hangover rather than intentional cheating. Nevertheless, it was inexcusable.

However, this friend's ethics were questionable in other ways. He had made his money on an illegal fee-splitting scheme involving lawyers and accident-claim awards. In addition, he was sailing alone and arranged to have a live-in girl in every port where he spent any time. His girlfriend back home continued to run his business while he sailed, and when she periodically flew out to spend some time with him, he moved his live-in girls out while he entertained her in luxury hotels.

The trade winds whipped up to 30 knots about the time we were ready to leave. We reclaimed our bonds, stocked up on fresh fruit and bread, anchored behind a picturesque *motu* near the pass with five other boats, and waited three days for better weather. We passed the time by socializing with friends on the other yachts. One of them was the

Japanese yacht of the turtle-fishing lure exchange. When the skipper heard I hadn't caught anything on his lures, he studied my gear and said, "You need swibble." He went back to his boat and returned with a bag of swivels and a wooden frame for winding up my line on which he had written, "*Tainui*, Good Eating."

Our Japanese friend was a strong believer in the weather fax charts that he received through his ham radio. Every day he showed me the chart and explained why it was not the right day to go. One day he climbed aboard beaming and waving his latest chart. He explained how the well-spaced isobar lines guaranteed light winds and calm seas. He was sure that it was the perfect time to leave for Japan. I was skeptical. The 8-1/2-x-11-inch chart covered most of the western Pacific Ocean, making it difficult to determine the conditions in a local area, but he was out of the anchorage in a flash. The next few days we had the worst weather of our entire stay in French Polynesia—so much for the weather fax.

CHAPTER SIX

SUVOROV AND PAGO PAGO

Gale-force winds held us in our beautiful anchorage in the lagoon at Bora Bora for three days after our Japanese friend sailed away. On October 3, 1989, the wind settled to a steady 15-knot trade wind, and I cranked up the anchor and got *Tainui* underway for Suvorov Atoll, 600 miles to the northwest. The sea had not calmed down from the recent gales and 12-foot ocean swells greeted us outside the pass through Bora Bora's reef. Our course put the wind on our beam and *Tainui* in the troughs, where she rolled severely, making life aboard miserable.

The rough start unsettled my stomach. I could hold my queasiness in check as long as I sat outside in the cockpit, but I became nauseated if I tried to work below. Therefore I stood watch on deck and Connie, who never became seasick, read charts, monitored the Sat Nav, operated the radio, and made meals below. However, when she needed help tuning the radio, I went below and tuned it for her. Soon, focusing on the radio in the rolling boat nauseated me. I climbed back on deck, leaned over the lee rail, and was startled when my denture went into the sea with my dinner! It was an upper plate I had as the result of an auto accident in my youth. Fortunately we had a spare aboard. When I got over my embarrassment, I joked, "Somewhere, a fish is wearing my smile."

Eating lunch in the cockpit the second day out (my stomach was back to normal), we saw a little *chi chak* scurry across the deck. When we lived in Malaysia, this type of chameleon was a welcome guest on the walls of our house, because it kept the insect population down. Our children liked to watch them dart out from behind a picture on the wall and snap up a bug. Our cats leapt up the walls trying to catch them, but seldom succeeded. Occasionally they grabbed one, only to find themselves holding a wriggling detached tail. The chameleon quickly grew another one. We hoped this one would thrive on the insect population aboard *Tainui.*

The belt from the engine to the refrigerator compressor broke early in the trip. I had spares for all of the belts aboard *Tainui*, but my replacement for this one was a little too long. It fit loosely on its pulleys and wobbled in a way that damaged its edges. I left it on and hoped that it would last until we got to Samoa, where I could buy or order another one.

We reached the halfway point in three 100-mile days, thanks to the steady trade winds. Connie had made a pressure cooker full of chicken before we left Bora Bora, so we celebrated the halfway point of the passage with a chicken curry dinner and a glass of wine.

Our radio was especially active on this passage. We chatted every morning on an informal local radio net with boats still in Bora Bora, boats en route with us, and some that were already in Suvorov. The net provided some useful information about the weather ahead and what to expect at Suvorov, but we used it mostly for neighborly chatting like an old-fashioned telephone party line. In addition to the morning net, we had frequent contacts with Jerry after the evening roll call on the Pacific Maritime Ham Net. Once we talked to all three of our children the same night, using Jerry's radiotelephone patch. It was great fun, even though the radio format made the conversations less spontaneous than regular phone calls; we had to remember to say "Over" when we finished talking and wait until the other person said "Over" before we could talk again. Nevertheless, these radio contacts were a great comfort to us. The hardest part of sailing so far away was separation from our family.

On the night of our fifth day out, our radar picked up Suvorov Atoll from eight miles away. I was startled to see that, if we maintained our present course, we would strike a point of land jutting out just south of the pass. I had put our Sat Nav arrival waypoint right in the pass, not noticing this intervening promontory. Without the radar we might have hit it in the dark. Close to land, the radar was our most valuable navigation tool. We altered course, hove to at a safe distance from the reef, and waited for morning before approaching the atoll. Thereafter, I put my arrival waypoints 10 miles offshore, and planned my landfall from there—another lesson learned.

The lagoon at Suvorov was difficult to enter because of its narrow channel and strong crosscurrent. We also had 25 knots of wind to contend with. Our pilot chart supplied us with very detailed information, and we needed every bit of it. We were instructed to stay in the channel by keeping a pole in the middle of the lagoon in line with a small *motu* called Entrance Island, at the back of the lagoon. When we had identified these makeshift range markers, we took down our sails to take the wind out of play, and motored in. At one point we had to steer 30 degrees off course and use full engine power to keep the crosscurrent from sweeping us out of the channel. When we reached the place where we were instructed to turn into the anchorage, the water looked too shallow for us. We held our breath and followed the directions on faith. To our surprise, the depth sounder never registered less than 10 feet. The illusion of shallowness was due to the absolute clarity of the water at this pristine atoll—unspoiled by civilization. We anchored among five other yachts off the pier on the main *motu*, Anchorage Island. We had come 600 miles in five and a half days—a fast passage for *Tainui*.

Suvorov, the northernmost of the Cook Islands, was an atoll with flora and fauna, above and below the surface of the water, that were unspoiled by contact with humans, and the Cook Island government was determined to keep it that way. Humans were restricted to Anchorage Island—all of the others surrounding the lagoon were bird refuges and off limits to visitors.

The only permanent residents were the Tangi Jimmy family, who performed all government functions. They were the Immigration Office, the Department of Wildlife, and the E.P.A. The family was composed of an older couple, their daughter and her boyfriend, their son and daughter-in-law, and six grandchildren—a total of six adults and six children. There were also three temporary residents on the atoll: Phillip, an Australian volunteer, who was conducting an experiment for the Cook Island Fisheries Department, and Taka and Poto, his two Cook Islander co-workers.

After a belated breakfast aboard and a short nap, I put the dinghy in the water and we rowed ashore and checked in with Mr. Tangi Jimmy. The process was informal—more of a social visit than official business.

The first human occupant of Suvorov was a New Zealander named Tom Neal. He lived alone on Anchorage Island for 15 years, seeing a supply ship only once or twice a year. The redheaded, fair-skinned Neal fought sunburn throughout his hermit existence at Suvorov and ultimately died of skin cancer at age 75. His book, *An Island to One's Self*, inspired us to put Suvorov on our itinerary. We were pleased to find that his house was preserved much as he left it when illness forced him to return to New Zealand. A visiting sailor had carved and painted a wooden bust of Neal and placed it on a post near his old residence. We signed a visitors' register, also provided by visiting sailors. Most of us, having lived Neal's dream and shared his sufferings through his book, had developed a feeling of kinship with him.

The day after we arrived, we went snorkeling on the reef with Chuck and Dottie from *Viki* and Bob and Joan from *Hunky Dory*. [Note: These two couples became lifelong friends. We recently visited both of them on a trip to the East Coast. Chuck and Dottie completed a circumnavigation, sold *Viki*, and are living ashore in Florida. Bob and Joan lost *Hunky Dory* to a hurricane in Guam and are living in South Carolina.] We anchored our dinghies near the reef, donned masks and fins, and dove off of our dinghies. The water was crystal clear, and the reef was alive with unspoiled coral and tropical fish of every size and color. The water was comfortably warm and buoyant. I relaxed on the surface with my hands clasped behind my back, my face in the water, and breathed through my snorkel tube. I propelled myself with the fins on my feet, making no effort to stay afloat. I occasionally dove down around an interesting coral formation or through a school of colorful fish, surfaced, blew out my snorkel tube, and continued cruising on the surface. Later, we snorkeled around coral heads at wading depth off the beach at Anchorage Island with equally exciting results. Snorkeling was our favorite cruising pastime, and Suvorov provided the best snorkeling of our trip.

The next two days, Phillip, the Australian volunteer, took me on fishing trips with his helpers Taka and Poto, and Tangi Jimmy's son, Sonny Jimmy. The first day, we went out in Phillip's12-foot aluminum boat with a 25-horsepower outboard motor. We trolled in the ocean near the pass into the lagoon on the incoming tide, when the fish were most likely to be feeding. The men used hand-carved wooden lures. They caught tuna, jack fish, barracuda, coral trout, and bonita—all large fish. It was heavy work reeling them in and hauling them aboard. I persuaded them to try one of the fancy lures given to me by my Japanese friend in exchange for the large turtle shell. It worked equally as well. Apparently when the fish were feeding, they were not fussy eaters. We fished until the sun went down in a pink sky behind the atoll, before bringing in our abundant catch.

The next day, Phillip took me along on a spearfishing expedition. He anchored his boat on the reef, and Taka, Poto and Sonny strapped scuba tanks on their backs, sat on the rail, and back-flopped into the water, holding their spear guns over their heads. I went overboard with my snorkeling gear and watched them from the surface. I could see them clearly, at a depth of 75 feet, and even see the reef disappear below them at more than 100 feet. This was a fantastic experience. There were only a few places in the world that had water this clear. Kudos to the Cook Islanders for their determination to preserve it.

When the divers' oxygen tanks ran low, they put them on the boat, and continued to spearfish by free diving. They speared fish at depths of up to 50 feet and surfaced holding up the spear with a fish neatly impaled just behind the head, which spoiled as little meat as possible. After a while, a large gray shark cruised into the area. Phillip explained to me that they ignored black-tipped reef sharks, but did not trust the grays. The shark slowly circled the group and then took an interest in a fish on Poto's spear. I assumed he would give the fish to the shark and retreat to the boat. I certainly would have—but not Poto! He put the fish in his backpack, faced the shark in a sitting position with his spear gun aimed at it from between his swim fins, and slowly backed to the surface. As the shark and diver approached, I scrambled back into the boat—only so I wouldn't be in the way, of course! Poto calmly backed up to the boat and rolled over the rail without incident.

Phillip's project was to test the feasibility of developing small commercial fishing projects on isolated islands by storing fish in freezers powered by portable generators and selling the fish to trading vessels that made infrequent visits to their islands. I was relieved to learn that they did not intend to establish a fishery at Suvorov.

One rainy day at anchor, I experimented with a way to improve our rainwater catchment system. We had rigged a sunshade shaped like a wall tent across the entire back half of the boat. Its shallow peaked roof normally drained the rainwater off each side of the boat. I flattened the roof, and installed a drain hole in the middle of each side of it. To each drain hole I attached a fitting with a hose that ran into a jerry jug on the deck. Finally, I pulled the fittings down toward the deck with ropes, turning the roof into two makeshift funnels. By the time I finished rigging it, the rain had quit, but a shower woke us in the middle of the night. We jumped out of bed and collected seven gallons of freshwater from our new catchment system.

About this time, we began to worry about our friends Bill and Kathy aboard *Affaire d'Amour*. They had not arrived from Bora Bora after nine days on what was normally a five-day passage. We decided to report them missing if they didn't show up in two more days, but the next day *Affaire d'Amour* limped into the anchorage. Ultraviolet light from the tropical sun had deteriorated the threads in their aging sails, causing some seams to give way. Only their small heavy-duty staysail had survived. Their engine was not working, so they had crept along on just that one small sail. They were on a tight budget, and many of us were worried about the neglected maintenance on their vessel. A cruiser with a sail-repairing sewing machine repaired the parted seams for them.

The day before we left Suvorov, I went fishing with the men again. We trolled just outside the pass. This time they handed me a pole. It felt like sport fishing, in contrast to towing our meat line behind *Tainui*. A barracuda soon struck my lure like a silver streak, and reeling it in as we continued through the water at seven knots was hard work. My back got a good workout that day. I reeled in several more big fish before we started back. When we got in, Phillip gave me a share of the catch.

The next morning we went ashore and paid our parting respects to the Tangi Jimmy family. Tangi Jimmy's wife, Luisa, was working on a decorative hanging basket for Connie, made by shrouding a coconut shell with decorative fiber weaving. She promised to send it on with one of the following yachts. It subsequently arrived in Pago Pago, American Samoa, and hung in *Tainui* as long as we had her.

We pulled up our anchor around noon, side slipped our way through the crosscurrent in the tricky pass, and set our course for American Samoa, 500 nautical miles to the southwest. We had anticipated the normal southeast trade winds that would give us a fast beam reach— but had no such luck. An 18-knot wind from the northeast immediately blew directly on our stern. The following seas caused *Tainui* to yaw back and forth so much that the self-steering wind vane had to fight to keep her under control. *Tainui* rolled mercilessly under these conditions. Sailing wing-and-wing was impossible, even with the staysail rigged tightly amidships to dampen the roll. Searching for a better strategy, I tried having only one sail rigged on one side of the boat. I hoped this would keep *Tainui* heeled more to that side and stop her from rolling so far back over to the other side. To avoid putting up the heavy whisker pole in these conditions, I rigged the genoa jib sheet through a block at the end of the mainsail boom, pulled the boom as far out to starboard as it would go, and took down the mainsail. The genoa filled with wind, heeled *Tainui* to starboard, and pulled her along on a fairly even keel— another seamanship trick learned by trial and error.

After we left Suvorov, we learned of an unfortunate incident involving a sailor visiting Suvorov. An arrogant yacht skipper (thankfully not an American) decided that there was nothing the Tangi Jimmy family could do to stop him from visiting the restricted *motus*. He went out in his dinghy and tramped around these prohibited *motus*, ignoring admonitions from Tangi Jimmy. However, Tangi Jimmy was in daily short wave radio contact with the Cook Island government at Raratonga. The trespasser was in for a surprise. The Cook Island Navy diverted a nearby destroyer, which entered the lagoon and expelled the offender. Unfortunately, it also expelled all other visiting yachts and temporarily closed Suvorov to visitors. As was the case of a few yachties cheating Greg at Bora Bora, the irresponsible behavior of one sailor negatively impacted many others.

Early on our first evening out, a sudden 50-knot gust knocked *Tainui* over onto her beam-ends. The wind put so much pressure on the jib sheet that I had difficulty jerking it out of its jamming cleat. I had no purchase for my feet on the steeply sloping deck, and I slid along on my seat until my feet found one of the lifeline stanchions, which gave me enough purchase to free up the line. The genoa jib flew out, flogging wildly in the wind. I could hear the sound of unsecured gear crashing about down below as I scrambled forward and pulled down the walloping jib. In the rocking bow pulpit, I stuffed the big jib into its sail bag and secured it with double lashings. By the time we restored order below, the wind had eased a bit, so I set up the small heavy-duty staysail. Squalls built up 10-foot waves during the night and Connie's log that night read, "What a terrible night! We rolled many, many times from gunwale to gunwale. It felt like we were in a washing machine." In spite of the motion, we managed to contact our daughter, Kathleen, through the ham net and wished her a happy birthday.

The squalls continued the next day and the seas built up to 12 feet. I ran up our rarely used storm jib and put a double reef in the mainsail. This combination gave us good speed, but a wild ride. We got a phone patch through to Larry's home in Seattle that night. He was out performing with his rock band, but we had a chat with his wife, Joyce, who caught us up on the family news. When Joyce asked, "How are you doing tonight?" we tried to sound nonchalant as we replied, "Oh fine, were just sailing along in a bit of a blow."

Lighter winds set in for the next day and a half, and the sea calmed down. Connie was able to cook again and we had pancakes for breakfast and fish curry for dinner, using up the last of the fish that I had caught in Suvorov. The wind was still blowing from dead astern, so I went back to my strategy of rigging the big genoa through a block at the end of the mainsail. Our next 24-hour run was only 75 miles, but it was comfortable.

When the wind picked up the following afternoon, I added the staysail, which increased *Tainui*'s speed to four and a half knots. The wind held the next day and we had a peaceful 100-mile daily run. We sighted the high green islands of Ofu and Olosega in the Manua group about 25 miles ahead of us on our fifth day out. Pago Pago was 50 miles beyond them.

We sailed through the night, arrived off the harbor at 3:00 in the morning, and hove to until daylight. At 7:00 a.m. Connie motored us into the harbor while I secured our sails. The harbormaster directed us by radio to the customs dock, but that dock was completely occupied by other vessels, so we radioed for further instructions. This time the harbormaster directed us to a big concrete commercial pier where full-sized ships tied up. That pier towered over *Tainui*. It was too high for me to reach from our deck, but the face of the pier was covered with old car tires hanging down on ropes to protect the hulls of ships. Connie watched with apprehension as I scrambled up this latticework of tires to the deck of the pier. The harbormaster was not immediately available, and we didn't complete our entrance formalities until mid afternoon.

After checking in we anchored with the cruising fleet at the back of the bay. Most of us were there for the hurricane season, because Pago Pago was the best hurricane hole in the South Pacific. The harbor was shaped like a giant boot, with the yacht anchorage in its toe. It was protected in all directions from ocean waves, and surrounded on all sides by high steep hills, which sheltered it from the wind. Forty yachts were anchored there for the Southern Hemisphere cyclone season, which lasted from December through April. During those five months, the sailors in the harbor became a close-knit community. Connie and I began many lasting friendships during that hurricane season in Pago Pago.

The sound of the anchor chain rattling out had scarcely died away before old friends dropped by to welcome us to Pago Pago. That first evening, a group of us went ashore to the happy hour at the Sadi Lounge, which featured free *pupus* (Polynesian snacks) and Monday night football (welcome back to America). A birthday party for Don from the yacht *Wind Dancer* added a festive spirit to the evening. We renewed old friendships and easily made new ones. The word "fellowship" was probably derived from "fellow shippers," and in our experience, there was, indeed, a common bond among sailors that created almost instant rapport.

Pago Pago was a seedy town. Many of the buildings were dilapidated wooden structures covered with peeling paint and black mold. A run-down dark and dusky tropical bar was the hangout of a crew of rough-looking characters. Some of the yachties paid it a visit to soak up the atmosphere and fantasize about the nefarious activities of its mysterious regulars, but Connie and I gave it a pass; they looked like a bunch of washed-out alcoholics to us. The water in the harbor was filthy because the residents dumped their trash into creek beds and the frequent heavy rains flushed it into the bay. Effluent from the two large tuna factories added a reddish-brown color and a foul odor to the mixture.

There were three attractive buildings in town: a modern bank, a police station, and the legislative building. The legislative building was done in an attractive Samoan style with a large oval-shaped domed roof. The only hotel was the Rainmaker, also built in Samoan style. It looked lovely on the beach as we sailed into the harbor, but on closer inspection it turned out to be in a sad state of disrepair. Large sections of it were closed due to low occupancy rates or malfunctioning water and electricity. The name was honest, given the prevailing climate, but did not seem like a welcoming invitation to tourists. Who would want to vacation at the Rainmaker?

Connie was pleased to find that prices were lower in Pago Pago than in the United States, in contrast to French Polynesia, where they were twice as high. She bought walking shorts for six dollars and blouses for four. There were two large grocery stores. One in particular was stocked with a full range of American goods, and of course there was no need to exchange money—American dollars were the official currency.

Somerset Maugham wrote his short story Rain while visiting Pago Pago. This was probably part of the reason for the name of the hotel, but it was well backed up by the wet weather. Rain was the story of a visiting fundamentalist missionary who committed suicide after being seduced by a notorious local madam, whom he was ostensibly trying to convert. We read the story and then enjoyed a production of the play enacted annually by an amateur theater group in Pago Pago.

One day we shared a rental car with Bruce and Mary from Impunity and toured the island of Tuituila, upon which Pago Pago was situated. Once out of Pago Pago, the scenery was beautiful. We climbed jungle-covered hills, dropped down into lovely lush green valleys, drove along the shores of sparkling blue-water bays with palm-fringed beaches, and passed through villages with oval meeting houses called fales (pronounced far-ayes). The fales had domed roofs held up by pillars around their perimeters, and open sides. Mats were rolled down the sides when it rained.

Toward evening, a group of men in one of these villages flagged us down and diverted us off the road into the parking lot of a church, where a lot of young people were hanging out on the porch. A policeman ordered us to remain there until a curfew was lifted. The thought of a curfew was frightening—especially for Bruce and Mary, who had been placed under curfew during their Peace Corps service in Africa when a civil war broke out around them. Finally, a bell rang and we were motioned on our way. We had no idea what had caused the curfew.

All seemed to be peaceful and quiet back in Pago Pago. At dinner in a restaurant, we asked our waitress about the curfew. She answered that that particular village holds an angelus every day from 6:00 to 6:15 p.m. It is supposed to be a time of prayer for the villagers, and everyone in the area is required to pray or observe silence. No one we saw in the village appeared to be praying—least of all the kids on the church porch. She told us that the villagers had once stoned a visitor who jogged through their village during the curfew. I wondered if you could pray and throw stones at the same time. Fortunately, the jogger survived with only cuts and bruises.

Once again, *Affaire d'Amour* was seriously overdue. Bill and Cathy did not have a long-distance radio, so we could not call them or monitor their progress on a maritime net and they could not make an emergency call that could be heard any farther than the 20-mile range of their ship-to-ship VHF radio. A group of us were about to call the authorities, when they crept into Pago Pago harbor under their single staysail just as they had done in Suvorov. The sail repair in Suvorov took care of the seams that were ripped out at that time, but more seams had ripped out on this trip and the motor was still out of order. Bill and Cathy planned to spend the cyclone season in Pago Pago, and we hoped they would be able to raise money for new sails and other much-needed maintenance before sailing on.

One Sunday we attended the big Congregational church in Pago Pago. The women and girls were dressed in crisp white dresses with brightly colored sashes. The music was beautiful, as was the case throughout the South Pacific, but the service was in Samoan so we did not understand much of it. A part that we did understand interested us. It was their annual stewardship Sunday, when the members' financial pledges were received. As the clerk called the roll, a representative of each family came forward with the family pledge card, which the clerk then read aloud to the congregation.

We were the only Caucasians in the service, and our reception at the church was cold and unwelcoming. No one greeted us or acknowledged our existence at any time. If the opportunity had arisen, I would have introduced myself as a retired Congregational minister and extended greetings from a sister Congregational church in Salem, Oregon. I believe this treatment was indicative of their attitude toward white people, including Americans. Many Samoans were unfriendly to us, and some were surly. Fred from *Janana* was assaulted without provocation while leaving a popular restaurant. Samoans liked the money that America poured into their economy, but many of them didn't like Americans.

The next Sunday we had a happier experience. We attended a potluck picnic in the park honoring the birthday of Marilyn from *Spindrift*. Cruising sailors from most of the anchored yachts attended. By now we were all well acquainted and easily got into a party spirit with food and drink, storytelling, and silly games. When a torrential thunderstorm rained out the picnic, we continued the party into the night at the Pago Pago Yacht Club, which most of us had joined. Back at *Tainui* that night, we found that the wind had flipped open the hatch over our bed and the rain had soaked our bedding. That night Connie slept on the galley table, which converted to a single bed, and I slept on a narrow settee. Fortunately, sunny, breezy weather quickly air-dried the bedding the next day.

As the holiday season approached, we helped organize a community potluck Thanksgiving Day celebration for cruisers and anyone else who wished to join us. We rented the Pago Pago Yacht Club and bought two big turkeys from the American supermarket. The yacht club had only one oven, so Bill, a local commercial diver, let us use the oven in his apartment across the street from the yacht club. The rest of the meal was a potluck. There was plenty of food, drink, and laughter. We enjoyed the party, but it was our first Thanksgiving away from home and we missed our family.

We spent the next week preparing for our two-month Christmas home visit. I was nervous about leaving our yacht in Samoa during the hurricane season. Samoa had not been hit with one for 10 years, but Samoa was in the tropical cyclone zone and we were exposing *Tainui* to that possibility. I prepared *Tainui* for the worst before leaving. I secured the use of a mooring buoy that was tied to a 1,500-pound ship's anchor that was buried so deeply in the mud on the bottom that only the tip of its shank showed. I had Bill, the diver, go down and replace the rope mooring line with double half inch anchor chains that led to a steel ring on a large flotation buoy. I was sure that no storm could break the chains or drag that anchor. The problem was to keep *Tainui* attached to the buoy. I shackled two heavy nylon mooring lines to the ring on the buoy and put leather chafing guards on them where they left *Tainui*'s deck. Finally, I shackled *Tainui*'s anchor chain to the mooring ring, leaving enough slack in it so that it would only come into play if the nylon lines broke. The springy nylon lines would absorb the shock of the boat bucking in the waves better than chain, but were susceptible to chafing. Feeling that I had done as much as I could do, I hired Ed from *Spindrift* to take care of *Tainui* while we were gone. He agreed to run the motor, air her out, and check her mooring lines once a week. This turned out to be a wise decision.

Just before we left, we cleared *everything* off the decks. I disconnected the boom and stowed it below with the mainsail lashed to it. I disassembled the canvas dodger and removed the weather cloth from around the stern pulpit and stored them below. I took the dinghy ashore, cleaned its bottom, and then lashed it upside down on the deck. *Tainui* looked strangely naked as we left her. I hoped that this wouldn't be Samoa's year for a hurricane, but as our Hawaiian Airlines flight lifted into the night sky at 2:00 in the morning on November 30, 1989, I felt that she was as well prepared as she could be.

On our way home, we visited our friends Hood and Doris Simon in Hilo. While we were there, we witnessed an eruption of Mount Kilauea. A park guide led us on an eerie walk across a field of hardened lava that looked like shiny black glass and was still hot and venting steam. He took us to a lookout point from which we saw glowing red lava fall off a cliff into the sea, sending up huge plumes of steam. The rare sight was worth the scary walk. A few days later, we heard that a fresh stream of lava had swallowed up that lookout point.

Back on the mainland we visited friends and relatives in Oregon and Washington. The day before our scheduled return flight from Seattle, a friend called and told us that Samoa had been hit by a devastating hurricane. I immediately called Al, one of the ham net operators, and asked him to try to contact any yacht in Pago Pago and inquire about the fate of *Tainui*. Waiting for his reply was nerve-wracking. Vivid images flashed through my mind of a videotape I had just seen of yachts piled up on a beach in the Caribbean by Hurricane Hugo. We faced the real possibility that it was all over—our beloved *Tainui* and everything on her might be lost. We had not been able to insure *Tainui* for this trip, so we had planned our finances to be able to survive the loss of her; our main concern was for our cruising dream. When the phone rang, I held my breath as I waited for Al to speak. He had great news. A sailor in the harbor told him that all the yachts in Pago Pago had survived the hurricane. In order to relieve me of any doubt, he told Al that he could actually see *Tainui* riding at her mooring as they spoke. What a relief!

After an overnight delay in Honolulu because the Pago Pago airport was closed due to hurricane damage, we were on the first flight into Pago Pago after the hurricane. We landed at night on February 13, 1990.

On our cab ride back to town, we could see the devastation in the light of the full moon. Trees were flattened, power lines were down, bits of buildings were scattered about, and the taxi had to dodge debris on the road. The scene was so scary that I had to see *Tainui* for myself before I could really believe she was safe.

It was nearly midnight when we reached the dinghy dock and bummed a ride to *Tainui* in a friend's dinghy. As we climbed aboard we could see no damage on deck. We unlocked the companionway hatch and climbed down inside. When we switched on the lights, a multitude of cockroaches scampered for cover. Every wood surface in the cabin was covered with a green velvet coating of mold from being cooped up in the warm, moist tropical air. The cabin felt creepy and dirty and smelled of mold. In spite of our jet lag, we opened all the hatches and portholes, got out our cleaning supplies, and washed off the mold before we fell into bed.

Our friends who had remained in Pago Pago told us many stories of Hurricane Ofa. Some had ridden out the storm on their boats, so they could monitor their anchor chains or mooring lines, and take defensive action if necessary. They said that the winds approached 100 miles per hour and blew foliage off of the hills that fell into the harbor like a green rain. However, the waves in the well-sheltered anchorage reached heights of only about two feet. This prevented the boats from breaking their lines by bucking in the big waves that developed in less protected places. One of our friends showed us a home video of *Tainui* skating violently back and forth on her mooring lines in the high winds. The yacht *Zingara*, with Jack and Donna aboard, dragged her anchor toward a rocky shore. Jack and Donna put their valuables and most important possessions in their backpacks and stood by to leap ashore when the boat hit the rocks. However, her anchor caught on a coral head and *Zingara* jerked to a stop 100 yards from shore. Another boat broke her mooring lines and drifted down on Ed's boat, *Spindrift*, causing some damage. He got a line on it and secured it alongside *Spindrift* before it could get away and run ashore or hit another vessel. Friends told us that Ed, our hired boat watcher, went above and beyond the call of duty— whenever the wind dropped below 50 knots, he launched his dinghy, fought his way to *Tainui* and checked her mooring lines.

Most of the cruising families with children chose to weather the storm ashore. Some slept at a temporary shelter set up in a church. They said they couldn't sleep at night because, when the lights were turned off, the floor crawled with giant cockroaches. Two families with small children took shelter in the house of a friend. While they were cooking a big pot of spaghetti, the wind ripped the tin roof off the house, creating a vacuum that sucked the spaghetti out of the pot, and showered them all with hot, half-cooked pasta. They then crawled on their hands and knees to a neighbor's house. The parents tried to keep the children calm and guide them to safety through the storm with coconuts flying by like cannon balls and tin roofing sheets making an ominous wow-wow-wow sound above their heads. One of these roofing sheets sliced a palm tree in two! They all reached the next house safely, only to lose that roof and have to crawl through the hurricane to yet another house. The roof stayed on that one, but the parents' nerves were shattered and the children were hysterical. Sleep was impossible in the shrieking wind and the fear that this shaking house might blow away.

Hurricane Ofa was 1,000 miles wide and its eye passed within 150 miles of American Samoa. Many homes and buildings were damaged. We took a bus to the end of the road and hiked to a village near the sea that had sustained the worst damage. Villagers told us that waves taller than their houses had come ashore. We saw wrecked houses hundreds of feet from their foundations and a historic church that was reduced to rubble. Fortunately no one was killed, although many were injured and hundreds were homeless. Most of the Samoan victims stayed with relatives—the villages were essentially extended families. Only a few stayed in the shelter in the church. Pago Pago was without electricity, water, and sewer for two weeks. Life on the yachts in the harbor, however, was not affected; we were all self-contained. We had propane tanks for cooking, generated our own electricity for lights and radios, and freshwater in our own tanks.

Western Samoa was not so fortunate. The eye came within 40 miles of the main island; there were several fatalities, and 90 percent of the buildings were damaged!

We saw some examples of devious local behavior when FEMA (the Federal Emergency Management Agency) came to provide financial relief to those whose property was damaged by the hurricane. For example, the wind tore the roofing iron off of the home of the American assistant manager of a grocery store. His Samoan neighbors went out in the night and took it to repair their own roofs. (Maybe theirs were blown farther away or someone else took theirs.) When the neighbors heard that FEMA was in town, they tore it all off and applied for FEMA's generous compensation. Another example involved two yachting families who had rented houses from Samoans. Their landlords knew that FEMA would not compensate for damage to rental properties, so they evicted these families without prior notice and installed relatives, who told FEMA that these were their family homes. FEMA money was given for the purpose of repairing hurricane damage, but the following month set a record for car sales in Pago Pago.

Shortly after our return, we took a break from boat work and joined a small group of cruising couples on a scuba-diving trip to Ofu Island in the nearby Manua group. Although we were not scuba divers, we enjoyed the opportunity to get back to beachcombing and snorkeling. We flew over in a twin engine 12-seater with a beautiful bird's-eye view of the islands and the ocean. The small plane landed on a bumpy grass field and taxied up to the gate of the rustic resort.

We stayed in individual small cabins, but took our meals and spent our evenings together in the lodge. In the mornings the scuba divers went off on diving expeditions to the reef, and we swam and snorkeled off the beach in front of our cabins. The water off the beach was crystal clear over pristine coral heads that were teeming with colorful fish. We cherished the opportunity to snorkel in these isolated, unspoiled, and unpolluted places that were becoming increasingly rare with the encroachment of civilization. We took leisurely beachcombing walks in the cool of the evenings, picking up shells and enjoying the sense of being on an island paradise. In our less active moments, we relaxed and read or napped in lounge chairs in the shade of palm trees or just hung out with our friends. It didn't get much better than that.

We came back to a busy social life and more odd jobs on the boat. There were social events at the yacht club, parties at restaurants, and get-togethers on each other's boats. We hosted several movie and popcorn nights on *Tainui*, showing TV movies that our daughter, Kathleen, had videotaped and sent us. A morning Pago Pago local radio net helped bind the boating community together. I served as net controller for much of the time. Connie took Tongan basket-weaving classes, and a group of boating wives trained for a women's dugout canoe race. They didn't win, but made a good showing by placing third out of six canoes.

I became concerned about a metal-to-metal vibration in the cutlass bearing where the prop shaft left the hull at the stern. The metallic sound meant that the rubber sheath inside the bearing was gone. Things corroded quickly in Pago Pago's rich (foul) water. Most likely the rubber had frozen to the prop shaft while it was idle and then was ripped apart when we shifted the engine into gear. Without it, we would be limited to emergency use of the engine on our upcoming trip to Tonga, because the prop shaft itself would be damaged if we ran it without the protection of the rubber lining.

At first, it seemed impossible to repair it in Pago Pago. I had a spare cutlass bearing, but the old bearing could not be removed underwater. The only haul-out facility in Pago Pago was for ships and charged a minimum of $1,500. I searched my mind for a temporary fix. I had read that old ships sometimes used hard wood or even soft metal sleeves for cutlass bearings, so I had a machine shop make me a brass sleeve that was the exact size of the missing rubber part. The brass was a softer metal than that in the shaft, so the shaft would wear the brass, instead of being worn itself. Our friend Steve from *Gwaihir*, who was a good scuba diver, made a temporary underwater repair. He removed *Tainui*'s prop and slipped the snug-fitting brass sleeve over the shaft. He then slid a long piece of pipe over the shaft and used it to hammer the brass sleeve into place. After he reinstalled the prop, the shaft turned noiselessly when we tested it. Yacht repairs were a nuisance, but I enjoyed the challenge of creative problem solving.

About this time Tropical Storm Rae passed within 1,000 miles of us and brought several days of 35-knot wind and 60-knot gusts. These were the strongest winds we experienced aboard *Tainui*. (*Tainui* had experienced stronger winds during the hurricane when we were away.) We stayed aboard on these windy days, partly to make sure *Tainui* was safe, and partly because the dinghy ride to shore would have been wet and wild. We used some of the time for maintenance work. For example, the pesky marine head stopped functioning one night. The saltwater inlet was not letting in enough water to flush it. The inlet was on the bottom of the boat and could not be cleared from above. Bill, the local diver, managed to get his workboat to *Tainui* through the wind and waves and dove under and cleaned out the marine organisms that were clogging it. He cleaned our prop while he was at it—all for only $10.

The ham radio also helped us pass time on the windy days. We listened to foreign broadcasts and made many ham contacts. But the radio use led to yet another work project. We got electric shocks if we touched the radio while it was transmitting. The cause turned out to be a broken ground wire from the radio to the steel hull. We replaced the wire with a perforated copper strap, which stopped the shocks and improved our transmitting power by strengthening the connection of the radio to its ground plane. Transmitters need a reflecting surface (the ground plane) to transmit properly—the bigger the ground plane, the stronger the signal. The ground plane had to be metal; therefore *Tainui*'s steel hull provided an excellent ground plane for our radio. I often served as a relay between vessels with weaker signals.

We yachts in the harbor kept our VHF radios on for local communication. While listening on one of the windy days, we heard a desperate call from a woman in our harbor whose boat was being blown away by the wind because her mooring line had broken. Her husband was ashore and she wasn't confident that she could handle the boat by herself. Bob from *Hunky Dory* picked me up in his inflatable dinghy and we bounced off under a leaden sky into steep, choppy waves with wind-whipped whitecaps. By the time we climbed aboard the drifting boat, the woman had the engine running. Her prop was so fouled from sitting on a mooring that her boat could only make a speed of three knots. She was trying to pass an anchored vessel on its windward side, and I could see that she didn't have enough speed to pass it. If she kept going, the wind would set her right down onto the other boat. She gave me the helm and I turned the boat downwind and steered safely under the lee of the other vessel.

We did not have enough speed to fight our way back upwind to the woman's mooring buoy, so I maneuvered her boat cautiously toward a large unoccupied steel ship's buoy downwind of us. I figured we had one chance to snag it before we would be blown by. When we were close enough, Bob took our bowline in his dinghy, raced ahead of us, climbed up on the large black cylindrical buoy, and attached the line. The drifting vessel blew downwind of the buoy, snatched up on its bowline, and held fast to the buoy with its bow into the wind. We doubled her lines for extra safety and beat our way laboriously back upwind, arriving at *Tainui* and *Hunky Dory* wet and windblown. The woman's husband was shocked when he returned to the dinghy dock and saw that his boat was not at its mooring, but he was relieved and grateful when he heard of our rescue.

Later the same day the wind struck again. Connie saw an empty dinghy blowing downwind and a man in the water. I called Bob, he picked me up again, and we raced to the rescue. The man's dinghy had broken loose from his boat and he was swimming after it, but it was moving faster than he could swim, and he was tired and struggling to keep afloat. By the time we picked him up, a dinghy from another yacht had corralled the stray and was towing it back.

Not wanting *Tainui* to be the next to blow away, I went back to *Tainui* and checked our own mooring lines. We were attached to our buoy by a single line that was backed up by a slackened anchor chain, which would only come into play if the line broke. I found that the line was chafed halfway through at the mooring buoy! It was evening by the time I rerigged it with a new line. After this exciting day, we relaxed with a gin and tonic in the cockpit and watched a videotaped movie before retiring.

American Samoa was the only place we visited where Americans could legally get jobs. Most countries gave work permits only for positions they could not fill with their own work force. Some cruising sailors worked clandestinely in these countries, usually doing diesel repairs, sail repairs, or other boat maintenance, in spite of the fact that they could be arrested and fined or deported if they were caught. In American Samoa, everyone who wanted work found it. It was cheaper to hire someone who was already in the country than to bring a worker out from the mainland. When the head of the Department of Social Services learned of my former occupation, he asked me to set up a drunk-driver program in American Samoa. I told him that I didn't think an outsider could succeed in that culture. He told me not to worry; they all had that problem—nobody cared and the pay was good. I wasn't looking for work, but I wouldn't have been interested in that kind of a rip-off if I were.

Sailors with medical backgrounds found work at the Lyndon Baines Johnson Center for Tropical Medicine in Pago Pago. While we were there, they included an X-ray lab technician, an emergency room nurse, a pediatrician, and an audiologist. The pediatrician eventually quit because he was so upset by the child abuse cases that he saw. Many Samoans were heavy drinkers, and some became violent when drunk. Unfortunately, they sometimes struck their children in the head, causing brain injuries. The head of social services actually put out a public service announcement advising parents to hit their children only on their backsides—never above the waist. He felt it would be futile to tell them not to hit their children at all, and that this would at least protect children from the most serious injuries.

The dental lab at the LBJ center made me a new denture to replace the one I lost overboard when I got seasick. The one I lost cost me $800. The LBJ center charged US$100. Subsequent events bore out the old adage, "You get what you pay for."

Bob, on a West Sail 32 named *Renaissance*, was teaching high school to build up his cruising kitty. He rowed out to *Tainui* one day and asked me what I had done for a living. It turned out that he had neglected to line up a speaker for his social studies class on his school's Career Day. It was just two days away. He thought my experience in the alcohol and drug field would be good, given the serious alcohol problem in Pago Pago. Although I believed that the drunk-driver job could not be done by an outsider, I saw this as an opportunity to encourage local youth to become trained in alcohol and drug abuse education and prevention so they could work with their own people.

Career Day began with an assembly under an outside playground roof. When the principal began introducing the Career Day guest speakers, Bob leaned over and whispered, "When they introduce 'Mr. Smith,' you stand up." When he had to submit my name, he realized that he had never heard my last name. Most of us sailors did not know each other's last names. I knew him as Bob from *Renaissance,* and he knew me as Vern from *Tainui.* He didn't call me Vern Tainui because his students would then have expected a native. Calling me "Mr. Smith" became a standing joke between us.

The Berlin Wall came down while we were in Pago Pago, which resulted in a couple of interesting experiences. We watched this exciting event on the television news. American Samoa was the only place on our trip where we could use our American television set. Unknown to most Americans, there are several TV broadcasting systems in the world, all incompatible with each other. The United States uses the NTSC system, Southeast Asia uses PAL, and in Europe it's SEACAM. Later that day we were walking to town with a young Czechoslovakian family. They had built a boat, ostensibly for recreation on the Danube River, but had escaped in it and were now cruising the world. When I asked them, "Did you hear that the Berlin Wall has come down?" the husband replied, " Oh, come on. You are surely joking!" They didn't believe me until they confirmed the news with some other cruisers. When the reality of its consequences for them and their families sunk in, they were in a state of shock, with tears in their eyes.

Not long after the Berlin Wall came down and the Soviet Union was experiencing glasnost and perestroika, a Soviet research ship anchored in Pago Pago. We motored over in our dinghy to have a closer look, and they invited us aboard. They gave us a tour of the vessel and invited us to join them for dinner in their ship's galley, where they served a substantial meal of fried chicken, fish soup, carrot salad, and Russian black bread. We invited two young sailors who spoke passable English to visit *Tainui* the next day. They came bringing gifts of vodka and glasnost and perestroika souvenir pins. They told us this was the first time they had ever been allowed to go ashore in a foreign country on their own, not accompanied by a party member, and that they would never have been allowed to visit an American vessel. They were in a state of euphoria at their newfound freedom. The next day the Soviet ship held a dinner party on board for anyone who wished to come. Many of us cruising sailors attended. The Russians gave parting gifts of liquor and souvenirs.

The largest yacht in our fleet was Walt and Bea's 70-foot ferrocement ketch *Galatea*. Walt had a complete machine shop in the bow compartment, with an impressive supply of odd hardware bits and pieces. The word in the fleet was that, no matter how unusual an item you needed for a repair job, Walt would have it. Before the fleet broke up after the hurricane season, we had a group picture taken of the 38 of us aboard *Galatea*. Years later someone sent us a copy of an issue of *Crossings* magazine with that photoraph in it and a"Where Are They Now?" article written by Debbie Howe, one of the group. She told as much as she could of the further adventures of those of us in the picture, based on responses to a survey she had sent out..

When we arrived in Pago Pago, a large wooden ketch named *Amazing Grace* was rotting away at the dock of the small marina that served as our dinghy landing. We were told that it had been used by a religious group to combat the growing Mormon influence in the South Pacific. They allegedly sailed around distributing anti-Mormon literature and preaching against the Mormons. Later, a young man named Craig got permission from the ketch's American owners to salvage it. There was a lot of wood rot, particularly at the base of the main mast, but Craig was more of an engineer than a sailor and worked mostly on the engine. He persuaded the Pago Pago Port Authority to declare the vessel to be salvage and to give him title to it for payment of its back harbor fees. When the boat appeared to have a future, its former owners changed their minds and Craig decided to get *Amazing Grace* out of American territory as soon as he could get her operational.

Shortly thereafter, Craig's girlfriend, Gwen, a lovely young woman of Fijian and Swedish parentage, took off with him and his dog for Fiji, where he hoped that her Fijian citizenship, along with the Pago Pago Port Authority document, would let them register *Amazing Grace* in their names as a Fijian yacht. Craig had not repaired the mast because he planned to motor all the way. The engine quit a dozen times en route because the rough seas stirred up gunk in the bottom of the diesel tanks, which clogged the fuel filters. Craig spent most of the trip down in the engine compartment cleaning filters. Unfortunately, the engine quit just as they were approaching the pass into Suva, Fiji, with 20 knots of wind blowing. Craig frantically pulled off the filters and cleaned them as the wind swept them toward the reef. He couldn't sail out of danger because the strong wind would have brought the rotting mast down. Unfortunately, he didn't get the engine restarted in time, and *Amazing*

Grace went up on the reef near the pass. Greg, Gwen, and the dog were rescued, but the surf quickly destroyed the fragile wooden hull.

We wanted to visit nearby Western Samoa while we were in Pago Pago. Because the harbor at Apia, the capital city of Western Samoa, was unsafe for small boats, we left *Tainui* in Pago Pago and flew to Apia on Polynesian Airlines. This was also a good excuse to spend a few days in a nice hotel. There were two to choose from in Apia. One was Aggie Gray's, a white colonial building named after an illustrious madam and entrepreneur who had died only a few years previously. We chose the other one, which was the Tusitala. Tusitala was the Samoan word for "storyteller," which was their nickname for Robert Louis Stevenson, who spent the last years of his life in Samoa. The Tusitala was done beautifully in Samoan style, with a large domed roof using native woods and no visible modern hardware. Lush flowering plants surrounded its pool and patios. We had wonderful meals in the hotel, swam in the pool, ate in restaurants in town, and took a tour bus ride around the island with a group of noisy German tourists. Our tour passed many old-style Samoan villages. We picnicked and swam at a lovely beach on the far side of the island, and stopped on the way back to wash off the salt by swimming in a cool freshwater pool at the base of a waterfall.

Traditional Samoan culture was better preserved in Western Samoa than it was in American Samoa. American Samoans were wealthier and more westernized. Many of them worked at one of Pago Pago's two big tuna plants—Bumblebee and Chicken of the Sea. Its second major employer was the U.S. government. They ate fast food, drove American cars, and watched American TV. Obesity was epidemic, starting at an early age. At a party in Pago Pago attended by local officials, I once quipped, "If Samoans were paid for being fat, they would be wealthy people!" The head of the local Social Security office coughed into his hand and looked uncomfortable. I said, "I'm not sure I want to hear this." He replied sheepishly, "Obesity is an SSI disability. When they get over a certain weight, they get Social Security disability checks." They actually were paid for being fat! That accounted for some of the people in the long lines at the post office the day the Social Security checks arrived.

There were still strong elements of Samoan culture in American Samoa, but its westernization stood out in contrast to what we saw in Western Samoa. Western Samoans were lean and athletic looking, and their villages lacked the trappings of Western civilization. Their social system was based more on sharing and trading goods than on cash. From our conversations with some of them, however, this was not necessarily because they wanted it that way. Many of them aspired to the more materialistic life of the American Samoans. Work permits for the tuna factories in Pago Pago were in high demand in Western Samoa.

The highlight of our trip to Western Samoa was a hike up Mount Vilima to the tomb of Robert Louis Stevenson. We started out at 6:30 in the morning to beat the heat. We were warned about mosquitoes and tried to dress appropriately—Connie wore the only long pants she had brought with her, which were white ones. They were soon stained with red mud as we climbed over and under downed trees and other debris that had not been cleared from the trail since Hurricane Ofa. The climb took us about an hour. The white tomb stood alone atop a grassy knoll at the summit. It was inscribed with a poem to his wife at one end and the epitaph, which he had written for himself, along one side. It looked down on the city and the harbor with the sea in the background. In the presence of this great man's tomb with its immortal words and the stillness of the mountaintop with its panoramic view, we felt we were standing on holy ground. We were pleased that we could be there alone, to think our own thoughts. I was inspired to memorize Stevenson's poetic epitaph, which read:

Under the wide and starry sky,
Dig the grave and let me lie.
Glad did I live and gladly die,
And I lay me down with a will.

This be the verse that you grave for me:
Here he lies where he longed to be;
Home is the sailor, home from the sea,
And the hunter home from the hill.

But for the cloud of mosquitoes rising out of the grass around the tomb, we would have gladly lingered in this hallowed place.

Back in Samoa, we began thinking about leaving Pago Pago. It had lost its charm. This excerpt from one of Connie's letters home says it all:

"We are really looking forward to getting out of here. I am so sick of smelling fish cooking from the tuna factories, seeing their blood and slime in the bay, seeing oil slicks, smelling diesel fumes from the fuel dock, watching garbage float by our boat because the people here throw their garbage into the streams which flush it into the bay, and listening day and night to the roar of the big diesel electric power plant on the shore. I am also tired of cleaning the tube worms and barnacles, which grow so profusely in the rich waters of the bay, off of the dinghy and the sides of our boat. And it is disgusting to walk around the garbage in town, which the people throw on the streets, often around, but not in, the garbage barrels, and which stray dogs strew everywhere. This place is filthy. YUCK!"

Boats were beginning to move out in early April, but we decided to wait until the end of April, when the Southern Hemisphere cyclone season was officially over, before leaving for Tonga. We were in daily radio contact with two of the couples who had left early for Tonga. They were caught in huge waves that were stirred up by the March storms. Both wives were seasick all the way. When their boat fell off a wave one of them was thrown across the cabin into a corner of the galley table and broke a rib. She lay flat on her back in pain for the final two days of their trip, leaving her husband on watch for 48 hours without sleep.

During the last week of April, we made our final preparations for leaving. I did routine maintenance including changing engine oil, replacing oil and fuel filters, replacing a worn cable on the wind-steering vane, and putting up new flag halyards. Connie took charge of provisioning. We took advantage of Pago Pago's American grocery stores and low prices by buying a three-month supply of nonperishable goods for $600. We were delighted to receive a fat mail package from our son Larry, with pictures of our grandchildren, just before we left. If we had missed it, the mail could have chased us across the Pacific for months. The night before we left, we participated in a work day at the yacht club, and the barbeque that followed served as a farewell party.

CHAPTER SEVEN

TONGA

We hauled the dinghy aboard and lashed it to the deck at 10:30 a.m. on April 28, 1990, cranked up the anchor, and set sail for the Kingdom of Tonga, 350 nautical miles to the southwest. We left in a lull in the recent windy weather, but a fresh series of squalls soon stirred up the sea again. Starting out in rough seas after six months in port was a tough adjustment for us. We both took Meclazine tablets, hoping to ward off seasickness. I discovered a tear in the working jib in the afternoon and took it down, and Connie began repairs immediately because it was our main jib. We lost speed as we continued to sail without it. Connie had pressure-cooked a whole chicken the night before we left, and she served a fine meal of curried chicken over rice that night, but neither of us had enough appetite to do it justice.

By 8:00 p.m. I was seriously seasick. My ears were ringing and my mouth was dry from the Meclazine. I was drowsy and lethargic, and my stomach was so queasy that I would throw up if I didn't lie down. Connie was a little queasy as well, but was not really seasick. She took over sailing *Tainui*, and I lay down on the settee with the canvas lee cloth rigged to keep me from falling off. Connie was on watch from 8:00 p.m. to 1:30 a.m. She slept on the cabin sole, set a timer, and got up and looked out at 15-minute intervals. I hated to ask Connie to do this. It happened four or five times in our seven-year cruise, and Connie always took over without complaining. By 1:30 a.m. I felt better and stood watch until 5:00 a.m., when Connie took over until daylight, about two hours later.

The next day dawned sunny and clear, and the seas quickly calmed down. After the stormy night, we enjoyed sitting in the cockpit with the warmth of the sun on our backs. We felt better, but we had not fully regained our appetites. I put the repaired jib up and we had smooth fast sailing, which did wonders for our stomachs and our spirits. When the wind and rainsqualls returned in the evening, I took down the jib, left the staysail up, and put an extra reef in the main as a precaution to eliminate the need to get up and make sail changes in the dark if the weather worsened during the night. It was another rough night, but I took my regular watches this time.

The weather improved again in the morning and remained good for the remainder of the trip. That day we had breakfast on May 1 and lunch on May 2—we had crossed the international dateline. When we charged our batteries that afternoon, the engine overheating alarm went off. My troubleshooting routine found no blockages in the cooling system, but no water was going through the engine. I took the water pump apart and found that it was full of broken impeller blades. This was a surprise because it was a new pump that I had installed in Pago Pago. It could have had a defective impeller. I had a replacement impeller, but I was concerned that, if something had caused the former impeller to fail, it might also destroy the replacement. I installed the new impeller, but as a precaution we sailed the rest of the way without using the engine, to save it in case we needed it for maneuvering in the potentially dangerous approach to the harbor.

We were headed for the town of Neiafu in the Vava'u island group, which was the northernmost of the three groups that made up the Kingdom of Tonga. Neiafu was the port of entry and the only town in the Vava'u group. The channel to the harbor made many turns, most of which were not marked with navigational aids, so as we came in we watched closely for landmarks onshore that were described in a pilot book. We made our initial approach under sail, which required repeated tacks in the narrow channel with fluky winds. I steered and Connie got a workout pulling the jib back and forth every time we tacked. It took our best seamanship to bring *Tainui* safely into the harbor under sail. In the harbor, I started the engine and motored up to the commercial dock. The water pump impeller functioned normally.

Checking into Tonga was comical. We were immediately boarded by a Tongan customs official. He asked the usual questions about things we would be bringing into his country, and when he was satisfied that we were not importing any dutiable goods, he signed the necessary papers. However, he did not leave immediately. He hung around making small talk and slyly looking over our possessions. We guessed that he was going to ask us for something. Sure enough, when his eyes lit on our racks of audiotapes, he said he liked jazz and asked if he could borrow some of my Miles Davis tapes. It wasn't exactly a shakedown—he had already signed off on us—but I didn't want to begin our stay in Tonga by irritating an official. I gave him two of my least favorite ones, knowing that I would never see them again. As he was about to leave, he spied a packet of M&Ms on the galley table. He said, "Oh, may I have these?" and scooped them up without waiting for a reply. He told us to check in with immigration on the pier, climbed up the companionway steps, and left.

We had heard lots of stories of officials abusing their position by demanding gifts of entering vessels. We thought we got off relatively easily—except for the M&Ms. It was our custom when we were at sea to treat ourselves to a packet of M&Ms every afternoon at 3:00. It gave us something to look forward to and broke the routine of the long days at sea. I had eaten my M&Ms at the wheel on the way in, but Connie had been so busy handling the sails that she left hers to eat when she had time. It was our last packet of M&Ms and she was hopping mad!

Next came immigration. We were tied to a huge concrete ship's pier that was empty except for little *Tainui*. We scrambled from our deck up over the rough cement onto the pier. The only building in sight was a large empty quonset-hut-style warehouse across an expanse of concrete large enough to stack the cargo of a fleet of freighters—had there been any cargo. The concrete was hot under our sandal-clad feet and suffocating heat from the afternoon sun reflected up at us. As we approached the warehouse, we saw three men just inside the huge open doors sitting on folding chairs around a dilapidated metal desk. This was the Immigration office. Each man wore part of a uniform: one wore khaki pants, another had a shirt with a badge, and the third sported a military hat with lots of gold braid. We presented our passports and official U.S. Coast Guard ship's document. The officials spoke good English as they greeted us and examined our papers. In the process, a question arose that required them to make a telephone call. An old rotary-dial telephone minus its rotary dial sat on a corner of the desk. The man with the hat took a bare wire from some part of the instrument and touched the end of it to the exposed rotary contacts, where the dial should have been. Sparks flew from the wire and he handed the phone to the man with the badge, who conferred briefly in Tonganese. He smiled and nodded as he replaced the hand piece on its cradle. We shook hands all around and the officials welcomed us to the Kingdom of Tonga. We crawled back down into *Tainui* and moved her to the anchorage in front of the town, among a small fleet of yachts.

The Kingdom of Tonga, a constitutional monarchy, claimed to be the oldest continuous kingdom in history. It was the only country in the South Pacific that had never been ruled by another country. When we arrived, the entire kingdom was holding a week of festivities in honor of Crown Prince Tupotu's birthday. It was a cultural feast for us. The beautiful Paradise Hotel in Neiafu was hosting special events every evening. The first night we attended a dance competition in which the 10 lovely young women contestants wore costumes made of natural Tongan materials. They were graceful and exotic as they danced in their outfits made from palm branches, banana leaves, and flowers. The next night there were two more competitions: a singing competition, which displayed the beautiful harmonies for which most South Sea islanders are justly famous, and a costume competition by a group of charming Tongan children.

We walked into the town of Neiafu on our first morning in port and spent time chatting with the friendly Tongans at the Visitors' Bureau, did a little shopping, and went to the Tongan Bank for a cash transfer on our Visa card. Visa cash transfers were available in every country we visited, but each country had its own procedures. In some countries, such as New Zealand and Australia, it resulted in immediate transfers. In Tonga, we had to leave off our application and Visa card and come back four hours later for our money.

That afternoon we went down to the big commercial dock to await the arrival of what we were told would be a big parade. When it arrived, it turned out to be two little improvised floats. One was a rag-tag Boy Scout band on a slightly decorated flatbed truck. They repeated the only two songs they knew, over and over. The songs were "Kumbayah" and a local tune. The other float represented the Tongan Cultural Society. It was a Volkswagen Campervan with local art and craft items hanging over it. To our embarrassment, the parade organizers commandeered Connie and me, as objective outsiders, to judge the floats. We put on a show of careful inspection, followed by consternation over the difficult decision. Then we solemnly announced that it was impossible to choose, and declared it a tie. This act of diplomacy brought cheers and smiles from everyone.

We had also been told that the parade would be followed by boat races in the bay, so we walked along the shore to watch. The races consisted of men throwing inner tubes off of a floating dock, and on a signal small boys leaping into the tubes with their paddles in their hands and flailing furiously at the water in a race to the shore.

The climax of the celebrations was a birthday grand ball in honor of the crown prince. He flew up from the capital city of Raratonga, located in Tonga's southernmost island group, 600 miles to the south of us. For $5 apiece, we bought tickets that advised, "Dress fancy." People did dress up. We wore the best that we had and seemed to fit in. I was one of the few men who wore a tie. All of the important Tongan people in town attended, as well as many visitors. At the ball, the winners of the weeklong contests gave command performances before the crown prince, who sat on a big chair decorated with fine mats and flowers. Then the grand ball commenced. Several young Tongan women approached the crown prince, curtsied, and asked him to dance. He graciously rose from his throne like chair and danced with each of them. After some egging on from her girlfriends, a young American tourist approached His Highness, curtsied, and was escorted to the dance floor by the crown prince. She had something special to write on her postcards that night. We danced late into the night. The music was recorded American golden oldies. I remember several repetitions of "The Tennessee Waltz."

His Royal Highness, Crown Prince Tupotu, a bachelor, was a large quiet man about 50 years old. The local people told us that he would never become king because of his problem. Sadly, he was reputed to be a homosexual pedophile who used his princely position to recruit young boys.

We spent two active and exciting months in Tonga. Our life was a constant round of interesting and fun experiences. The following accounts are grouped more by subject than by the calendar.

We were anchored near the shore in a bay on the island of Vava'u, for which the whole group was named. A steep 50-foot bank rose immediately behind the beach. We left our dinghies at the dock at Coleman's boatyard. A steep cement stairway started next to Coleman's and reached the top of the bank alongside the Moorings International Yacht Charter Service's office. Up on the bank the outdoor picnic tables of the rustic little Double Dolphin Café and Gift Shop looked down on the bay.

From there the main street went straight inland to the town of Neiafu. On the way it passed the Catholic church, which looked down on the harbor from the top of a higher hill. Each day at noon its campanili wafted belled hymn tunes over the yachts anchored below. Then the road dropped down into the village of Neiafu, which was about a mile from the bay. Neiafu was a small town with dirt streets and few cars. Its services were barely sufficient to support its local economy and small tourist trade.

We had been warned that Tonga was a conservative Christian country that expected visitors to observe the Sabbath. We were advised not to be seen working on our boats on Sunday, because we could be arrested and fined for breaking the Sabbath.

From the top of our bank, another road led off to the right along the shore for about a mile to the Paradise Hotel. We preferred to reach it by dinghy. It was an attractive and well-maintained hotel with gardenlike grounds that sloped down the bank to the bay. There was no beach, but the hotel maintained a dock where yachts could tie up and fill their water tanks. The Paradise Hotel boasted a cocktail lounge and one of the best restaurants in town. The front half of a small twin-engine airplane jutted out from the wall above the bar in the lounge. The owner was a pilot whose plane had been damaged in a crash landing. He had salvaged the front end of the plane to become a conversation piece in the bar.

Across the road from the hotel was the rustic Vava'u Guest House. It had cottages and a common dining room. Affluent tourists stayed at the hotel, and the guesthouse entertained everyone else, from backpackers to middle-class folks. We ate with the guests in the common dining room several times. The food was served family style at common tables, which enabled us to have conversations with an international mix of adventuresome people.

The Vava'u Club, a private bar frequented mostly by American and European expatriates, was located on the same road between the harbor and the Paradise Hotel. With an introduction from David, owner of the Double Dolphin Café, we occasionally spent an evening there, socializing with cruising friends and hobnobbing with the town dignitaries.

We were in daily radio contact with yachts coming down from American Samoa. Late one afternoon, Fred and Lon, our Dutch friends on *Janana*, reported that their engine had quit and they were sailing in. They would arrive at night and were afraid to negotiate the tricky entrance in the dark. They figured that we knew the way in and asked us to come out and tow them. We quickly got *Tainui* under way and motored out to *Janana*. I maneuvered *Tainui* close alongside and Fred heaved us a towing line. I cleated it off to a stern mooring cleat, and *Tainui* began towing *Janana*. I was nervous about towing them because it was fast becoming dark and I would have to rely on my memory of the landmarks from the pilot book. Also, *Janana* was a 40-foot heavy-displacement full-keel steel boat that was hard to control. I told Fred to stay in my wake as closely as possible to keep *Janana* from veering out of the channel. Between some lights ashore and my memory, I got us safely to the final turn. This turning point was very close to shore. A navigational marker onshore marked the place to turn, but it was unlighted. I ran *Tainui* toward the shore as long as I dared and then turned toward the anchorage, hoping we were in the channel. I never saw the shore. I held my breath as *Janana* swung in toward the shore behind me. We both made it into the anchorage without bumping into anything.

Connie had been making chicken curry for dinner when Fred called for help. I could smell it and got hungrier and hungrier as we towed *Janana* in. Connie figured that Fred and Lon had not had time to make dinner so, once we were both anchored, she invited them to join us. They protested that we had already done enough, but she prevailed, and we all relaxed from our adventure over a meal of Connie's chicken curry and some fine wine from our Dutch friends.

Vava'u was a renowned yacht cruising ground. People from all over the world flew in to charter boats from Moorings. Dozens of islands of all sizes were encased in an outer reef, making an inland sea with smooth sailing and calm anchorages. Except for the tropical climate, it reminded us of the San Juan Islands in Washington's Puget Sound. Vava'u's islands had white sand beaches for picnicking and beachcombing, and the surrounding waters were warm and clear with pristine coral reefs for snorkeling and fishing. There were also caves that could be explored by dinghy or by diving into them. All of us cruisers used the Moorings company's <u>Vava'u Cruising Guide</u>. It contained chartlets of all the main islands, showing how to approach them and where to anchor, and highlighting reefs and other navigational hazards. Navigating these waters would have been difficult without the guide. The guide identified the islands by number rather than name because their names, such as Pangaimotu and Euakafa, were difficult to pronounce. A typical radio conversation between two cruising boats might have been: "Let's meet at number 10 tonight for a barbecue on the beach and then go over to number 22 for snorkeling tomorrow."

Whenever we didn't need to shop or work on the boat, we headed out into these islands. The snorkeling was wonderful. We saw many varieties of coral, including fire coral, stag horn coral, fan coral, tube coral, and many others that I can't name. Swimming around and within the coral, there seemed to be an unlimited variety of tropical fish. We snorkeled by swimming back and forth between yachts in the anchorages and by swimming off of our dinghy near the big coral reefs. Snorkeling was our favorite cruising activity, and Vava'u was replete with snorkeling opportunities.

Sometimes I dove down to the bottom to pick up shells. Shelling was a popular but controversial activity among sailors. It was not strictly ethical. So many shells were being collected for gift shops that many species were endangered. Some people ignored this, including us at first. Even though shells could not legally be brought into the United States, most people had no difficulty getting them in. Some managed to bring home huge shell collections. However, the process of getting rid of the live creatures that inhabited the shells was a smelly business. Some people buried them in sand boxes until they rotted out, but even in the sand, we could smell them on one another's boats. Other people tried putting them out where ants could get at them. They still stank. We made a feeble beginning at shelling, but soon thought better of it. We switched to picking up dead shells that were washed up on the beaches by the tide. This provided an added attraction to beachcombing—another of our favorite activities. Many of the shells we found on the beach were in just as good condition as live ones. I foolishly declared some of these when passing through U.S. Customs at the end of our cruise. When I told the official that they were only dead ones that we picked up off of the beach, he said that that did not make any difference—anyone could claim that. I thought I was in big trouble, but he kindly suggested that it would save us both a lot of inconvenience if I would just scratch the shells off my customs declaration.

I enjoyed sailing among the yachts in quiet anchorages in our wooden sailing dinghy. It was usually peaceful, relaxing, and convivial. People sitting out in their cockpits called out greetings as I ghosted by. It was not so relaxing one time when the sky suddenly darkened and a stiff wind came up. I was downwind from *Tainui* and tried in vain to beat my way back up to her. The wind overpowered my little single sail and I lost ground on every tack. To keep from being blown out of the anchorage, I sailed to a small island downwind, beached the dinghy, and sat down to wait for better weather. Connie had been watching my struggle through our binoculars, and she radioed one of our friends on a nearby yacht for help. He came to me in his outboard-motor-equipped dinghy and towed me back to *Tainui*.

Two of the islands had interesting caves. Connie and I went into Swallow Cave in our dinghy accompanied by another couple in their dinghy. The tunnel into the cave could be entered only at low tide, and even then we had to duck our heads as we motored in. The low tunnel opened into a huge dome-ceilinged, stone amphitheater with rock columns and side rooms. It was dimly lit by eerie greenish light coming in through the tunnel. Without the reflection of the sky, we could see deep down into the dark water. It would have been possible to beach our dinghy on a rock ledge and walk about or swim, but the cave was the nesting place of a variety of sea snakes. They swam around us and a few even struck at the sides of our dinghies. They were about the size of garter snakes. Some were black and white banded and others had black, white, and yellow bands. They had paralyzing venom that was usually fatal, but they were not as dangerous as they sounded. Their mouths were so small that they could only bite a small extremity. Fishermen pulling fish out of their nets were most likely to be bitten in the webbing between their fingers. Connie is terrified of snakes and was relieved that we couldn't stay long because the tide was rising.

I also visited Mariner's Cave with some of the better swimmers. The entrance into this cave was always underwater so we would have to dive down and swim underwater into it. I had practiced in the anchorage before the trip by making surface dives, swimming under *Tainui*, and coming up on the other side. We went at low tide to make the dive as shallow as possible. A Tongan guide led us to a cliff on the side of an island. We anchored our dinghies on a rock ledge, donned masks and fins, and rolled over the sides of our dinghies into the water. Our guide swam to a spot on the cliff marked with white paint. He paused there until we were all in line behind him, then he dove beneath the surface. Another member of our group dove right after him, and I filled my lungs with air and went in third. Five of us entered in single file, each person maintaining visual contact with the one in front of him. It was hard for me to see up to the rock surface above me, and I didn't want to bump my head or scrape skin off my back, so I went a little deeper than the man in front of me. When he started up, I kicked up hard, broke the surface, and let out a big burst of air. We climbed out on a rock ledge and took in our surroundings. Fortunately, there were no snakes in this cave, but, even so, it was also an eerie place. The light that filtered in through the water had a blue cast that shimmered due to the wave action. I felt constant changes in the air pressure in my ears because swells pushing into the underwater mouth of the cave compressed the air inside. We walked about on the rocks and swam around a bit before leaving. The swim out was easier, partly because I knew how deep and how far it was, and partly because we were swimming toward the light.

We met some interesting people in Tonga. Surprisingly, some of them were from Oregon. One Saturday morning when we were shopping in town (all stores closed at noon on Saturday), a young American named

Don stopped his motorbike and introduced himself. We struck up a conversation, and he took us to his Tongan-style house and introduced us to his family. They were his wife, Norie, and their children, Alan and Ona, aged nine and seven. The house was primitive and run-down. The doors and windows were just openings. Their free-running pigs and chickens had turned their yard into mud. A large sow stood in the open kitchen doorway as Norie made us coffee.

We spent the afternoon visiting with them. We were surprised to learn that Don had once taught at Sprague High School in Salem, Oregon. They had been living in Tonga for 10 years and planned to settle there permanently. Norie taught school and Don farmed. Both the children spoke fluent Tongan. Don told us that when they came there, there were no real roads and few vehicles. They traveled by horseback, as did most Tongans. (There were still only dirt roads, and they were full of potholes and mud puddles.) They were originally attracted by Tonga's primitive lifestyle and were not thrilled by the encroachment of civilization that had caused them to trade the horse for a motorcycle. We had lots of questions. Connie asked them how their parents felt about their decision to stay in Tonga. It was not a happy situation. Their income was too meager to allow them to fly home for visits, so they were isolated from their families. I wondered if their children would be content to stay on when they grew up. We both wondered how they would survive without Social Security, pensions, or investments when they were too old to work. However, they seemed happy and contented in their situation. When we thought about the contrast between how little they needed to live a decent life and the surfeit of goods and luxuries that so many of us Americans took for granted, we were not surprised that America appeared to be a greedy and materialistic culture to so many people of the world.

On one of our trips out in the islands, we spotted a couple in a tandem sea kayak fighting choppy seas and strong winds. They were making no progress, and their kayak appeared to be taking on water, so we motored over and offered them a lift to town. They gladly accepted and we helped them up on deck from their kayak, which sat so low in the water that it became unstable when they stood up. Then we pulled the kayak on board and lashed it to the side deck. They were wet, cold, and exhausted. We gave them towels for drying off and a hot drink to warm them up inside. They had flown out from Eugene, Oregon, with their take-apart, folding kayak in two duffel bags. We had a pleasant two-hour trip back to Neiafu as *Tainui* made light work of the sea chop that had stalled out their kayak. They were staying at the Neiafu Guest House and treated us to dinner there when we got in.

I was standing near the Moorings office one day when an attractive red-headed woman shouted my name and ran up and threw her arms around me and gave me a big hug. She was another Oregonian, Rhonda, the long-time manager of the Embarcadero Marina in Newport, where we had moored *Tainui*. She had no idea that we were in Tonga and was as surprised to see me as I was to see her. She and her husband and another couple had come to charter a yacht in Vava'u.

We also had Oregon visitors. Bill Mayhall, a friend from our church and my personal orthopedic surgeon, came to Vava'u with two other families from Salem and chartered yachts from Moorings. Altogether they were six adults and seven children. They had timed their two-week charters to be in Tonga when we were there. We shared anchorages and partied on each other's boats almost every day. The men in Bill's group were eager to experience ocean sailing, so they often moved from one numbered island to another by sailing outside the reef in the open ocean. Their families did not appear to share their enthusiasm for ocean swells. On these occasions Connie and I, not lacking in ocean sailing experience, waited for them at our next scheduled rendezvous.

We had read the book My Tonga by the widow of a Scottish doctor who had spent his career serving the people of Vava'u. She was still living in their house across the bay from Neiafu and we wanted to meet her. We took our dinghy over one afternoon. She had no phone, so we went unannounced and hoped that she was in and that it was an opportune time. We landed the dinghy on her beach and walked up the trail to her house, where we found her working in her flower garden. It was obvious from the profusion of flowering plants around her house that gardening was a passion of hers. She appeared to be about 80 years old and in vigorous health. She asked us to forgive her gardening clothes and invited us into her spacious house, where she served tea and cakes as we sat on rattan chairs in her living room. She graciously signed our copy of her book and told us more tales of Tonga. One that particularly amused us was the fact that Tongan people thought that we white people got money just because we were white. Most of the white people that they saw were visitors like us, who just went to the bank and got money when they needed it. As far as they could tell, she just sat at home and got money—they couldn't understand how writing could be work. Since they never saw any of us work for our money, they concluded that it must be a white person's birthright. Oh, that that were true!

We became well acquainted with David, the proprietor of the Double Dolphin. His café served as a popular meeting place for those of us whose yachts were anchored out in front of the stairs leading up to the café. We passed it coming and going every time we went to town or to the hotel. When *Tainui* was hauled out at Coleman's Boatyard, we ate lunch and took coffee breaks there almost every day. In appearance, David could have been the cartoonist's model for Duke in the comic strip "Doonesbury." His wife was a large Tongan businesswoman who was well connected with Neiafu's important families. She ran the gift shop and David ran the restaurant. David and I had long conversations. He was a source of insider knowledge about Tongan economics, politics, and the foibles of its main characters. David trolled in the bay every evening for coral trout and the next day the woman who cooked in the restaurant turned them into delicious fish burgers, which she called *ika bekkas*. *Ika* was Tongan for "fish" and *bekkas* was her transliteration of "burgers." I ordered them every time she had fresh coral trout. Soon, when she saw me coming, she didn't even ask. She laughed and shouted, *"Ika bekka!"* We did our Christmas shopping early that year in the Double Dolphin's gift shop. A three-foot-tall wide-mouthed woven basket served as the container for an assortment of smaller handicrafts. It still functions as our clothes hamper. We bought all of our Christmas gifts from local craftspeople while we were cruising.

When we got to Australia two years later, we were saddened to learn that David had been lost at sea. He had helped two friends attempt to sail an old wooden boat from Vava'u to Pago Pago. It was only 350 miles and the weather report was favorable, but they were hit with an unpredicted storm and never heard from again. We knew the crews of eight yachts that were lost on reefs, but David was the only person we knew personally who perished at sea.

There had been no haul-out facility for yachts in Pago Pago, so we hauled out at Coleman's to check the bottom paint, install a new depth sounder, and replace the emergency brass cutlass bearing that we had installed in Pago Pago. The brass bearing worked well on the way to Tonga, but we had a proper new one with a rubber bearing that would cause less wear on the prop shaft than the metal one. To be hauled out, we motored *Tainui* over an underwater flatbed railroad car and tied her dock lines to vertical poles coming up from the corners of the car. Then Don Coleman's big winch pulled us up inclined tracks into his work yard on a strong steel cable. He could haul only one boat at a time. It rained too much to work on *Tainui* for the first two days, so we spent our time walking to town, attending church to listen to the music, and having some of our long conversations with David at the Double Dolphin. Returning from a trip to town one wet day, we found that the rain had sunk our dinghy with the outboard engine on it. I bailed out the boat and clamped the motor onto the boatyard's outboard motor barrel, pulled the starter rope until it sputtered to life, and let it run for an hour to dry it out. This was not the first time I had to do this, nor would it be the last.

Large flakes of the coal-tar epoxy we had applied in Raiatea eight months earlier had already come off. I spent a lot of time sanding the hull and applying two new coats of coal tar epoxy paint between rain showers. Ironically, David, the boatyard manager from Raiatea, and his wife sailed in while I was doing this. He had quit his job and gone cruising. He was embarrassed and appalled that the paint that was applied at the *carenage* had failed in just eight months. After eight days in the boatyard, *Tainui* splashed into the bay and we immediately struck out for the islands.

We had heard tales of the beautiful singing in the churches in the South Pacific and attended the big Methodist church in Neiafu to find out. We attended with our friends Chuck and Dottie from the vessel *Viki,* who were retired music teachers from New York. The service was in Tongan, which made it boring for us, but the music made up for it. We knew from the first strains of the opening hymn that we were in for a musical treat. The congregation sang in such rich, resonant four-part harmony that it was no surprise that the choir anthem was a masterpiece. They gave a masterful a cappella rendition of Handel's "Hallelujah Chorus." They sang in Tongan, but words like "hallelujah" and "amen" came through untranslated. After the service, we congratulated the choir director and asked to see the choir music. There was nothing on the pages but numbers. The choir director explained that a missionary had translated the notes for each part into numbers. The system did not require any musical notation like clefs, lines, staffs, sharps or flats. The choir members memorized the words.

We music lovers got a special bonus when the Methodist District Meeting was held in Neiafu while we were there, featuring an evening choir competition between eight churches. Each choir director's introduction included impressive academic credentials. The contest consisted of two rounds—sixteen anthems. They were all Western-style pieces—many by classical composers—and were performed to perfection. At the end of the contest, the congregation and all eight choirs joined in singing the closing hymn. The harmony was so strong that we could feel the vibrations in the floor and in the pews we sat in—it gave us goose bumps.

We also had a church experience on the small island of Hunga (I can't remember its number). Hunga was a circular island about five miles in diameter, formed by the rim of an extinct (we hoped) volcano. The entrance was a small break in the volcano wall that could be entered only at high tide. With her four-and-a-half-foot draft, *Tainui* easily slid over the bar into the completely sheltered lagoon and joined a half dozen other yachts at anchor. The crater was so deep that we had to anchor near to the shore to find anchoring depth. This proved to be a problem in the night. We had entered at high tide, so we had to put out a lot of chain. When the tide went down in the night, we had too much chain for our depth, and *Tainui* swung toward shore. The depth-sounder alarm awoke us when *Tainui*'s stern was 10 yards off the shore and we were at a depth of five feet. We had just six inches of clearance from the bottom. I pulled us offshore by winching in some chain, and let it out again at high tide in the morning.

The next day was Sunday, so about a dozen of us dressed up and went to the village for church. From the dinghy landing we had to climb up a steep wet bank. It was slippery going, and by the time we reached the top, our shoes were great balls of red clay and our Sunday attire was sporting red stains. Nevertheless, we carried on. Most of the group went to the Methodist Church, but not wanting to overwhelm the small congregation, a few of us went to the smaller Free Tongan Church. We were afraid that we would be disappointed in the music when we saw that the entire congregation consisted of only fifteen adults and fifteen small children. However, when the music began, all the parts of the harmony came through loud and clear. Even the children could sing their parts. An elder preached what sounded like hellfire and damnation sermon. For once I was glad I didn't speak Tongan. When they took the offering, the elder announced what each person had given, but when they got to us, they announced the lump sum from visitors.

Early in our stay, we attended one of the feasts that Isaiah and his wife, a local Tongan couple, occasionally held at Lisa's Beach on the far side of Vava'u Island. Isaiah himself made the rounds of yachts and personally invited us. We took an ancient bus that bumped and rattled through the potholes and rocked precariously on the hairpin turns down the steep bank to the beach. Lisa's Beach was at the bottom of a high cliff. A rumor was going around that the pig for the feast was killed by throwing it off the cliff. We hoped it wasn't true. The feast consisted of many pork dishes, lots of seafood, including squid and octopus, baked papaya and breadfruit with coconut sauce, and many fresh fruits. There was also a display of local crafts, and music. After the feast we danced into the night to the music of a three-piece orchestra that consisted of a guitar, a banjo, and a violin. Isaiah's wife decorated Connie's arm with a bracelet of pandanus leaves and danced with her. When it got dark, the Tongans lit torches made from beer cans filled with kerosene.

We had another group eating adventure at the Spanish restaurant on Tapana Island. It was a rustic building with walls made of tapa cloth. We had eaten there before when we were anchored nearby and had enjoyed food and the company of the Spanish couple who owned and operated it. The cuisine featured paella, Spanish omelets, and homemade bread. This time we joined a group traveling by taxi from Neiafu to Ano Beach on the far side of the island, where a chartered boat would take us to Tapana. Our outboard motor quit on the way to the hotel, where we were to pick up a taxi, and Bob from *Hunky Dory* towed us the rest of the way. We had a rough taxi ride over the poorly maintained dirt road with huge potholes. When we arrived at Ano Beach, I told the taxi driver that we would not pay him until he picked us up at 10:30 p.m., in order to guarantee his return. I did not relish the prospect of being stranded at Ano Beach in the middle of the night. The wooden powerboat was waiting and took us across the channel to Tapana Island. We approached at low tide and beached the boat a long way from shore in two feet of water. A husky Tongan man gave the women piggyback rides to the beach while we men waded in.

At the restaurant we joined the crews of several yachts that had anchored off of Tapana Island. There was a huge buffet of Tongan and Spanish dishes, a well-stocked bar, and music and dancing. At about 10:00 the party broke up. By then the tide had come in and waves were breaking on the beach. The cruisers who had anchored off Tapana Island got wet as they launched their dinghies into the breaking waves. Even our larger wooden boat took waves over its sides on the rough crossing back to Ano Beach, soaking us all. The unpaid cab driver was waiting as instructed. He probably would have come back anyway, and I was embarrassed by my lack of trust, but I regarded it as a case of better safe than sorry. Our outboard motor ran smoothly all the way back to *Tainui* from the hotel dock, but a tropical shower hit us at mid-passage and we were soaked again, this time with freshwater.

We hated to leave Vava'u. It was our most fun cruising experience so far. We stayed until we had just enough time for a short visit to Fiji before making the passage to New Zealand before the next cyclone season. Connie directed our provisioning. Neiafu boasted a small Burns Phillip store—part of an international grocery store chain that was popular in South Pacific countries. They had frozen chicken pieces that would last most of the way and fresh baked bread, and there were ample fruits and vegetables in the open-air markets. After I cleared with customs and immigration, we sailed out to Port Murielle near the outer reef where we anchored for the night alongside our friends Ed and Marilyn and their young daughter, Laura, on *Spindrift*. Marilyn invited us over for her extra-special lamb curry, and Connie brought a carrot and apple salad. Thus we celebrated our last night in the quaint and beautiful Kingdom of Tonga.

Vern takes the helm on *Tainui's* sea trials in B.C., Canada. (above)
Sailing our new "bare-bones" *Tainui* on our own. (below)

Moored stern-to Mediterranean-style at Cabo San Lucas alongside *Sasaparilla*. Note the addition of cockpit dodger, stern pulpit canvass and wind vane. (above)
Happy hour at the Hotel Finestero in Cabo San Lucas. (below)

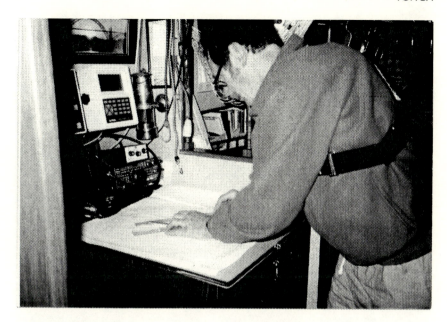

Off for the South Pacific. Can we find Nuku Hiva 3,000 nautical miles away? (above)
Early fishing success. Fresh meat for dinner. (below)

Not again! Connie's all too familiar view of Vern at sea. (above)
The devastation caused by hurricane Ofa in American Samoa. (below)

The tomb of Robert Louis Stevenson on Mt. Vilima in Western Samoa.
(above)
One of the two floats we judged in "the big parade" in Neiafu, Tonga.
(below)

Lobster "home delivery" in Tonga. (above)
The entrance to Swallow Cave in one of the numbered islands of
Vava'u, Tonga. (below)

CHAPTER EIGHT

FIJI

On the morning of July 7, 1990, I changed the oil filters on the diesel engine and secured the deck gear for sea, and Connie put *Tainui* in shape below. The crew of *Spindrift* waved good-bye as we weighed anchor and departed Vava'u, Tonga, for Suva, Fiji, a journey of 450 miles. Our trip began with an eight-knot breeze and flat seas, and the wind conveniently went dead calm at bedtime and remained that way through the night. We took two-hour watches, and when off watch, we slept well in the balmy tropical night with a full moon. We didn't make any progress, but we were glad for the gentle reintroduction to ocean sailing; we began our trip with settled stomachs and good appetites.

We awoke to a day of constant tacking and sail trimming as we tried to milk every bit of progress from light headwinds and intermittent calms. Toward evening, a steady wind filled in and backed a bit to starboard. I put *Tainui* on a starboard tack under a singled-reefed main, working jib, and staysail. *Tainui* was so well balanced under this configuration that she held her course without the autopilot. We were doing so well at bedtime that I took a chance and didn't reduce sail. As a result, we were awakened at midnight by *Tainui* crashing into big waves as she beat her way into a 35-knot headwind. Connie stood watch in the cockpit while I crept forward through the spray in the dark of night to the bucking bow pulpit and pulled down the jib. Without the jib, *Tainui* quieted down enough for us to get some sleep during the remainder of the night.

The following morning the wind backed to a 25-knot beam reach, and *Tainui* sped along at six knots under a double-reefed main and staysail—our heavy-weather configuration. We had a great ride all day and were pleased to be making up for lost time. Again, I was so excited about our progress that I didn't reduce sails at night, and again in the middle of the night, the wind blew harder. It was a noisy and wild ride, but we were still flying along, and I wanted to tough it out. Connie felt otherwise. We had a little discussion, and, as no further sail reductions were possible, I begrudgingly hove *Tainui* to for the rest of the night. Heaving to was a good decision. We were in an isolated area, out of all shipping lanes, so we increased our on-watch sleeping periods to 30 minutes between lookouts instead of our usual 15, and started the next day rested and ready to sail on.

The wind abated slightly in the morning, so we took off again under a double-reefed main and staysail. An hour later the wind backed to a broad reach, and I shook both reefs out of the main, took down the staysail, and poled out the jib, which pushed *Tainui* to her maximum speed. Our Sat Nav clocked us at seven knots for most of the day, which was exceptionally fast for *Tainui*, so I suspected that we were aided by a following current. It was an exhilarating ride, and toward the evening of this, our fourth day out, we sighted the islands of Onega and Nariti on the eastern fringes of the Fiji group.

The direct route to Suva would take us through the Lau group, which was about a day's sail southeast of Suva. These islands had a reputation for strong unpredictable currents and dangerous reefs, so we decided to sail south of the group and then up to Suva. This approach would take a little longer, but I felt the faster route wasn't worth the risk. More yachts were lost on the reefs in Fiji than any other place on our route. However, at the speed we were traveling, we would make the turn around Totoya Island, at the south end of the Lau group, in the night. Therefore I slowed *Tainui* down enough so that we would round Totoya in the morning.

In the early morning light, we rounded Totoya and turned northwest toward Suva. This short passage should have been an easy one-day sail, but light winds and an adverse current made it frustratingly slow going. We were still 25 miles out at sunset, so we hove to at a spot 10 miles off the island's big reef, well clear of local shipping and with good clearance for unknown currents. We had a peaceful night, taking turns sleeping and looking out, and began motoring the remaining 10 miles at dawn. As we entered Suva's harbor, the sight of three wrecks on the reef confirmed the wisdom of our conservative approach.

We anchored well out in the harbor, ran up the yellow Q (for quarantine) signal flag, and waited for our health clearance. The original purpose of this practice was to keep ships' crews from bringing the plague or other communicable diseases ashore. Many of the 15 countries that we visited on our seven-year cruise had given up on harbor quarantine and allowed yachts to check in onshore. However, in Fiji we were not allowed to leave our boat until we received our health clearance. Four hours after we anchored, the Health Department launch pulled alongside, and the port health officer climbed aboard and signed our Health Clearance Certificate. He was courteous, polite, and efficient, with no hint of the shenanigans we experienced when we were boarded at Tonga. Before departing, he directed us to the Prince's Wharf for customs and immigration clearance.

There was no dock space at the Prince's Wharf, but we were directed to tie up to the outside of a tugboat, and a New Zealand sailboat soon tied up outside of us. I got our passports and ship's papers together and set off with Terry from the New Zealand boat, while our wives stayed aboard as required. Fiji followed the custom that only the captain could go ashore until the vessel was completely cleared into the country. As Terry and I were crossing the broad open stern of the tug, some crewmembers insisted that we share a cup of kava with them before continuing. Kava was made from smashed pepper-tree roots and looked like muddy dishwater. Not sure what it would be like, I held my breath and gulped it down in one draught. It had a green, muddy taste that reflected its earthy origin. We soon learned that kava was the national drink of Fiji. Every government office had a huge kava bowl for regular kava breaks. Fortunately, Fijian kava was mild compared to what we found later in Vanuatu. Vanuatuan kava would have brought the Fijian government to a halt in a drunken stupor.

Checking in required long waits in the unair-conditioned offices of multiple government agencies. In the late afternoon, when we were officially entered into Fiji, we cast off Terry's lines, untied *Tainui* from the tug, and motored over to the Royal Suva Yacht Club. Suva was a major crossroad for yachts traveling in the Pacific, and the Royal Suva Yacht Club was their main gathering place. Boats of every size and description from all over the world crowded the marina docks and the off-lying mooring buoys. We immediately spotted a dozen or so yachts of our friends from previous anchorages. The farther we traveled, the more people we knew, and entering a new country was like a mini class reunion. We tied up at the guest dock and signed in at the yacht club office. The manager assigned us to a mooring buoy half a mile from the club's dock. We secured *Tainui* to our buoy, then launched our dinghy, and hurried back to the evening barbecue at the yacht club. The barbecue was a great opportunity for us to link up with our friends from previous ports.

The Royal Suva Yacht Club charged US$20 per week, which included the mooring buoy and the use of their showers, laundry tubs, bar, and restaurant. We did most of our laundry by hand in their wash tubs and sent our sheets, towels, and heavy clothes out to a laundry that picked them up one day and returned them the next for 30 cents per item. With the exception of Pago Pago, where there were laundromats, we had been doing our washing by hand aboard *Tainui*—an onerous and time-consuming task. From Fiji on, however, we hired it done by local people. We found more exciting things than to do laundry in the exotic places we visited!

Fiji was a large country, consisting of 300 islands dotted across 200,000 square miles of ocean. Its ethnic makeup was Fijian, East Indian, and Chinese. With a population of 73,000, Suva was the largest city we had encountered after leaving Mexico. The only other sizeable city in the South Pacific was Papeete in French Polynesia, with a population of 65,000.

After a good night's sleep at our peaceful mooring buoy and a quick breakfast aboard *Tainui*, we hopped into our dinghy and motored through the fleet of moored boats to the landing at the yacht club. A couple we had met in Pago Pago shared the short taxi ride into Suva with us. Before we shopped, we all exchanged money at an Indian jewelry shop, where we got the best exchange rate. Indians had originally been brought to Fiji to work in the sugarcane fields, but over time they had become the majority. The recent election of an ethnic Indian prime minister outraged the native Fijians. Colonel Rambuka led a bloodless coup, kicked out the Indian prime minister, and installed a Fijian one. The government then enacted laws that gave Fijian tribal chiefs control of the Parliament and discriminated against Indians. As a result, the more well-off and better-educated Indians were leaving Fiji. However, government regulations prohibited them from taking large sums of money out of the country. Therefore, Indian jewelers, who were also moneychangers, were paying high rates of exchange for American one hundred dollar bills, because they were easier to smuggle out of the country than large quantities of smaller bills. We heard that some Indian business owners had managed to smuggle out as much as US$200,000. We had saved five one hundred dollar bills for this purpose, and later our son Larry brought us 10 more when he and his family visited us in Fiji.

After exchanging our money, we ate lunch in a Chinese restaurant. The Chinese were Fiji's third-largest ethnic group. As elsewhere in the South Pacific, the Chinese in Fiji were concentrated in towns and cities, where they operated shops and restaurants. We wondered if there were any place in the world that didn't have a Chinese shop or restaurant. After lunch we shopped at a bakery and at a large open-air fruit and vegetable market—the biggest and best one that we found on our entire trip. That evening we ate a curry dinner at the yacht club restaurant. It was too bland for the taste in hot curry we had cultivated when we lived in Malaysia. Chinese and Indian restaurants tended to serve mild curry to Westerners unless they were specifically asked to make it hot. As a result, I had the following conversation in a Chinese restaurant where the proprietor didn't speak much English:

"Is your curry hot?"
"Don't worry, I won't make it too hot for you."
"But I like it hot."
"You like it too hot?"
This was a tough question. I took a chance, "Well, … er… yes."
"Okay, for you I make it too hot!"
I guessed right. It was just the way I liked it.

Our introduction to "Rainy Suva," as it was often called, began immediately—it rained and blew hard all night and all the next day. Local people claimed that, out of spite, their ancestors had tricked the British into establishing Fiji's capital city on the wettest and most mosquito-infected part of the island. We were eager to see more of the town, but didn't brave the weather. We took advantage of the rainy day to straighten up the boat and get some more rest to recover from our night watches at sea. In intermittent rain the next day, I went to the Department of Communications, where I got a temporary ham radio license, which allowed us to use our ham radio while we were in Fiji. When I launched the dinghy to return to *Tainui*, the outboard motor quit and I rowed back in the rain.

We made the most of the first sunny day by running errands. We took the radar to an electronics repair shop, found a denturist who replaced a tooth that had fallen out of my economy Samoan-made denture, and located a marine store, where we bought new oarlocks for the dinghy. After the rain, the weather was oppressively hot and humid. We treated ourselves to ice cream sundaes at a snack bar in the mid-afternoon, and later we had a relaxing dinner at an excellent Indian restaurant.

After dinner we walked to the venerable old British-colonial-style Grand Pacific Hotel for a drink and to soak up the atmosphere. It was much like the Eastern and Oriental Hotel in Penang, Malaysia, and the Raffles Hotel in Singapore. We were struck by the sense of great space and quiet as we entered the lobby with its large rattan-meshed ceiling-fan blades slowly rotating high above. It reminded us of a scene from an old Humphrey Bogart-Sidney Greenstreet movie. Elderly white-jacketed Chinese staff members, moving about with quiet dignity among the potted fan palms, imparted the impression of decaying British colonialism. We sat in cane chairs in the plush lounge and sipped our gin and tonics as we studied the lounge denizens. The well-off British gentlemen who were drinking at the massive mahogany bar were reminiscent of English planters of old at their private club. We felt as though we had been transported back in time to the age of the British Raj.

We had our six-person life raft serviced in Fiji. After we saw how small and cramped two people would be in a four-person raft, we had bought the six-person model. Our life raft was packed in a fiberglass canister that was installed on teakwood chocks on the coach roof with quick-release straps and secured to the mast by a tether. In the unfortunate event that we needed it, we would release it from its chocks and throw it into the sea. The pull on its tether would trigger its opening mechanism. The canister would pop open and an internal air cylinder would inflate the raft, which would float in the sea tied to *Tainui* by its tether. We would toss in the man-overboard containers that we kept by the companionway stairs. These comprised a sealed bucket containing valuables, such as money and passports, and a sail bag filled with emergency rations. We would then board the raft and cut the tether with a knife that was tied to the outside of the raft for that purpose.

Life rafts needed to be periodically blown up, be checked for leaks, and have their emergency supplies of drinking water, flashlights, fishing gear, and flares inspected and replaced as needed. We had bought our raft second-hand in Seattle and had it serviced for US$250. In Suva, it cost only US$100, and we participated in the process, unlike in Seattle, where it had been sent away for servicing. The Fijian service staff left the raft inflated for 48 hours to check for leaks, and then reviewed its contents with us so we could make our own decisions about needed replacements. Then they installed a new compressed air-inflating cartridge and repacked the raft in its canister. We were surprised to find that there were no emergency rations in the raft. Thereafter, we kept a sealed container of emergency food near the companionway stairs.

In Fiji we heard the rest of the *Amazing Grace* story. After sailing *Amazing Grace* from Pago Pago and crashing her on the reef at Suva, Craig and Gwen and their dog got safely off the boat and were rescued from the reef. Craig managed to salvage most of the equipment, but the government of Fiji impounded it due to a claim that had been filed by its original owners. Craig got none of it back and had nothing to show for the money and effort he had put into restoring *Amazing Grace*. He went to Australia to look for work, hoping that Gwen would eventually join him there. Gwen moved back aboard *Galatea* with Walt and Bea, who were now in Fiji, and went along with them as crew on a lengthy charter expedition. On the trip she fell in love with one of the passengers, a wealthy Swede, and ultimately married him and moved to Sweden—completing Craig's loss.

While we were eating at the yacht club one evening, a weather system with gusts of wind up to 25 knots brought waves straight into our anchorage. On our way out to *Tainui*, our dinghy splashed head-on into the waves, and sheets of spray blew back into our faces. It was like riding a bucking horse in a rainstorm. As the night went on, the wind and waves increased, causing the boats on the yacht club moorings to buck and roll wildly, and making sleep impossible. Some yachts took off in the night for the more sheltered part of the bay, in front of the Trade Winds Hotel, but we did not attempt it in the dark. At first light we cast off from our mooring buoy and motored toward the Trade Winds Hotel. Visibility was so poor in the driving rain that I could not find the small navigational aids that were supposed to guide us to a gap between the two reefs that separated us from the anchorage near the hotel. We wandered around anxiously in the storm not knowing where the reefs were, until we made radio contact with the skipper on one of the yachts already anchored at the hotel, who talked us safely through the opening. Once inside, we anchored in much calmer water among a small fleet of other yachts seeking refuge from the storm.

We parked our dinghy at the hotel dock that evening and went out to dinner with a group of friends. The Trade Winds Hotel was up for sale and was temporarily closed to the public but they still charged us US$3 a night to tie up at their dinghy dock. Our party returned late in the evening and found that the tide was high and waves were crashing into the dinghy dock and the hotel's concrete sea wall. The waves threw up huge showers of seawater that ran down the front of the hotel like a waterfall. The hotel staff had pulled all of our dinghies up on the dock to keep them from being smashed by the waves, but the wet and slippery floating dock was rolling so violently that none of us dared to venture out on it to launch a dinghy. The 10 of us had no choice but to spend the night at the defunct hotel. We rearranged the overstuffed furniture in the lobby to create makeshift beds and prepared to bed down for the night. However, when the part-time interim hotel manager, who was also the pastor of a local church, stopped in and saw our plight, he opened up some of the rooms, provided us with linens, and gave us all a free night's lodging.

The tide was out and the weather had calmed down in the morning, so we all returned to our boats. Connie stayed aboard to catch up on her sleep, while I dinghied back to the hotel, took a cab to town, and retrieved our life raft. The next day we moved *Tainui* back to the Royal Suva Yacht Club in preparation for the arrival of our son Larry, his wife, Joyce, and our grandsons Colin, six, and Graham, two.

Suva is situated on the eastern side of the island of Viti Levu, and the airport is located at Nadi (pronounced Nandi) on its western side. Our kids rented a car, drove the 87 miles from Nadi to Suva, and met us at the yacht club. They stayed at the venerable Grand Pacific Hotel while they explored Suva with us for three days, and then they wanted to sail out of the city and see some village life.

We set out for the island of Bega (pronounced Benga—see a pattern developing?) about 18 miles from Suva. It was a fairly rough crossing, with winds ranging between 20 and 25 knots and waves to match. Joyce and Graham got seasick as soon as we hit the open sea. We gave Graham Dramamine, which put him to sleep for the remainder of the trip, but Joyce passed on the medication and toughed-out the three-hour crossing without complaint.

Bega was surrounded by a fringing reef about a mile and a half offshore. We were told that a stick with a triangle on top of it marked the pass through the reef. Larry helped me douse the sails, and I motored along as close to the reef as I dared in search of the stick. We were all looking out for the marker, but no one saw it on our first pass. I turned *Tainui* around and tried again. The stick was so small that Larry, standing in the bow pulpit, didn't spot it until we were 10 yards from it. The primitive marker didn't follow the international system for marking reefs, i.e., it didn't indicate on which side of it the pass was. I held my breath and steered toward shore, passing a few feet from the marker, while everyone looked out for shallow water. We were all tense until we were sure we were inside the reef. Late in the afternoon we anchored off a village in Malumu Bay along with one British yacht and two others flying New Zealand flags. Malumu Bay was actually a fjord. The steep hills on its sides provided good protection from the wind, but its steep banks meant deep water near the shore. The least anchoring depth we could find was 10 fathoms (60 feet), which was much deeper than we were used to. In order to get our usual scope of five times as much chain as the depth, I paid out all of our 300-foot anchor chain.

Our passengers' upset stomachs settled down quickly in calm water, and we all enjoyed dinner aboard. It took all of our available bunk space and the cabin sole to make beds for the six of us. In the middle of the night, a violent blast of wind shook *Tainui* and knocked her far over. Sailors call these nocturnal blasts "williwaws." Technically they are catabatic winds. After the sun goes down, the air on the steep hills cools quickly, while the sea stays warm. The warm air above the sea rises, and the heavier cold air rushes down the hillsides to take its place. The bigger blasts heeled *Tainui* so far over that it was difficult for us to stay in our bunks. We kept a radar watch through the night to make sure we didn't drag anchor in the gusts and tidal current, and no one slept much that night.

We went ashore the next morning and paid our respects to the chief. Fijian custom dictated that we must first do a kava ceremony called *savasavu* with the village chief and elders, and then request permission to visit the village and use its beaches. Before the ceremony began, we gave our required gift of pepper-tree root to the chief. The ceremony was usually for men only, but this chief invited Connie and Joyce to join in. The kava was made by mashing the pepper root and squeezing its juice through cheesecloth into a kava bowl filled with water. Kava bowls were large hand-carved, wooden, basin-shaped three-legged bowls. They were popular souvenirs in Fiji; we brought home a large one.

We all sat crossed-legged on the floor, while the chief presided. It was considered impolite for a man to refuse kava, but a woman could abstain. Connie and Joyce gave it a try this time—but never again! One of the elders dipped a half coconut shell into the kava bowl and served the chief. He then served the other elders, and we visitors were served last. Each person drank the kava down in one draught, handed back the bowl, and clapped his or her hands three times. I tried not to make a face or appear to be gagging the kava down. It made my lips and tongue slightly numb, but I felt no other effect. When the ceremony was over, the chief formally welcomed us to his village and invited us to use its beaches.

The village people were fascinated with our two little grandsons. All of the children wanted to play with them and touch their white skin and blond hair. A village couple, Isaiah and Servatu, invited us all to their home for tea and pancakes. Their house was a one-room shed-type dwelling made of a single layer of boards that served as its inside and outside walls, which was typical of village houses in the tropics. Inside the house, there were only a few pieces of furniture. Their 18-year-old daughter made the tea and pancakes for us in a kitchen area that was in one corner of the room. They had an old couch, but she served us as we sat cross-legged on the floor, along with Isaiah, Servatu, and their three younger children. Before we left, Isaiah gave us permission to use a beach that he owned across the bay from our anchorage.

We went back to *Tainui* in the afternoon for a late lunch. Connie and I ate aboard, but Larry and Joyce packed a lunch and took their family across the channel in our dinghy to Isaiah's beach for a picnic and a swim. While we were eating, we saw the village passing by our portholes. Our anchor was dragging, and the current was taking us out of the bay. We motored back up to the village and reanchored. This was the only time in our entire cruise that we dragged our anchor, and it was also the only time that we had not tested it. It was our custom to put the engine in reverse and back down hard on the anchor chain to make sure it held. Fortunately we were aboard *Tainui* when the anchor dragged. If it had happened while we were in the village, we would have been chasing *Tainui* out to sea in our dinghy. Larry and Joyce returned at sunset after having enjoyed excellent swimming and snorkeling on Isaiah's beach.

Because of the williwaws and poor holding in the deep water, we decided to seek a better anchorage. Yachts anchored off of the village of Vaga ("Vanga," of course) on the other side of Bega reported that they had much better anchoring conditions, so we took *Tainui* back out through the reef, made the short trip around the island, reentered the reef, and anchored near Vaga. The anchorage at Vaga was ideal. There were no hills, which eliminated the williwaws. The bay was wide, which eliminated the strong tidal currents that we experienced in fjord-like Malumu Bay. Finally, the long shallow beach gave us a reasonable anchoring depth and was perfect for beachcombing, swimming, and snorkeling.

This time Larry and I went to the village without our wives, presented our gift, and did *savasavu* with the chief and elders. One of the elders, Patema, nicknamed "Pat," invited us to bring our family to his home. We visited inside the house with Pat and his wife, Sarah, while their kids took turns pushing Colin on a big rope-and-tire swing hung from a tree on the edge of the beach. Pat gave us permission to use his beach, and Sarah insisted that we come back for dinner that evening to try a special Fijian dish, but mentioned that she did not have any meat for it, implying that we should supply it. We got her message. Larry and I took our dinghy a mile up the shore to tiny Rukua Village and bought four cans of corned beef.

Before dinner we spent the afternoon swimming and snorkeling on Pat and Sarah's lovely beach. Connie cooked a macaroni salad to share in the meal, and we all went back to their house for dinner and a pleasant evening. Sarah's special dish was delicious. We reciprocated by having Pat and Sarah join us for tea on *Tainui* the next afternoon. Connie served American-style apple crisp and Sarah provided some local snack food. Pat brought a guitar, and he and Sarah sang some Christian songs for us.

One day some people from Vaga asked us to join them on a hike to a neighboring village. They said that it was an easy hike on the beach, so we all went with them. It turned out to be a much more ambitious undertaking than we had been led to believe. It was a long walk on the beach, followed by a jungle trail up over a steep hill and down into the village. The hike was too much for little Graham, so we took turns carrying him. The village was isolated and very primitive. Once again, Colin and Graham were a big attraction. Crowds of children followed them wherever they went, and women took turns holding Graham. We got back to *Tainui* late and tired that evening, but felt that the experience of visiting the isolated village was worth the effort.

Sarah supplemented their meager income by weaving mats. Before we left Bega, Larry and Joyce ordered a large floor mat from her for US$100, which was a lot of money in the Fijian village economy. The mat arrived in Seattle as promised. It didn't last long in Seattle's climate, but Larry and Joyce bought it mostly to help out Pat and Sarah. However, Pat and Sarah were not through asking for help. It soon became clear that they thought their new American friends could somehow bring them to America. They had no concept of the necessary immigration procedures, the cost of moving their family halfway around the world, or how they would support themselves in America. It took Larry and Joyce a long time to convince Pat and Sarah that they were not able to bring them and their family to the United States.

We had smooth sailing back to the yacht club in Suva, much to the relief of our *mal-de-mer*-prone passengers. Colin and Graham stayed on the boat with us, while Larry and Joyce slipped away and spent their last few days in Fiji at the Hide Away Hotel on the Coral Coast midway between Suva and Nadi. We appreciated having the time with our grandchildren, and Colin quickly found playmates among children from other boats at the Royal Suva Yacht Club.

When it was time for Larry and Joyce to leave Fiji, we rented a car, picked them up at the Hide Away Hotel, and saw them off at the airport in Nadi. We spent that night at the Sea Breeze Hotel in nearby Laotoka, and then continued around the island by car. The next night we stayed at the Raki Raki Hotel in Raki Raki Village. It was a resort hotel with a swimming pool, a lawn bowling field, and a half-sized tennis court. We enjoyed the company of a family of four from Brisbane, who were returning from four years of voluntary service in Raratonga, the capital city of the Cook Islands. We had great fun playing half-court tennis with their two attractive teenaged daughters. We were impressed with the wholesomeness and politeness of these young women. In their cabin that night, at their bedtime, without being coached by their parents and with no apparent reluctance or embarrassment, they kissed all of us adults good night before retiring. We were touched by the naturalness with which they did it. Our children had refused to keep doing this long before they were teenagers.

Our road trip around the island continued through vast sugarcane fields on the flat, dry, west side of the island. The cane was hand cut by Indian laborers and hauled out of the fields on a mini railroad system. The little open gondola cars were about the size of the cars used in coal mines, and their engines were built to the same scale. Before we had gone very far, we had a flat tire. I changed the tire, and then the air conditioner quit. The heat was bearable driving with the windows down in the cloudy weather. The middle part of the trip was through jungle-covered hills with many native Fijiian-style, grass-roofed houses. Three days out of Nadi, we came out of the forest and drove into the usual rain on the Suva side of the island.

Back in Suva, we celebrated our 39th wedding anniversary with dinner at the Swiss Tavern Restaurant. An American couple at the table next to us introduced themselves as Ken and Ramona Larsen, Mormon missionaries living in Suva. They were fascinated by the story of our sailing trip and gave us a ride back to the yacht club in their car. I was surprised when they eagerly accepted my invitation to take them on out in the dinghy to see *Tainui*. They were both large people, and all four of us rode out in the dark with our small dinghy riding very low in the water. Once on board, they seemed to be genuinely thrilled to be visiting a world-cruising yacht.

The Larsens reciprocated by inviting us to dinner later in the week. At their home we met their house girl, Tekua, a 19-year-old Kiribati (pronounced Kirabass—don't ask me why) girl, who did light chores in return for room and board while she went to school in Suva. John Cook, a university professor, and his Fijian wife also joined us for dinner. During the evening, we took advantage of the opportunity to learn as much as we could from them about Fijian politics and culture. In response to our interest in Fijian culture, they invited us to join them on an upcoming trip to a major cultural event in the interior.

About a month later, Ken and Ramona picked us up in a van, along with Tekua, John Cook, and his wife. They drove us up a winding road through the jungle deep into the mountainous interior of the island. We arrived at a village in a clearing in a little mountain valley. The occasion was a regional bazaar that was attended by people from all of the surrounding villages. General Rambuka, who had led the bloodless coup that deposed the first (last and only) Indian elected prime minister, was to be the guest of honor. The village elders seated us on the ground with the visiting dignitaries under the shade of a makeshift canopy, and we awaited the arrival of the general. After an hour of hot, sweaty waiting, an army major arrived with the news that General Rambuka's helicopter had broken down, and that he had been sent in his stead.

With the arrival of the substitute guest of honor, an elaborate, traditional kava ceremony began, presided over by the village chief. We had been warned to keep our heads lower than the chief's head at all times. Traditionally, the penalty for violating this taboo was death. Two warriors, with bands of leaves around the biceps of their bare arms and the calves of their bare legs, entered from the back of the group carrying a huge kava bowl down the center aisle. They approached the chief, knelt down, and placed the bowl at his feet. They remained crouched low as they retreated, facing the chief, until they were well out of his presence. Two more warriors then came in carrying the entire root system of a pepper tree. This traditional gift had been brought by the major to present to the village chief. Then an elder brought water in a tall section of bamboo, knelt down, and poured the water into the kava bowl. Immediately, four young women, who had been sitting near the chief, moved to the bowl, keeping their heads down in a crouching position. They sat on the ground, mashed the pepper tree roots with a mortar and pestle, and squeezed the juice into the kava bowl through cheesecloth. In ancient times, the roots were masticated by virgins, who spat it into the cheesecloth—we were relieved that this custom was no longer practiced.

Before the actual kava ceremony began, visiting chiefs had their gifts presented. Two of their warrior-like men carried large baskets of taro and manioc roots down the aisle and laid them before the chief. Next, two others brought in another massive bundle of whole pepper-tree roots, and, finally, two warriors from another village struggled past us carrying a full-grown hog trussed up in vines.

A village elder dressed in a loincloth, possibly a priest or shaman, dipped out a half coconut shell of kava, raised it with his arms fully outstretched at shoulder level, slowly turned in a complete circle, and presented the bowl to the chief. The chief drank it down, gave back the bowl, and clapped his hands three times. The server repeated this process until all of the Fijian guests were served. Apparently he was exempt from the head-above-the-chief taboo. We outsiders were not served kava in this ceremony, but it was later offered to us at a tent at the bazaar. Speeches followed the drinking of the kava. A talking necklace, made of a ring of small cowry shells with one large one in the center, was given to each speaker when it was his turn to talk. The chief spoke first, and then handed the necklace to the major. It was not worn around the neck, but held in the speakers' laps. As they spoke, they ran their fingers over it in a way that reminded me of a Catholic with a rosary or Muslim with prayer beads. The speeches were long and in the Fijian language. We outsiders grew bored and were hot and aching from sitting on the ground for so long. However, no matter how stiff or restless we became, we kept our heads down; none of us wanted to test the injunction against getting our head above the head of the chief. Even if it no longer called for capital punishment, it would have been an inexcusable cultural gaffe.

After the speeches, the army band played for us as they marched up and down a wide grassy field that served as a parade ground. This was followed by an exhibition of slow, stately dancing by the women of the village, who were dressed in colorful floral-print dresses. To the accompaniment of drums, the dancers acted out village activities, such as the harvesting and threshing of grain. Toward the end of the dancing, some of the guests walked out to the dancers and stuck paper money in various places on them while they were dancing. Most people put the bills into their hair or waistbands, but the major and some of the soldiers got giggles when they tucked their money into the women's low-necked tops. Placing money on dancers was a common method of donating to charitable events in the South Pacific. (It has a different connotation in certain bars in the Western world.)

After the formal program we ate lunch in tents at the bazaar, where crafts and food were sold, and I drank kava with the men in our party at the common people's kava tent before our long ride back down the mountain to Suva. We never saw the Larsons again, but a *Book of Mormon* showed up in our mailbox at the yacht club one day.

Back in Suva, we spent a couple of weeks on boat maintenance and purchased some new electrical equipment. All of our American AC power tools were 110-volt ones, but the power in most of the countries we visited was 240 volts. In order to use our power tools when we were plugged in to shore power, we had to use a heavy-duty transformer.

I bought a set of new 240-volt power tools and replaced my aging, corroded 110-volt Honda portable generator with a new 240-volt model. In addition, we bought a new 2.5-horsepower Mercury outboard motor for our dinghy.

About this time we heard on the radio that Steve and Tina had run *Gwahir* up on the reef at Totoya Island, in the Lau group. They arrived in Suva, after two miserable weeks on the island, with a sad story to tell. Instead of passing below Totoya as we had done, they attempted to cut through the Lau group on a more direct route to Suva. In the process, they had to pass close to the northern shore of Totoya Island in the night. (I had actually slowed *Tainui* down, so that we would round Totoya in the daylight, because of the Lau group's reputation for unpredictable currents.) Steve and Tina had been so busy with steering and navigation that they had worked through the dinner hour. They got a Sat Nav fix at about 8:00 p.m. that indicated that they would pass safely about four miles off of Totoya's northern reef and went below to eat. They were both below when *Gwahir* passed closest to the reef, which turned out to be a tragic mistake. While they were eating, they felt a juddering bump, followed by a scraping sound. With an empty feeling in the pits of their stomachs, they rushed up on deck and discovered, to their horror, that *Gwahir* had sideswiped the reef. Steve grabbed the wheel and tried to turn *Gwahir* back out to sea, but could not turn the bow against the incoming breakers. Soon, a breaking wave picked *Gwahir* up and set her on the reef. At that point, there was no hope of saving *Gwahir*. They watched helplessly as the relentless waves bashed *Gwahir* farther and farther up the reef. The abrasive coral quickly tore through *Gwahir's* hull, and the vessel flooded. Her hull was cold-molded, i.e., made of thin crisscrossed wooden strips saturated in epoxy resin. That system produced the maximum strength per weight of any hull material, but as was the case with wood and fiberglass, it was subject to abrasion by coral. Only a steel hull was hard enough to abrade the coral.

Steve tossed their life-raft canister into the water on the inside of the reef and successfully activated its automatic inflating system. They grabbed their cat and a bag full of their most important possessions, leapt into the waiting raft, and attempted to paddle toward the shore. Progress was difficult because the raft was covered with a domed canopy, and they had to paddle through the small door opening. The raft's round shape made it difficult to steer, and the wind caught the dome and blew the raft sideways. When it looked like they were being blown back out to the reef, Steve, a commercial scuba diver, put on his fins, took a line, dove into the water, and began to tow the raft to shore. He made good progress, but was soon surrounded by sharks. He retreated into the raft, and they both paddled with all their strength until they landed the raft on the beach. They crawled out and lay on the sand until daylight, exhausted, cold, wet, and in a state of shock.

When Steve and Tina took stock of their surroundings in the morning, the sight of the wreck of *Gwahir* on the reef brought back the cold reality of their situation. Looking around, they found that they were on an isolated beach where there were no signs of human activity. There was nothing to indicate the way to a village, so they picked a direction and started walking. I don't know what they talked about on that walk, but it must have been a sad conversation. Their world had been turned upside down. They had lost their boat, which was a part of their financial security, and they might not be able to recover its contents. Their cruising life was surely over. They must have asked themselves over and over again: how could they have been far enough off course to hit the reef? What had they done that had been so terribly wrong? What were they going to do with their lives now that their cruising dream was over? Their future looked bleak. They were a long way from home. They had not gotten any money off of their boat, and they needed a place to stay in Fiji and airfare home. Three miles down the beach they found a path through the tall grass at the back of the beach. It took them up a wooded hill and down into Totoya's main village. A villager took them in while they waited to leave on the weekly mail boat, which was due in five days.

Meanwhile, Steve arranged to have the village men help him salvage what he could from the wreck of *Gwahir*. The men of the village agreed to take him to the wreck in a large canoe, and in return he would give them his tools and outboard motor—items that were too heavy for him to bring home. The seas had calmed down when they anchored the motorized canoe beside the reef, and the wreck of *Gwahir* was out of reach of the waves. From his first trip aboard the wreck, Steve brought out a sail bag filled with their most valued personal possessions and placed it in the canoe. He explained to the men that these were personal items, and that he would then go back and get some of the things he had promised them. However, when he came back with his tools, he was shocked to see that the village men had emptied the sail bag and were just finishing dividing his personal possessions among themselves! In spite of their behavior, he continued the salvage and managed to keep some boat gear and personal possessions that the villagers did not steal.

Steve and Tina wanted to get away from these people as soon as possible, but a storm canceled the next mail-boat run, which meant that they had to stay another week in the village. Their host family gave them a mattress under a mosquito net, but they had no privacy. Villagers watched every move they made. Everywhere they looked, they saw people staring at them, even in the middle of the night. Although their host family was friendly and sympathetic, many of the village men were openly hostile. Once, when Steve saw a man wearing one of his shirts, he went up to him and said, " Hey, that's my shirt you're wearing!" The man snarled back, "Oh, do you want it?" Steve said, "Of course I do!" The man took off the shirt, tore it to shreds, threw it in Steve's face, and shouted, "Here!" This was a frightening situation for Steve and Tina. The village men were large and intimidating, and there was no place for them to turn in the event of trouble.

Tina was heartbroken at the loss of some cherished jewelry that had been in her family for many years. Steve explained its significance to the village chief and pleaded for its return. The chief denied that his men had stolen it, but the jewelry mysteriously appeared at their house the next day. On a lighter note, the village women coveted Steve and Tina's beautiful Persian cat. One of them actually offered to trade her baby for it! Steve feigned indignation and countered, "Why, this cat is worth at least two babies!" Fortunately no one called his bluff!

Finally, the mail boat arrived. They had no money, but a technician from the Fiji Electric Department paid their passage home, and helped them put the gear they had saved onto the ferry. Back in Suva, we cruising sailors helped them sell their salvaged boat gear at the Royal Suva Yacht Club to raise money for their airfare home. I bought *Gwahir's* roller-furling gear. It was a series of four-foot hollow aluminum extrusions that slipped over the forestay and rolled the jib up. Steve told me that the village men had tried to get them from him to cut up for curtain rods.

We discussed the causes of the accident with Steve. He thought there was a combination of factors that added up to a four-mile error: a four-knot current may have set them toward the reef, the reef may have extended farther out from the island than its charted position, the Sat Nav may have given an unreliable fix, and they might have been steering off course due to a mistake in reading the compass (pilot error). We felt that he left out some important factors. In spite of the above possibilities, he had taken the risk of cutting through this channel in the dark, and he had compounded that risk by not keeping a watch on deck when they expected to be closest to the reef. A lookout might have seen the white breaker line or heard the roar of the surf in time to change course. Their accident could also have been prevented if they had had radar. Even though we did have radar, I hadn't thought the risk was worth the few miles the shortcut would have saved. Also, we tried not to rely on our radar to the point of putting us in situations that would have been dangerous if the radar failed.

As time went by, we became frustrated with sitting in the constant rain in Suva while our friends on the western side of the island were reporting on the local radio net that they were having a wonderful time in beautiful sunny weather. On the first clear day, we cast off from our mooring buoy at the Royal Suva Yacht Club and headed out, but within an hour smoke began pouring out of the engine compartment. It smelled like burning oil, and it was. Engine oil was seeping onto the hot exhaust manifold from an unknown leak. Reluctantly, we returned to the yacht club for repairs. Two diesel mechanics from other yachts diagnosed it as a worn-out oil seal on the cam-follower shaft. It took me two days to tear the engine apart and replace the seal, by which time it was raining night and day again. We sat through fifteen more days of rain, agonizing over the good weather we were missing on the other side of the island, but we were reluctant to attempt the trip in bad weather.

On one of those rainy afternoons, I walked into the bar at the Royal Suva Yacht Club and ordered a drink. The bartender smiled, reached up, and yanked three times on a short braided rope that rang a loud brass bell. Suddenly, everyone in the bar looked at me and laughed. I was totally confused. The bartender pointed to my head and explained, "If you come into a yacht club bar with your hat on, you must buy a round of drinks. Obviously you didn't know it, so we might let you off this time." Not wanting to be a bad sport and noticing that there were only six other customers in the bar, I shouted, "No problem, the drinks are on me!" I doffed my hat to the group and they gave me a round of applause. An Aussie customer gave me a thumbs-up and said, "Good on you, mate. Good job it wasn't Saturday night!"

The new headsail I ordered to go with *Gwahir's* roller-furling gear arrived from New Zealand while we were waiting out the rain. The morning I tried to install it, a dinghy came alongside and a pleasant man asked permission to come aboard. He introduced himself as Paul from the steel yacht *Elanoa*, and explained that he was a professional sail maker from San Diego. He said that he had heard over the radio several times how I had helped other people and decided someone should do something for me. I was flattered by his remark and grateful for his assistance. Paul's expertise in setting up the leads that controlled the new sail so that it would perform best in all points of the wind was invaluable.

We became good friends and shared our steel-boat philosophies in conversations aboard each other's yachts. Paul had opted for steel after the tragic loss at sea of his classic wooden yacht, *White Cloud*.

In desperation, we finally left Suva in the rain. We cautiously poked our nose out of the harbor in limited visibility. The shortest route would have been due west between the main island of Viti Levu and Kadavu Island (you guessed it, Kandavu) a few miles offshore. (I wonder if the "n" was missing on the typewriter of the Brit who originally translated these names.) The Kadavu Channel was narrow with rocky outcroppings and a strong current, so we headed south around Bega for the much wider channel between Bega and Vatu Lailai. We made good time under sail in 15-to-20-knot winds, but by the time we turned into the Vatu Lailai Channel, it had become dark and rainy with near zero visibility.

At the narrowest point of the channel, the chart showed a generous 14-mile clearance between the two islands. We relied on our Sat Nav to help us navigate safely through the channel. However, the frequency of Sat Nav fixes varied because satellites passed overhead at irregular intervals. In addition, if they were too high or too low in the sky, or too close together, the fixes were labeled unreliable. On this occasion, when we needed it most, we had to wait an unusually long time for a fix. Our tension mounted as we sailed on in the dark, not knowing exactly where we were. The Sat Nav was located below, on the wall above the chart table. When it finally beeped, Connie rushed below and found that we had a good fix. She plotted it on the chart and rushed on deck, reporting that, according to the Sat Nav, we were just two miles off the island of Viti Lailai, and its reef was charted to be about two miles offshore! If the Sat Nav fix was accurate, a strong current must have been pushing us rapidly toward Vatu Lailai. We both strained our eyes and ears but could not pick up the sight of white water or the sound of waves pounding on the reef. I quickly started the engine, turned away from the island, and motored out toward what I hoped was the middle of the channel. We don't know how close we came to repeating Steve and Tina's disaster, but it was a frightening and humbling experience. My recent criticism of Steve and Tina's seamanship suddenly seemed a little smug.

Our next obstacle was a large rock that was situated near mid-channel at the far end of the Vatu Lailai Channel. We hoped to find the rock with our radar, but, as we approached the end of the channel, our radar screen was so full of echo returns bouncing off of the waves and rainsqualls that I could not identify the rock. I hated to go ahead blind, but had no desire to turn around and go back. Fortunately, a timely Sat Nav fix helped me steer clear of the rock, and we passed safely out of the

Vatu Lailai Channel without seeing the rock or the shore of either island. Outside the channel, we were still in rain, strong winds, big seas, and the dark of night. We both stayed on deck and kept a double lookout for another 10 miles to make sure we were really in the clear. Even then, it was hard to relax, and we only got two hours of fitful sleep apiece that night. In the morning the sun came up with no sign of rain and not a cloud in the sky. We were happy to have escaped the interminable rain of Suva, but were not pleased to have exposed ourselves to so much risk in the Vatu Lailai Channel during the night.

Our destination was the Musket Cove Yacht Club on the island of Malolo Lailai. Malolo Lailai was inside the big reef surrounding the main island of Viti Levu, but Malolo Lailai also had a reef of its own, so we had to negotiate two passes. The first one, Nevula Passage, was the main shipping channel for the western ports of Viti Levu, and large range markers on a hill above the pass guided us safely through. However, the pass through the reef surrounding Malolo Lailai was hard to find. We had to pass at high tide between two low-lying islets that were scarcely visible above whitecaps that were kicked up by a brisk wind. As we approached the pass, we radioed the yacht club and informed them of our intended arrival, and John and Gudrun aboard *Speedwell* kindly motored out and guided us through the tricky channel.

We anchored off the beach among a small fleet of yachts, several of which were well known to us. After guiding us in, John and Gudrun came aboard for a drink and a brief visit. John was an accomplished English yachtsman who was known in Great Britain for having been the skipper of a boat in the prestigious Whitbread Around the World Race. We were pleased to hear their enthusiastic confirmation of the wonderful time cruising sailors were having at Musket Cove. They left in the late afternoon, and we took a nap. We got up long enough to eat some spaghetti, and then crashed for the night.

We awoke to a clear and cool morning with a light trade wind rustling the palm branches. The view from the anchorage was all that we had hoped for—a gleaming white-sand beach shaded by palm trees and backed by lush green hills. We ate breakfast in the cockpit as the sun rose above the mountains of Viti Levu to the east of us, whence we had come. Our coffee pot was busy all morning as friends from our previous ports of call came aboard to welcome us and catch up on each other's news. They advised us to join the Musket Cove Yacht Club as soon as we went ashore.

I left the outboard motor on the stern rail and rowed Connie the short distance to the yacht-club pier. On an arch over the end of the dock the words "Musket Cove Yacht Club" were inscribed under a painting of an old-fashioned musket. The yacht club was part of the Musket Cove Resort owned and operated by Australian entrepreneur Dick Smith, who had a soft spot in his heart for sailors. He made us lifetime members of the yacht club at the price of one US$1 for the captain and five US$5 for the crew, complete with laminated membership cards carrying the musket logo. Many privileges went with the membership, and we took advantage of one of them immediately—showers in the club's clean and comfortable bathrooms. In addition, the swimming pool and the resort's sailboards were free to members and their children, we got a discount on the weekly pig roast buffet, and the restaurant put on a weekly barbecue on the beach for sailors. We brought our own meat to the barbecue, and they supplied lighted charcoal barbecues, salads, and baked potatoes. We sailors also had the use of the yacht club lounge and library. Dick Smith had the names of members' yachts carved on the beams of the resort buildings, and he and his wife invited sailors into their home for cocktails on Tuesday evenings. We spent 19 days of relaxation and fun in the sun at Musket Cove. It was worth the scary exit from rainy Suva—we only wished we had done it sooner!

During our stay at Musket Cove, friends joined us for occasional dinners or movies aboard, and we attended the weekly pig feasts and the beach barbecues for sailors, hung out with friends in the library/lounge reading the scrapbooks filled with entries from previous visitors, and searched the carvings on the beams for familiar yacht names.

One morning we hiked a mile down the beach to the only other resort on the island, the Plantation Hotel. It was bigger than Musket Cove, and its beach was packed with tourists of all ages sunbathing, swimming, snorkeling, and paddling surfboards. We ate delicious hamburgers for lunch that were charcoal-grilled in a thatched-hut kiosk on the beach. We enjoyed a day of absorbing the holiday atmosphere, but were happy to return to the much quieter Musket Cove Resort, where we were among friends and not just another pair of faces in the crowd.

One evening Don, who had sailed alone from his native England, invited us aboard his cruising catamaran *Blue Goose of Arn* for a dinner of pikelets, which turned out to be pancakes. Later, on the grocery-store shelves in New Zealand and Australia, we found boxes of pikelet mix that looked very much like our Betty Crocker mixes. Unfortunately, while we were in Australia, *Blue Goose of Arn* collided with a freighter off the coast of that country and sank, resulting in a harrowing saga for Don, which I will recount in a later chapter.

Shortly after our arrival at Musket Cove, Ed and Marilyn from *Spindrift* and their12-year-old daughter, Lara, led us to their favorite snorkeling spot. Lara was a tall athletic youngster, polite and mature for her age. She was an expert free-diver, spear-fisher, snorkeler, and sailor. We followed them in our dinghy to a spot where the time-bleached white wreck of a large wooden vessel sat on a sandbar near the reef. The coral reef was an ecosystem for a profusion of colorful marine flora and fauna. We snorkeled, swam to the sandbar and examined the wreck, picnicked in our dinghies, and dove in and snorkeled again in the afternoon. We wore T-shirts when snorkeling to avoid burning our backs from the long exposure to the sun as we lay face down on the surface with water gently washing over us.

When the boat supplies I had ordered from the United Sates arrived at Nadi, I went to Malolo Lailai's airport and took the short flight across the water to collect them. The airport was an amusing sight. Its landing strip was a pair of tire tracks in a grass field, and the ticket office was a desk sitting on the bare ground with a thatched roof over it. Aboard the single-engine plane, I enjoyed the view from the air of the beautiful stretch of water between Malolo Lailai and Nadi. In the bright sunlight, the water color was dark purple over coral heads, dark blue over deep water, aqua at lesser depths, and a translucent light green over white-sand shallows. The surface was broken by a scattering of coral reefs with white water breaking on them, and tiny sandy one-or-two-palm-tree islets.

In Nadi, I went first to a travel agency and reserved tickets for our holiday flight home from New Zealand, which was to be our next port of call, and then I went back to the airport and cleared my goods through customs. Generally, goods for yachts in transit were exempt from import taxes. In order to ensure that the goods were not illegally imported, some customs offices kept the merchandise until that yacht was ready to leave or sealed it in a storage locker aboard the yacht until the vessel departed. In Nadi, a polite, professional customs officer released my goods to me duty-free with no such conditions. After clearing customs, I caught a return flight to Musket Cove on the same day.

As the hurricane season approached, we prepared to sail to New Zealand, which was south of the tropical hurricane belt. We began with a short sail to the nearby town of Lautoka on the main island, for provisioning. On this four-hour trip in calm seas and light wind, *Tainui* was beset with mechanical problems. The radar blew a fuse, the pulley that ran the belt to the refrigerator compressor made a disturbing metallic rattle, and when we anchored, I found a crack in our heavy-duty bronze anchor winch. Connie and I were becoming increasingly discouraged by the extent to which boat maintenance was dominating our life.

It took me three days to complete these repairs. The radar problem was easily fixed—it was just a short in the plug to its power supply. But the refrigerator compressor pulley noise was the beginning of a continuing problem that came to a head when we returned to Lautoka from New Zealand eight months later. The pulley was attached to a short projection of the crankshaft. A thin rectangular piece of metal, called a "woodruff key," was fitted into a slot in the shaft and a matching slot in the pulley hub to keep the pulley from slipping on the shaft. That key had broken in two, and the slot in the shaft was slightly damaged. I made a new key and fitted it in the shaft, but the pulley split in two while I was reattaching it. I unbolted the anchor winch from the bow and hauled the hefty winch and the broken pulley to a welder. These things accomplished, we made several provisioning trips in the dinghy in the oppressive, humid heat.

Our final task was to go to Nadi and pay for our airplane tickets to the United States. A friendly Indian gentleman who was going there on business gave us a free ride to Nadi. This dry side of the island was predominantly Indian, because Indians had originally been brought there to work as laborers in its sugar-cane plantations. After we paid the travel agent, we enjoyed an excellent Indian curry meal—our favorite international cuisine. With some creative bargaining, we negotiated a cab ride back to Lautoka for the price of two bus tickets.

We sailed back to Musket Cove, and I prepared for the passage to New Zealand by cleaning the accumulated growth of marine flora and fauna off of *Tainui*'s bottom. In the Marquises, I had done this job by free diving, which was a lot of hard work and took a long time. This time, Bob on *Hunky Dory* loaned me his hooka. The hooka was a gasoline-powered air pump mounted on an inflated inner tube, with a long air hose that allowed me to breathe underwater. When the hooka was in the water, it was important to keep the exhaust away from the intake to the breathing hose. A diver using a hooka in a shipyard at Pago Pago actually died when the exhaust got upwind of the intake and fed him carbon monoxide instead of fresh air. There was a wind vane on the hooka to keep the exhaust downwind, but it was useless on calm days. Taking no chances, I kept the hooka on deck where it wasn't free to turn, and Connie monitored the wind direction. I strapped a pair of scuba-diving weights to my waist to keep me submerged, jumped into the water, and quickly cleaned *Tainui*'s bottom.

CHAPTER NINE

NEW ZEALAND

The 900-mile trip to New Zealand would take us across the dreaded Tasman Sea—dreaded because a constant parade of depressions swept across it, bringing frequent gales and occasional storm-force winds. We left Musket Cove on the afternoon of November 4, 1990, cleared the reef around Malolo Lailai, and headed for the pass in the outer reef. A blinding rainsquall hit us as we approached the pass. Not wanting to challenge the reef with limited visibility, we ducked into little Momi Bay near the entrance to the pass. The bay was well protected, with good holding in mud at a depth of 25 feet. We anchored for the night alongside the boat that took harbor pilots out to ships wanting to enter the pass. After the rainsquall moved on we had a peaceful night in flat, calm water.

We got our weather reports from Harry, an amateur radio operator on *Whale Song*, who did weather reports for cruisers as a hobby. *Whale Song* was in New Zealand at the time, and Harry got his weather information from the high-seas forecasts of the New Zealand Coast Guard and from charts printed by a weather fax machine that was connected to his ham radio. We sat in Momi Bay for three days waiting for better weather while Harry continued to predict a 35-knot blow right off our coast. We were anxious to get started, but hated to leave in bad conditions. On the fourth morning I asked Harry, "When do you expect this wind to die down?" He replied, "Not for a while, Vern. But it doesn't extend very far from Fiji. You might as well get out there now. You may be seasick the first day, but after that you will have smooth sailing." We took Harry's advice and motored through the pass at 9:30 that morning. We were soon to learn that Harry was an optimist.

The throttle cable broke in the middle of the pass. Fortunately the engine kept running. It would have been a dangerous place in which to maneuver without power. The main inconvenience of the break was that in order to shut off the engine I had to go below, pull the companionway stairs away from the engine compartment, and manually close the throttle. Our small diesel yacht engine did not have an electrical ignition system. There were no spark plugs; the pistons fired from the heat of compression. Therefore I couldn't turn off the key to stop the engine. The only way to kill the engine from the cockpit was to shut off its fuel supply, which required a functioning throttle cable.

Outside the pass the wind was blowing 25 knots off the stern quarter, so we made good time with two-thirds of the furling jib rolled out and one reef in the main. The ride was wet and bouncy because the waves had built up over the windy days. At evening time we got Harry's predicted 35-knot wind with gale-force gusts of 45 nautical miles (about 50 statute miles) per hour. I put the second reef in the main and rolled the furling jib down to the size of a storm jib. The roller-furling system was a godsend. I had to go out into the weather to reef the mainsail, but I no longer had to go up into the plunging bow pulpit to pull down one jib and hoist up another—I just sat in the shelter of the cockpit dodger and adjusted the size of our new furling jib by pulling in or letting out on the roller-furling line.

That night I checked in to two ham nets. One was the Keri Keri Net run by hams in New Zealand, who tracked yachts on the way to and from New Zealand and gave daily weather reports for the Tasman Sea. That night John, the Keri Keri Net operator, predicted that we would have two or three more days of gale-force weather before reaching calmer seas. We also checked in to the Pacific Maritime Net, which had tracked us on our big crossing from Mexico to the Marquises. It was the net by which we got in touch with our family through our ham friend Jerry in Salem. The night was noisy and rough as Connie and I took our regular two-hour watches. The off-watch person slept on the settee with the lee cloth rigged to keep from falling off, and the person on watch dozed on cushions on the cabin sole in the 15-minute intervals between lookouts.

The conditions were the same the next day, with on-and-off gale-force winds of 40 to 45 knots. Neither of us could eat. My stomach was close to nausea all day, but I was able to keep it under control as long as I stayed outside. However, when the engine overheated while I was running it to charge the batteries and run the refrigerator compressor, I had to go below and work on the cooling system. That was too much for my stomach. I made a quick trip up to the lee rail before completing the job. I found nothing wrong with the cooling system, so I put it back together, and the engine ran for an hour without overheating. We suffered through another miserable night, taking our normal watches.

There was no improvement in the weather as the sun rose on the third day, but our appetites had recovered enough for us to eat breakfast. We sat in the cockpit and ate our cereal from half-filled bowls and drank our coffee from half-filled mugs, to keep their contents from sloshing out as *Tainui* pitched and rolled and occasionally fell off a wave and landed with a tooth-rattling thud. The sky was black and threatening, and blinding rainsqualls swept the deck. The lead gray waves grew steadily higher until they were 9 to 12 feet high with breaking white crests at their tops. With the wind and waves coming off the stern, we were making good progress, and the self-steering wind vane was working well, so we didn't heave to. It was intimidating to look back and see a wall of dark green water towering over us, but *Tainui*'s stern would lift high and the wave would magically slip beneath us and roll on ahead with a loud "Whoosh!" *Tainui* would roll away from the wave, dive down into the trough, and roll back as she rose up on the next wave. Life in this constant motion was uncomfortable and tiring.

Most of the time we hunkered down out of the weather in the cabin below decks. We went out to the cockpit regularly to look out, and only went beyond the cockpit if there was a need to. When one of the pulleys that controlled the roller-furling line broke loose near the bow and fouled the line, I reluctantly donned my harness, attached its tether to the jack line, and cautiously worked my way forward. In the process of untangling the line, I discovered that the line itself was frayed. It was important that this be repaired, because if the line broke, the entire jib would unroll, leaving *Tainui* so over canvassed in the gale that she could be knocked flat on her side, the sail could be destroyed, or the mast could come down. I tied the furling line securely to the bow pulpit so that the sail could not unwind and worked my way back to the cockpit, where I picked up a new line and then went forward again and rerigged the entire system.

Contrary to the predictions of Harry and of the Keri Keri Net, the weather did not relent on the fourth day—it got worse. The wind started at a steady 30 knots in the morning and increased throughout the day. The waves also increased in size, sometimes reaching a height of 15 feet. Wave heights were determined by three factors: wind velocity, fetch (how far they traveled), and duration. Because of the duration of this storm and the almost unlimited fetch of the southern ocean, the waves were higher than they would have been from 30 knots of wind in more restricted waters. Waves often crashed into the side of the boat and threw up sheets of water, which soaked me when I went on deck. With the wind mostly behind us, we continued to sail under a scrap of jib and a double-reefed mainsail, making between five and six knots. It would have been impossible to sail to windward in these conditions, which concerned us, because we planned to return through these same waters after the hurricane season.

It was extremely noisy in the cabin. Waves hit the side of the boat with a crash that sounded as if we had collided with a truck. We got so we could anticipate these collisions. There would be an ominous silence when we slid into an unusually deep trough, which temporarily blocked the wind. This meant that a monster wave was about to strike. The motion in the cabin was wild. Once in a while *Tainui* balanced on a wave in such a way that the wave slid out from under her and she fell through the air and landed in the trough below with a bone-jarring crash. These falls were unpredictable and shook loose everything that wasn't tied down and some things that were. The cabin was a total shambles. Books, audiotapes, wet clothing, pencils, and other items were strewn everywhere. We spent our time lying down or wedged into a corner to keep from falling or being tossed about. Moving around under these conditions was dangerous. I worried about accidents more than I did about the boat sinking. It was absolutely imperative that we observe the sailors' maxim, "One hand for yourself and one hand for the boat." I repeatedly cautioned Connie not to move about with both hands full; we needed to always have one hand free to hold on with.

Of course it was too dangerous to cook. I had visions of a pot of scalding hot food falling on Connie. Our meals in these conditions consisted mostly of crackers and peanut butter or cheese. Finally, this life was horribly boring. There was very little that we could do to pass the time. It was impossible to read without getting motion sickness, and most other activities were either too dangerous or too hard to accomplish in the unsteady environment. Time passed incredibly slowly; it felt as though the storm had lasted forever, and there was no sign of a letup. Unfortunately, we had plenty of time to worry. I trusted our steel hull, but worried about the stress on the vessel's gear. For example, a shroud could break and the mast would come down. One of our worst fears was that the self-steering mechanism would be destroyed, and we would have to hand-steer day and night in all weather. Fortunately, that unit did not fail and our mast didn't came down.

That afternoon we discovered that the water in our freshwater tank had a slightly salty taste. Based on a similar experience on our big ocean crossing, I assumed that the water system's deck-filler cap was leaking. I remedied the problem by disconnecting the hose that ran from that fitting to the tank, so any seawater that leaked through the cap would run into the bilge instead of the water tank. We were not concerned about a lack of fresh- water, because we had enough drinking water in jerry jugs lashed on deck to reach New Zealand. We would use the slightly salty water in the tank for cooking and washing up.

By evening, the wind was screaming in the rigging at 45 knots and the waves were 16 feet high. Many of them were breaking and sounded like freight trains as white water roared by on both sides of us. It was too dangerous to keep on sailing. We might surf down the face of a wave and broach, that is, slide sidewise, and then be rolled over when we hit bottom. The waves were also too big for heaving to, so we had to lie a-hull. I completely rolled up the jib and then climbed up on the cabin top and pulled down the mainsail and lashed it securely to the boom. The waves were splashing water over the cabin top, so I was thoroughly soaked as I crept below and changed into dry clothes. With no sails up, *Tainui* reacted by lying in the troughs sideways to the oncoming waves— hence the term 'lying a-hull.' *Tainui* rolled a lot more than she had while we were sailing, but with no forward motion it was quieter and less scary. Nevertheless, we were too tense to sleep much that night. It was our worst day at sea so far. With the lack of sleep and substantial meals and the fear that gear on the boat might break or that the conditions might worsen, we were worn out physically and mentally.

On the morning of day five, the wind came down to 25 knots, gusting to 30, so I put up a little bit of sail and got *Tainui* moving again. On the roll call of the Keri Keri Net that morning, we learned that the other yachts bound for New Zealand were experiencing the same severe conditions, and most of them were as frustrated and tired of it as we were. However, there was one exception. The report of our British friend John on *Speedwell* embarrassed us. John had left for New Zealand a day before us. John was an experienced skipper who had captained a yacht in an around-the-world race. He gave his report to the net in his best British style, "I say, we're having bracing weathah out heah! We are taking green watah over the bow with every wave, and all the othahs aboard are sick below [John and his Swedish partner, Gudrun, had picked up two young women backpackers as passengers] but we are having a

161

dashing sail. Yesterday, *Speedwell* made her best daily run evah—220 miles in 24 hours!" He was glorying in the same conditions that we were cowering in and whining about. I envied his experience of racing in all kinds of weather and his knowledge of just how much punishment his boat could take. However, even if I had had the confidence to push *Tainui* to her limits, I would not have done it. Life aboard would have been intolerably uncomfortable, and the bragging rights of a record daily run would not have been worth it to me.

I had a repeat of the engine-overheating problem when I charged the batteries later that day. It heated up; I took the cooling system apart, found nothing wrong, put it back together, and it ran normally for an hour. Intermittent problems like that were especially frustrating. That afternoon, I also got a shock when I checked the bilge. It was full of water—probably about 200 gallons. I rolled up the carpet, removed all the floorboards, and traced the leak to the chain locker in the peak of the bow. The only opening to that locker was the hawse pipe on the deck. Its brass cap had an opening on one side, where the chain passed through it on its way to the anchor. This opening was larger than the chain, and water leaked through it when waves washed over the deck. While the electric bilge pump pumped out the water, I rummaged around in a spare-parts locker, where I found a roll of refrigeration insulation tape that had the consistency of putty. The thick black stuff was so sticky and oily that it appeared to be waterproof. I crawled up to the bow and squeezed it liberally around the chain in the opening where it went through the hawse pipe cap, and that stopped the leak. By the time I finished, the bilge had been pumped dry.

On the morning of the sixth day, the weather was just the same. Connie's log entry was a repeat of every morning's entry so far: "Another terrible night." On this day, humidity in the cabin caused a problem. Condensation on the windows ran down the cabin walls and got into our electronic equipment. The radar blew a fuse, the Sat Nav worked only part of the time, and the ham radio transmitter wouldn't tune up. At first the radio would receive but not transmit; later in the day it also stopped receiving. Loss of the radio created two serious problems. We had lost our ability to call for help in an emergency—rough weather was not a good time to lose contact with the outside world. And, the ham nets would report us missing if we stopped checking in, which would trigger an expensive search-and-rescue operation and cause our family needless worry. I wiped the radio as dry as I could, wrapped it in plastic, and left it and the Sat Nav on all night to dry them out. (Normally I turned these devices off at night to conserve our batteries.) To our great relief, they both worked in the morning.

This was also a day to fight depression. Connie announced, "I have had it! When we get to New Zealand I will never get on this boat again! I want to sell it and fly home." She had been discouraged before, but never to that extent. I gave her my usual answer, "Okay, but let's talk about it when we get to New Zealand." With any luck I could bring it up again when we were having a drink in the cockpit and watching the sunset in a beautiful anchorage after a day of fun in the sun with good friends.

Unfortunately, the weather did not help my cause. We had one of our worst nights. The wind built back up and screeched through the rigging at 40 knots. *Tainui* sped along at six knots, even though I had up only a tiny scrap of jib and a double reefed main. The extra speed made the motion even noisier and more violent. The conditions did not seem quite as bad to me as they did the time we lay a-hull, so we kept sailing. Our wonderful wind-powered autopilot performed so well that we never broached. Sometimes we began to skid sideways down a wave, but the autopilot straightened us out so quickly that we never got into trouble. Words cannot fully express my admiration for this self-steering system that kept *Tainui* under control in these conditions.

It was no surprise that Connie's log on the morning of day seven read, "Another terrible night. I was really scared last night. Six days straight. When will it end?" By this time, my mind was numb. A kind of lethargy came over me as I sat below listening to the howling wind, the crashing waves, and the creaks and groans of the boat. I had a hard time making decisions and a harder time bestirring myself to act upon them. I would sit below and wonder for hours if I should further reduce sail or take it all down and just lie a-hull, without taking any action. Other sailors have reported this same mind-numbing malaise after days of heavy weather.

On the brighter side, Connie's next log entry acknowledged, "We have only 385 miles to go. At least we are making a fast trip!" We also had a bit of sun that day and got our hopes up because the wind dropped to 20 knots. We hoped this would be the end of the stormy weather. Once again, I found water in the bilge, but not very much this time. I roused myself and found it dribbling in from the freshwater filler cap on deck. It was full of pinholes from corrosion. I had already disconnected it from the hose to the water tank, so it was leaking directly into the bilge. In our spare-parts locker, I miraculously found an identical cap from some other fitting. (In my mind, this justified the fact that I seldom threw away anything that might prove useful someday.) The cap was a flat disk that was flush with the deck when it was screwed in. I screwed the substitute cap into the deck plate and it made a perfect seal.

As the day went on, the wind backed until it came from straight behind us and blew directly into the canvas dodger that sheltered the companionway. The wind tore some of the canvas away and finally collapsed the frame. I stitched the canvas back onto the frame with heavy sail twine and tied the framework back in place with rope. The wind was taking a toll on our equipment, and we worried about how *Tainui* would hold up if it kept on much longer or, worse luck, blew even harder.

One of Connie's log entries describes eating aboard in a gale: "Eating is a problem. Breakfast usually consists of a bowl of cold cereal in half-filled bowls. But, occasionally I manage to cook some oatmeal by holding the pot over the propane burner with one hand and holding on to the boat with my other hand. I call lunch a picnic. We sit on the settee and eat cold cuts, cheese and peanut butter on crackers and rice cakes and drink a diet Coke from a can. We place the food on the seat between us. Dinner is very hard to fix. One day I managed to open a canned chicken and make a stew with cabbage, onions, and carrots, again holding onto the pot with one hand and the boat with the other. I had to sit on the settee to cut up the vegetables. I can't stand up at the galley counter because it is too rough. The stew was quite good and lasted for two days. Some days I can't cook at all. On really bad days Vern is afraid to have me use the stove for fear that I might burn myself."

On the eighth day, the wind dropped down to 15 knots, and the sun shone all day. We actually enjoyed sitting out in the cockpit. It was so calm that we took sun showers on deck—a refreshing relief after seven days and nights in a hot humid enclosure with only an occasional sponge bath with a damp cloth.

In the evening, however, our hopes that the storms were over were dashed. Once again the wind built up to 40 knots. In the middle of the night, we ran into a stretch of water with the biggest waves we had ever seen—steady 16-foot crests with an occasional 20-footer. When Connie got up at 2:00 a.m. to take her watch, she climbed up into the cockpit, took a look back at a towering wall of water, and came below with a frightened and apologetic look on her face. She said, "I'm sorry, Vern. I can't do it this time. It's just too scary out there. The waves coming up behind us are as tall as the mast." I knew how hard it was for her to say this. It was the only time she had failed to take her watch. I not only didn't mind taking her watch for her, I felt I owed it to her. She had taken several extra watches for me when I was seasick or on the verge of becoming sick. I told her to go back to bed and climbed out and took a look around. The waves were not as high as our 50-foot mast, but in the middle of the night, when we were in the bottom of a trough with a 20-foot wave rising up behind us, it seemed like it. The waves were spaced wide apart and were not as steep as some of the earlier ones. *Tainui* was riding over them without any signs of broaching, so I let her sail on. I have to admit, however, that the waves were scary to me too. My strategy was simply not to look back. Connie came on deck at 6:00 in the morning and told me that she had been able to get a little sleep, but that she had been frequently awakened by "that terrible freight train noise when a huge wave roared past."

We have been frequently asked, "Were you ever scared?" This, the scariest part of our trip, is a good place to talk about fear. It is impossible not to be aware that there is some danger when you are in the ocean in a small boat. I believe there are degrees of reactions to danger ranging from worry to fear to terror. Worrying about what could happen was limited only by our imagination. We dealt with it by dissecting accounts of sailing disasters to see what could have prevented them, researching other people's solutions to emergencies, and rehearsing what we would do "if." For example, what would Connie do if I became incapacitated? Our solution was for Connie to become completely competent to carry on by herself. In addition to learning to sail the boat during her years of recreational sailing, she had learned to operate the ham radio, the radar, the Sat Nav, and to read navigational charts. I experienced anxiety, approaching fear, when something important malfunctioned at sea. For example, initially I got an empty feeling in the pit of my stomach every time the engine unexpectedly lost revolutions or died. After a while I got so used to it that I took it in stride. I was actually frightened a few times when we lost our bearings in the dark near a reef and emotionally held my breath until we were out of danger. Connie was scared when I fell overboard off of Coos Bay, Oregon, on a rough day. I was in the water only a minute or two and was so busy getting back aboard that I was only scared in retrospect by what might have happened.

So how scared were we on that night with the 20-foot waves? Sitting below listening to the shrieking of the wind in the rigging, the crashing of the waves on the hull, and the creaking and groaning of the vessel, worrying about things that could happen became fear that they might really happen. However, I never experienced terror, where I feared that *Tainui* might sink. I feared that we might be dismasted in a storm by being knocked down or rolled over. We would then lose our radio antenna. But this fear was tempered by the knowledge that we would still survive. If we lost our mast, we could motor to port. If our motor failed, we could drift until somebody found us. The ham net would report us missing at our last reported position, and we would activate our EPIRB (Emergency Position Indicating Radio Beacon) to help guide a rescue airplane to us. Finally, if *Tainui* sank, we would get into our self-inflating six-person life raft with our EPIRB, our hand-held radio, and our survival supplies.

The question remains, "Why take the chance?" My answer is that life is a series of risk/benefit decisions. For example, when we fly on a commercial airliner, we are calculating the benefits of access to so much of the world, being able to get to a loved one's funeral, etc., against the slight risk of flying. To us, the benefit of realizing a lifelong dream was worth the remaining risk after we had done everything we could to reduce it: buying a steel boat, installing all kinds of emergency and safety equipment, studying dozens of books, and acquiring years of experience before setting out. For us, as for many others, a life devoid of adventure would be a life not worth living, and there is no adventure without risks. The safety of the adventure depends on how carefully the risks are calculated and prepared for.

On day nine, conditions actually improved. The wind dropped to 25 knots at dawn. The morning light also revealed a three-foot tear in the mainsail. To prevent further damage, I took it down and put up our tiny storm trysail. This was its first time out of the bag. It was designed for weather even more severe than what we had been experiencing. *Tainui* performed fairly well under the trysail and a medium-sized jib. By 11:00 in the morning, the wind calmed down even more. We kept our fingers crossed that the gales were finally over. That night was our first calm night—9 days out on an 11-day trip.

Day 10, the last full day of the passage, was a beautiful sailing day. The wind eased and backed so that we had a blissfully quiet, smooth, dry, downwind sail. Our ham radio operated intermittently, but we managed to get a phone patch through to Seattle and wish our son Tom a happy birthday. We took advantage of the improved conditions by sorting things out and putting the boat back in shape in preparation for our arrival. Connie worked on the mess below, and I worked on a leak in our forward hatch. This hatch was on the foredeck right above our double berth and had soaked it. We hadn't faced the problem on this passage because the bow was so active and noisy that we never slept there at sea. It was also impossible to work on it in rough weather with water splashing over it. On that calm, sunny day, I removed the old rubber seal, sanded the hatch surfaces, and installed new rubber.

When I dogged the cover down tightly, it looked better, but in heavy rain or extreme sea conditions it still leaked a little. That hatch turned out to be a continuing struggle—I was never able to make it completely watertight. Our last night at sea on this passage was even more peaceful than the previous one.

On the morning of day 11, I predicted that we could reach port before dark if we had really good sailing. One of our battery banks was low when I checked them that morning. The cause was that the solenoid relay that engaged the refrigerator compressor had accidentally been left on all night. Fortunately our two 200-amp-hour battery banks were isolated from each other, so we still had one fully charged bank. I started the engine to charge up the weak battery bank, and it ran for only a few minutes and shut down. This time it had not overheated. The small diesel engine had no electrical ignition, so an interruption in the fuel supply was the most likely cause of the problem. I traced the fuel lines from the injector pumps on the engine through the fuel pump and the fuel filters to the fuel tank in the bilge. In the tank I found that a blob of soft plastic material had been sucked into the fuel intake line. It had probably been stirred up by the rocking of the boat in the rough weather. While I had the system apart, I changed the fuel filters.

On the final day of the passage, the sky was clear and the sea was bright blue. A group of dolphins leaped along in the distance. It was hard to believe that this was the same ocean that had battered us for eight consecutive days. We opened all the hatches to air out the cabin and hauled the soaked bed linens on deck for drying. The winds became so light and fluky by noon that we motored the remaining 52 miles in order to arrive before dark. It would be a good test of the engine, and we still needed to charge up our low battery bank. If the engine failed again, we would spend another night out and sail in the next day.

Happily, the little diesel engine purred flawlessly all the way. Soon we saw the faint blue-green image of the North Island rising above the hazy horizon. Then we putt-putted past the high, pointed 10 Mile Rock, which marked the entrance to the Bay of Islands. We felt a little silly coming in on a flat and windless sea flying a storm trysail designed for near-hurricane weather. Actually, it was amazing to me that, after all the battering she took, the only damage *Tainui* had sustained was a crumpled canvas dodger and a three-foot tear in the mainsail. Daylight began to fade, but the whole Bay of Islands had easy anchoring depth. If it got too dark to continue, we would just drop our anchor wherever we were, spend a peaceful night, and go to the dock in the morning. Thanks to daylight saving time and New Zealand's long summer days (their November was equivalent to our May), we just made it. We were showing our running lights and the lights of the town were visible as we approached the long customs pier at Opua, Bay of Islands, North Island, New Zealand.

The pier was fully occupied, but George and Janet invited us to tie up alongside their vessel, *Apogee*. We had been on the radio with them almost daily, so they were well aware of the trials and tribulations of our passage; in fact, they had experienced the same conditions, having arrived one day ahead of us. After they took our lines, George and Janet handed two gin and tonics over to us, and a group of their New Zealand friends passed warm welcomes between our vessels. We couldn't actually get together, because we were not allowed to leave our boat or have any one else aboard until we were officially cleared in. But the trip from hell was over. What a relief!

At 11:00 that night, the New Zealand Health and Agriculture officers came down to the pier to clear us in. As we had anticipated, they filled a large black plastic bag with our remaining eggs, cheese, and fresh produce. They didn't seem the least put out by being called to work so late; in fact they extended us a warm, friendly welcome to their country. New Zealand officials were the most understanding and flexible officials we had met. That night we slept on the settee and cabin sole once again, because the mattress in the double berth in the bow was still soaked. These were not the most comfortable beds, but we slept long and hard, our first peaceful, uninterrupted night's sleep in 11 days.

We awoke to a bright sunny day and took in our surroundings as we ate breakfast in the cockpit. We had arrived in a beautiful place. The Bay of Islands was an inland sea dotted with islands, as the name implies, for as far as we could see. Opua was situated on a picturesque crescent beach. The town's long pier, where we were rafted to *Apogee*, was full to capacity with yachts, and many more were anchored or tied to mooring buoys in the harbor. A steep hill rose up behind the village dotted with summer homes peeking out of lush green foliage. As we sat in the cockpit and gazed at this tranquil scene, a sense of relief sank in—the trip was really over and we were safe and sound in New Zealand, where we would be settled in for the next six months.

We were free to leave the boat but, in addition to the previous night's Health and Agriculture clearance, we had more checking in to do. We scrambled across *Apogee* to the pier and tried our legs on solid ground. Customs, immigration, and the harbor board were all within easy walking distance of the pier. Everyone ashore was friendly, and life in the village of Opua appeared to move at a relaxed pace. After finishing our official formalities, we did a load of washing at some public laundry tubs at the back of the pier.

At noon, we bought fish burgers at The Great New Zealand Take-away and ate them on a bench by the ferry dock, which was next to the town pier. Seagulls landed near our feet and begged for our fries. These were the first seagulls we had seen since we left the Northern Hemisphere. After lunch Connie went to the public phone at the ferry dock and placed a call to let our family know that we had arrived safely. I soon realized that she was having an extended conversation with the operator. When she told the operator that she was calling home to report that we had arrived safely by sailboat, the operator became fascinated with our adventure and discussed it with Connie for five minutes before she put through the call. When Connie hung up, she said, "Wow! Life really does move at a slower pace here. Imagine such a conversation with a telephone operator at home!" Just then, three young women came by carrying on a rapid-fire conversation with strong New Zealand accents. After they had passed, we looked at each other and shook our heads—we hadn't understood a word they said.

That night, we joined a group of sailors at the Opua Cruising Club for dinner and drinks. We paid our dues, joined the club, and signed up for the community turkey feast on the upcoming American Thanksgiving Day. At the club, we encountered Harry, the amateur weather forecaster from *Whale Song*. I had been waiting for this opportunity. "Harry," I asked, "What happened? When we were holed up in Fiji waiting for better weather, you said, 'Go ahead and leave, Vern. You may be seasick for one day, but then you will have good weather for the rest of the trip.' We took your advice and were blasted with gales for the next eight days!" Harry looked surprised, shook his head, and said, "Oh, it must have been a local condition." I replied, "I've got news for you, Harry. We can only sail in the local condition!" This confirmed my skepticism about weather fax charts. They cover a large section of the ocean on a letter-sized piece of paper. They would show a major disturbance, such as a hurricane, but they were useless in predicting local conditions.

That night we moved *Tainui* off the government pier and anchored among a fleet of about 50 yachts a half mile from town. I wrapped our still soggy mattress in plastic so we could sleep in our double berth. It was a real luxury! When the wind came up in the night and blew at 35 knots, we were glad we were safely anchored in a sheltered bay. In the limited fetch of the bay, the wind only kicked up two-foot waves. I got up twice to make sure that the anchor was holding—a minor inconvenience compared to nights of riding out gales at sea.

In the morning, after coaxing our outboard motor to start, I helped Connie haul another load of laundry ashore. It was a rainy day, but Connie managed to dry the load on board between showers. While she was handling the laundry, I took inventory of the maintenance chores that inevitably followed an ocean passage: the throttle cable on *Tainui's* diesel engine needed to be replaced, the generator was putting out only half of its rated amps, the TV had succumbed to the humidity, and I needed to buy a new power grinder for working on rust spots.

The next several days I set about completing my maintenance tasks. The only place in Opua to shop for boat supplies was a small yacht chandlery at the nearby boatyard. The chandlery had such a limited inventory that they had to order most things from Australia or the United States. Limited inventory was a problem in New Zealand marine stores. The entire country had a population of only two million, and a quarter of them were islanders on the dole. It was not economically feasible for most of their shops to carry the large inventories that we were used to in the big marine stores in the United States.

Shortly after our arrival, George and Dorothy, commodores of the Opua Cruising Club, invited us to tea at their home along with other new arrivals. They were widely acclaimed in the cruising community for their hospitality and helpfulness to visiting yachts. The welcome mat was always out at their spacious home on the hill overlooking the bay. They also operated a local radio net every morning at 8:00 to assist yachts in the harbor. It was a pleasure and an honor to be entertained in their home.

Opua had very few shops, so we did most of our shopping in the town of Pahia, eight miles from Opua. Pahia was a pretty little town, across a narrow neck of land, on the west coast of the North Island. We enjoyed shopping in Pahia. Instead of supermarkets, Pahia had individual meat markets, greengrocers, bakeries, dairies, etc. In these shops, the owners or their families, rather than hired clerks, waited on us. There were also cozy teashops with tempting pastries. Our favorite lunch spot was the Fifth Avenue Café, which had New York theater décor, American jazz on the stereo, and posters of American movie stars and musicians on the walls. We ate there so many times on our shopping trips that we became well acquainted with the proprietor, who was a devotee of American jazz. We usually hitched rides back and forth with friends, but one time, for exercise, we walked all the way back through a beautiful hardwood forest on a well-maintained trail that occasionally crossed wetlands on boardwalks.

With our most important boat maintenance projects completed and the less urgent ones deferrable, we took a little time to enjoy the Bay of Islands before our trip home for the holidays. One evening, we sailed the short distance from Opua to the quaint little town of Russell. We arrived after dark and tied up to the dock at the Russell Boat Club. In the morning, Julie, from the yacht *Interlude*, walked down the dock, introduced herself, and invited us to breakfast with her and George on their vessel. After breakfast we walked the short distance from the Russell Boat Club to downtown Russell and spent a leisurely sunny summer day browsing in quaint British-style shops and snacking in bakeries. At the end of the day we treated ourselves to dinner at the classic Tudor-style Gables Restaurant, where the food was expensive but worth the price.

While we were in town, we met Pat Henry, the woman solo sailor who was working her way around the world on a shoestring by trying to sell her paintings. We had crossed wakes with Pat several times from the Marquises to New Zealand. She told us that she had reached a point of desperation in New Zealand. She had gotten down to her last $3 and had no idea how she would be able to go on. Just then the owner of a gallery where she had placed some of her paintings asked her to manage his gallery while he was away on an extended vacation. She sold her own paintings at the gallery and got commissions on the other paintings that she sold. While we were chatting, Pat gave Connie some interesting newcomer advice. She told Connie, "Don't refer to that little pouch strapped around your waist as a *fanny pack*." Struggling to explain what "fanny" meant in New Zealand, she pointed to Connie and said, "You have one," and then pointed to me and said, "You don't." We got the message.

When we got back from Russell, I learned that George and Dorothy needed help with their morning radio net while they were on vacation, so I ran the net for them until we left for the United States. Other sailors volunteered for the remainder of their vacation.

In preparation for our visit home for Christmas, we moved *Tainui* to a commercial mooring buoy so we wouldn't worry about her anchor dragging. Our neighbors in the moorage offered to watch her while we were away. On December 3, 1990, we hitched a ride to Pahia and took a bus to Auckland, 120 miles to the south. The bus was a new Volvo with plush seats and relaxing music. As we rode along, we got a look at a cross-section of New Zealand's North Island. It was heavily forested and sparsely populated, with mostly small towns and villages. We were surprised that none of the houses had shake or composition roofs; their roofs were all tile or metal. The climate and countryside were similar to the coastal area between Los Angeles and San Francisco, minus the heavy population and smog. We spent a night in a backpackers' hotel in the city and flew home on December 4.

During our two-month home visit, we stayed for two weeks at a time with the families of each of our three children and two weeks visiting friends. It was especially important to us that we stay in touch with our grandchildren as they grew up. We would never have gone away for seven years if it had not been possible to make these annual trips home. Fortunately, having sold our house, cars, etc., we were left with no monthly bills and were able to save enough money to make these annual trips, in spite of having taken early retirements.

We arrived back in Auckland on February 8, and checked in again to the backpackers' hotel. It was on Queen Street in a colorful, hippie-like area of Auckland. We crashed for 12 hours to recover from the 14-hour flight and the five-hour time change. When we finally dragged ourselves out of bed, we were delighted to find that all of the things we had ordered while in the United States were waiting for us at the hotel desk.

Tainui was in better shape when we returned this time than she had been when we left her in Pago Pago during the hurricane season. There was no mold, and there were no cockroaches. However, neither of our two outboard motors would start, the head wouldn't flush, and the engine cooling system was clogged. These problems were easily dispatched. I quickly flushed out the cooling system and cleared the salt crystals out of the valve in the head. The outboard motors both started after I took their carburetors apart and cleaned them with solvent. This kind of maintenance had become routine through lots of practice.

In search of better produce, we got a ride to Keri Keri with Bob, from *Renaissance,* who had bought a car. Keri Keri had the biggest fruit and vegetable market in the area. Bob still referred to me as "Mr. Smith" from my career-day appearance at his high school during our Pago Pago days. Keri Keri was a tiny town that was noted for a historic stone building standing on the shore of its inlet. The old inn had become a general store in recent years. Its picture was popular on postcards in New Zealand souvenir shops.

No one could fix our portable Honda gas generator in Opua or Paihia, so we rode along with a group of sailors in *Renaissance* Bob's car to Whangarei (some New Zealanders pronounced it Fongarei, but no one could explain why). Whangarei was 50 miles to the south and had a large boatyard and many specialty marine repair shops. We stopped at the boatyard and found two of the yachts that had spent the hurricane season with us in Pago Pago up on the hard having osmosis blisters in their fiberglass hulls repaired. Almost all fiberglass yachts in the tropics eventually had to deal with this problem. The outer gel coat was not completely impermeable, so seawater eventually got through the gel coat, and by osmosis it soaked the inner layers of fiberglass. Gases released in this process raised blisters on the outer skin and created pits in the fiberglass under the blisters. Grinding out these blisters often left deep holes. Our steel hull could not get blisters, but we were not smug about it, because we ground out our share of rust. Every hull material had it plusses and minuses. If there were one perfect material, there would have been only one kind of boat hull. We had lunch at a pizza parlor with our friends, left our generator off at a marine electrical shop, and rode back to Opua with Bob.

Another Bob, also an American, had sailed to New Zealand on his vessel *Sunrise Sunset*. He had traded his house in Florida for a house on the hill above Opua overlooking the Bay of Islands. When he moved into his new house, he threw a big house-warming party for us sailing people and several of his New Zealand friends. He provided food and drinks and hired a professional jazz pianist. He wanted to immigrate to New Zealand, but New Zealand immigration rejected him. They required him to bring in NZ$200,000 of new business in order to qualify for immigration. He was retired and didn't want to go back to work, so he countered with an offer to invest in the country by purchasing NZ$200,000 worth of New Zealand bonds, but the New Zealand government turned this offer down. He was only able to get a six-month tourist visa like the rest of us. As a result, he sailed *Sunrise Sunset* back and forth between Fiji and Opua every six months.

This was the way the New Zealand immigration was treating all retired applicants, no matter how well off the retired people were. Most of us thought that this policy was short-sighted. Retired people did not take jobs away from New Zealanders, and they did not drain money out of New Zealand. On the contrary, they put foreign money into the New Zealand economy. The New Zealand government eventually woke up to the obvious. We heard two years later that they had changed this policy and made it easier for retired people who met a basic means test and purchased health insurance to retire there. Duh!

By the time we reached New Zealand, *Tainui* needed some work that required the services of a boatyard. There were only two boatyards in Opua: a large government operation and a small private yard run by Brian Elliot. We chose Elliot's because of his reputation for being honest, hardworking, and competent. His yard was a mile down the beach from town. Most of our work could be done at the dock, but we would need to haul out and renew our antifouling paint before going back to sea. Our biggest job was to remove *Tainui's* teak decks. I had worried about the decks since our problem with steel rusting under our wood trim in Raiatea. Black liquid was oozing out between the teak boards when we walked across the bow, where seawater most often washed across the deck. We loved the salty look of the teak decks and hated to remove them. The salesman who sold *Tainui* to us said that the teak was glued down on a bed of epoxy so thick that wood would never touch the steel and that no screws were used, so there were no holes in the steel. Neither of these things was true. The epoxy bedding had completely broken down, and there were hundreds of brass screws through the steel. Both of these things were bad. Wood creates an acid environment, which accelerates rust, and the combination of brass and steel, being dissimilar metals in a saltwater environment, causes electrolysis. Being inferior to brass on the galvanic scale, steel was the metal that would be sacrificed by electrolysis. This situation needed to be corrected before any further damage was done.

Tainui's deck was covered with two-inch-wide teak planks that were held down by dozens of brass screws, with teak plugs hiding the screw heads. Taking the screws out one at a time would have been tedious and time-consuming. To speed up the job, I bought an electric skill saw and set the blade to cut into the teak to one-sixteenth of an inch from the steel hull. I made long parallel cuts in the teak about three inches apart. I tried to miss the brass screws, but once in a while the saw blade screeched through one of the soft metal fasteners. I then ripped up the strips of teak with a crowbar. Gordon from *Nepenthe* saw me tearing up the teak and offered to help me strip the deck if he could have some of the larger pieces of teak. I offered him all the teak he wanted without working for it, but he got his crowbar and worked alongside me until all the teak was off. Gordon was a retired Welsh doctor who had practiced in the United States. When his wife died, he bought a Norsea 27 and set out to sail around the world alone in that small but seaworthy 27-foot boat.

The next task at the boatyard was to sandblast and paint the deck and house. Connie and I unscrewed all of the hardware fittings, masked the wood trim and teak steering pedestal, and fitted plywood covers over the portholes. Brian then sandblasted the deck, cockpit, and house and sprayed on seven coats of two-part epoxy paint. The glossy white finish made *Tainui* look like a new boat.

There were no public accommodations in Opua, and we had no car, so we slept aboard during this process. Eating was not a problem, because there were a few restaurants in Opua, but sleeping aboard during sandblasting and painting was no fun. Each day we rolled up our bedding and wrapped it with a tarp. At night when we tore the masking tape from the forward hatch and crawled in, a fine white talcum powder-like dust coated everything. It even got into our wrapped-up bed linens. Sleeping in the dark, hot, stuffy, cabin on gritty sheets was barely tolerable. We vowed never to stay on the boat in a boatyard again, even if we had to rent a car to get to other accommodations.

Before we could go to sea again, we needed several other repairs: the hydraulic steering system needed new seals, the radar needed a new part, the damaged dodger needed repairing, the mainsail cover needed stitching, and brackets needed to be welded to the lifeline stanchions to hold the pulleys for the roller-furling line—they had been temporarily installed with hose clamps. Our main problem was transportation for taking equipment to repair shops and searching for parts. We bought a 1966 Ford Cortina station wagon that had been passed from cruiser to cruiser. The body was rusty, but the motor sounded good. We shared the car with Gordon, who split the US$300 price with us.

We took a break from boat work and used our vehicle to spend a night in Whangarei at the home of Keith and Graham Wright, an older New Zealand couple we had met when they visited Elliot's boatyard. The Wrights had a lovely big house. They were Scottish dancing enthusiasts, and their home had a room with a special suspended hardwood dance floor. To our surprise, they were close friends of Bill and Kathy from *Affaire d'Amour*, who were also Scottish dancing enthusiasts. Keith was the owner of a fleet of gravel barges. In the morning they took us on a sightseeing ride in their new Mercedes. They stopped at their private pier and showed us their immaculate US$250,000 45-foot steel yacht. *Tainui* must have looked like a toy to them. Next they stopped by the airport and showed us their twin-engine airplane. Finally, they drove us to the Kauri Museum 40 miles away on the west coast of the North Island. Kauri wood was an especially durable hardwood that was prized by boat builders, but it had become so scarce that it was protected. Later the Wrights' airplane and yacht would play significant roles in the rescue of *Affaire d'Amour*.

After removing the teak from the deck and painting it with glossy, but slippery, epoxy paint, we needed a new nonskid surface on our decks. We used Aquatread, made of a composition of cork and rubber. It came in 4-X-8-foot sheets with a pattern of small raised diamond shapes for tread. I cut out pieces shaped to fit *Tainui*'s curves and glued them on to the deck and housetop with epoxy glue, leaving about three inches between the pieces. Brian provided me with a heavy roller to squeeze out the voids and excess glue. In the end *Tainui* had attractive and durable nonskid decks.

After completing the work on the deck, we took time out to see the country. Gordon joined us on a three-week tour of the North and South Islands in our jointly owned, ancient little Ford Cortina station wagon. Its last owners had just taken it on a 2,000-mile tour of the South Island, and our friends in Opua were skeptical about its ability to make another such trip. Undaunted, we loaded it up and set off on a 4,000-mile sightseeing trip.

The country was absolutely delightful. New Zealand had high scenery density, meaning that it was not far between its many scenic wonders. One of the highlights of the trip was the discovery of a small Maori village named Tainui on the southwest coast of the North Island. It was populated by the Tainui tribe, which was named after the boat their ancestors arrived on. We asked them about the meaning of the word "Tainui," but they were not sure what it meant. Their guesses were that it was "just a name" or it meant "big water" or "little cry." The people in the general store were impressed when we told them that we had arrived in New Zealand in a sailboat named *Tainui*, just as their ancestors had. They directed us to a cemetery on a hill overlooking the sea, where we found a sacred site dedicated to the memory of the original *Tainui*. Inside a small plot enclosed by a five-foot-high wrought-iron fence, the anchor stone from that ancient double-hulled canoe was set in concrete in a small open-boat-shaped concrete container. It was a large black stone with a waist worn around its middle for holding the anchor rope, giving it a kind of fat figure-eight look about the size of two basketballs fused together. Two bronze plaques on the gate described the *Tainui* and recounted some of its history. I photographed them and later framed them and mounted them on a bulkhead in our *Tainui*.

On our motor tour we stayed mostly in New Zealand's motor camps, which had a range of accommodations. They had tent sites, where the toilets and bathing facilities were in an ablution block; dormitories, where the facilities were down the hall; and tourist flats with kitchenettes and bathrooms. We stayed in the tourist flats. I was startled at one of these motor camps when I heard someone shout, "Hey, Mr. Smith …. Vern Smith!" Bob from *Renaissance* and his girlfriend Thalia were putting up their pup tents in the camping area.

When we were driving, Gordon, the retired physician and widower from Wales, sat in the backseat and honored a family tradition in his late wife's stead by knitting a christening blanket for a grandchild that was due to be born within the month. He was a neophyte at knitting, and we were amused by the groans coming from the backseat when he counted a row of stitches, got the wrong number, and had to pull them all out. To his credit, Gordon persevered and finished the blanket in time for the christening.

Contrary to the local skeptics, our little car made the 4,000-mile trip with only minor repairs. When we returned, Bob, the man with the big house on the hill, was having car trouble and offered to buy our little Cortina for a second car. However, in New Zealand, when the title to a car changed hands, the car had to pass a test to obtain a Warrant of Fitness. When we took our car in to have it "woofed," the inspector poked a screwdriver through its rusty frame and declared it unfit to sell. Legally, we should have driven it to the junkyard, but we gave it to Bob to use and dispose of as he wished. Gordon and Connie and I had no regrets. We had gotten more than our US$300 worth.

The final step at the boatyard was to haul *Tainui* out and renew her bottom paint. Brian hauled *Tainui* out on his ingenious marine railway system. He lowered a little flat car into the water on submerged rails, and we maneuvered *Tainui* over the car and tied her to four poles sticking up from the corners of the car. A steel cable ran from the car to the drum of a diesel-powered winch up on the hill. Connie and I stood on deck and held on to the shrouds as Brian fired up the winch and pulled *Tainui* up to a turntable on a flat space partway up the hill. We climbed down and helped Brian push the turntable around until its tracks lined up with one of four siding tracks that led to separate workstations. Brian removed the cable, threaded it through a new set of pulleys, and pulled us to our destination, where the railroad car was now *Tainui*'s work cradle. Each workstation had its own flat car. Brian's fifth rail car ran up the track past the turntable into a side-hill A-frame building, where Brian could work inside on powerboats or sailboats with their masts down.

I blasted the marine growth and slime off the bottom of *Tainui*'s hull with a power washer. Then I sanded some rusty spots and touched them up with coal-tar epoxy. When that paint was dry, Brian sprayed on two coats of antifouling bottom paint and lowered *Tainui* back into the water, ready to sail the oceans of the world again.

About that time, we discovered that our visas would expire before our planned departure date. We contacted the New Zealand immigration officer, who came up to Opua from Wellington only once a week, and asked him if we should send our visas in to be renewed. He said, "If you send them to Wellington for renewal, it will take so long that your departure will be delayed. Go ahead and overstay your visa. I am immigration here, and it's all right with me."

We waited for the yachts in the annual Opua-to-Fiji race to leave the bay before leaving New Zealand. There were about 30 boats in the race. A few years later, the boats in this race were caught in a killer storm. Several boats were lost, there were dramatic rescues at sea, and some sailors perished. The leading boats got through safely, but the trailing boats were hit hard. We would have been in the worst part of the storm if we had left New Zealand after the yacht race that year!

Once the boats in the race were gone, we contacted the immigration officer again and told him that we were ready to check out, but that the racers were reporting bad weather. We asked him if we had to wait to check out until he came back in a week. He said, "No problem. I'll check you out now, and you just go out into the Bay of Islands and hang out until you like the weather. I wouldn't want you to leave in a storm." What a nice guy! Most other countries' officials were strict about yachts leaving immediately after they checked out. One sailor told us that, in a Mediterranean country, immediately after they checked him out, the officials came down to the dock, untied his lines, and pushed his boat off the dock!

Our last evening in Opua, we took the ferry to Russell and strolled around the village in the cool of the evening. It was now June, which was Opua's December. The temperature reached 70 degrees F in the daytime, but the nights were cool. We ate our departure dinner at the Victorian Marlborough Hotel and lingered over a drink by the fireplace in their warm, cozy lounge, soaking up all the comfort we could before tackling the Tasman Sea again.

High winds were still blowing at sea, caused by a slow-moving high-pressure cell over New Zealand. We sailed to Matauphi Bay in the Bay of Islands and anchored for two nights waiting for better weather. We went into the little village each day for muffins and coffee in the morning and for lunch in the afternoon at an outdoor café. From there we sailed to Robertson Island, which was close to the ocean. The marine radio weather report still predicted high northerly winds and nine-foot seas. We took a hike up a high hill to a point where we got a panoramic view of the Bay of Islands with *Tainui* anchored off Robertson Island's crescent-shaped beach. From that vantage point, we took the picture that we featured on our Christmas letter that year.

Finally the Keri Keri ham net announced that the wind was down to 10 to 15 knots and the sea conditions had improved. We had used up some of our perishable supplies and freshwater while waiting for good weather, so we returned to Russell, topped up our water, and bought some fruits and vegetables. We said goodbye to civilization by stopping at the bakery for a last coffee and pastry before returning to the dock. On June 3, 1991, we sailed out of the Bay of Islands into the dreaded Tasman Sea once again.

CHAPTER TEN

BACK TO FIJI

Twenty knots of wind whipped up a steep chop in the Bay of Islands as we headed toward the open sea under half a jib and a reefed mainsail. However, outside of the bay our reintroduction to the Tasman Sea was a pleasant surprise. Unlike the gale we had encountered when we embarked from Fiji, we glided out onto a calm ocean under a bright blue sky with a 10-knot breeze on our beam. I let the furling jib all the way out, shook the reef out of the mainsail, and hoisted the staysail. With all her sails flying, *Tainui* sailed smoothly along, while Connie and I sat in the cockpit with the weak winter sun warming our backs. We couldn't have had a more pleasant start to an ocean passage.

The wind quit altogether at dusk. Instead of motoring, we let *Tainui* drift so we could have a quiet dinner and a peaceful night. Even in these peaceful conditions, after six months ashore we were not very hungry and ate only soup and canned fruit cocktail for dinner. That night we enrolled in the Pacific Maritime Ham Radio Net and reported our departure to our family through Jerry in Salem. We also checked in with the Tasman Sea Net out of Keri Keri in the Bay of Islands. John, the net operator, predicted winds of 15 knots gusting to 20, which would have made fast sailing, but the winds did not come, and *Tainui* sat dead in the water all night. Drifting so close to land, we were extra conscientious with our night watches because of the local ship traffic.

The next morning our appetites returned, and we ate a hearty breakfast of pancakes in the cockpit while *Tainui* sat still in the morning sun on a flat sea without a breath of wind. Harry, the amateur ham radio weather forecaster on *Whale Song,* reported that a high-pressure cell was currently blocking the wind in our area, so we motored for four hours, then rested the motor, and drifted in the afternoon. While we were drifting, an albatross landed on the sea alongside of us. We thought it might be looking for a handout, because these birds often followed ships to pick over the garbage that had been thrown overboard. We threw bread and apple cores into the sea, but the bird showed no interest, and after watching us for three hours, it flew away. A light wind came up at bedtime, which allowed us to sail slowly through the night at about three knots.

The wind quit again after breakfast, but Harry predicted that a gale forming in the Coral Sea between Australia and New Zealand would reach us in 36 to 48 hours. We mentally crossed our fingers and hoped that it would change course. With no wind in the immediate future, we motored all morning. In the afternoon, we played with various sail combinations, trying to make progress in light and variable winds, but had little success. We tried to call our family after the maritime net, but Jerry's phone patch had quit working. Jerry informed our family of our progress that night by phoning them after the net. The Keri Keri net that evening confirmed Harry's warning of an imminent gale. A 10-knot headwind came up later in the evening, and *Tainui* beat to windward through the night. She heeled enough that we rigged the lee cloth to keep us from falling out of our bunk when we were off watch. We had a comfortable two hours when we were becalmed in the middle of the night, but the wind soon returned, and we went back to life on the slant.

Tainui continued to beat into a 10-knot wind all the next day. There were still no signs of a gale, so we clung to the hope that it might miss us. Connie took advantage of the light wind by cooking a macaroni and cheese dinner. We enjoyed the comfortable ride, even though our slow progress toward Fiji was disappointing

During the night, the wind increased and backed a bit, which allowed *Tainui* to fall off the wind and pick up speed. However, as time went by, *Tainui* struggled against bigger and bigger waves. The waves were much too high to have been caused by our local winds. This was an ominous sign; we knew that the strong winds that had stirred up these waves would soon reach us. We braced ourselves for what was coming.

A late-afternoon weather report confirmed our suspicions; the high-pressure cell had given way to a deep low that was sending a gale our way. I double-checked the lashings on all of the gear on deck, and Connie secured everything loose below. As evening approached, ominous black clouds darkened the horizon, and white crests broke on the dark seas. Intermittent gusts whistled through the rigging. In preparation for the storm, I double-reefed the mainsail and rolled up the jib. There was so much wind pressure on the big jib that it wound up more tightly than usual. This seemed like a good thing at first, because the smaller it was, the less wind resistance there would be on the bow, making it easier to keep *Tainui*'s bow into the wind if we hove to. However, rolling the jib up so tightly required more turns of line on the drum than usual, and I ran out of line before the sail was completely rolled up. We were stuck with a small jib. At that time, the small jib did not present a problem.

As the night fell, the wind built to gale force with 40-knot gusts, and dramatically bigger seas crashed violently into the hull, often breaking over the deck and flooding the cockpit. Before long, the wind shifted toward the bow, and *Tainui* ceased to make progress against the wind and waves. It was time to heave to, but we could not heave to with a jib on the bowsprit. The bow would blow downwind, and *Tainui* would race back toward New Zealand, surfing down the face of the waves. She would be in danger of broaching and being rolled over when the waves hit her broadside. I needed to finish rolling up the jib as quickly as possible.

I went forward with my safety harness tethered to the jack line that ran along the deck. The trip to the bow was wet and slippery, and working in the bow pulpit in the dark was difficult. The wild up-and-down ride made it hard for me to manage my flashlight and keep one hand free to do my work. I was dipped into the water up to my waist when the bow plunged into a wave and chilled by the gale force wind when the bow rose up. By the light of a flashlight, I secured the roller-furling drum so that, when I untied its furling line, it couldn't unroll the big jib—which would have been a disaster in the gale. The line had been secured to the drum by poking it through a small hole and tying a figure-eight stopper knot. I untied the knot, pulled out the line, and took some extra turns around the drum. I wanted to secure the line onto the drum again and roll up the sail, but the wet line had swollen and would not go back through the hole.

I came back to the cockpit, pulled the old line out of its pulleys, and installed a smaller line in its place. I put a dozen turns of the smaller line around the drum, poked it through the hole, and tied a stopper knot. That line rolled the jib all the way up, and *Tainui* hove to under a sheeted-in double-reefed main. The mainsail was aft of the mast, so her stern blew her downwind, and *Tainui* lay comfortably with her bow about 50 degrees off the wind.

By the time we were hove to, it was 1:00 a.m. I was tired, wet, and cold from working out in the gale. The combination of lack of sleep, physical effort, and nervous tension made working under these conditions physically and emotionally exhausting. Connie had also been on deck all this time (we were always both on deck when either of us went forward, which was especially important at night), but she insisted on taking the next night watch so I could get some rest. Even with our tri color navigation light shining at the top of the mast and our radar reflector in the rigging to alert ships to our presence, we kept a particularly vigilant night watch when hove to. Dead in the water, we would not have the maneuverability to dodge an approaching ship. Instead of awakening me in the usual two hours, Connie let me sleep until I woke up at 5:30 a.m.

On the morning ham net, the skipper of the vessel *Seraphim* reported that the storm had done serious damage to his vessel. We were the nearest boat to him, and even though we were hove to in the storm, we offered to attempt to provide assistance. The skipper thanked us but declined. He was nearing New Zealand, and he felt that he had enough sail power to limp into port. The wind was still howling in our rigging and we were tired, so we remained hove to and slept, waiting for better weather. Finally, at 4:30 in the afternoon, the wind slackened and shifted to the aft of us, and I sent *Tainui* off on a fast broad reach.

On one of my daily rounds, I lifted up the floorboards and found that the bilge was half full of water. I checked the through-hull fittings first, because they would have been the most serious cause of the leak, but all of them were dry. The through-hulls were openings in the hull that brought water into the boat for the engine, galley, and head or drained water out. They had valves called "seacocks" that opened and closed with just a quarter turn of their handles. *Tainui* had five of them. I had wired a round, tapered, softwood plug to each through-hull, so that it would be readily available to be hammered into the hole in an emergency. Otherwise, I might be rummaging through the lockers grumbling, "What did I do with those #*@! plugs?" while the boat filled with water. I didn't need a plug this time, so I turned my attention to the gap in the hawse pipe cover on the foredeck where the anchor chain left the chain locker. It had leaked on the way down to New Zealand, so I had sealed it with waterproof putty in advance this time, but waves crashing over the bow had washed it away. I stopped it up again and checked it periodically thereafter.

By midnight, we were hove to in a full gale. We slept fairly well even though we were sloshing around in big seas. On her early morning watch, Connie spotted a ship heading toward us and called me on deck. It passed so close to us that we could read the name on its stern: *"Forum Samoa."* We raised the skipper on the radio and found that he was headed for Lautoka, Fiji, which was also our destination. We were skipping rainy Suva this time and heading straight for the sunny side of the island.

We got *Tainui* under way again in the morning on a downwind run in a 20-knot following wind. The overtaking seas rolled us severely, making life difficult aboard. When Connie set a bowl of scrambled eggs on the galley counter and reached for a cup of coffee, the bowl slid off, and the eggs splattered on the cabin sole. The day was windy, but the sun was out, and it was a pleasure to sit in the cockpit again. An albatross soared in the sky above us for a while and then came closer and closer until it came alongside and glided a few feet from us for three hours. We were mesmerized by its ability to ride the wind for hours at a time without flapping its wings. It was a magnificent bird with a huge wingspan— much larger close up than we had expected.

On the ham net the next morning, a nearby boat gave us a bit of a scare. The skipper reported that his weather fax showed a severe low with 50-knot winds heading right at us. We had survived wind of over 50 knots at anchor, but 45 knots was the highest wind we had experienced at sea. We were not looking forward to this, but our anticipated doom did not last long. We contacted the official weather station on Norfolk Island and learned that the predicted low had already passed over us. It was likely that the wind in which we had hove to during the past night was the 50-knot wind, but we had no wind indicator aboard, so we couldn't be sure. Improving conditions inspired Connie to make a fine evening meal of lamb steaks, boiled potatoes, and coleslaw. It was a treat to have fresh meat six days out of port. Our meat had been vacuum-sealed by a New Zealand butcher, who said it would last for six weeks—several times the duration of our passage. All the meat survived the trip except the chicken, which went bad before we reached port.

The wind and sea conditions that night made it difficult for our usually reliable wind vane system to steer accurately. The wind vane needed to be set for the velocity of the wind, but the wind was fluctuating between light breezes, violent squalls, and calms. In these changing conditions, the wind vane required constant adjustments. In addition, the waves coming from behind pushed our stern from side to side, requiring the wind vane to work extra hard to bring *Tainui* back on course. We decided not to heave to again, because heaving to was making this a very slow trip. In order to make as much progress as possible, we were busy adjusting the wind vane and changing the sails all night. At 3:30 a.m. I pulled down the jib and sailed with just a boomed-out mainsail, which slowed us down a little, but gave us a steadier ride and less work to do.

The next day we had 600 miles to go—about one week of sailing. The sea conditions stayed about the same all that day—big following seas—but the wind settled down to a steady 25 knots from directly behind us. With the steady wind, the wind vane performed better and our reduced sail gave us a fairly comfortable ride. That evening, Keri Keri radio reported that a low-pressure cell, packing 50-knot winds, was moving slowly along the coast of Australia. We heard the skipper of the vessel *Hamlin* report that they were caught in it. They said they had been knocked down three times and were taking on water. They had contacted the Australian Coast Guard and were attempting to reach port somewhere along the Australian coast. We did not hear the outcome of their ordeal.

By evening, we had made good 130 miles in 24 hours—a very good run for *Tainui*. The conditions aboard were marginal for cooking, but we had been only snacking for two days and wanted a hot meal. Somehow, Connie managed to keep the pressure cooker on the stove in the rolling galley long enough to make chicken stew, and we had a hot meal. Life aboard had improved—but not for long. Once again the wind increased through the night until it reached gale force by 2:00 a.m. In spite of our desire for progress, we were too tired to try to sail through the gale, so we gave up and hove to again. That night the wind ripped out a set of reefing points in the mainsail. The damage was not repairable, so we would have to get along without the mainsail for the rest of the trip. We would be looking for a new mainsail when we got to Fiji.

The worst gusts were gone by morning, and the wind was down to a steady 20 knots, with occasional 30-knot gusts. We stayed hove to for breakfast and got underway at around 8:00 a.m. We had not made much progress during the night, so we were still 525 miles from Fiji. With the wind coming from behind us, we didn't miss the mainsail. We often sailed on the jib alone when we were running downwind. However, the seas had not yet calmed down, and I could not find any sail configuration that kept us from rolling from gunwale to gunwale. We were both tired from not having slept much the previous night, but we were too tense to relax. At dinnertime, Connie warmed up some canned beans and even cooked a pot of cabbage, carrots, and onions—another impressive feat in difficult conditions. The wind dropped to 15 knots by sunset, and the ocean calmed down around 10:00 p.m. *Tainui* made a steady four knots through the night. Without the wind howling in the rigging the night was more peaceful, but *Tainui* still rolled too much for comfort. Connie tried lying on some cushions on the cabin sole, but couldn't stay on top of them. She didn't get any sleep until I took my 2:00 a.m. watch, and she slept on the settee with the lee cloth holding her on.

The wind dropped steadily during the next day. Connie and I took turns napping during the morning, and by noon the wind was down to five knots—disappointing for progress, but a welcome opportunity to catch our breath. We motored for two hours to charge the batteries and gain a few miles and then rolled the big jib all the way out for the first time in several days. The wind was then on the beam and filled both the jib and the staysail, but even then we barely made enough speed to steer. That night, Connie made hamburgers using our vacuum-packed meat. At nine days out, this was the longest time we had ever had fresh meat on a passage. It was a comfortable 76 degrees in the cabin that afternoon; the weather was getting progressively warmer as we sailed north.

Finally, we had a good night. The wind picked up to an ideal 12-knot breeze, and we made a steady five knots all night. Our morning Sat Nav fix showed that we had only 350 miles to go. We had warm pleasant weather with good sailing in the morning, but the wind died in the afternoon, and we were totally becalmed by dinnertime. The sun that afternoon had warmed the water in our sun shower, so we hoisted it up and showered on the foredeck. After much appreciated—and much needed—showers, we sat on the deck in the late afternoon sun, comfortable in our shorts, and watched a school of dolphins play in our bow wave. The last two days had greatly refreshed us, which was a good thing; it would have been tough to face the next two days without some rest.

We were back into 30-knot winds all the next day, and there was another ominous weather forecast. The weatherman predicted that two approaching troughs were about to intersect right on top of us. There was a slight chance that they might pass south of us, but the weatherman thought we were already in the beginnings of them. He didn't know how much wind they packed, but he was sure that, with waves coming from two directions, there would be confused seas. Around midnight, the first depression hit, and we lay a-hull in a screeching wind. Without a mainsail *Tainui* didn't have enough windage aft to heave to, so we wound up wallowing crosswise in the troughs—which was much less comfortable than heaving to.

Conditions were a little better in the morning and we started sailing again after breakfast, but a fierce gale hit us within an hour. I raced forward and got all sail down as quickly as possible and let *Tainui* lie a-hull—wallowing in the troughs again. This time the wind was accompanied by torrential rain. The rainsqualls sounded like the boughs of a huge tree sweeping over our cabin top. Soon we saw lightning flashes in the distance and heard the thunder. They appeared to be heading our way, so I unplugged all of our electronics and disconnected all of their antennas and grounds. Our engine was still vulnerable because it was sitting on steel motor mounts. I had read of lightning strikes that had "fried" all the electronics on boats—even after they were disconnected—but I had done all that I could.

The lightning came closer and closer until it was striking all around us. One blinding streak hit so close that we could hear the electricity sizzle in the sea a split second before the ear-splitting thunder that accompanied it. Sitting in a steel boat watching the lightning hitting all around us was frightening. We tried to sit on the wood surfaces, afraid that the steel would be dangerous if we were hit. I tried to remember what I had heard and read about lightning striking boats. We were likely to get hit because our 50-foot aluminum mast was the tallest thing in the area. If the lightening struck the mast, it would try to get through the boat and ground itself in the water. Wood and glass boats actually were more dangerous than steel boats, because the only way for the lightning to pass through them to the water was through their metal through-hull fittings. Lightning's powerful current could melt these fittings, burning a hole in the hull that would cause the boat to flood. A steel boat offered a more diffuse path to the sea, producing a less concentrated current at any one point.

The lightning slowly moved away without touching us, and we relaxed a bit as we watched the spectacular light show recede into the night. Two hours later, the wind shifted to the west, and we sailed off on a beam reach—a fast, comfortable ride that lasted through the night. The night was not without incident, however. The alternator quit charging during a battery run.

There was no wind the next day, which made it easy to work on the alternator but was discouraging, because we made no progress toward Fiji. I found that the pulley that drove the belt to the alternator seemed to be slipping on its shaft. In order to get at it, I needed to remove the refrigerator pulley, which ran off of the same shaft. I was unable to pry or pull the refrigerator pulley off, and when I tried loosening it by tapping it with a hammer, it split in two. This meant that we would have no refrigerator until we got to port, but we were (we hoped) only two or three days out. Having disposed of the refrigerator pulley, I tightened the bolt that secured the alternator pulley to its shaft and started the engine. The pulley slipped again in a few minutes. Unless I could fix it, we would have to conserve our batteries to ensure the use of our radios, electronic navigation, running lights, and the engine starter. That night, we didn't show our running lights and used oil lamps in the cabin. I reported our problem to the Seafarer's Net, and they moved us to first on their roll call, so we wouldn't have to run our radio while listening for our turn.

On the brighter side, a whale surfaced twice near our boat that day, and a brown booby circled us and settled down for the night on one of our spreaders. Contacts with sea life always brightened our days at sea.

We had a very quiet night, and in the morning we sailed slowly for a while in a light breeze but were soon becalmed. We had only 115 miles left and I wanted to get going, so I tightened the alternator bolt again and motored. The alternator put out a weak charge for four hours and then wobbled and made a loud knocking noise, so I stopped the engine. I hoped it had brought the batteries up a bit. After the engine cooled down, I pulled the pulley off its shaft and found the root of the problem. The bolt only kept it from coming off the shaft; the pulley was kept turning by a thin metal key that slid into matching slots cut into the shaft and the pulley hub. The key was broken, and the slot on the shaft was slightly damaged. I made a new key by filing down a piece of steel and tried motoring. It worked for a while and then slipped again.

We drifted through another windless night. There wasn't much to do, so I took the pulley off again. One end of the new key had been damaged, so I turned it around and figured that I could run the alternator until the other end gave out.

The next day was the same—no wind, so we motored. After four hours, the alternator gave out a loud vibration. This time the slot in the shaft was so damaged that it would require major surgery. We were frustrated to be so near our destination, yet unable to get there. However, we enjoyed the warmth of the tropical sun and the lack of the discomfort and tension from storms. Our mechanical problem was a nuisance, but not a major concern. We knew that we could eventually sail the rest of the way and even if we lost our satellite navigation, the island of Viti Levu was too big to miss.

Our deliverance came the next morning in the form of a 10-knot breeze. We sailed all day at two to three knots and even faster through the night, when the wind freshened. We arrived off the reef at Nevula

Pass on a calm sea at 6:30 a.m. We were unable to see the range markers on the hillside, because the sky was hazy and the sun was in our eyes. But with flat calm seas, we sailed through the wide ship's pass without incident and anchored off Lautoka at 1:30 p.m. on June 19, sixteen days out of the Bay of Islands. We loved New Zealand, but we were glad to have seen the last of the Tasman Sea.

We notified the port control, health, and agriculture officials by radio of our arrival. We had time for lunch and to straighten up the boat, before they came out together in a launch and boarded us at 4:30 p.m. That evening our friends John and Gudrun invited us aboard *Speedwell* for a light supper. (John was the professional racing skipper who had embarrassed us when he gloried in the gales in the Tasman Sea on our way down to New Zealand). Back aboard *Tainui,* we enjoyed what had become almost unimaginable—a night's sleep in a comfortable berth without interruption: no night watches, no emergencies, no rocking and rolling!

We slept in the next morning and then went ashore to check in with customs and immigration. Immigration was busy with a big ship and couldn't get to us until 2:00 p.m., so we walked to town for lunch. It felt good to walk on solid ground again, and it was a treat to relax and have a meal served to us.

Most of our seven-and-a-half-week return visit to Fiji was consumed by boat work at the new Neisau Marina in Lautoka. We arrived in time for the marina's grand opening, which featured a Fijian feast called a *lovo,* in which all the food was cooked in an underground pit. Because the marina was not yet fully operational, all services at the marina were half price, including the new Maytag washer and dryer in the laundry room, the hot showers, and the cost of our slip. Great flakes of plaster were already falling off of the ceiling in the shower rooms, which didn't bode well for the quality of the new construction.

A series of three engineers with dubious qualifications worked on our alternator and refrigerator pulley problem for most of the time we were in Lautoka. The first one installed three setscrews, which he thought would grip the shaft in place of the damaged key and slot system, but the shaft fell off after running the engine for five minutes. The second engineer put a new sleeve over the shaft to strengthen it, made a new hub for the pulley, and installed a new key and slot. Shortly after his repair effort, the shaft fell off on a day trip out to Musket Cove. The third one, an Australian who claimed to be a mechanical engineer, decided that it needed bigger setscrews, which he called "grub screws." They had pointed ends that fit into dimples he drilled into the shaft. His fix appeared to solve the problem, but at our next port the shaft broke in two where his dimples had weakened it.

During the repair, one of the engineers accidentally punctured the engine's front oil seal, and a huge puddle of smelly black crankcase oil leaked out onto the cabin sole carpet. This was too much for Connie, who had made it abundantly clear that she didn't appreciate having a diesel engine in her living room and that she was becoming increasingly tired of boatyards. She left on an overnight trip to Suva with a another cruising wife, and I cleaned up the leaked oil before she got back.

While walking in town one day, Connie and I were hailed by Rafiq, an Indian taxi driver who had driven us several times on our previous visit and had taken me to his house for lunch. He was overjoyed to see us again and invited us to his house for dinner on the next Sunday. They were a Muslim family, and that Sunday turned out to be an Islamic holiday called Eid, which celebrated the end of the pilgrimage to Mecca. Their small house was decorated with framed writings from the Koran in ornate Arabic script. Rafiq's wife, Zobra, served us a delicious beef curry dinner, and we were charmed by their attractive, well-behaved children ages eight, five, and three.

In return, we invited Rafiq and his family to a Sunday dinner aboard *Tainui* featuring authentic American food. It took two tries to get them aboard. When they failed to show up the first time, friends from another yacht accepted our last-minute invitation to help us eat up the hamburgers, French fries, and potato salad. Rafiq said that on that occasion the guards at the gate wouldn't let them in. I think they were just shy. I had alerted the guards to watch for them, and the guards said they had not seen them. They came the second time when I assured Rafiq that I would personally be at the gate to see that they were admitted. Zobra looked frightened as she walked on the floating dock and even more uneasy when she reluctantly climbed aboard *Tainui*. She became queasy as soon as she sat down below and immediately went out and threw up. As far as we could tell, *Tainui* was sitting perfectly still. She waited on the dock while the rest of her family quickly ate their meal, and Rafiq took them home. We thought her motion sickness was caused more by nervousness than by the motion.

One evening a French couple invited us aboard their luxury 50-foot yacht. Their three daughters, a 10-year-old and three-year-old twins, had been on the yacht since birth and didn't know any other lifestyle. This visit led to an amusing experience. The family had just had their boat reupholstered by a local auto shop, run by an Indian family, for a fraction of what it would have cost in the United States. We were pleased with the results, so we gave it a try ourselves.

We invited the foreman from the auto upholstery shop to come to our boat and give us an estimate. We chose an expensive rose-colored velour material, and he said he would do our nine cushions for US$183. (At the Seattle Boat Show, we had gotten a US$1,000 estimate for the same job!) When I asked him, "How long will it take?" He replied, "We will do it in one day, sir." This was patently ridiculous. I figured he was afraid that we might be on a tight time schedule, and if he told the truth, he would lose the deal, so I said, "Look, we're not leaving soon. You don't have to promise to do it that fast. How long do you think it will <u>really</u> take?" He said, "It will be no problem, sir. I will put all nine of my men on it." He put the nine cushions in his pickup truck and left.

A week later, having heard no word about the cushions, we walked up to the shop to see how they were doing. The scene was hilarious. They did in fact have nine workers. However, they had only one sewing machine! "Putting all my men on it" turned out to mean one man sewing and eight watching. It took another week for them to finish. While we were waiting for the cushions, we recarpeted the cabin sole, which had never fully recovered from the oil spill. Finally installed, the cushions were beautiful and significantly brightened *Tainui*'s cabin.

There was a company at the marina making small fiberglass boats. I asked the Aussie woman manager if they could make a hard dodger for *Tainui* to replace our aging canvass one. They had only made small fiberglass boats from a mold, but she wanted to start servicing the yachts that were arriving in the marina, so she was eager to try. I drew up the design and we agreed on a price of US$750. She promised it in a week. I was sure that it would take longer and told her that time was not an issue, but she insisted that it would only take a week. The job ultimately took six weeks—she didn't have a clue about how long such a job would take. As a result, she under-bid the job—to our considerable advantage.

Initially she sent two local carpenters to *Tainui*. They climbed aboard armed with a plumb bob and a spirit level, which were useless on a boat that didn't sit level in the water and rocked every time a workman changed positions! They had no idea how to begin. Retrofitting equipment on a boat was especially difficult. *Tainui* had no square corners to work from. The house roof was curved, its back and sides sloped, and the deck was curved. I sent them away, and the manager fired them. Two days later the Aussie manager sent two men whom she promised were more competent, which shouldn't have been hard to do!

This pair brought two large plywood sheets for the sides of the dodger and cut them out according to my plan. But they made the cutout where they fitted over the house bigger on one side than the other. When they put the sides in place, there was an eight-inch gap above the housetop on one side. They fixed it by cutting eight inches off of the bottom of that side. This eliminated the gap, but put an eight-inch slant in the roof. I had the manager make them build the short side over again. We called the finished product our "Third World dodger." Although it was crude looking, it was sturdy and served us well.

When the dodger was finished, we sailed to Musket Cove on the island of Malolo Lailai to have some fun. As we were approaching the pass through the reef around the island, our engine quit. I quickly determined that the fuel filter was clogged. I always bought several filters at a time, but I had run out of replacements, and the ones I had ordered from the States had not yet arrived. There were 20 knots of wind against us, which would have made it difficult to negotiate the pass under sail, so I radioed Musket Cove for assistance. The yacht *Hobo* came out and towed us in. It was getting dark, so Ed from *Illusion* and George from *Wind Dancer* came out in their dinghies and shone flashlights on the rocks and navigational markers. *Hobo* was a small fiberglass sailboat with a small engine and struggled to pull the much heavier *Tainui* through the pass. At one point *Hobo* lost control and glanced off the reef. Fortunately, only minor damage was done. I paid the skipper of *Hobo* US$80 for the tow.

We stayed 10 days at Musket Cove, where we had become lifetime members of the yacht club on our previous visit. We did a lot of socializing and snorkeling. Before we left, I wanted to meet an elderly ham radio operator who lived alone on a hill high above Musket Cove. We were told that he was an eccentric retired hotel owner who practiced nudism. I can't remember his name, but I'll call him Henry. We were told that Henry used to ride down to the resort in the early morning on his motor scooter in the nude and take a dip in the pool before the guests got up. At the request of the early morning women hotel workers, Dick Smith, the owner of the resort, put a stop to it.

I wanted to meet this eccentric radio buff (but not necessarily in the buff), so when Connie and I hiked to the top of the hill, I stopped at his house. Connie waited outside while I visited with Henry. Sure enough, he was clad in a cigar, a pair of glasses, and sandals. It was a little disconcerting, but he had a fascinating radio room. All of his equipment was of tube-type World War II vintage; there was not a transistor in the lot. It all worked, and he had a great signal out to sea. Henry was a highly skilled radio technician and gave me some good advice on how to solve one of my transmitting problems. After the visit, Connie and I hiked on up to the top of the hill and got excellent still and video pictures of *Tainui* lying off the beautiful beach in the transparent green water among the other visiting yachts.

One afternoon, a group of us dinghied to the neighboring island of Malolo Levu to visit a craft fair at a local school. Malolo Levu meant "big Malolo" in contrast to Musket Cove's Malolo Lailai, which meant "little Malolo." School was in session, and we could hear the rote-style teaching as we passed the lightly constructed classrooms. The teacher would read a line, and the class would repeat it in unison. This process was repeated over and over for as long as we were there. The children sounded as though they might be fourth or fifth graders.

When the time came to leave Musket Cove, I managed to clean up the clogged fuel filter enough to motor back to the marina at Lautoka. When we got there, we found that mail had arrived from the States with a new supply of fuel filters and that the new mainsail we had ordered from Australia had also arrived. Our filters had been clogging up so fast I suspected that our fuel tank was fouled. I removed the small round inspection plate in the top of the tank and poked a broomstick down to the bottom of the tank. It came up with an inch-thick coating of purple sludge on the end of it. The tank needed a thorough cleaning. The fuel tank was in the bilge, and most of it lay back underneath the engine. The only access was the six-inch inspection plate, which was too small for the job. In order to gain enough access to clean the tank, I cut a hole one foot in diameter in the top of it with my angle grinder. I bought a piece of stainless steel and made a steel cover for the new hole. I didn't want the tank to leak fuel in rough weather, so I made threaded screw holes one inch apart all around the hole in the tank, and when I finished cleaning the tank, I screwed the lid down over a rubber gasket.

Cleaning the diesel tank was a filthy, smelly task. First I pumped as much of the fuel as I could into a 50-gallon drum. Next, I cut the handle of a mop in half, reached through the new access hole, and mopped out the rest of the fuel. Then I poured water and detergent into the tank. This time I shortened a long-handled floor brush and reached in and scrubbed the bottom as far back under the engine as I could reach. I repeated this process until the gunk appeared to be gone and then flooded the tank to overflowing with water to rinse out the detergent. After I pumped the water out, I dried the tank with a couple of fresh mops. It still looked moist so I poured in five gallons of alcohol as a drying agent. I wiped out most of the alcohol and let the remainder evaporate. Satisfied that the tank was as clean and dry as I could make it, I reattached the access plates and filled it with fresh fuel. In order to make sure we were starting with clean fuel in the tank, I ran the new fuel through a three-stage filter. The whole process took a week and the stench of diesel fumes was nearly nauseating. Connie stayed away from the marina as much as possible during the tank cleaning. Once again I realized how lucky I was to have Connie—some women would have given up on the boating life.

The Europa '91 Around the World Regatta made a pit stop at the Neisau Marina while we were there. They were a group of about twelve yachts sailing around the world together in nine or 10 months, led by Jimmy Cornell. Cornell organized these around-the-world regattas, and an annual Christmas regatta from the Canary Islands to Bermuda for yachts returning from a season in the Mediterranean. He had been influential in our decision to buy *Tainui*. He had published two books six years apart, giving the results of extensive surveys of cruising sailors regarding their satisfaction with boats and boat gear. In the first survey, published before we bought *Tainui*, the ideal boat came out to be a 35-foot steel-hulled cutter, and that was exactly what we bought. As time passed, we noticed that we were seeing a richer group of sailors with bigger boats. The ideal boat in Cornell's second survey had grown to be a 40-foot steel-hulled cutter.

Several of the Europa boats were hauled out while we were at the boatyard. They got priority treatment at the marina because of their tight schedule. One man decided to paint the entire hull of his steel 50-footer. He was in such a hurry that he let the yard make two cardinal errors in painting a steel boat. The top authorities on steel hulls advised that steel should be as dry as possible when painted, because rust bloom formed very quickly on moist steel. In the tropics this meant that steel should be sandblasted and painted in the hottest part of the day, and even then, blasted steel should be primed every three hours. I was shocked to see this 50-foot steel hull completely sandblasted at night under floodlights before any paint was applied. If the experts were right, it would turn out to be a wasted paint job.

Connie and I couldn't imagine sailing around the world that fast. These sailors had almost no time for exploring the countries they passed through. If their stop at Lautoka was typical, they spent most of their time in port, getting their boats ready for the next leg of their trip. I think they joined Jimmy Cornell's fleet because they wanted the prestige of being a circumnavigator, and they didn't have the time or the skill and courage to do it on their own. Jimmy Cornell made all of the advance marina arrangements, dealt with the officials, and brought along a diesel mechanic and a boatwright to take care of problems along the way. In addition, there was the security of being in a group, which eliminated navigational errors and meant that there were always other boats standing by to assist in the event of an emergency. We felt that these conveniences made them second-class circumnavigators.

We heard later that the Neisau Marina went bankrupt. We were sorry but not surprised. The manager had bought expensive equipment with reckless abandon—to the dismay of his investors. He felt that this equipment was necessary in order to attract the big boats, which was where the big money was. Unfortunately, they didn't get enough business to keep up their loan payments, and the banks foreclosed.

We celebrated our 40th wedding anniversary with dinner at the upscale Waterfront Hotel in Lautoka, and twelve days later we were ready to leave for Port Vila in Vanuatu. Many of our friends waited to participate in an upcoming race from Fiji to Vanuatu, but we decided to go on ahead.

CHAPTER ELEVEN

VANUATU AND NEW CALEDONIA

After a light lunch on board *Tainui* (we had discovered it was not a good idea to eat a heavy meal before the first day at sea), on August 29, 1991, we untied our dock lines and set off on the 500-mile trip from Lautoka, Fiji, to Port Vila, Vanuatu. Outside the marina, the water was dark blue with brilliant whitecaps that gleamed in the sun. *Tainui*'s heavy-displacement hull easily pushed through the two-foot wind chop as we motored south toward the reef around the island of Viti Levu with a stiff breeze in our faces. When we reached the reef in the late afternoon, there was a 20-knot headwind in the pass, so we pulled into nearby Sweeny Bay and anchored for the night. We would tackle the pass and the ocean in the morning when the wind was usually calm and in the meantime get a good night's rest. We shared the bay with a small sailboat named *Osprey*. Her skipper, Gordon, brought us some steaks from a four-foot wahoo that he had just caught. There was more meat on it than he, his wife, and their one-year-old child could possibly eat.

Well rested and in no particular hurry, we ate a leisurely breakfast in the cockpit on a sunny, calm morning before I cranked up the anchor and Connie got *Tainui* under way. There was no wind at all, so we motored through the pass and turned due west toward Vanuatu. About five miles out, an ideal 17-knot wind from the northeast filled in. I called Connie up from the galley, where she was cleaning up after lunch, and she took the wheel while I raised the sails and eased the sheets for a fast, comfortable broad reach. That evening, Connie cooked a wahoo steak dinner—a real treat. Wahoo was one of our favorite eating fish.

Although the wind politely dropped to 12 knots for the night, neither of us slept well—typical for our first night at sea.

We awoke to another sunny morning. The wind had veered to the north, which put it directly on our beam, so I hauled the sails in a little, and *Tainui* swished along at over five knots on a beam reach. We heard a growling sound when we motor-sailed at battery-charging time. It sounded like a metal-to-metal vibration in the cutlass bearing, where the prop shaft passed through the stern. If so, it would not be a serious problem; it could be replaced the next time we hauled out, but any unusual event like this planted a little seed of concern in the back of my mind. Fortunately, it did turn out to be the cutlass bearing. The reaching wind continued through the night, and we caught up on our sleep. We were enjoying a very pleasant trip so far.

Early the next afternoon the wind backed until it was directly from our stern. Connie took the helm again while I went forward and set up the sails for a wing-and-wing downwind run. Managing the heavy aluminum whisker pole was heavy work. I snapped its inboard end onto a ring six feet up on the mast, attached the jib to the its outboard end, and hoisted the whole thing up until the sail stuck straight out from the side of the boat. It took all my strength to pull it up. Then I pushed the mainsail straight out on the other side. Our biggest sails, now rigged straight out on both sides of the boat, caught the wind from behind and pushed *Tainui* swiftly downwind like a giant bird; hence the term "wing-and-wing." As usual, we rolled a bit downwind, but not severely in these light conditions. The wind conveniently dropped to 10 knots again in the evening, and we got another good night's sleep. This trip was still going very well.

And yet another day of glorious sailing followed. The sun shone in a clear blue sky and the wind backed to a 10-to-15-knot beam reach, which was smoother and faster than running downwind. The ride was so smooth that Connie put her heavy pressure cooker on the galley stove and cooked up a hearty beef stew. As usual, the pot was held on by clamps called "fiddles," but they could not have held this pot if the weather had been rough. Jerry, our ham radio friend in Salem, had replaced his ailing telephone patch, and that evening we talked to all three of our children—another highlight of the trip for us. Our children told us that they found these contacts reassuring when we were at sea.

The smooth sailing continued through our final day. We spotted the island of Efate (pronounced e-far-tay) at 6:30 p.m. The sun had set when we reached the island. We sailed slowly along the shore in the dark toward Port Vila, the capital city. To give ourselves a good clearance from the reef, we hove to when our radar put us 10 miles off the pass into the harbor. It was a good thing we had radar, because the Sat Nav did not give us a position during this landfall—just when we needed it the most. As usual when we were close to land, both of us were awake much of the night, watching for traffic and checking our position.

At daybreak we motored through the pass, passed between the red and green navigational buoys that marked the harbor entrance, and dropped anchor near the yellow quarantine buoy. The health officer came out and satisfied himself that we were not bringing in the plague, dead bodies, or dead rats (apparently live rats were okay). He was using a "one-size-fits-all" form designed for (ancient?) merchant ships. Clearing in with the customs and immigration officers ashore was simple and efficient, and by 10:30 a.m. we had officially entered Vanuatu.

We had really enjoyed this smooth, trouble-free passage—it was as good as sailing gets. We were sleepy from our night watches, but not exhausted the way we had been after our battles with the Tasman Sea. If all sailing were like this, there probably wouldn't be room enough in places like Vanuatu for all the visiting boats.

Port Vila was an attractive small town situated on a mile-long concrete seawall. The harbor was well protected by capes that extended out from both sides and by some islands near the entrance. Tiny Iriki Island in the middle of the harbor was the site of an upscale resort. With no polluting industry and few visiting ships, the water in the harbor was clean and clear. When I rowed our dinghy around Iriki Island for exercise in the cool of the mornings, I saw fish swimming beneath me, and the bottom below them.

Vanuatu, formerly known as the New Hebrides, had been under joint British and French control in what was called a "condominium" government (locals referred to it as "pandemonium"). All government services were duplicated. There were both French and English immigration departments, police departments, etc. The country had achieved independence and changed its name to Vanuatu about 10 years before we arrived. Port Vila, the capital, had French restaurants and sidewalk cafés, plus formal English restaurants and pubs serving fish and chips and ale. We enjoyed the best of both worlds.

There was little that the French and English agreed on. The French were Catholic and the English were Protestant. The French-speaking Catholics and English-speaking Protestants could not agree on either of those languages, so they adopted a form of pidgin English called Bislama as their national language. Bislama was originally developed by slave runners, called "black birders," as a common language for the diverse group of islanders they rounded up. The picturesque and sometimes humorous words were loosely based on English. For example, a guitar was a "smol (small) bokis (box) yu scratchem belly he sing out," and "bra" became the more descriptive "titti basket." The word "long" served for every preposition, often occurring over and over again in a sentence. For example, "Yume (We) went long (to) town long (to) buyem drink long (at) pub long (by) dock long (on) waterfront." Their money bears the same motto as ours: "In God we trust," translated as "Long God yume stanup." This was the language of the newspapers, the radio, and all public and private business. We could decipher it in its written form but could not keep up with the locals when they talked fast. Fortunately, as in most parts of the world, persons dealing with tourists spoke English, and many businesses were run by Western expatriates.

Vanuatu comprised a dozen large islands and hundreds of smaller ones. Efate in the south, site of Port Vila, was the most developed. The second largest town was Luganville on Espirito Santo, Vanuatu's biggest island. Tanna Island boasted the world's most accessible active volcano. Pentecost Island was the home of land divers who dove off rickety bamboo towers with vines tied to their ankles, sometimes with crippling results. Other islands had exotic primitive villages where the men wore nothing but penis sheaths tied to a belt around their waists, and witch doctors danced in long, shaggy cone-shaped grass robes wearing tall, carved masks. A yachting couple showed us an impressive video of a two-day ceremony in such a village.

We were excited at the prospect of visiting these islands and began with a 55-mile trip to Moso Island, off the northwest coast of Efate Island. We sailed southwest around the cape protecting Port Vila's harbor, turned north into a strong headwind, and then motored the rest of the way in order to arrive before dark. Connie and I sat in the cockpit and enjoyed the scenery as the electric autopilot steered *Tainui* along the shore. Late in the day we entered Havana Harbor, a long narrow waterway between Efate Island and Moso Island. It became narrower and narrower and appeared to close down completely at its north end. We anchored in Esema Bay, off the village of the same name, on Moso Island.

That evening a parade of outrigger canoes crossed the half-mile-wide channel from their garden plots on Efate Island to their homes in Esema Village. A couple in one of them paddled up to *Tainui* and sold us some lettuce, cabbage, and tomatoes.

We had become worried about Bill and Kathy on *Affaire d Amour*. We had heard on the radio that they were 25 days out of Fiji en route to New

Zealand and had not been heard from. We expected them to be slow because their sails were in bad shape, and we knew their radio seldom worked, but they were long overdue. That night we got some good news on the radio. A Japanese freighter had sighted them 250 miles from New Zealand and had refilled their freshwater tank. Later on we heard more of their story. A week later, the New Zealand Coast Guard launched an air search and found them with tattered sails fighting a losing battle against the wind just off the north end of North Island. After the Coast Guard repeatedly urged *Affaire d'Amour* to accept a tow, and Bill stubbornly refused, they gave up on them, and *Affaire d'Amour* went missing again. Finally, their Scottish dancing friend, Keith, from Whangarie, initiated his own search. He located them with his twin-engine airplane and went out and towed them in with his big steel sailing yacht. The New Zealand government was so upset by this event that they subsequently required all visiting yachts to pass an inspection before leaving port.

After our cruise, Bill's partner, Kathy, told us of the tragic end of *Affaire d'Amour*. While she was at home trying to earn some money for their always meager cruising kitty, Bill lost *Affaire d'Amour* on a reef while attempting to sail alone. He returned to the United States and soon died of cancer. In spite of Kathy's urging, he had stoically refused to ever see a doctor as long as she knew him—even when the symptoms of his cancer had become obvious.

In the morning, we beached our dinghy on the shore of Moso Island at Esema Village. A friendly young man named Gary greeted us and gave us a tour of the village. Living conditions were primitive. The village's facilities consisted of a primitive health clinic that was open one day a month, a board shack convenience store that was open only on request, a rustic primary school, and an equally rustic Presbyterian church—they were all basically spartan wood-frame buildings with dirt floors and window openings without glass. Gary showed us his house, which was of similar design, with a kitchen shelter attached to the back, a outdoor stone bread-baking oven, and a privy. He proudly displayed his most valued possessions, which were his throwing net, his machete, and the rifle with which he hunted wild pigs in the hills behind the village.

Freshwater was scarce in Esema Village. Moso Island had no well water, streams, or lakes. Gary showed us a faucet in the middle of the village. It was connected to the water supply on Efate Island, but its pump had broken down two years previously, and the villagers had not been able to raise the US$1500 to repair it. The only water in the village was the rainwater they collected on their tin roofs or carried in jugs from the "mainland" in their dugout canoes.

One rainy morning a couple named Thomas and Celia stopped by on the way to their garden plot in their dugout canoe to ask if we wanted to order any produce. We invited them aboard to get out of the rain and served them tea. On their way home that evening, they gave us a gift of a large yam. That afternoon Gary took me across the channel to the village's garden plots on Efate Island. They grew taro root, manioc, yams, garden vegetables, and fruit. Due to the lack of irrigation water on Moso Island, the Vanuatuan government had given each family a garden plot on Efate Island. The family plots were about half the size of a city block.

Gary, an elder in the church, invited us to attend the Presbyterian church on Sunday. He said that worship was at 10:00 a.m., but we were the only people in sight at that hour. A little before 11:00, a shy primary-school girl in her Sunday dress came timidly down the path, eyeing us suspiciously. Before long a dozen children flocked around us. One of them wore a T-shirt with a picture of two white feet sticking out of a cooking pot, with a caption in English that read, "Cannibal Stew"! The children eventually went into the building and began singing gospel songs with corresponding hand motions. They sat facing the front of the church, but they twisted their heads around to watch me videotaping them from behind. At the same time, out the window, we could see the not so faithful kids spending their Sabbath diving and swimming from their canoes.

The service began about 11:30. We sat with half a dozen adults and a dozen children on backless wooden benches on the dirt floor. A wooden table about the size and shape of a card table served as altar and pulpit. We were surprised that it was decorated with a small vase of plastic flowers in a country with such a profusion of real blossoms. Two elders conducted the service in rapid-fire Bislama. For once I was glad that I could get only a few words at a time. It was obviously an impassioned hell-fire-and-brimstone sermon. The congregation sang the hymns enthusiastically and in surprisingly full harmony for such a small congregation.

Back at our dinghy, Connie opened a bag of hard candies and passed them out to children on the beach. They gave us a great send-off, laughing and waving as we motored away.

While we were there, we visited back and forth with a few other yachts that came into Esema Bay. One was a British yacht with Charles and Diane aboard. From their names, we would have expected a more regal yacht than their little 30-foot *Mr. Percifal.* Harry, our infamous weather forecaster on *Whale Song,* also dropped in.

About the time we planned to leave, I came down with a fever that kept us there for four more days. Gary heard that I was ill and came aboard with another elder to help me. They had recently taken a course on healing and wanted to try it out on me. I let them go ahead and tried to keep an open mind. The healing service, which they conducted out in the cockpit, was so noisy that another yacht called on the radio and asked if we had some trouble aboard. The elders' healing efforts produced no noticeable results, and the fever ran its course. They probably figured I didn't have enough faith.

During my illness, I also had my first experience with an ulcerated tropical infection. We had been advised to treat every scratch seriously because of this possibility, and the scars we saw on the legs of most children were graphic evidence that it was a serious problem in the tropics. However, when I worked on the engine I invariably got scratches on my knuckles and soon gave up on treating them. Fortunately none of them became infected. But this time, a scratch on my leg below the knee did not heal; it grew quickly by expanding around its edges. At the same time, a large purplish streak spread along the underside of my leg as I lay in bed. This was one of the few times we needed to use the prescription drugs in our medicine chest. We treated the infection with an antibiotic ointment and oral antibiotics, and it began to heal.

We had a pleasant sail south down the coast of Efate Island with a following wind before we rounded the point, and then we powered slowly back up to Port Vila with a stiff wind in our faces. A crosscurrent created by a swift ebb tide made it difficult for us to stay on course amid the rock- and reef-strewn channel, but there were adequate navigational markers and *Tainui*'s engine performed well. We picked up a mooring buoy in front of the Waterfront Restaurant for easy access to town and consulted a local doctor about my leg. He approved of our treatment, but switched me to a more broad-spectrum antibiotic which, incidentally, cost only US$5.

Shortly after we moored in front of the Waterfront Restaurant, boats began arriving as they finished the 500-mile Fiji-to-Vanuatu race. *Princess del Mar* came in with engine trouble. They did not trust their engine for anchoring in the wind and current among a crowded fleet of yachts, which was difficult enough even with an engine. We were on a secure mooring, so we had them raft up to us for a week while Jim repaired their engine. Jim and Gwen were pleasantly surprised by the official checking in of the yachts that were in the race. Jim described the process in his self-published book, <u>Circumnavigation of Princess del Mar</u>. "Customs came aboard and, in the true spirit of the race, not only cleared us easily, but presented us with a package of goodies: a six-pack of local beer, two T-shirts, a bag of fruit, and several coupons from local businesses."

We attended the official Pig Feed and Award Ceremony for the racers at the Waterfront Restaurant. It was a festive event. Although it was called a race, it was much more informal than that name implied. Every boat got a prize for something. *Princess del Mar* was awarded the prize for the first boat to finish with a cat aboard. Jim captured the nature of the event in his book when he said, "We did not win the smallest fish contest, however. We were beat out by just a few millimeters by someone who very skillfully cut out the middle portion of a flying fish and joined it together, all in the outlandish spirit of this whole event."

We enjoyed the week of their company, and we also visited back and forth on more yachts than we ever had before. The farther we traveled, the more the gatherings of yachts in these ports took on the character of class reunions—we even referred to ourselves as "classes" according to the year we first crossed the Pacific. For example, we were the class of '89. Boats were scattered at times, but Pago Pago, Suva, and Port Vila were the major natural "crossroads" on the main South Pacific sailing routes. At Port Vila we were reunited with yachts from virtually every port we had visited.

On our daily engine run one day, we heard a crash in the engine compartment. The troublesome crankshaft extension that supported both the alternator and refrigerator pulleys had broken off where the Australian engineer in Lautoka had drilled deep dimples for his "grub screws," and the stub of the shaft with its two pulleys had fallen into the bilge. This was a major disappointment for us. We had already begun provisioning to depart Port Vila for some of Vanuatu's exotic outer islands. But it turned out that by the time we found a solution to the problem, received parts from the United States, and completed the repairs, we had to leave for Australia to escape the approaching hurricane season without exploring any more of Vanuatu.

Meanwhile, we did our best to enjoy our extended stay in Port Vila. We could run the engine because the water pump ran from a different pulley, but we had no alternator for charging our batteries and no refrigeration. We solved the electrical problem by tying to the seawall in front of the Waterfront Restaurant and hooking up to shore power for a reasonable fee. We converted our refrigerator to an icebox and hauled ice from town on foot. There was no block ice available, and the crushed ice melted so quickly that hauling ice became a daily chore. Actually, though, we didn't mind the walk, because it was a pretty town, and we always stopped along the way at a French sidewalk café for a demitasse of strong coffee and a pastry.

The Waterfront Restaurant was a popular gathering place, featuring wonderful steak dinners from local beef. An American rancher had helped establish beef-cattle ranches in Vanuatu. On our excursions out of town, we saw fat beef cattle standing belly deep in lush grass. They yielded excellent steaks. At the restaurant we selected our steak from their refrigerator and paid only US$10 for the steak and salad bar. They also featured coconut crab, which was considered a rare delicacy. A live one was always tethered to a coconut palm tree beside the restaurant. We never tasted that delicacy: its US$25-a-plate price tag was too rich for our pocketbooks.

The seawall extended from the Waterfront Restaurant along the entire shore of the town—a distance of a little over a mile. The seawall was a beehive of activity. There were about 20 yachts tied up to it, with frequent arrivals and departures. One day a large crane hauled a damaged Japanese yacht up onto the seawall. It had gone up on a reef in the Malakula Islands; high winds and a high tide had then washed the yacht over the reef into the lagoon. Several yachts went to the rescue. Because there was no pass through the reef, they had to haul the yacht back over the 300-yard-wide reef. To lighten their boat and show their appreciation, the Japanese couple gave the villagers all of their canned goods and dry stores. A large aluminum catamaran became the main rescue boat. The captain tore out the built-in flotation air bags that made his yacht unsinkable, and secured them under the Japanese yacht. At high tide, the crew of the catamaran ran two long towlines from where their boat sat in the ocean, across the reef, to the stranded yacht. After several unsuccessful attempts at towing, the captain of the catamaran decided that he needed a lower angle of tow to lift the Japanese yacht's bow up onto the reef, so he cut holes for the towlines in the transoms of his twin hulls near the waterline. About 100 villagers came out to help. When the catamaran was ready to pull, a dozen villagers hung on lines from the mast of the Japanese vessel to heel the yacht over and keep its keel from sticking down too far. Dozens of other village men went out onto the reef, grabbed the towline, and helped pull. Many of them got bleeding coral cuts on their feet. Amazingly, all working together, they succeeded in dragging the stricken yacht over the reef and into deep water. The Japanese yacht then sailed back to Port Vila without taking on water.

We checked out the yacht when it was up on the seawall and found that the extent of the damage was a badly scratched-up hull, part of the keel pulled away from the hull, and a bent rudder—surprisingly light damage for such an encounter with a reef. It was a minor miracle that the boat was salvaged at all. When the captain of the catamaran refused to take the compensation that the Japanese couple offered, even to offset the damage to his vessel, the couple were grateful, but embarrassed. Culturally it was extremely difficult for them to accept gifts without being able to reciprocate proportionally.

One Sunday morning, walking along the seawall, we met a redheaded young man wearing a Chicago T-shirt. He told us he was an American Peace Corps volunteer and confided that he was frustrated with his Peace Corps assignment. I told him that I was a former Peace Corps volunteer supervisor, and we all went back to *Tainui* and talked it over. He was an outgoing, sociable city guy from Chicago who had been assigned to a small village on an isolated island—a situation for which he was ill suited. He was suffering from loneliness and homesickness. He was further isolated because there was no Peace Corps office in Vanuatu—the Vanuatu volunteers were under the Peace Corps office in Honiara in the Solomon Islands, 1,300 miles to the north. He couldn't drop in to the office for a chat and had been reluctant to make a long-distance call. He was also embarrassed to acknowledge that he was not adjusting to his assignment. I told him to go ahead and call his Peace Corps office. They were there for his support and would want him to call. The next day he made the call, and the Peace Corps immediately flew him up to the Solomons for a consultation. A few days later he stopped by *Tainui* and told us that he was on his way home. He and the Peace Corps had decided that this assignment would not work for him.

Cruise ships visited Port Vila about once a week. We met two Vanuatu Peace Corps volunteers who were posted to Port Vila. They told us, "We can always tell when there is a cruise ship in port by the 'cadaver legs' in town"! These attractive young women boasted that they had dressed in their Sunday best and ridden out to a cruise ship with a returning shore party. They mingled with the crowd at the ship's lavish buffet and took another launch back to shore. These volunteers had adapted very well to their Port Vila assignment.

I went one evening with a small group of cruisers to a place said to serve an especially potent form of kava. We walked about a mile to a crude hut enclosed in a palisade-style bamboo fence. They served us their kava in half coconut shells. I drank a small amount, and my lips turned numb, which was enough for me. However, some of our group imbibed liberally and became seriously wasted. A few threw up. On the walk back, some said that their legs felt like stone. After 16 years in the substance-abuse field, I wasn't surprised that half the group went back for more the next night.

Eventually Larry, our son in Seattle, in consultation with a factory representative for our engine, worked out a solution to the broken pulley-shaft problem. They sent us a pulley for the alternator that could be added to the camshaft along with the water pump pulley, instead of working off the broken crankshaft. It was larger than the original pulley, meaning that the alternator would turn faster, which was not a problem. It also rotated in the opposite direction. I was surprised to learn that alternators could turn in either direction. With the alternator functioning, the engine was fully operational, but we still had no way to run the refrigerator compressor. We would be without refrigeration until we reached Australia.

By the time we had the engine running properly, we needed to leave in order to reach Australia, via New Caledonia, before the start of the hurricane season in the tropics. However, yachts at sea were reporting gales on that route, so we waited out five days of bad weather. Finally, on October 21, 1991, conditions improved. We went to town in the morning and did our last minute shopping, copied some charts of the waters ahead and sent a departure fax to our children. After a shower and a good lunch at the Waterfront Restaurant, we got away in mid-afternoon, after seven weeks in Vanuatu. *Princess del Mar* had left several hours ahead of us. The replacement head gasket that they needed for their engine was being sent to Noumea, in New Caledonia, and we agreed to keep in touch with them on this passage in case their engine failed and they needed a tow.

It wasn't long before I regretted having eaten a big lunch at the Waterfront Restaurant. We had good sailing in wind ranging between 15 and 20 knots, but the confused seas leftover from the recent gales knocked *Tainui* around with a jerky motion, causing one of my worst bouts of seasickness. Connie stayed below and checked in with two ham nets, while I stayed outside where I had easy access to the lee rail.

Conditions were the same in the morning, but I had recovered sufficiently to enjoy a light breakfast of cereal and papaya. The sky had cleared, but the wind headed us so that we had to point well south of our intended course. The wind remained steady all day and the seas calmed down enough that Connie was able to make a chicken stew for dinner. On the radio, *Princess del Mar* reported from a position 23 miles ahead of us that their engine was working well. *Tainui* sailed swiftly all night in a steady 12-knot wind under a brilliant full moon.

The morning of our third day out dawned sunny and warm. The wind dropped to10knots and the seas became smooth and comfortable. The wind continued to head us, so we were still sailing south of our intended course. In the afternoon, we passed between Lifou and Tiga islands of the Loyalty group. Our Sat Nav had stopped giving fixes, so I plotted our position by taking compass bearings on these two islands. By the time we cleared Lifou, the wind had backed enough that we were able to lay a direct course again. The wind dropped below 10 knots during the night, which made for slow sailing but restful sleep.

The next day we sailed and motor-sailed, as dictated by fluky on-and-off winds. We reached the southeast end of Grande Terre, New Caledonia's main island, late in the day. Grand Terre was a narrow island about 250 miles long, lying at a 45-degree angle from southeast to northwest. Noumea was 45 miles up its west coast. The approach to Noumea was through the Havannah Channel, which ran through a complex of reefs. *Princess del Mar* was anchored for the night partway up the channel in Prony Bay. A favorable current moved us quickly through the channel and we anchored alongside them at 7:30 p.m. We had come far enough south that it was still light—in the equatorial tropics the sunset at 7:00 and it was completely dark by 7:15.

We got up at 6:00 a.m. and were under way alongside *Princess del Mar* in less than an hour, in order to catch the ingoing tide in tricky Wooden Passage. Our Sat Nav, which had worked intermittently the day before, apparently benefited from the night's rest and gave frequent fixes, which were most useful as we motored all the way to Noumea through a minefield of reefs. We checked in at the Port Moselle Marina at noon. Like all places French, it was expensive, but we didn't plan to stay long and wanted easy access to shore for carrying ice and running errands. We were finished checking in by 4:30 p.m. and walked to town to look around, send a safe-arrival fax to our family, and buy a few groceries. We returned to an impromptu cocktail party aboard *Princess del Mar*, along with crews of three other yachts.

As usual there were a lot of our longtime friends in the marina. We invited Bob and Maria from *Countess Maria* for dinner on Halloween Day. They showed up in costume. Bob, or "Roberta" as he called himself, came in drag, complete with wig and lipstick, and Maria wore white slacks that showed the face of the devil on the seat of her pants when she bent over. We had a good laugh when a South African friend, unfamiliar with our Halloween custom, dropped by. He was nonplussed by "Roberta's" repeated advances. We did our best to explain what was going on, but he went away shaking his head.

We were only six days in Noumea, and I spent most of it working on *Tainui* at the marina. My major project was to overhaul the mounting struts for the wind-steering vane. They were stock sections of aluminum pipe railing about two inches in diameter. The problem was that they were attached to the transom by L-shaped brackets, which supported them on only one side. (U-shaped brackets would have held them firmly from both sides.) In the case of our L-shaped brackets, the single bolts supported the two-inch struts on only one side and could not keep them from twisting when the system's heavy steering rudder was subjected to strong forces in violent seas. The steel bolts had elongated the bolt holes in the aluminum struts, and the looser they got, the more they moved and the larger the holes became. By the time we reached Noumea, the vane assembly rattled constantly. I removed the entire assembly, rotated all of the struts 90 degrees, and drilled new holes. This took two days and was only a temporary solution. I planned to replace the L-brackets with U-brackets when we got to Australia.

Noumea was a pretty little town. It had a very clean public market with a blue tile roof near the marina. The downtown had the usual French expensive look, with upscale boutiques, coffee shops, and restaurants. Old men played a game something like bocce ball in a park in the center of town. They threw steel balls onto bare, hard ground. They were adept at using the irregularities in the rough field to get their balls where they wanted them. Sometimes to blast an opponent's ball away they threw them so hard that we heard the loud crack! from a long way off. We went to town often because the bank would give us a VISA card cash advance of only US $35 worth of francs per day. This was not a problem for our short stay, but we still needed to go almost daily to accumulate enough money to cover our marina bill and provisions for our passage to Australia.

Fruit and vegetable market in a rural town in Fiji. (above)
Connie and Vern snorkeling at Musket Cove, in Fiji. (below)

Our "Third World" dodger freshly installed at Lautoka, Fiji. (above)
Off to see New Zealand. Gordon and Vern change a tire on our ancient
Ford Cortina station wagon. (below)

The anchor stone of the original *Tainui* in the town of Tainui, North Island, New Zealand. (above)
Goodbye to the Bay of Islands. *Tainui* rests at anchor as we await fair weather to attack the Tasman Sea again. (below)

Tainui anchored in Esema Bay, off the village of the same name, on Moso Island in Vanuatu. (above)
Esema villagers coming to sell us produce as they return to their village from their farm lots on the main island. (below)

Back of Gary's house on Moso Island. (above)
We wait for boat parts moored at the Waterfront Restaurant in Port
Vila, Vanuatu. (below)

Enjoying a pleasant meal in the cockpit in Port Vila.

CHAPTER TWELVE

AUSTRALIA

We backed *Tainui* out of her slip, spun her around, and motored out of the Port Moselle marina at noon on November 5, 1991, to begin our 800-nautical-mile passage from New Caledonia to Australia. The channel before us wound through a labyrinth of rocks and coral heads on its way to the pass through the outer reef. We had some anxious moments when we missed a navigational marker and wound up in a kind of no-man's-land in which we had no idea where the hazards were. We cautiously backtracked until we found a channel marker and paid closer attention to our navigation as we motored the remaining 12 miles to the pass. Outside the pass, we sailed into a cloudless sunset with a perfect 12-knot wind on *Tainui*'s beam. Our wind vane piloted us flawlessly, with nary a vibration or rattle in the struts, which I had overhauled in Noumea. That evening we enjoyed croissants, wine, and chocolate from a care package that Maria had given us at departure. Following our check-in on the evening ham net, friends on five other yachts contacted us to wish us well on our passage to Australia. We slipped comfortably back into our night-watch routine at bedtime. How nice it was to start a passage in such pleasant conditions!

I awoke in the night to the sound of the sails slatting; we were totally becalmed. I got up and took down the sails to quiet them and stop them from chafing on the spreaders. There was no wind for the rest of the night, so we each slept well when we were off watch and looked out for ships when we were on. In the morning, *Tainui* still bobbed up and down on a windless sea, so we motored for two hours to make a little headway and give the battery a charge. Light, fickle breezes teased us through the early afternoon. Each time we saw a little "cat's paw" of wind spread across the glassy sea, we hoped in vain that it would be the beginning of a real wind. Finally, in the late afternoon, *Tainui* beat slowly but steadily into a light headwind. We ate a big tossed salad for dinner that night in order to consume our fresh vegetables, because for the first time we were sailing without refrigeration. On the evening radio net, we thanked Maria for her thoughtful care package.

The wind picked up a little at night, and we sailed along quietly at four knots until 4:00 a.m., when once again the wind quit and left us dead in the water. While I was on deck taking down the sails, I saw the lights of a merchant ship heading toward us. Our radar confirmed that she was on a collision course with us. I started the engine in case we had to get out of her way and hailed the ship on the VHF radio. The captain responded and graciously altered course. Technically, sailing vessels had the right-of-way over power vessels in the open ocean, but we knew that a ship might not see us at night and that those aboard did not always listen to the radio. I always attempted to contact ships to make sure they were aware of us and offered to get out of their way if I was able to, because I knew they were hard to maneuver. However, most of them gave way to us. When a ship did not respond to our radio call, I held my course according to the nautical rules of the road as long as it was safe to do so. I was concerned that if I did something that would not be expected of me, we might get into a dodging game that could be disastrous. However, when it became clear a ship was not going to alter course, I made a turn so decisive it would have been impossible for the ship to mistake my intentions.

The pattern of windless mornings continued the next day. We motored from 9:00 a.m. until 1:00 p.m., and then shut down the engine and drifted. When light, variable winds came up later in the day, I put up all of our sails, and we hand-steered and played with the sails in order to squeeze as much progress as we could out of the fluky breezes. A steady six-to-eight-knot wind came up in the late afternoon, and we gratefully turned the helm over to the wind vane and relaxed and enjoyed the evening while *Tainui* plodded along on her own at three knots. In these light conditions, we were eating well. That evening Connie cooked up a spaghetti dinner with salad and French bread. Radio propagation was exceptionally good that night, so we had a good conversation with our son Tom and his family in Seattle. When the wind quit again at dark, I took all of the sails down, and we enjoyed another comfortable night.

We had on-and-off light variable winds the next 24 hours. Keeping *Tainui* moving was frustrating. Connie steered, and I trimmed the sails to match the changing winds. When we were becalmed, I took down the sails to keep them from slatting and chafing and put them back up every time the breeze returned. We wore ourselves out keeping this up all day. Had it not been for the roller-furling system that we installed in Fiji, repeatedly hauling the big jib up and down would have been too much for us. That night we talked to our son Larry at radio time. This was the last passage in which we could reach our family by radio. We were unable to make radio contact with the West Coast of the United States after Australia. Fortunately, there were no more long passages, and we were able to make telephone calls and send faxes to them from our ports of call.

Connie made a lot more comments about food in her log on these calm days. That night it read: "Canned ham, yams, cabbage, carrots, and onions for dinner." Such a meal would have been far too ambitious in rough weather. Once again, we made no progress at night. This trip was taking a lot longer than we had planned—we were averaging only 60 miles a day compared to our usual 100. There was no danger that we would run out of supplies, because we carried food, water, and fuel for three times the estimated duration of our passages. However, we were eager to make progress, because the longer we were out, the more we were exposed to the possibility of a freak storm or mechanical failure.

The next day we finally got a sailing wind. It was on the nose at first, so we couldn't lay a true course, but it backed off in the early afternoon, allowing us to sail directly toward Bundaberg, our chosen landfall in Australia. During the day a small seabird called a noddy tern was attracted to our wind vane, and interfered with our self-steering. It would land on the big black double-aluminum wind vane, causing it to swing down until the bird fell off, whereupon the vane would right itself. Each of these movements of the vane caused *Tainui* to make a sharp turn. When I shooed the bird off of the vane by hollering and waving my arms, it hovered six inches from my face for a few minutes before it flew away. That night Connie made a chicken and noodle casserole with coleslaw—we were eating almost as well as at home. The good sailing continued that night, with the exception of one rainsquall that got me on deck to roll in some jib and put a reef in the main.

A sperm whale surfaced 20 feet from us early the next morning. It was a giant creature with a high Moby Dick-type forehead. 35-foot *Tainui* seemed very small alongside it. The whale took a long look at us with one big eye, then slowly slipped beneath the water, and disappeared.

We were thrilled to be so close to this magnificent creature. The comfortable sailing wind continued, but the waves became bigger and bigger. This was worrisome, because they were probably coming from a low-pressure cell in the Solomon Islands that was showing signs of becoming a cyclonic depression. We had been following its progress on the radio and were hoping it would pass to the east of us. By evening, we had made an 85-mile daily run—not great, but the best run of this trip. That night we had the first uncomfortable night of the passage as *Tainui* rolled heavily in the building seas.

The wind remained far enough to the north to allow us to stay on course the next morning. Without refrigeration, we were out of fresh meat, so I put out two fishing lines. Almost immediately, I had a dorado on each line. While I struggled to net one of them, the other shook itself loose, which was a good thing, because without refrigeration we couldn't have kept them both. In fact, we cut fillets for two meals off the one we caught and threw the rest into the sea. The fillets gave us two delicious evening meals; this was our first dorado, and we immediately put it high on our list of favorite fish. By afternoon, the wind headed us to the point that we could longer sail our intended course toward Bundaberg and continued that way at 12 to 15 knots all night. We were being forced well south of our course and knew that if the wind didn't back off, we would have to do some tacking to reach Bundaberg, but we thought that we could still get there in a reasonable amount of time.

The next day the wind increased to 15 to 20 knots from the same direction, and we continued to beat to the south of our course. *Tainui* periodically stalled to two or three knots as she plowed into the steep oncoming waves and increased wind. One of our Sat Nav fixes showed us to be even farther south than I thought we should be. It might have been one of the spurious readings that Sat Navs were prone to, so I ignored it and waited for the next fix, but that fix put us even farther south. This meant that we were in a strong south-setting current. By then, we were so far off course that we knew it would take days of tacking against the wind and current to reach Bundaberg. We consulted our chart and altered course for Brisbane, 120 nautical miles farther down the Australian coast than Bundaberg. The course change put us on a close reach, and *Tainui* took off at five knots. We could be in Brisbane in two days if the wind held.

We had chosen to enter Australia at Bundaberg because friends had recommended it to us as smaller, less formal, and easier to check into than Brisbane. They had warned us that the immigration office in Brisbane was used for training new officers, which meant closer scrutiny, sometimes resulting in delays and stricter treatment. Having altered course for Brisbane, we would soon find out.

Our slow, peaceful passage was over; we had lots of wind the rest of the way. The nights were especially rough. The first night we had rainsqualls accompanied by thunder and lightning and didn't sleep much. The squalls were gone in the morning, and we sped quickly toward Brisbane in a favorable15-knot wind. The wind increased again at night, and *Tainui* crashed along in the dark at six and seven knots—seven knots was her maximum rated hull speed. It was noisy and bouncy and a little scary, but we put up with it because we were making excellent progress. That night a ship came alongside us and shined a spotlight on us for a while. We thought it might be an Australian Coast Guard vessel, but it didn't identify itself. We had had a similar experience with a U.S. Coast Guard ship off the coast of Washington one summer. Connie's log entries stopped describing dinner menus—canned beans with peanut butter and crackers wasn't worth mentioning.

We were only 50 miles out in the morning. The wind remained steady all day, and we sighted Moreton Island off the coast near Brisbane at 5:30 p.m. The approach to Brisbane was through Moreton Bay to the mouth of the Brisbane River and up the river to the city with a stop on the way at the customs dock. We couldn't reach Brisbane in daylight and didn't want to spend the night anchored in the narrow channel in Moreton Bay, so we hove to for the night near the Moreton Bay entrance buoy, 10 miles offshore. Because we knew that customs would confiscate all of our meat products, we ate our last can of beef stew. We had bought it in Noumea, and the French version, packed in a mushroom sauce, was a gourmet delight compared to the American Dinty Moore variety. After the ham net that night Don, a retired Australian harbor pilot, gave us detailed instructions for crossing Moreton Bay and navigating up the Brisbane River. We were told that Don's radio shack in his home near Sydney was a replica of the navigator's station on a ship's bridge, complete with a huge flat file containing marine charts for all of Australia. Yachts were welcome to call him for his assistance.

Keeping watch near the entrance to a major harbor required special attention. We monitored the courses of several other vessels during the night and kept a periodic radar watch to measure our distance from shore. Lack of sleep was a problem. We had not slept well the previous two nights because of the rough weather and keeping watch for ship traffic as we closed with the coast. I stayed awake all night, as I often did when we hove to near a major seaport, and I felt groggy and spaced-out when we got under way in the morning and faced the twisting channel through Moreton Bay.

Moreton Bay was large, but shallow. Even a vessel as small as *Tainui* would run aground if it strayed from the dredged channel. We left the sails furled to eliminate the effect of the wind and motored through the bay, ticking off the navigational markers on our harbor chart until we reached the mouth of the river. The Brisbane River was deep and wide and easily navigable. We motored up to the customs dock, which was on high pilings because it was designed for full-sized ships. The officers climbed down a ladder and boarded us. They took away our pork, vegetables, and dairy products—even though some of the identical products were sold in their stores. However, contrary to the rumors we had heard about them, they were courteous and friendly.

As we motored on up the river, our engine's heat-warning alarm sounded just as we approached a Sunday afternoon sailboat race. I unrolled the jib, and Connie sailed us through the race while I got the engine running. She was very tense at the wheel. We were supposed to give racing boats the right-of-way, but without the engine that was not always possible. If we had obstructed the progress of an avid racing skipper, we might have gotten an interesting Aussie vocabulary lesson. Connie feared that we would have a collision if one of these boats tried to force its right-of-way. Fortunately, I had only to tighten the water-pump drive belt. Connie wrote in her log, "Whew! What a relief when Vern got the motor running. I was trying to steer through a sailboat race, up-current in a strange river in a strange city in a strange country."

We soon arrived in downtown Brisbane. About 30 yachts were tied up between pilings in front of the beautiful Brisbane Botanical Gardens. As we approached an unoccupied pair of pilings, a couple from a moored yacht came out in their dinghy and took our lines to the pilings for us. They didn't know us, but after seeing others struggle to catch the pilings in the current, they rushed out to help. This kind of unsolicited assistance from fellow cruisers no longer surprised us.

As usual, it was a relief to secure *Tainui* after an ocean passage. Once we were tied up, we relaxed and took stock of our surroundings. The botanical gardens had ornamental flowerbeds, lush green trees, brick walkways, and fountains. A manicured lawn ran downhill to a brick walkway that extended upstream along the river's edge as far as we could see. To our right, downstream, the late afternoon sun glinted off the windows of the tall buildings in Brisbane's beautiful modern skyline. Bridges spanned the broad Brisbane River upstream and downstream of us, connecting the two sides of the bustling city.

We were tired from the trip and decided to finish checking in the next day. However, it was still daylight, so we launched our dinghy and went ashore for a quick look at the city before we crashed for the night. The dinghy landing was on a city dock downstream from the park at the foot of one of Brisbane's main streets. We were delighted to be moored in a lovely park setting so convenient to the city center. We walked off the dinghy dock into a crowded Sunday afternoon street fair that extended along the waterfront for several blocks. We shuffled along elbow to elbow in the crowd, as interested in the people as we were in the arts and crafts. After treating ourselves to a cold drink and a pastry, we returned to *Tainui* and went to bed early for a wonderful night of "no worries" sleep. We were to hear the expression "No worries, mate" over and over again during our nine months in Australia.

We felt energized in the morning and dedicated the day to taking care of business. We had cleared customs on the way up the river, but still had to check in at immigration and the port authority office. Immigration went smoothly because we had gotten our visas in advance, as required. At the port authority office, we were pleased to learn that our berth at the pilings cost only US$15 per week, including free showers and laundry facilities. We had paid US$18 a day in New Caledonia without the showers and laundry. Officially in Australia, we walked to the post office and arranged to have our mail forwarded from Bundaberg, where we had told our family to send it. Along the way we visited a travel agency and reserved airplane tickets for our trip home for Christmas. Because the flight would leave from Sydney, we walked on to the bus station and bought our bus tickets. While we were eating lunch at the modern West End Shopping Mall, Connie broke a tooth, so we completed our walking tour of downtown Brisbane by locating a dentist on fashionable Queen Street. The next day he put a gold crown on her tooth for a fashionable US$800. Ouch!

Yachts were arriving daily from New Caledonia. When *Princess del Mar* came up the river, we helped Jim and Gwen tie to the pilings and accompanied them ashore, where they introduced themselves to Australia by eating at McDonald's. We tried to stay away from American things in other countries but, since we didn't eat at McDonald's at home, we rationalized that we were having a new cultural experience.

A few days after we helped Ralph and Phyllis tie *Fram* to the pilings, we celebrated an American-style potluck Thanksgiving dinner with five other couples aboard the spacious 50-foot ferrocement *Fram*, which we called a floating condominium. Celebrating Thanksgiving in the hot Australian sun felt strange, but we had a splendid time with a turkey dinner, good wine, and the company of people who had become, and still are, among our best friends. Connie was amused that she had to cook the turkey on 35-foot *Tainui*, because the oven on 50-foot *Fram* wasn't big enough.

Just as we were getting ready to fly home, an American cruising couple told us a worrisome story about their attempt to get permission to leave their yacht in Brisbane while they flew home. The port captain asked for a bond based on a percentage of the value of their boat. The amount of the bond was so high they couldn't pay it. They pleaded, but the port captain was adamant. When the cruising wife broke down and cried at the prospect of not being able to be with her family at Christmas, the port officials were so embarrassed that they decided it was a family emergency and made an exception. When our turn came, they asked us for a US$15,000 bond—at least we had been spared the shock. The port captain explained that it was to cover the cost of disposing of our boat if we abandoned it. To us, this was ridiculous—the yachts on the Brisbane pilings were all worth far more than the cost of disposing of them, and none of us would abandon our yacht for 20 percent of its value. We kept our cool and negotiated until they accepted our round-trip airplane tickets as sufficient assurance of our intention to return. We paid them US$54 in advance for two month's moorage, and they checked us out.

Later, a fellow sailor, Joe Fern, had an amusing experience when he asked the port captain for permission to leave his expensive yacht, *Champagne*, while he went back to work in the United States for nine months. They took this very seriously and would not relent on the bond. Unlike the rest of us, Joe, an attorney, knew what to do next. He said, "Okay. I give in. Where have people been buying their bonds for this purpose?" The port captain looked embarrassed and mumbled, "Ah … that is … well … er … we've never actually collected one." Apparently in all previous cases, either they had given in or the sailors had given up. Following this admission, they gave Joe permission to leave *Champagne* without posting a bond.

After our port office experience, we took the bus to Sydney, 430 miles south of Brisbane, and caught a 14-hour nonstop United Airlines flight to Los Angeles en route to Seattle. After two busy months of celebrating Christmas and a seemingly endless round of visiting family and friends, we arrived back in Sydney on February 12, 1992. We spent a night in a hotel in Sydney to recover from the long flight and flew to Brisbane the next day.

Our successful experience of buying a used car in New Zealand inspired us to try it again in Australia. We were planning major boat work, which would require a lot of shopping for supplies. We also wanted to see the country. I read in the newspaper that there was an auto auction every Saturday in Brisbane, and Connie and I went there the next Saturday morning. We arrived late and had only 15 minutes to examine the cars. We were allowed to start the engines, but could not test-drive the vehicles. We hastily checked out some four- or five-year-old midsized station wagons and wrote down the numbers of our prospects. As we approached the bidding area, one of our choices was already on the auction block. The station wagon had a bottom price of A$2,500, but the bidding was stalled at A$2,000. The auctioneer tried for A$2200, and I raised my hand. Connie was shocked and asked, "What are you doing? The auction has just started!" I explained that I had decided to bid on the first one of our choices that was at a good price and not risk being outbid on the others. It turned out to be a good decision. The auction agency phoned the owner, and he let us have the car at our price. After license, insurance, and a certificate of roadworthiness, we paid A$3,000 (about US$2,200) for a late-model Toyota Corona station wagon and sold it four months later for the same price.

Parking in downtown Brisbane was difficult—we could park free overnight at a parking meter, but we had to get up early in the morning, plug the meter, and move the car from meter to meter all day. This was a terrible nuisance, especially when 11 days of rain followed our car purchase. We soon learned that other cruisers were parking their cars on the other side of the river on a little dirt lane that had no meters. The little lane was near the landing of a small pedestrian ferry. The landing even had a little brick waiting room that sheltered us from the rain. Thereafter, we drove across a bridge, parked in the lane, and commuted to the car on the ferry. The fare was only A$1 per roundtrip—a lot cheaper than plugging parking meters all day.

One rainy day we drove up the coast to the Cabbage Creek Boatyard in Sandgate to arrange a haul-out. The yard owner convinced us to wait and haul out after the rainy season, so we decided to take an auto tour of Australia before we hauled out. We bought an air mattress for sleeping in the back of the station wagon and an "Eskie" (Aussie for our "Igloo") cooler so we could make our own lunches, and set out to see Australia. We traveled for 25 days in the month of March—early fall down under. We drove inland on our way south through Canberra to Melbourne and came back up the east coast to Brisbane via Sydney.

Our route south to Melbourne took us along the edge of the outback. The outback is a red earth landscape sparsely dotted with gum (eucalyptus) trees. (There are many varieties of eucalyptus trees, but koalas eat the leaves of only one of them.) The eucalyptus trees had the amazing ability to survive fire. Their oily leaves burned quickly, but the trees regenerated after the blaze passed. The outback was crossed by miles and miles of straight red dirt roads lined with road-kill kangaroos. These animals were nocturnal and hard to miss on the road at night, especially because Aussies tended to drive very fast on the long straight roads. Fortunately, we did not drive at night on our trip. It would have sickened us to have hit a kangaroo. Some of them were as large as a person. Australian cars that traveled the outback had strong metal frames attached to their front bumpers called "roo bars."

We took the car ferry from Melbourne across the 150-mile Bass Strait to Tasmania and drove to the beautiful seaside city of Hobart. The passage over was rough, and half the passengers got seasick. Due to the stormy weather, they were unable to go outside and lean over the rail, so they barfed below, which created a very unpleasant atmosphere. Fortunately, the sea was flat calm on the return passage.

Buying used cars in Australia and New Zealand was one of our best cruising decisions. Walking and public transportation were adequate in Third World countries, where most people did not own cars, but not in the more developed countries of New Zealand and Australia. Having a car gave us leisurely access to the countryside and the convenience of transportation for our many errands when we were at a boatyard. After reselling the cars, the net cost of our cars for three months in New Zealand and four months in Australia was only US$500—most of which was for insurance, fees, and repairs—a fraction of the cost of renting or leasing.

After our road trip, *Tainui* remained on the pilings at the botanical gardens in Brisbane for two weeks while we waited for dry weather before hauling her out at Sandgate. Most of our boat work would be done on the haul-out, but while we were waiting I did some tasks that could be done while *Tainui* was in the water. I installed the GPS (Global Positioning System) that we had bought on our home visit. GPS promised to be a significant upgrade of our electronic navigation. I also overhauled the outboard-motor carburetor and rewired the bilge pump, which had been shorting out. In addition, I hired Ron, our new neighbor on the pilings, who had just completed a circumnavigation on *Ma'Leish*, to make some shelves in *Tainui's* V-berth area. We had been storing small clothing items like socks and underwear in string hammocks slung on each side of our double berth. These hammocks were unattractive and awkward to use. Ron replaced them with beautiful mahogany shelves that had removable railings. We stored clothes on some of them and books on others.

The Port Office Tavern, a block from the dinghy landing, offered a Tuesday-night steak dinner including a free glass of beer or wine for A$10 (about US$6.50). It was a favorite night out for yacht crews. Connie and I attended whenever we were in town on Tuesday. One night a male sailing friend of ours walked up to the bar wearing a tank top. The bartender told him, "Sorry, mate. We don't allow singles in the bar." Not understanding the Aussie term, our friend replied, "Oh, I'm not alone. That's my wife right over there." The bartender shrugged and, with typical dry Aussie humor, said, "Oh well, mate, in that case I guess it'd be all right," and let our friend stay.

One morning we saw a picture in the newspaper of our friend Don, from *Blue Goose of Arn*, in intensive care in the Marysville Hospital. His boat had been run down and sunk by a freighter. We read that he had survived with only the clothes on his back and his life jacket and that people in Marysville were donating clothing. We bought him a couple of soft travel bags for his new clothing and drove up the coast to Marysville to see him. He was out of intensive care and receiving visitors by the time we arrived.

He told a chilling story. As he approached the coast of Australia late one day, he spied a southbound freighter on the horizon. When it appeared to be well south of him, he went below to prepare food for the night. Sailing alone in a heavy-traffic area, he knew he would be on deck all night. He was only 35 miles out and expected to be in by morning. While he was below, the ship made a U-turn and came back and collided with *Blue Goose*. The collision knocked Don's mast down. The ship stopped and dropped two crewmembers aboard *Blue Goose* to help Don clear away the debris. Don felt he could still motor to port, so he exchanged insurance information with the captain, and the ship pulled away. But, in maneuvering away from *Blue Goose* in rough seas and 30 knots of wind, the ship struck her again, this time tearing the bow off of one of the catamaran's two hulls. At that point, the captain of the ship pleaded with Don to abandon *Blue Goose* and come aboard the freighter, but Don refused, and the ship left.

In the investigation that followed, the Coast Guard was suspicious that the ship may have been engaging in some kind of clandestine activity. Its reported destination was Newcastle, hundreds of miles to the south, and there was no legitimate reason for it to have turned back to the north and struck *Blue Goose*.

After the ship left, Don forced his inflatable dinghy into the damaged bow of his catamaran and inflated it. He hoped that it would keep enough water out to allow him to motor to port. However, before Don had motored far in the rough seas, the jagged edges of the damaged hull punctured the dinghy. It collapsed, and water flooded that hull. It was then clear to Don that he could not make it to port, so he prepared to abandon ship. He inflated his emergency life raft, tied it to the leeward side of *Blue Goose,* and went below and gathered up his important documents and most treasured mementos. While he was below, the wind turned *Blue Goose* around and put his life raft on her windward side, where waves bashed it against the damaged hull and shredded it. Catamarans do not sink as easily as monohulls do—sometimes they remain afloat for days while fully submerged. Don activated his EPIRB (Emergency Position Indicating Radio Beacon) and wisely stayed aboard as long as he could—his catamaran would be easier to spot from the air than a man in the ocean. But *Blue Goose* eventually filled with water and stood on end with only her damaged bow above water. Don then went into the water and clung to that bow, wearing his life jacket and holding on to his EPIRB. He was badly scratched and bruised as the waves dashed him against the jagged bow. After a few hours, *Blue Goose* slipped out from under him and Don was left afloat in the sea. His only hope was that he could stay alive until daylight when a search plane would respond to his beacon.

Australian Search and Rescue picked up the distress signal that night and launched a helicopter at dawn. Don had registered with them at the start of his voyage, giving them a description of his vessel and emergency equipment. They thought he would be easy to spot from the air because he had listed two dinghies and a life raft. The helicopter crew homed in on the beacon and searched the sea, but when their beacon detector indicated that they had passed over the beacon, they had seen nothing. They made another pass, this time looking for a man in the sea, but still did not see Don. At that point they considered the possibility that Don had drowned and his EPIRB was floating in the sea. However, they turned around and came back again, lower and slower, with a crewmember standing outside on one of the landing skids. He spied Don in the water weakly waving an arm.

A rescuer dropped into the sea from the helicopter and swam a lifting sling to Don. He tried to remove Don's life vest and get him into the sling, but Don did not part easily with his life-saving vest. He had been locked into a fetal position for hours hugging the EPIRB and depending on his life vest for his survival. He was also weak from hypothermia, had water in his lungs, and was disoriented. After a struggle, the rescuer got him out of his life vest and into the sling, and the helicopter pulled him up and delivered him to the hospital.

Don was very popular with the nurses in the hospital. He was a widowed, solo-sailing grandfather from England with a cheerful, indomitable spirit. His attitude toward the accident was, "It's just a boat; it's not me life." He mostly regretted the loss of his personal mementos. The nurses were furious with immigration for trying to get to Don in intensive care to ask him for his passport and visa, which of course, had gone down with *Blue Goose*. The intensive-care nurses successfully protected Don from officials and the media. Later we heard two interesting postscripts to his story. Don made a public service TV video for Australian Search and Rescue on the importance of life vests and EPIRBs, but it was never aired. The Australian Actors' Union blocked it on the grounds that Don had taken a job from an actor. Even though he did it as an unpaid volunteer, their rules required that a paid actor play his part. The happy ending to the story was that, the last we heard of Don, he was living in southern Australia, sharing his settlement from the shipping company with a new bride—his former intensive-care nurse!

Finally, the time came for the haul-out at Sandgate. We said good-bye to our friends in Brisbane when we left, because we would be going north from Sandgate up the Great Barrier Reef and on to Indonesia. We motored down the Brisbane River and threaded our way through a marked channel in shallow Moreton Bay. Out at sea we turned on our newly installed GPS. It was a fantastic navigation system. When one of our sailing friends got his GPS, he exclaimed, "It's not the best thing since sliced bread; it's the best thing since bread!" Our Sat Nav gave us a position whenever an acceptable satellite passed overhead, but sometimes these fixes were hours apart. The GPS was in constant contact with a group of 23 geosynchronous satellites and gave us continuous data including position, speed, course, time, and distance to our destination with an accuracy of 60 feet. If we had had GPS as we approached Australia, we would have immediately discovered the south-setting current that swept us toward Brisbane and tacked in time to make Bundaberg. With the GPS, I used our ship's compass only to set a starting course; the GPS then served as compass, knot meter, and position tracker, unaffected by tides and currents. Because all things electronic were subject to failure, we kept our Sat Nav going as a backup to the GPS.

On our short trip up the coast, the GPS guided us spot-on to the mouth of Little Cabbage Creek, which led to Sandgate. The Cabbage

Creek Boatyard was rustic in the extreme. It looked like a junkyard in a cow pasture. Bits and pieces of rusting equipment, some functioning and some not, lay about in the dirt and unmown grass. The manager helped us tie up to a rickety wooden dock for the night. At dusk, a flock of white sulfur-crested cockatoos flew in and roosted in the bleached white branches of a nearby tree that they had completely stripped of leaves and bark.

In the morning, I looked up the manager to discuss the haul-out and check out the facilities. I found him sitting outside of his office in a wooden chair with his pet cockatoo in a cage beside him. Having been warned that he was a temperamental sort who could be hard to get along with, I made an extra effort to be polite and cooperative. We got along well, but I had the feeling that I was walking on eggshells whenever we conferred about the work. He said he would haul us out at 5:00 that afternoon, when the tide was right. Looking at the facilities, I knew that Connie would find the bathroom disgusting and the prospect of climbing off the boat and finding it in the night totally unacceptable.

Our major task was to repaint the hull. The paint and deck tread we had put on in New Zealand had held up beautifully on the deck and house, but the coal-tar epoxy on the hull required major touching up, as it had done every time we hauled out. This time I planned to paint the entire hull with high-quality two-part epoxy paint. I hired Ron from *Ma'Leish* to do the painting, and he and I consulted with a technical representative of a company that made such a paint system. Ron followed their specifications for the standard of sandblasting, the type and amount of metal etch-primer, and the number of coats of high-build filler needed to create an impermeable water barrier before applying the glossy blue topcoat.

During the week of sandblasting and painting, Connie and I stayed in a caravan park in a nearby town. I had promised her in New Zealand that we would never stay aboard at a boatyard again, and promise or no promise, I knew she would not stay in this one. The caravan park units were small, square mini mobile-home trailers. They were almost new and were well furnished. I commuted to the boatyard daily to supervise the painting, and Connie usually stayed in the caravan and read or watched TV. I came back for lunch, and sometimes on my way back to the boatyard I stopped at a pie shop in Sandgate and bought a bag of savory pies for the workers. In Australia "pies" generally meant meat pies rather than dessert pies; they were the Aussie equivalent of our hamburgers.

Burger King and Mc Donald's were, however, becoming increasingly popular in Australia. In fact, American fast-food restaurants were springing up everywhere. We were disappointed one day on our auto tour when we drove into an Australian town and found its main street lined with Burger King, Mc Donald's, Pizza Hut, Kentucky Fried Chicken, and Jack-in-the-Box. We looked at each other with an unspoken, "We sailed 10,000 miles to find an Aussie imitation of an American town?"

When we no longer needed to be out of the water, we moved back aboard and berthed *Tainui* at the Little Cabbage Creek Marina. It was clean with good facilities and a pleasant staff. While we were there, we had a stainless-steel arch built over the stern pulpit to hold a pair of solar panels we had ordered in Seattle. Several months after our original order failed to arrive, the solar-panel company had acknowledged that the shipment was lost and sent us another pair. We also replaced our lifelines, had new wind vanes made for our self-steering system, and got our refrigerator back on line by adding a third pulley to the camshaft. While we were installing our replacement solar panels, the original pair caught up with us. The solar-panel company didn't want them back because they then belonged to the insurance company, and the insurance company decided that I was not obligated to ship them back so we mounted all four on our new arch. They gave us 30 to 40 amp-hours of battery charging a day, which made a huge difference when we were sailing at night. We could run our running lights and use the stereo, ham radio, and radar without additional battery-charging time on the engine.

Tainui was now as ready as she could be, so we drove the car to Brisbane and turned it over to Ron, who paid our original wholesale price for it. We had lunch in the Queen Street Mall and took the train back to Sandgate to start our final journey in Australia, which would take us north to Cape York and across the Gulf of Carpentaria to Gove—a journey of 1,800 miles.

We planned to begin with a leisurely 800-mile run to Townsville, where our friends Steve and Linda Gallon from Corvallis, Oregon, were joining us for the leg from Townsville to Cairns. We would be cruising inside the Great Barrier Reef in a protected inland waterway dotted with many islands, several of which had resorts. On the mainland, there were many towns, river mouths, and bays where we could anchor and go ashore. Coastal harbor hopping was our favorite kind of sailing, and in these protected waters it promised to be as good as it gets.

On June 7, 1992, we cast off our lines from the dock at the Little Cabbage Creek Marina, took on a full load of diesel and water at the fuel dock, and motored down Little Cabbage Creek. When we reached open water, we hoisted all of our sails, killed the engine, and headed north on a sunny afternoon with a mild breeze. After over six months at Brisbane and Sandgate, it was exhilarating to feel the sense of the freedom and adventure of being under way again. We had planned to stop every night, but conditions were so good that when night fell, we kept on sailing. The wind increased to 20 knots at midnight, but caused only a light choppy sea because of the protection of the Great Barrier Reef. What a pleasant change from sailing in the open ocean!

Around noon the next day, we entered the Sandy Straits—a significant shortcut on our way north. The straits cut through the base of Sandy Cape, which extended 100 miles into the sea. The channel was too narrow and twisting to negotiate under sail—even motoring required constant attention. We didn't feel up to that challenge after our overnight sail, so we dropped anchor in the afternoon in Pelican Bay, just inside the entrance to the straits. We took a nap and spent a quiet afternoon at anchor. During dinner we watched the evening news on our little black-and-white Aussie TV, and then went to bed early and slept peacefully in the sheltered little bay.

We awoke to another beautiful sunny morning. At 28 degrees south, June in Australia was warm but not hot—roughly equivalent to December in Florida. Motoring through the Sandy Straits that day was like driving the boat through a ditch in the desert—bright white sand flats extended on each side of us as far as we could see. The strait was a labyrinth of waterways, many of which were false leads. We strained our eyes to identify the numbered navigational aids that marked each turn in the channel. Once, when we hadn't seen a marker for a long time, we weren't sure whether a marker was missing or we had passed one without seeing it. We motored cautiously on, feeling for the channel with our depth sounder. We soon found ourselves in five feet of water. *Tainui*'s draft was four and a half feet! We cautiously turned *Tainui* around without going aground, retraced our path, and found the channel. We anchored for the night at Big Woody Island, still in the Sandy Straits. A New Zealand couple aboard *Foxy Lady*, a pretty red yacht from Wellington, invited us over for a drink and a chat before dinner. They were also working their way north. That evening we were still able to pick up the news on Brisbane TV during dinner.

The next day dawned dark and threatening and we ate a breakfast of hot oatmeal. The dark clouds soon drifted south, and the sky opened up to a sunny day. The sandbanks officially terminated at Hervey Bay, which was a huge expanse of water, but the sandbanks still lurked just below the surface. We followed numbered channel markers through the bay for two more hours before emerging into truly open water. Once free of the narrow channels, we put up our sails and made a short pleasant run to Bundaberg. We took a slip for the night at the Burnett Heads Marina, which was at the mouth of the river that led to Bundaberg. There were only two other boats in the little marina. Later in the afternoon, a couple from one of them dropped by and shared some fresh sautéed prawns that they had just bought from a fishing boat. We served them drinks and munched on the prawns with them. The prawns were delicious, and we had a lot left over. We showered at the marina and walked the half mile to town for dinner at a hotel that had a great salad bar. They played Johnny Cash songs while we ate, which didn't surprise us. In many ways, Australia reminded us of American frontier culture.

We topped off our water at the dock and left the marina in mid-morning. After rounding Burnett Heads, we had smooth sailing all day on a broad reach in a moderate southwest wind. Sailing conditions were ideal because the weather was warm and the offshore breeze made the sea unusually calm. Conditions were still perfect at dusk, so once again we sailed through the night. We snacked on our leftover gift prawns on our night watches. It was cold enough that we wore a sweatshirt when we were on watch, but we expected warmer weather as we sailed north toward the equator. At 1:00 in the morning, the wind died and we motored toward Roslyn Bay, our next stopping place. When I began my 4:00 a.m. watch, I checked the GPS and discovered that we were a long way off course. The electric autopilot had quit. I had to wake Connie up and have her steer while I replaced a blown fuse in the autopilot. I turned it on again and crossed my fingers. If there were a short circuit, it would have immediately blown the new fuse. However, it worked perfectly. I had no idea why the first fuse had blown. We anchored in Roslyn Bay the next evening with no further problems.

The weather changed the next day. We awoke to cloudy skies and a light drizzle. We reluctantly ate breakfast below instead of in the cockpit. One of the pleasures of coastal cruising was eating outside and enjoying the scenery in the anchorage. The light rain stayed with us all day, but a good 10-to-15-knot sailing wind came with it. We spent the day crouched under our dodger watching out for traffic through the windshield, while the wind vane steered *Tainui*. In the late afternoon, the wind picked up to 20 knots and the sea became choppy, so we made for the nearest anchorage, which was Clinton Bay—a small well-protected harbor on the mainland. After getting the sails down and setting the anchor in the wind and rain, I was glad to go below to warm up and relax for the evening. We appreciated being able to find a place to anchor when the weather worsened instead of having to tough it out at sea.

The evening weather report predicted that the 20-knot wind would continue for another day. It didn't, but a misty drizzle stayed with us as we sailed along in a moderate wind. About 4:00 in the afternoon, still a few hours from our next planned stop, we decided to get out of the rain and pulled into Supply Bay on the mainland. We anchored behind Townshend Island, which protected the entrance to the bay. I spotted some signs on the shore and read them with the binoculars. They warned, "DANGER! BOMBING RANGE!" Since there was no activity in sight and it would soon be dark, we stayed for the night.

There was no wind at all in the morning. We didn't like the prospect of motoring all day and would have relaxed at the anchorage, waiting for the wind, if it were not for the warning signs onshore. Reluctantly, we cranked up the anchor and motored out from behind Townshend Island. There was a little breeze outside of the bay, so we hung out our full complement of sails and drifted slowly away. Around noon, we heard airplanes followed by the thud-thud of bombs exploding on Townshend Island. We wondered what would have happened if we had still been there.

At the speed at which we were sailing, we wouldn't make our scheduled stop at South Percy Island by dark, so we motored the rest of the way. So far on this trip, we had seen very few boats at sea and had had most of our anchorages to ourselves, but there were two sailboats in the anchorage at South Percy—a junk-rigged craft and a large ketch. We communicated briefly with each of them by radio and learned that the junk was headed north along with us, but the ketch was southbound. Now out of range of Brisbane TV, we ate our dinner of baked beans listening to the BBS World News on the short-wave radio. The anchorage was exposed to the weather and a bit rolly, but tolerable on the windless night, and we slept well.

Our sailing hopes rose the next day when a beautiful broad-reaching wind greeted us as we left the anchorage, but in two hours the wind died. We wanted to make Digby Island that night so we could reach Brampton Island, where we planned to stop over and enjoy its resort, the next day. Unable to sail fast enough, we started our diesel engine and motored all day. With no wind, we were also beginning to feel the heat. The days were becoming warmer as we traveled north. We anchored at Digby Island at dusk and had a drink before dinner, watching a beautiful crimson and orange sunset. Brampton Island was still 60 miles away, which meant a long day's sail. It would take 12 hours at our normal cruising speed of five knots. This would mean arriving after dark, because there is not much twilight in the tropics, and we were approaching the shortest day of the year in the Southern Hemisphere.

We left at 7:00 a.m. the next day and ate our breakfast under way. We could only make three knots in the light wind, so we motored, hoping that the wind would increase during the day. A good sailing wind finally came up at 5:00 in the afternoon and gave us good sailing for the last three hours of our passage. We approached Brampton Island in the dark at 8:00 p.m. Using our GPS, radar, and depth sounder, we felt our way toward some lights ashore that we thought were from the resort. Fortunately, we were moving slowly when our keel bumped a rock. No rocks were shown on the chart where we thought we were, so we had guessed wrong about the lights. We stopped *Tainui,* turned her around, and backtracked into deep water, where we shut down the motor and let *Tainui* drift while we ate a late dinner. After dinner, we reviewed our situation. Replotting the GPS position on the chart exposed our error. Encouraged by a rising full moon that gave surprisingly good visibility, we proceeded cautiously toward the actual lights of the resort. We soon found a small fleet of anchored boats and, much relieved, we dropped our anchor among them by the light of the moon.

After breakfast the next day, we swung our dinghy over the side and motored to the resort. A high tide made it possible for us to motor all the way to the dock. The beach was so long and shallow that the dock was inaccessible at low tide. We checked in at the resort office and got permission to use its facilities—a restaurant, a take-out food stand, and showers. We started with the showers—cold water only—and then had a cool drink at an umbrella table by the pool, where we lingered to enjoy the scenic beauty of the island. A flock of brightly colored lorikeets was eating at a large bird feeder nearby. They were so tame that they landed on our head and shoulders and took food from our hands. We would have stayed longer but had to go back to *Tainui* before the low tide stranded our dinghy.

In the afternoon we went back to the island for a hike and dinner. It was low tide, so we took our dinghy to a deepwater dock about a mile from the resort. This dock was the landing place for the boats that brought tourists to the resort. We walked back to the resort on a trail beside a little tramway that transported resort guests between the dock and the resort. Before dinner, we took a three-mile hike up Mount Brampton on a switchback trail that had many scenic turnouts. The sea was especially beautiful from above. Coral heads, rocks, and white sandy patches on the seabed were plainly visible through the sparkling, transparent blue-green water.

The trail back to the resort took us along the 18th hole of the golf course. We were amused to see an emu and a kangaroo on the fairway. I wondered what golfers thought about that. Could an emu swallow a golf ball? Back home I told people, "The kangaroos pick up the golf balls and put them into their pockets." Some half believed me until I added, "Then they sell them back to the golfers for 50 cents apiece."

That evening we were joined for dinner at the resort restaurant by Rhona, the skipper of *Cacique,* and two women who had joined her for two weeks of cruising behind the Great Barrier Reef. Rhona was from England and had been cruising—mostly alone—for 10 years. A typical single-hander, she was an independent, self-sufficient person. The restaurant building was of indoor/outdoor tropical-style with a grass roof and open sides and was adorned with colored lanterns. We ate, drank, talked, and laughed into the night. We had enjoyed our 12 days of smooth sailing and quiet anchorages, but we also found this taste of resort life to be very pleasant.

The moon was not up yet when the five of us left the restaurant. We had to walk back to our dinghies in the pitch-black night with no flashlights. We couldn't see the trail, so we walked on the tramline's cross ties. We had to feel for each cross tie with our feet. At one point, Connie stumbled and rolled down a small embankment. She climbed back to the track, shaken up but unhurt. An unusually low tide had left our dinghies high and dry at the deepwater dock, so we dragged them a few yards over sand and rocks to the water.

During the night, an onshore wind came up, setting up a steep chop and making the beach a lee shore. *Tainui* bucked hard on her anchor chain in the choppy waves. I got up and set up a snubber to take the shock. The snubber was a length of stretchy nylon line that bridged a loop in the chain so that the nylon, instead of the chain, took the shock when a wave jerked *Tainui*'s bow. It made it much quieter below, but we had to interrupt our sleep by taking turns keeping an anchor watch to make sure we did not drag toward the lee shore.

There was no wind in the morning, and not being in a bombing range, we sat in the cockpit and took our time at breakfast before making a late departure. This leg of our trip reminded us of sailing among the San Juan Islands in Washington State—fluky winds and lots of islands. We sailed when we could and motored when we had to. Our electric autopilot quit, so we hand steered when we motored. By late afternoon we were tired of the constant sail changes and anchored beside a small island. Based on the previous night's lee shore experience and the marine weather forecast, we anchored on what should have been the lee of the island. Around midnight, however, a strong wind blew onshore, bouncing *Tainui* on the incoming waves. The V-berth was so active and noisy that we left it. I slept on the settee, and Connie made her bed on the convertible galley table. This arrangement was reasonably comfortable, but because we were again on a lee shore, we had another night of anchor watches.

We slept a little later the next morning before making a short downwind run to the town of Airlie Beach on the mainland. I had not been able to repair the electric autopilot, so we were happy to be able to relax in the cockpit while the wind vane steered us. A group of dolphins entertained us for over an hour by surfing off of our bow wave. One of them repeatedly surfaced and smacked the water with its tail. We wondered if this was to flick off parasites or just a part of its frolicking. We arrived at the little town of Airlie Beach in the early afternoon, glad to have had a short sailing day. Connie helped me lower the dinghy into the water, and I rowed us the short distance to the town dock. We browsed in the touristy little gift shops and had an excellent curry dinner at a restaurant called Charlie's Around the Bend, where all meals were half price that day to promote its new menu. We wondered if the name referred to the restaurant's location or the owner's mental condition.

We were then about three days' sail from Townsville, where our friends Steve and Linda Gallon were to join us for two weeks. Anxious to get there in time to finish our maintenance chores before the Gallons arrived, we decided to try to reach Townsville in one overnight sail. In the morning we stocked up on groceries and washed clothes at the coin laundry, where we met an Australian couple from a 54-foot steel boat. Our conversation centered on cruising in steel boats, and they invited us to have a look at their vessel. It was a luxurious new yacht with every possible convenience, but at 54 feet they felt it was too big for the two of them to handle, and they had hired an extra crewmember. We were not envious. We preferred our cozy and easily manageable 35-foot *Tainui* and had no desire to have another person aboard.

We went back into town in the late afternoon to shower and eat out again. Connie used the women's public shower on the beach, which was a cold shower. As I stood looking at the "out of order" sign on the men's shower, a friendly gentleman gave me directions to the Whitsunday Sailing Club, where I got a hot shower. After our showers, we went to a Greek restaurant and feasted on kebabs, pita bread, and a Greek salad.

The next day we went to the telecoms office and faxed our son Larry instructions to have a new compass unit for our electric autopilot sent to Steve and Linda Gallon in time for them to bring it with them to Townsville. By the time we topped off with fuel and water, it was early afternoon and we could not reach Townsville in one overnight, so we sailed 10 miles up the coast to Double Bay and rested up for a nonstop overnight run the next day.

We left Double Bay at daybreak in unseasonably cold weather. It was winter, but at 20 degrees south latitude—equivalent to Mexico City's 20 degrees north—the weather should have been warm. We wore sweatshirts during the day and slept under two blankets at night. A moderate favorable wind moved us along comfortably throughout the day. With the wind vane steering us under sail, I worked on the electric autopilot, but had no luck. We didn't need it as long as the wind held up, but we dreaded the prospect of taking turns hand-steering through the coming night if the wind quit. Not only did the wind not quit; it increased in the night, gusting to 25 knots, which made for a fast passage, but rough sailing and poor sleeping. The strong wind produced short choppy waves in the protected waters. Much larger, but well-spaced, open ocean waves produced a smoother ride than the jerky, jolting, rapid bang-bang-bang of the short, steep wind chop that we were experiencing. Nevertheless, as long as the wind vane could handle it, it was better than hand steering. We made excellent time as the wind continued through the next day. In the early afternoon, we radioed the Townsville Motor Boat Club and reserved a slip. An hour later we dropped our sails near Magnetic Island at the entrance to Horseshoe Bay and motored the 10 miles across the bay to the town.

The Townsville Motor Boat Club was friendly and attractive, with good facilities for sailors. In spite of its name, which was painted on a full-sized motorboat raised high above the street entrance, many sailboats were moored there. Jeff and Margaret from the sailboat *Horn* stopped by, welcomed us, and briefed us on the yachting supplies and services in the town. They were planning to head north about the same time as we were.

When we arrived at Townsville, we had 10 days to get ready for the arrival of Steve and Linda Gallon, who would sail with us from Townsville to Cairns. We did the usual cleaning up of the boat, changing the oil and fuel filters, and inspecting all other gear. Our major task was to clean *Tainui*'s stainless-steel chain plates. The cables that held up the mast were attached to these plates, which were bolted to the sides of the boat. Rust had gradually built up under them. I tied rope halyards from the top of the mast to the scuppers on each side of the boat to hold the mast up while I took off the plates and cleaned, primed, and reattached them. Connie and I also ground out and painted a few dozen small rust spots that had accumulated on the house and deck. While we were in Townsville, I bought an inexpensive electric autopilot as a backup to the main unit.

Steve and Linda arrived July 3, and we all stayed aboard *Tainui* at Townsville for the next two days to give them time to recover from the long flight and to take advantage of the tourist amenities in Townsville. We attended an Omnimax film of diving on the Great Barrier Reef. Our seats were tilted back and the screen was a dome over our heads, which gave a very realistic sensation of diving on the reef. The simulated motion was so realistic that some people (not us sailors, of course!) got motion sickness. We had another realistic underwater experience at the aquarium, where we walked in a Plexiglas tunnel on the bottom of the sea.

We celebrated the eve of our departure from Townsville with a dinner in one of the city's finest restaurants and cast off from our mooring at the Motor Boat Club the next morning. There was no wind, so we motored 10 miles through Horseshoe Bay to Magnetic Island. After lunch aboard, we went ashore and took the bus to the Koala Park, where we watched these living teddy bears eat eucalyptus leaves. Some tourists took pictures of one another holding a koala in their arms. Back in the town, we had a drink at a small outdoor café, returned to *Tainui,* and sat on the stern deck watching a colorful sunset.

The weather report the next morning warned of winds of up to 25 knots. Connie and I were reluctant to start Steve and Linda out in rough weather, but they urged us to go for it. We needn't have worried about the weather. The wind was from abaft the beam, and we flew along with a partially unrolled jib poled out to leeward. We didn't have to worry about Steve and Linda either. They were a joy to have aboard—enthusiastic about sailing—and eager to learn and to help. They regarded this trip as a rare opportunity and embraced every bit of it—the rough sailing as well as the smooth. Seeing our cruising experience through the eyes of such appreciative people helped us to appreciate anew things we had come to take for granted. At lunchtime, we dropped our anchor in white sand and crystal clear water in a little bay on uninhabited Palm Island.

After lunch, we rowed ashore and swam and snorkeled off the beach. With no coral reef or coral heads, there were not many tropical fish, but we swam in the clear warm water, sunned ourselves, and beach combed for shells or whatever else the tide might have brought in. It was a lazy, relaxing afternoon.

The anchorage at Palm Island was calm and peaceful that night until about 1:30 in the morning when a stiff wind kicked up. The bay was protected from the waves, so *Tainui* sat comfortably in the water, but the wind whistled in her rigging. The high-wind warning was still in effect in the morning, so we spent most of the day relaxing on board and enjoying our protected anchorage. Connie baked banana bread in preparation for celebrating Steve and Linda's 25th wedding anniversary aboard that evening. When the wind dropped in the early afternoon, we got *Tainui* under way and made a short, fast downwind trip under sail to Juno Bay on Fantome Island. The first few times we dropped our anchor, it bounced off the rocks on the bottom. We motored around the bay until we found a spot free from rocks near Jeff and Margaret on *Horn*, the couple who had welcomed us to Townsville. After dinner Connie served banana bread on wedding anniversary napkins that Steve and Linda had brought, and we toasted the occasion with wine. The wind came up strong again that night, and this anchorage was not well protected, so *Tainui* rolled uncomfortably. None of us slept very well, but Steve and Linda accepted the conditions without complaint.

In the morning, we assessed the weather, discussed our options with the Gallons, and decided to head for Little Ramsey Bay on Hinchenbrook Island, which appeared to offer shelter from the prevailing wind. Again it was a short trip under perfect conditions—a 15-knot favorable wind stayed with us all the way. At the bay, Connie showered on board, while the Gallons and I went ashore for a combination swim and bath in the sea. We had guessed right about the bay; it sheltered us from the wind and waves, so we caught up on our sleep.

The next leg of our trip was a longer run to Cardwell on the mainland, where we could pick up some supplies, so we left early and ate breakfast under way. The wind was 10 knots out of the east, which gave us a beam reach. So far Steve and Linda had been treated to only perfect sailing conditions. They probably wondered why everyone wasn't out cruising the world. At Cardwell, we wanted to tie up to the pier, but the tide was so low that the water near the pier was too shallow. We anchored out and waited for high tide, but by the time the water was deep enough for us to reach the pier, a strong wind had come up that would have made it difficult to maneuver *Tainui* to the dock, so we gave up and took the dinghy to the pier. The dinghy ride was bouncy and wet, and climbing up on the slippery dock with the dinghy jumping around was challenging—another adventure for Steve and Linda.

We strolled around the pleasant little town shopping and sightseeing, and Linda made a telephone call home. Drinking water was available on the pier and our tanks were running low, so I decided to try to get *Tainui* to the pier after all. I anchored *Tainui* upwind of the pier, and Steve slowly paid out the anchor chain while I backed *Tainui* down with the engine until we could tie a line from her stern to the dock. This got us close enough to bring the water hose aboard and fill the tanks. Not wanting to spend the night in the rough water at Cardwell, we made a short sail up the coast and anchored off the resort at Cape Richards, but the sleeping conditions did not turn out to be much better.

We relaxed aboard in the morning, watching the weather. It was a little rough at sea, but the Gallons were not intimidated, so we set out on the 20-mile run to Dunk Island, where there was a resort that welcomed yachts. On the way, *Tainui* rocked and banged into the choppy waves, and the wind blew spray across our faces as we bounced along. The trip lasted four hours, and everyone took it in stride. By this time our visitors had adjusted to the motion of the boat.

We anchored off the resort in a sheltered bay, went ashore, made reservations for dinner at the resort restaurant, and took cold showers in a bathhouse for visitors. Steve and Linda took a hike in the hills behind the resort before dinner, and we joined them for a four-course gourmet meal at the resort restaurant. It cost A$35 each (about US$24) and was worth the price. Back aboard Tainui, the bay provided protection for a blissfully peaceful night's sleep.

After an early breakfast aboard, we got under way on a 30-mile run up the coast to Moorilyan Harbor on the mainland. We poked our nose out of the bay at Dunk Island into a brisk 15-to-20-knot headwind. We had a rough eight-hour sail to windward under dark skies. When we anchored at Moorilyan Harbor, there were several boats already anchored there. A solo sailor named Ivan, from the vessel *Navi* (Ivan spelled backwards), rowed over to say hello and came aboard for an extended conversation. (We figured that, being a single-hander, he was hungry for human contact.) Steve and Linda plied him with questions about solo sailing. After he left, we all agreed that sailing alone was not for us. Connie and Linda cooked up a delicious chicken masala for dinner, and we slept well again that night.

Moorilyan Harbor was about 60 miles from our destination of Cairns (Aussies don't pronounce the "r"). We decided to make the trip in two easy sailing days, but the weather gods had a different idea. We began by heading for High Island, 30 miles away, in no particular hurry. Reasonable winds of 15 to 20 knots were predicted. But, outside the harbor, we met 30-knot gusts under black, threatening clouds. It was a reaching wind that produced a fast but wild ride. In the 30-knot gusts, *Tainui* was hard to control. She wanted to round up into the wind, which turned her toward shore. Gusty weather was one of the few conditions in which our self-steering wind vane was overwhelmed. I had to hand-steer and constantly fight *Tainui's* weather helm (the tendency to turn to windward when the wind blew harder). Cold rain and spray swept across the deck, and we all wore yellow foul-weather gear.

To our amazement, we reached High Island at noon—averaging over six nautical miles per hour. Actually, I should have said we passed High Island at noon. Its anchorage provided no shelter from the prevailing wind, so we consulted our charts and decided to go on to Fitzroy Island. The weather remained unchanged, and *Tainui* roared through the 10 miles to Fitzroy in record time, only to find that it was also totally unprotected and unsafe. We went back to the charts.

This time we chose Turtle Bay on the mainland, another 10 miles toward Cairns. The wind was still blowing hard, so it was another wild ride with the wind whistling in the rigging, the waves roaring by, and the helmsman—most of the time me—muscling the wheel to keep *Tainui* from running toward shore. The wind was also blowing into Turtle Bay, but we were tempted to go in anyway. We were all tired from the work of sailing in rough conditions. Even those not at the wheel had to use considerable energy to hang on in the rocking boat, and we were feeling stress from the noise, tension, and uncertainty of our situation. We talked it over and decided to give Turtle Bay a pass and look ahead again for a safer anchorage. At that time we were only 20 miles from Cairns, but we could not make it in daylight, and I wouldn't enter a strange harbor in the dark—especially under these conditions. If the wind held, however, we could make Mission Bay, another 10 miles away, before dark. It couldn't be any worse than Turtle Bay, and it might be a more tenable anchorage.

As we plowed ahead, the waves became increasingly menacing. The Gallons remained calm and even appeared to find the wild ride exhilarating. Feeling the responsibility for the safety of the boat and its crew, I was probably more tense than they were. We reached Mission Bay at dusk. The anchorage was protected from the sea by a long, low sand spit. It was not high enough to shelter us from the wind, but it was a good breakwater. Steve helped get the sails down—by now the Gallons were accomplished crewmembers—and I motored *Tainui* into the wind toward the beach, hoping to get maximum protection from the waves by tucking in close to the spit. We crept in cautiously, watching the depth sounder. I didn't know the state of the tide, which made it difficult to choose the correct anchoring depth. Unfortunately, the beach was shallow, so we had to anchor a few hundred yards from the spit. The waves were tolerable but the increasing wind shrieked in the rigging. We had covered 50 miles in eight hours—a remarkably fast passage for *Tainui*.

We were all exhausted and slept well that night in spite of the noise of the wind in the rigging. There was no letup in the wind as we motored the remaining 10 miles to Cairns. Under way we contacted the Marlin Marina on the radio and reserved a slip. The marina was on the waterfront of the city in the mouth of a river. When we arrived, we saw that it would be difficult to safely enter our assigned slip in the prevailing wind direction, so we circled out into the river and requested a more accessible slip. The marina obliged, but even then we needed help from people onshore to corral *Tainui* when she came close to the dock. We were soon snuggled securely in our slip—a great relief after our wild ride to Cairns.

We spent the next two days ashore sightseeing in the pretty little town of Cairns and waiting for the wind to die down so we could sail the Gallons to the Great Barrier Reef. After three days, the wind was still up, and Steve and Linda were running out of time, so they took a cruise to the barrier reef on a huge ocean-going catamaran. The ship supplied the snorkeling gear and took them to the best diving areas. They returned ecstatic about their experience.

Steve and Linda still had a couple of days before their flight, so we sailed to nearby Fitzroy Island. Beating back and forth into light and fluky winds, this 15-mile trip took us six hours. We anchored off a friendly resort and enjoyed their hot showers and cheap happy hour. The next day we snorkeled off a coral reef that ran along one side of the anchorage. It was alive with colorful fish. I saw a beautiful but poisonous lionfish. I had seen lionfish in aquariums, but never in the sea. It was a very fancy-looking fish with oversized, lacey, multistriped fins that appeared to be designed more for beauty than for propulsion. It didn't swim but drifted to and fro with the motion of the waves near the coral. Even though I knew it could hurt me only if I grabbed one of its barbed fins, swimming so close to it gave me an eerie feeling.

We all took a long hike up a hill behind the resort. At each switchback on the trail we got a glimpse of the resort and the sea, and at the top there was a panoramic view. We could see the mainland to the west and far out toward the Great Barrier Reef to the east. We took pictures of *Tainui* resting at anchor far below.

We stayed at Fitzroy the last two days the Gallons were with us. We liked the little resort. It had a beautiful swimming pool surrounded by umbrella tables and palm trees, some of which grew through the canvas roofs over the patios. We ate our meals aboard *Tainui* to use up our extra supplies, which meant macaroni with cheese and sausage, and chili con carne with the last of our hamburger. Each evening we enjoyed our own happy hour sitting in deck chairs on the stern of *Tainui* watching the sun go down. It was a lovely ending to Steve and Linda's visit. Their last morning we sailed them back to Cairns and saw them off on their long flight back to Corvallis, Oregon. We were sincerely sorry to see them leave. *Tainui* seemed empty when we got back aboard.

I had worked for over a week before Steve and Linda arrived so that I wouldn't have to do any boat work while they were with us. As soon as they were gone, I went back to routine maintenance to get *Tainui* ready for the next stage of our journey. Our visitors could easily have gotten the impression that cruising was all fun and games—all you did was sail, swim, snorkel, visit exotic places, meet interesting people, relax in quiet anchorages, sip gin and tonics, and watch the sun go down. Steve and Linda were too savvy to be fooled by this, but if this carefree impression were to inspire anyone to buy a boat and sail away, reality would soon set in. I figured that boat maintenance was about a half-time job. This time, a few days of grinding out and repainting some rust spots on the ribs and stringers under the floorboards and a routine oil change were all that was needed.

We spent nine more days in Cairns—a few more than we had planned. When we were ready to leave, 30-knot winds and frequent rainsqualls kept us in port for an extra four days. Waiting for the weather to improve, we indulged ourselves in one of our favorite pastimes— hanging out in a small seaport town. We browsed in shops, ate in good restaurants, stopped for coffee and pastry in coffee shops, and hung out with the other cruisers in the marina. Joseph and Lucia, a fun couple on the large yacht *Out to Lunch* (the name fit their sense of humor), joined us on some of these outings, and we frequently shared sundowner drinks on each other's vessels. They were also on their way north.

When the wind finally dropped to 20 knots, we made a short, rough passage to Port Douglas. The seas had not quieted down from the former strong winds, but we had a following wind, which made the short trip go quickly. After so long ashore, we were a little queasy as *Tainui* rolled her way downwind, but we were soon securely moored at the new marina in Port Douglas. We immediately took a walking tour of the small town. Along with the marina, there was a railroad depot, three or four business streets, and a sprinkling of private residences on the outskirts of the town. We bought fresh-baked bread and treated ourselves to coffee and pastries at a bakery near the railroad station. As we strolled back to the marina, Lucia and Joseph hailed us from a cocktail lounge. We joined them for the happy hour and some laughs before returning to *Tainui*.

At Port Douglas, we were able to pick up an Australian TV station out of Cairns that was broadcasting the summer Olympics. Watching the Olympics on TV outside of the United States was a learning experience for us. Australia, of course, gave priority to the progress of its own athletes, which made it difficult for us to follow the American participants. This gave us a glimpse of the frustration of viewers from other nations when they had to watch the games on American TV.

We bought a few groceries in town in the morning and cast off at noon for a short trip across the channel to the Low Isles. It was a short, smooth passage in much-improved weather. We dropped our anchor among a small group of yachts on the lee side of the island. The wind drifted us too close to another vessel, so I tried to pick up the anchor and move. I cranked the anchor winch until the chain was straight up and down, but it refused to move another inch. I guessed that it was stuck under a coral head. I tried everything I could think of to break it loose. First, I just kept it snubbed up tight until the wake of a passing boat hit us, which put an enormous upward pressure on the chain, but it didn't budge. Next, I motored around and pulled from different directions to see if I could unwind it, and it still didn't come free. Finally, a young man named Kim, from the yacht *Willow* out of San Francisco, volunteered to help. He put on his snorkeling gear, pulled himself hand over hand down the chain to the anchor, and dislodged it.

The Low Isles were aptly named. At high tide that evening, the larger waves swept right over the island and into our anchorage, rocking and rolling us as we watched the Olympic games. Fortunately the tide went back down during the night, and the island sheltered us as we slept.

The next day we set off for Cooktown with an overnight stop at Undine Reef. We beat into 15-to-20-knot winds all day and were glad to join *Willow* in the lee of the Undine Reef in the late afternoon. The reef was completely bare of vegetation. There was nothing on it but gleaming white sand, a flock of large black birds, and a small wooden tower with a navigational marker on it. In the morning we found out why *Tainui* had rolled so heavily during the night and why the island needed its own navigational marker. When we went on deck and looked around, the tide was high and the island had completely disappeared.

Except for the navigational tower, we might have been anchored in the middle of the ocean—there was not a speck of land in sight.

Unable to sleep with *Tainui* rocking and rolling, we were up at 5:45 a.m. and out of the anchorage by 6:00. We were not surprised to see *Willow* making an early departure along with us. It was just as well that we got an early start, because we had to reach Cooktown by 3:00 p.m. in order for the tide to be high enough for us to cross the river bar. The weather cooperated with a lovely 12-to-five-knot favorable breeze, but we still arrived off the mouth of the river with only 10 minutes to spare. I put out a radio call to anyone in the harbor who could direct us across the bar, and a local fisherman called back and talked us through. *Willow* was already anchored off the town. Captain James Cook, whom I, along with many others, consider to be the greatest navigator of all time, had come into this river to make repairs after his ship had struck the Great Barrier Reef. He named the river after his vessel, *HMS Endeavor*, and the Australians who later founded the town named the town after Cook. Cooktown was essentially a small fishing village built along the banks of the river. We walked to a store and brought some groceries back to *Tainui*. Later, we went back to town for dinner at a cozy restaurant filled with a group of convivial local folk—Cooktown was too isolated to be a tourist town. Back aboard *Tainui* that night, we had a last look at the Olympic games. Even little Cooktown had one TV station.

The people of Cooktown were justifiably proud of their relationship to James Cook. In his book <u>Blue Latitudes</u>, Tony Horiwitz gives an account of his participation in the town's annual celebration of Cook Day in 1991. According to Horiwitz, local people dressed in period costumes and reenacted Cook's visit to their river, imbibing liberally through the preparations and festivities, himself included. (He was impressed into service as one of Cook's sailors.) Horiwitz portrays the festival as a bawdy drunken party in which great irreverent liberties were taken with history, to the delight of spectators and participants.

Cooktown was the last town between us and Cape York, 1,000 miles to the north. Our first anchorage was to be Cape Bedford, only a 17-mile run up the coast , so we slept in and had coffee with Kim aboard *Willow* before we left. We stopped at the fuel dock for diesel and water and then rode the ebb tide out the Endeavor River. A strong wind blowing in against the outgoing tide created a rough bar. After *Tainui* crashed through the breakers in the bar, sea conditions improved, but it was still a rough passage. Cape Bedford was a high headland that jutted out from the mainland far into the sea. We dropped anchor in the mid-afternoon on what we hoped was the sheltered side of the cape. The wind died down to 15 knots in the evening, but fierce williwaws came rushing down the cliffs at night with a frightening roar, shaking *Tainui* and leaning her far over.

At first light, we gave up on sleep and got under way for Lizard Island, where we planned to spend two days at one of its resorts. One was a public resort and the other was an ultra exclusive resort that catered to the rich and famous. After a pleasant sail with fair winds, we arrived off the public resort in the early afternoon. We wanted to eat dinner ashore that night, but a rainstorm confined us to *Tainui*. Connie salvaged the evening by making a lovely curry-honey-chicken dish for our dinner. We consumed the last of our fresh meat, and there would be no place to shop for almost 1,000 miles. Unless we caught a fish, we would be eating canned food for several days.

Connie's bare feet got wet as she washed dishes in the galley after dinner. I discovered that the freshwater foot pump was cracked and leaking. I didn't have a spare, so I replaced it with the saltwater foot pump and capped the saltwater inlet. If we needed saltwater, we could get it from the sea with a bucket.

The next morning I went ashore to fax Larry instructions for sending a new foot pump to a future port. It turned out that fax service was available only at the exclusive resort on the other end of the island. I hiked over the hill to the exclusive side of the island anyway, figuring that the worst they could do was to turn me away. The palatial main building was set in the midst of immaculately manicured grounds. I screwed up my courage, walked boldly through the grand entrance, and explained to the woman at the desk that I had an equipment failure on my yacht and needed to send a fax. She was friendly and sent my fax at once, refusing to take money for it. She explained that they did not accept drop-in visitors because they did not keep any cash at the resort. Each of their guests paid US$800 per day by credit card and was then entitled to all of the amenities at the resort (I had noticed cut-glass decanters of port or sherry on the coffee tables in the lobby). There were no established prices for the restaurant and bar, because guests were entitled to anything they wanted without further payment. She explained that the reason for their exclusiveness was their clientele. The hostess dropped the names of celebrities who had been their guests, including Princess Diana. These people paid the resort's high prices in order to have a vacation free from public scrutiny.

Connie and I spent the rest of the day enjoying our side of the island. Connie showered on board, but I preferred a combination swim and bath at the beach. We hiked up to a lookout point at the top of a high hill behind the resort. A plaque at the lookout explained that Captain Cook had climbed to this point to scan the barrier reef in search for a pass large enough to return *Endeavor* to the sea after his men had completed her repairs at what is now Cooktown. On the way down the hill we caught a glimpse of one of the large lizards for which the island was named; it looked to be about four feet long. That evening we joined a small group of sailors for dinner in the restaurant. At night, williwaws swept down from the high hill that we had climbed and rattled our rigging and rocked our boat.

The morning weather report predicted winds in the 15-to-20-knot range so we set off for Howick Island, 35 miles away. The actual wind turned out to be at least 30 knots, but it blew from abaft the beam, pushing *Tainui* along at a remarkable seven knots. *Tainui* would rise up on the backs of the overtaking crests and surf down their faces, sometimes landing with a bang in the troughs. The waves roaring by on each side sounded like a pair of passing freight trains. But making a passage at seven knots was exhilarating. We did the 35 miles in five hours.

When we arrived at Howick, five of the boats that we had seen at Lizard Island were already anchored there. We were not well acquainted with their crews yet, but we got to know them as we shared anchorages on our way north. At Howick, we all tucked in between the reef and the island, which worked well until high tide at 4:00 a.m. when waves rolled across the reef and into our anchorage.

The next day we crossed back over to Cape Melville on the mainland. The wind was down to 15 knots—a perfect sailing speed. Connie must have been impressed. Her log reads, "It was the most beautiful sail we ever had." It was a joy to relax in the cockpit while the wind vane steered a perfect course and *Tainui* glided smoothly over calm seas. We called an oncoming freighter on the radio to make sure that the helmsman was aware of us. The skipper answered with a cheery "G'day, mate." He assured us that he would pass well to starboard of us and wished us a pleasant voyage. We circled behind Cape Melville and anchored in Bathurst Bay among a fleet of yachts and fishing boats. Rhona on *Cacique* had caught a fish under way and shared it with the yachts in the anchorage. Afterward, she and her lady crewmember, Jackie, came aboard *Tainui* for a drink. That night wind whistled though the rigging, but the water stayed calm and we slept well.

Our next destination was a fuel barge anchored in Owens Channel between Flinders and Stanley islands. Connie sat in a low-cut camp chair on the stern deck shaded by an umbrella as we motored the 10 miles on a hot and windless day. After we anchored in the channel, I rowed to the barge to fill our water jugs and check out its supplies—the fuel barge was also a limited convenience store. Water was in short supply, but I was told that we could shower, wash clothes, and fill our water jugs at the National Park on Flinders Island. Connie was delighted when I returned to *Tainui* bearing chocolate candy, ice cream drumsticks, and a box of wine. Australians were proud of their invention of the cardboard wine boxes with the plastic bladders inside. We called them "chateau cardboard."

On a round-table radio conference in the morning, the yachts in the channel organized a group outing to the national park on Flinders Island. Our five-dinghy convoy was composed of *Cacique* (with two English women) *Tethys* (with an all-woman crew from Seattle), *Freebooter* and *Rumoolu* (both with Aussie couples aboard), and *Tainui*. We motored two miles to the National Park on Flinders Island and washed our clothes and bathed in a freshwater stream. Then we crossed over to Stanley Island and hiked to some caves with aborigine paintings on the walls. The oldest paintings were primitive depictions of hunting scenes, and the more recent ones had pictures of the tall-masted ships of the earliest explorers. We returned to the national park on Flinders Island and filled our jerry jugs with freshwater. After our hot, sweaty hike, we all bathed again before we hauled the water back to our yachts in our dinghies. The day was a satisfying combination of social picnic and safari. Tired from the day's activities, we went to sleep early, which prepared us for a nighttime start on the extra-long 67-mile run to Morris Island.

In order to arrive in the daylight, we forced ourselves out of our bunks at 1:00 a.m. and were under way in a half an hour. We motored, sailed, and motor-sailed slowly in light, fickle winds through the night, and picked up a sailing breeze in the morning that brought us to Morris Island in the late afternoon. *Cacique* had caught another fish, and this time we made a group decision that whoever caught a fish could give it to another boat to cook. Connie cooked this fish and made a salad, Rhona and Jackie brought rice and a vegetable, and I broke out the chateau cardboard. The fish was short on meat and long on bones, but it was a good excuse for an evening get-together.

From Morris Island we made a two-day trip to Portland Roads on the mainland in company with *Cacique*. We stopped overnight at Night Island, a popular fishing-boat anchorage, and arrived at Portland Roads late the next afternoon. The community of Portland Roads consisted of a few houses scattered along a narrow dirt road. There was no town, but we had heard that there was the possibility of getting some supplies at one of the houses. After we were safely anchored, we picked up Jackie and Rhona in our dinghy and went ashore to find out. We landed the dinghy on a shallow beach at low tide, jumped out in knee-deep water, and pulled the dinghy up past the high-tide line. We walked down the narrow, dirt, deeply rutted track, which appeared to be the community's only road. Perhaps the community should have been named Portland Road instead of Portland Roads. We could see only two houses, but some lanes that lead off the road probably led to houses that were hidden from view. One of the houses had a café sign with the promising information that it was still a few minutes before closing time. We hurried in, but they refused to serve us anything but cool sodas. On the way back to the boat, a woman in the other house sold us some scones. It was hard to imagine a more isolated and ingrown community than Portland Roads. There appeared to be less than a dozen houses, and they were over 800 miles from the nearest town to the south, and that was the village of Cooktown. The resort at Cape York was 100 miles of dirt track to the north, and it had very limited services.

We hoped to reach Cape York in three days and spend a day enjoying the resort. We began with a relatively short trip to Margaret Bay in good conditions. The entrance to the anchorage was a veritable minefield of rocks, islets, and coral reefs, and our new GPS quit in the midst of the most critical part. We managed to negotiate the channel following the written directions in the <u>Pilot Book of the Queensland Coast</u>. The GPS revived itself once we were safely in—"Thanks a lot, GPS!" *Cacique, Canapus, Tethys,* and a 70-foot luxury yacht named *Sassenach* were already anchored there. *Sassenach* was owned by a wealthy Englishman who paid a crew of four young people to maintain his yacht and sail it to anyplace in the world that he requested. *Cacique* had caught yet another fish—this time a four-foot-long mackerel. *Sassenach*'s owners were not aboard, so her young crewmembers barbecued the mackerel and hosted a potluck dinner and cocktail party aboard the incredibly spacious and luxurious *Sassenach*.

The next day we left at 2:30 a.m. and sailed and motored 73 miles to Escape River. After a peaceful night in the river, we left for a short sail to Cape York. As we approached the cape, the crew of *Tethys* contacted us on the radio and passed on the disappointing news that they had been turned away from Cape York. For some reason, the Cape York Resort no longer welcomed yachts. We reluctantly continued on toward Thursday Island in the Torres Strait.

The Torres Strait was a narrow waterway that separated Cape York from Papua New Guinea in Indonesia. This straight was infamous for its narrow, winding channel through shoals and its adverse currents. The

GPS worked perfectly as we rounded Cape York through Albany Passage, but when we got into the Torres Strait, it functioned intermittently. Our transit of the strait was further complicated by a 20-knot wind with gusts up to 30 knots. I suspected that the main electrical-system ground was corroded, but it was not easily accessible, and I didn't dare divert my attention from navigating long enough to fix it. The intermittent GPS fixes could not make us instantly aware of the effect of currents, so we were very tense as we negotiated the strait. Fortunately, the GPS gave us just enough information to find our way to Horn Island. With great relief, we took shelter from the wind for the night in the protected harbor at Horn Island. As I had suspected, the electrical problem was easily corrected by cleaning the corroded ground connection.

We took the ferry to Thursday Island the next morning because Thursday Island had no safe anchorage. We bought fresh bread at a bakery and, as usual had coffee and pastry. At the bakery, we chatted with a local public health nurse and a schoolteacher, both Aussies. They directed us to the Anglican Church of Australia, where there was a memorial to the ship *Quetta*, which had hit a reef in the Adolphus Channel in 1890 and sunk in three minutes. Of the 254 people aboard, 133 perished. Some artifacts from the wreck were hanging in the church. We walked from the church to the Jardine Hotel and made reservations to stay there the next day, which was our wedding anniversary. The hotel was happy to have us—if we could get there. Our anniversary, August 18 was on a Sunday, and the ferry did not operate on Sunday. The hotel clerk promised to try to find us a ride. We finished our day on Horn Island with an excellent lunch at the Federal Hotel and took the ferry back to *Tainui*.

The hotel called us on the radio in the morning and had us go to the airport on Horn Island and join a group of arriving hotel guests. From there they brought us all to Thursday Island on the hotel's launch. We really enjoyed the hotel. Compared to our cramped sleeping quarters on *Tainui*, our spacious and lavishly decorated hotel room was a great luxury. We were settled in to the hotel in time for cocktails in the lounge before having a slow, relaxing dinner in the hotel's fine dining room. Later we watched an old movie, "There's No Business Like Show Business," on the TV in our room. Thursday Island had the luxury of two television stations. It was a treat to sleep in a real bed on dry land after so many nights on *Tainui*. We topped off the occasion with a late breakfast at the hotel before the ferry ride back to Horn Island on Monday morning.

From Horn Island, we embarked for our last destination in Australia, the bauxite-mining town of Gove. Gove was 400 miles across the mouth of the Gulf of Carpentaria, which took a Hudson Bay-like bite out of the northeast coast of the continent. We had a lovely sail in the morning in optimal 12-to-15-knot winds, but the radio weather report predicted that an unusually strong high-pressure cell moving across southern Australia would cause winds of up to 30 knots in the Gulf of Carpentaria. We were 15 miles into the gulf when we heard the weather report and considered heading for the nearest shelter, but we were making good time in fair weather and had faced worse winds before, so we pressed on knowing that the going might get rough. The night came and went with no winds over 15 knots, and we made an excellent 125-mile run in the first 24 hours. The next morning's weather report still predicted an imminent big blow in the gulf, but our second day out also passed peacefully, and we hoped that we had escaped the blow. However, the storm hit us with full force that night.

The Gulf of Carpentaria was much shallower than the ocean—less than 200 feet deep where we crossed it. Instead of building up well-spaced, long ocean swells, the strong winds in the gulf created a short choppy sea. The waves were only five or six feet tall, but they were almost vertical and were close together. The wind direction put us on a close reach, slamming into the wind and waves at about a 60-degree angle. Connie described the conditions in our log:

"The seas got very choppy. It was like being in a washing machine—waves were coming from all directions, and they were very close together. We pounded into the waves on a close reach all night. Neither of us slept very much. I couldn't stand watch that night—it really scared me—hearing the wind howl and being violently tossed around, with *Tainui* crashing into rough seas. I didn't feel that I could handle the boat alone in those conditions. I felt sure that, if I ever got to land, I would never cruise again." [This was one of only two times in seven years that Connie was too scared to take her watch.]

I kept watch all night, setting the timer for 15-minute intervals so I could nap between lookouts. I know Connie felt that she was letting me down, but I tried to make it clear to her that I didn't feel that way. I was pleased and impressed with how much she was able to do. She was helping me live my dream, and I never felt she had a duty to carry a certain share of the sailing load. Few sailors could have had a better sailing mate than I had in Connie.

The strong wind continued through the next day and night. Connie wasn't sure whether the wind wasn't as strong or she was just getting used to it, but she took her watches that night as usual. During the night, the 30-knot wind periodically dropped down to 20 knots, giving us moments of relief. The storm was still blowing hard the next morning when, with great relief, we doused the flapping sails and motored into the protected bay in front of the Gove Yacht Club. When I went forward to drop the anchor, I discovered that five jerry jugs filled with fuel and water had been swept off the port side of the boat. They had been tied to a plank that was lashed between two of the forward lifeline stanchions. The plank had been ripped off and jugs went with it. The five similar jugs on the starboard side had survived. This was the only time any gear was ever washed off of our deck. That six-foot chop in the Gulf of Carpentaria did more damage than the 20-foot seas that built up during our seven days of gales in the Tasman Sea en route to New Zealand.

We were exhausted after our two wild nights, but went ashore for a steak dinner at the yacht club. The yacht club was very accommodating to us. They offered a complimentary one-month membership that entitled us to use their free hot showers, washing machines, and inexpensive bar and restaurant. The clubhouse was situated on a lovely crescent beach, but the beach was off limits for swimming, and we were even warned not to walk on it after dark. The problem was the presence of one of the estuarian crocodiles that Aussies called salties. These were extremely dangerous animals—thought by many to be the most dangerous creatures in the world. The biggest ones were 20 feet long and 6 feet wide at the shoulders. Their huge jaws were enormously powerful, and perhaps most frightening of all, when any creature entered their area— animal or human—they almost always attacked. The salties also moved surprisingly quickly on land, which was the reason the beach was off limits at night. Every year, these creatures killed several people, usually tourists who didn't take the warnings seriously. Near the major cities in Australia the beaches were protected with steel nets, but as we sailed north we passed hundreds of miles of inviting white-sand beaches posted with round signs showing the universal red diagonal slash over the figure of a swimmer. There was a crocodile trap on the beach in front of the Gove Yacht Club. It was a 25-foot section of corrugated metal highway culvert with raw meat bait at the closed end and a spring-loaded gate poised above the open end. Before we left Gove, a crocodile was trapped and transported several hundred miles away.

The yacht club was located near a bauxite-processing 10 miles from the town of Gove. The red powdered ore was transported from the mine to the plant by a giant pipeline, supported about 10 feet above the ground. It looked like a tall version of the Alaskan oil pipeline. Loudly droning engines moved the powdered ore through the pipeline 24 hours a day. The noise was annoying at first, but faded into the background as we became inured to it. Gove is an entirely company-owned town. The company ran a free bus from the plant to town, which we caught after a short walk from the yacht club to the pipeline. Most other services in the town were also free, including schools, a swimming pool, and utilities. These perks were needed in order to attract workers to this isolated town in a desolate area with no freshwater, and virtually no other attractions. The pay was good, and there was not much for the workers to spend their money on, so many of them signed on for a few years to get out of debt or to save money to start their own businesses. We spent a week at the yacht club and made liberal use of its facilities. As the time for our departure neared, we made several trips to town to replace our lost jerry jugs and to provision for our passage to Indonesia.

CHAPTER THIRTEEN

INDONESIA

By the time we left Gove, there were only two months left on our three-month Indonesian cruising permit. The permit had to be secured well in advance and its dates could not be changed to accommodate our late entry. We were disappointed that we did not have time to sail on to Darwin and visit Australia's Kakadu National Park, which had been highly recommended to us by friends who had been there.

We sailed out of Gove on August 28, 1992, in the late morning in fine weather. The direct route lay between Wessel Island and the mainland, but if we took that route, we would reach its narrow rocky passes at night, so we took the longer route around the outside of the island. That evening, the wind strengthened and turned against us, and we fought hard all night to beat our way north.

At 4:00 a.m., Connie became sick to her stomach. By 5:00, she was vomiting and had diarrhea. We hated to give up the hard-won miles we had made against the wind and return to Gove, but did not want to get farther away from medical assistance if it should become necessary. We called Don, the retired ship's pilot who was now an amateur radio operator assisting yachts, to discuss anchoring at Wessel Island and watching Connie's condition for a while before going on. He reported that a sailboat had recently drug anchor and gone aground there at night. We thought we could anchor there safely during daylight, but by the time we got there Connie was feeling better, so we sailed on. However, a little later in the day, Connie had another attack of the same symptoms, this time with a fever. We called Don again, and he got a doctor on the telephone and relayed messages between the doctor and us. The doctor's diagnosis was "probably just the 24-hour flu." He recommended that Connie take aspirin for her headache and fever, and Lomotil (which we had in our medicine kit) for the diarrhea and let the flu run its course. At Don's suggestion we altered our course and sailed west along the Australian coast toward Darwin to stay in the range of help, in case it was needed. Connie recovered quickly, and after she had been without symptoms for four hours, we returned to our northerly course.

Sickness or an accident at sea worried me more than the dangers of sailing in storms and navigating through reefs. These were things we had prepared ourselves to deal with, and *Tainui*'s steel hull was strong and watertight. But sickness, fire, or accidental injury could happen without warning when we were far from help. Our defenses were our well-stocked medicine kit and our ham radio. We were grateful for the volunteers who operated the ham nets and the doctors who gave of their time to be available when needed. Connie's flu was not serious, but it was reassuring to find that help was available when needed.

The passage to Tanimbar, our first port of call in Indonesia, featured light winds, headwinds, and no wind—it took us seven days to make the 500 miles. Some days we made only 50 miles in 24 hours, and we were becalmed several times—once for 18 hours. In most of the calms, I motored for about five hours. This gave us 25 miles of smooth sailing right on course and kept the batteries topped up and the refrigerator cold enough to make ice. On two afternoons, schools of dolphins entertained us by frolicking in the sea around our boat. Most evenings, we played a word game called Crossword before we took our formal night watches from bedtime at 11:00 p.m. until sunup around 7:00 a.m. We also took advantage of our well-charged batteries to make extended contacts with our family through radiotelephone patches arranged by Jerry, our ham radio contact in Salem.

The disadvantage of the slow trip was the heat. We were within 10 degrees of the equator. (Indonesia straddles that line with Java and Bali a degree or two to the south of it and Borneo and Sumatra extending well to the north of it.) The heat was, of course, most oppressive in the windless periods. We had 12-volt fans in the cabin that helped us sleep at night, and we rigged a canvas sunshade over the stern deck in the daytime when there was no wind, but these efforts brought only slight relief from the stifling heat and humidity.

The most exciting part of this trip was our arrival. The island of Tanimbar stood tall before us at dawn on the morning of our eighth day out of Australia. We sailed slowly through its long and deep bay to the town, which was far back in the bay and well protected from the sea. I took down the mainsail and rolled up the furling jib as Connie turned *Tainui* in toward the long pier that extended out from the town. The depth sounder showed over 60 feet alongside the end of the pier, which was deeper than I liked to anchor, so we proceeded slowly toward shore. I took the helm, and Connie stood out over the water on the bow pulpit looking down at the water while holding onto the forestay with one hand and shading her eyes with the other. I kept a sharp watch on the depth sounder. I glanced at the pier and saw some men waving at me to go back, but it was too late. The depth sounder went from 45 feet to 4 feet in a few seconds, and *Tainui* bumped up onto an old, extinct coral ledge.

I reversed the engine, but *Tainui* would not back up. We had bumped over a ridge and dropped down behind it—*Tainui* was trapped. I saw a local fisherman in an outrigger canoe nearby and motioned for him to come over. This would be a test of my Indonesian language skill. I had learned the language 20 years before, while working for the United States Peace Corps in Malaysia (the two countries speak the same language) and I had had no opportunity to use it thereafter. I expected (correctly) that the fisherman would speak no English—Indonesia had been a Dutch colony. When the fisherman brought his canoe alongside, I began the following conversation in Indonesian:

"Good morning. How are you?"

"Fine, thank you."

"Is the tide going up or down?"

As I suspected (*Tainui* was already tilting), the answer was, "The water is going down."

"How far down will it go?"

The man showed me with his hands that that there would be about only two feet of water at low tide. This was bad news; it would be dangerous for *Tainui* to lie flat on her side. When the tide came in, she could flood through the companionway hatch before the water was deep enough to right her.

My new Indonesian friend handed me his bowline and climbed aboard. He helped me prop *Tainui* up by pushing our heavy-duty aluminum whisker pole down to the ocean floor on *Tainui*'s low side and tying it to her shrouds. Then I attached an anchor to a halyard from our masthead, rowed it out on the high side, and stuck it behind a coral head. Back aboard, I cranked that line as tight as I could with the halyard winch.

Even with these precautions there was a danger that *Tainui* would twist around and wind up flat on her side. While I was pondering what to do next, the fisherman offered to go get some long poles, if he could borrow my dinghy with its outboard motor. Considering our position, I decided to trust him and sent him off in my dinghy with some Indonesian money. He was back in half an hour with six long poles, accompanied by a friend and the friends' 11-year-old son in another canoe. They all came aboard, and using a special non-slipping knot that they were proud of, they did a fine job of tying three "legs" on each side of *Tainui*. Actually, only the ones on the low side were needed, but they were enjoying themselves, so I let them do both sides. In the process, they used up every bit of spare line that we had. Thanks to their special knot, *Tainui* held firmly at about a 60-degree angle.

I figured that it would take about seven hours to float us off, so when the men had finished tying the poles in place, I thanked them for their help and told them they were free to go back to their fishing. However, they found us to be more interesting than fishing, so they sat contentedly on our side deck as we waited for the tide to lift us. As time passed Connie felt we should feed them something, but our supplies were depleted after seven days at sea. She managed to find some crackers and cheese, cold sodas, and fresh fruit. They said that they had never eaten cheese and called it by their word for butter. I tried the Malay word for cheese, and they said they had heard of it but had never eaten it. I found it hard to believe that the Dutch had not brought cheese to Indonesia. It would have been like the French not bringing wine to Tahiti. The men ate up all of our crackers and cheese, drank all of our remaining sodas, and finished off our apples and oranges.

At about 6:00 p.m. we floated off the reef and anchored at a depth of 60 feet. When we took the poles down, fisherman number one guessed that I wouldn't want to keep them on board and asked if he could have them. I had paid US$20 for them, but I gladly donated them to him in return for his help. With some difficulty, I managed to send the men home so we could go ashore and eat dinner. We soon learned that these people had no concept of personal privacy. They would have been happy to have accompanied us to dinner. In addition, we were a special attraction; they were excited that we could speak their language. Lack of privacy became a constant problem in Indonesia. Sometimes, when we wanted to be by ourselves, we gave no indication that we spoke their language.

Before we left for dinner, Dhani, a young Indonesian boy, came out in a powerboat operated by another young man. He climbed aboard and introduced himself as an English-speaking friend of all visiting yachts and offered his services free of charge. Before he left, he invited us to shower and have dinner at a hotel as guests of his family, whom he said owned the hotel and the airport.

The tide was high, so we were able to motor our dinghy all the way to the hotel dock at the back of the pier. We had brought along a bag of non-biodegradable trash, which we would not throw into the sea. We asked a man on the pier how we could dispose of it properly, and he said, "No problem I will take care of it." I handed it over, and he walked to the end of the dock and tossed it into the bay. So much for ecology!

The hotel that Dhani directed us to had an Asian-style bath. We squatted on a tile floor, dipped water from a large, square, tiled tub and poured it over our heads. The water was refreshingly cold on the hot, humid night. We had a meal of chicken and rice with cooked veggies. All we were asked to pay was the Indonesian equivalent of US$2.50 for two Cokes. After dinner we strolled around the town and found that most stores were open at night. This was often the case in equatorial Southeast Asian countries, where the midday heat was oppressive. We bought bread and candy bars in a shop and bananas and grapefruit at an open-air produce market where the vendors sat cross-legged on the ground beside their piles of fruit.

Dhani invited us to breakfast at the hotel the next morning. He ordered us coffee, pomelo, and sweet bread and refused to take our money. With Dhani as our guide, we cleared in with the port officials and the police. He was obviously disappointed that we didn't need his services as an interpreter. Then Dhani took us in a *bimo* (tiny minibus) to his school. We learned that he was a 14-year-old high school student. He introduced us to the teachers, who were all sitting around chatting on the porch and in the school lobby—it was a party day in celebration of the anniversary of the founding of the school. The English teachers wouldn't let me speak Indonesian to them, because they wanted to practice their English. One of them asked us to come to his English class on Monday so that his students could hear some native English speakers. However, when we came on Monday, the staff looked surprised and uncomfortable and told us that class was not meeting that day because the teacher was sick. Their uneasy manner made us feel like this was an on-the-spot excuse for something, but we had no idea what it was.

A few days later, Dhani arranged to take us to a remote village where he said that wood-carvers would display their best work. (We assumed that he got some kind of a finder's fee from them.) It was a long and expensive *bimo* ride—US$25 for the three-hour round-trip—but the opportunity to see the countryside and visit the village was worth it. The landscape was surprisingly dry for the tropics. Foliage was sparse, the farms had meager crops, and the farmhouses were little more than shacks. At the woodcarvers' village, we sat on the floor in a stiflingly hot one-room house, where a half-dozen carvers showed us their works. Most of their pieces were small carvings of tall skinny human figures. Their most distinguishing characteristic was that they were anatomically correct, which was exaggerated on the male figures. In *Tainui*'s limited space, small was good, so we bought a selection of them for souvenirs and gifts.

The next day at the hotel the manager blew Dhani's cover. She informed us that he was not the son of the owner and that he had no business offering us free meals. Then she handed us a bill for our meals at the hotel. We apologized and paid the US$12. Then she officially invited us to use the hotel showers. Her tone of voice gave the impression that she was irritated with Dhani, but her story did not add up. If it were true, why had she only billed us for our Cokes at dinner that first night? We were embarrassed by the position we had been put in, but we did not appear to have been overcharged or taken advantage of, so we let the matter drop.

The day before we left Tanimbar for Ambon, we took our laundry to the hotel. At U.S$20, the price was steep, but we were not willing to do it by hand aboard *Tainui* in the heat. Later that day, the Turkish sailboat *Deriska* arrived. We met the crew—a British woman married to a Turkish man and their two small children—in town and went with them to check out while they were checking in. They invited us aboard *Deriska* for drinks that evening. We warned them about Dhani, and we were not surprised that later we met others who told the same story about that rascal.

The passage to Ambon was slow and peaceful. We ate breakfast in the cockpit in the cool of the morning as we motored through Selat Jasi (Jasi Straight) between Tanimbar and a neighboring island. We caught a fish as we sailed slowly along during the day. Connie said its red flesh tasted like salmon, but I thought it had a fish-oil taste. After a brief rainsquall rinsed off our decks, a light breeze moved *Tainui* slowly through a peaceful night and into the morning hours. I used the peaceful sailing time to track down an engine-overheating problem. A partially blocked hose appeared to be the cause. The hose was too damaged at the point of the blockage to clear it out, but the problem was near enough to the end of the hose that I was able to cut off the bad part and reattach it. After three hours of motoring without overheating, I declared the repair a success. Toward evening an old wooden Indonesian fishing boat altered course and passed very close to us, apparently to satisfy the crew's curiosity. They waved and shouted greetings as they went their way. We drifted through the second night at one to two knots on light and variable zephyrs—great sleeping, but slow progress; we made only 55 miles in 24 hours.

In the morning, we were beating into a 10-knot wind at three knots as we passed between two islands that had been formed by volcanic eruptions. Our chart labeled them as active volcanoes, but we saw no smoke or steam. The chart also showed an anchorage on the coast of one of them, where we could have stopped for the night, but we gave it a pass because the trip was progressing so slowly. The three-day trip turned into a six-day passage.

The rest of the trip was uneventful until we approached Ambon, when the incidence of marine life increased dramatically. A loud splash attracted Connie's attention, and she turned and saw a giant whale's tail rise high in the air and sink slowly into the sea about 50 yards away. A little later, a school of dolphins passed close to us. As we sat becalmed in the afternoon in sight of the island of Ambon, whales spouted all around us. It was calm enough to use the oven, so Connie baked a pudding cake to spruce up our canned beef-stew dinner. We hadn't made much progress by nightfall, so I motored during the night until we were 16 miles off Ambon and let us drift until morning.

When we got under way in the morning, we were surrounded by hundreds of dolphins and dozens of whales. Some of the dolphins came within inches of *Tainui*'s hull. A young sperm whale—the Moby Dick-type with the high forehead—surfaced and came directly at us amidships. A few feet away, it dove and passed underneath us. It was an eerie feeling, knowing it was down there and wondering what its intentions were, but we never saw it again. An outboard-powered outrigger canoe with two people aboard came close to us to have a look and disappeared over the horizon as we entered Ambon Bay. We anchored in front of the Tirta Kencana (ken-cha-na) Hotel next to a large Danish sailboat with eight young people aboard. It took us two tries to set the anchor. The first time it just bounced along on the rocky bottom. The next time, when I gave Connie the full-reverse signal, the chain jerked *Tainui* to a halt.

The anchorage at the Tirta Kencana was in a village a few miles from the city. We caught a *bimo* to town in front of the hotel. We could barely squeeze ourselves onto its narrow bench seats, and in spite of its open side windows and back end, the heat and humidity were oppressive in the little van.

Ambon was a small city—much larger than the town on Tanimbar. The streets were lined with shops and markets, and the sidewalks were crowded with people. Most of the shops were open in the front, and we could see piles of goods on the floors and pots, pans, and multi-colored plastic ware hanging from the ceilings. The traffic in the streets was a mixture of trucks, taxis, private cars, motorbikes, and bicycles—all going at their own speed. Vehicles drove on the left side of the road—I was glad I was not driving.

After lunch at the Halim (Muslim) Chinese Restaurant, we tried to check in with the local officials, but it was Saturday afternoon and government offices were closed. We had the same luck when we tried to get cash at the bank. We took a *bimo* back to the Tirta Kencana Hotel, where we drank cold sodas in their lounge and negotiated bathing privileges. The bath was another Asian-style splash bath. As darkness fell aboard *Tainui* that night, we saw dozens of men carrying oil lamps to small open boats. As they drifted out into the bay, all we could see in the dark was hundreds of floating lights and their reflections in the water—a scene from a fairy tale. We assumed that there was a run of a kind of fish that were attracted to the lights.

We were able to conduct our business in town the next morning. Indonesia was a Muslim country in which the Sabbath was Friday evening through Saturday, and government offices and banks were open for half a day on Sunday. We cleared in with the officials, got money from a bank, had lunch in a nice restaurant, and then checked out a supermarket. By our standards, it was more like a convenience store. Its biggest attraction for us was that we were able to get Best Foods mayonnaise and shortening, which we had not seen since Pago Pago, American Samoa. Otherwise the selection was very poor.

On the beach on our way back to our dinghy, we met a man named Simone. He was friendly and offered to assist us in finding any services that we might need. Simone also told us that our boat would be safe because we were anchored at a Christian village. Indonesians at that time prided themselves on religious freedom for all—Christian and Muslims were living together peacefully. Subsequently, there have been communal riots in which Christians have been killed by Muslims. We wonder how this friendly little village fared.

The following day, we tested Simone's offer of assistance. Connie asked where we could get our laundry done, and I asked for help finding diesel fuel and a new alternator belt. He said, "Leave it all to me. My wife does laundry, and I can get the fuel and belt for you." He took our laundry to his wife and then went with me in our dinghy to a dock where

I filled five jerry jugs with diesel. Later, he went to town and came back with the wrong belt, but got it right on the next try.

One day I discovered that I could see our anchor on the bottom in 40 feet of water. This surprised me because there was no pollution control in Indonesia and the water was usually dirty. What I actually saw was that the anchor chain had wound around a large rock as *Tainui* had drifted in circles in the wind and tides. I tried to unwind it by motoring *Tainui* back around the rock, with no success and gave up and went off looking for a diver. I had no luck finding a diver, but while I was gone, some men who had been watching from the beach went out and unwound the chain by free diving on it. We gave them cold drinks for their efforts and reanchored in a place where we could see that the bottom was free of rocks.

Later that day Simone told us that his wife had burned three of our towels while ironing them. He claimed that she had left the ironing to tend to a child. When she returned the laundry, we found that she had replaced them with three thin Chinese towels. She apologized profusely and insisted that we come to dinner at their house the next night. We suspected that she had taken the opportunity to trade three cheap towels for our more luxurious ones. It was not necessary to iron the towels, and we doubted that she could have left the iron in such a way that it burned through three big bath towels at one time.

We had a pleasant evening at dinner with Simone's family the next evening. They were a middle-aged couple with eight children and three grandchildren. One of their daughters had married an Australian and was living in Australia with him. Their house was a simple board house, typical of Malay and Indonesian village houses. They served a mostly cold dinner. The main dish was a bowl of meat, vegetables, and prawn crackers, all mixed together and served with plain cold rice and cold fish. The drinks were mugs of hot water. All talk was in Indonesian, but we were able to manage a good conversation. The experience was worth the loss of the towels.

We spent the next day preparing for our departure. We checked out with customs, immigration, the port captain, and the health officer. The health officer scolded us for forgetting to check in first with him but forgave us. Oops! We knew better. We stocked up on fresh fruit and vegetables at an open-air market, and meat, cheese, and canned goods at another poor excuse for a supermarket. A wind change brought big seas into the anchorage that night, making the motion aboard *Tainui* so wild that it was hard to sleep—not the best preparation for going to sea again. Fortunately, the conditions had calmed down by morning.

We got the anchor up and were under way from Ambon at 8:00 a.m. We were headed for the Butung Strait, 300 nautical miles westward across the Banda Sea. We motored out of the bay at Ambon into a flat, calm sea. There was no wind, and it was already hot. I kept on motoring, just because it would have been depressing to sit there in sight of land. Three hours later a lovely 10-to-15-knot wind came up from aft of our starboard beam, sending us along smoothly at five knots. In the afternoon, Connie called my attention to a whale spouting a few hundred yards in front of us. The next time we saw it, it was only a few yards from us. The whale spouted with a loud "whoosh!" and filled the air with its foul-smelling, fishy breath. The whale disappeared, but the following wind stayed with us through the night. *Tainui* rolled quite a bit, which was not good for sleeping, but in the morning our GPS put us 110 miles out of Ambon.

The next day was much the same, but the wind dropped to 10 knots at night, allowing us to catch up on our sleep. Two local ships approached us at the same time from opposite directions during the night. They came very close to us, and it appeared to us that they almost collided after they passed us.

The wind picked up the next morning and backed further until it was coming straight over our stern, which dramatically increased the rolling of the boat. I felt a little nauseated most of the day, but staved off seasickness by staying out in the cockpit as much as I could. Connie handled the inside chores—the radio, navigation, and meals. The wind calmed again at night and a good sleep settled my stomach. However, the night was cut short when Connie woke me at 4:00 a.m. with the news that the GPS put us 10 miles from Butung Island. We sailed slowly ahead until our radar gave us a clear image of the island and hove to eight miles offshore. We kept a radar watch for the rest of the night and discovered that a current was setting us slowly toward the island but, it had advanced us only one mile by dawn.

The Butung Strait was a narrow north-south waterway between Butung and Raja Muna islands, which were just off the southeast corner of the island of Sulawesi (formerly Celebes). We skirted the north end of Butung Island, turned south, and sailed slowly toward the strait in a light breeze. Three whales surfaced in the entrance to the strait as we approached. One of them raised its giant fluke high in the air as it dove. Our peaceful entrance into the strait was shattered by a violent rainsquall. Connie and I scrambled to ease the mainsail and furl the jib. I started the motor, turned *Tainui* into the wind, and hove to. After the squall passed, we motored 12 miles down the strait with Butung Island on our port side and Raja Muna Island to starboard. Although it was still morning, we entered a little bay on the shore of Butung Island called Labuan Belanda ("Dutch Harbor" in Indonesian) to anchor early and rest after our interrupted night. Except for its name, this harbor near the equator bore little resemblance to our Dutch Harbor in the Aleutian Islands of Alaska.

A 50-foot local wooden sailing vessel trailing a dugout canoe for a dinghy was already anchored in the harbor. Before we got our anchor down, three of its sailors paddled over to *Tainui* to pay us a visit and advise us where to anchor. We took their anchoring advice and exchanged greetings, but asked them to postpone their visit, as we needed some rest. Being fellow sailors, they understood and graciously returned to their boat. After lunch, three canoes came alongside carrying seven Indonesia men, some from the sailing vessel and the others from a nearby village, and we welcomed them all aboard. Word had gotten out that there was an American yacht in the harbor with a captain who spoke Indonesian. They asked a lot of questions about our trip, boat, and equipment. I showed them around *Tainui*, explaining everything the best I could. From their response, it was evident that there was no modern equipment on the local vessel. I asked them questions about the local ship, and its crewmembers invited me to visit it.

After they left, I took two nautical charts of that area, for which I had duplicates, and rowed to their boat. It was a cargo ship. They bought goods in the markets in the city and sold them in the outer islands, where few goods were available. The primitive nature of their vessel fascinated me. They made these trips without an engine. Their pumps were wooden boxes with wooden diaphragms and were operated by hand levers. They used manpower instead of winches to raise the sails, trim the sheets, and raise the anchor. The head was an outhouse on a frame behind the stern, just aft of their charcoal-fired galley. They had no charts. Their families had sailed these routes for generations, and they could have written the pilot book for these waters. When I gave them my charts, the crew gathered around and took turns pointing at various features and calling them by their Indonesian names. They gratefully accepted the charts, but I knew they wouldn't use them. The charts were just a novelty.

I asked them how they went about sailing without an engine. The strait was narrow and had tidal currents and wind conditions that included calms and headwinds. Their main strategy was patience. At that moment they were waiting for the tide to change in the strait. They were also skilled at playing the land-and-sea breezes. Fishermen the world over have used this phenomenon for centuries to go out to sea in the morning, when heavy cold air from the land was sucked out to sea by the air rising over the warmer water, and to return in the evening when the reverse was true. I had the greatest respect for their seamanship. These men were true sailors. It was a special treat to sit on their boat and discuss the universal fundamentals of sailing with them in their own language.

Later in the day, one of the men from the cargo vessel went ashore with me in my dinghy and took me to a small village, where he introduced me to the chief and explained that I needed water for washing clothes and bathing. The chief gave me permission to use a nearby waterfall for laundry and bathing and to fill our boat's water tanks. Connie and I did wash clothes and bathe at the waterfall, but we passed on his invitation to take the water for drinking. Local people no doubt drank that water, but in Indonesia we drank only bottled water because we knew the water was unsafe for us.

Our chart of the Butung Strait showed a sizeable town called Raha 20 miles south of us across the strait on Raja Muna Island, where we hoped to get provisions and send a fax home. We left Labuan Belanda an hour after the Indonesian vessel left and chased it down the strait all afternoon without catching up with it. Their clumsy-looking craft sailed surprisingly well.

There was no bay at Raha, and the wind was blowing onshore. There was no anchorage on the other side of the strait either, but not wanting to anchor on a lee shore, we motored across the strait and anchored in the lee of a mangrove thicket, in 35 feet of water with good holding in mud. The wind whistled through the rigging, but the sea was flat calm. The wind calmed down around 6:00, and our refrigerator had managed to make a tray of ice cubes, so we sipped gin and tonics on the stern deck and watched the sunset over Raha across the strait.

It was calm in the morning, so we motored back to the town. Some men on the town pier beckoned to us to come closer. We motored over to them, and they showed us where to anchor. After anchoring we returned to the town dock in our dinghy and checked in at a police station, which was conveniently located on the pier; the police said no other clearing in was necessary. Raha was a large village with all the facilities of a medium-sized town. The central market was large and well stocked. We bought fruit, vegetables, bread, and a case of drinking water and had an excellent Chinese lunch at the Hawaiian Restaurant. The market had only live chickens, and we were not up to killing and dressing our own, so we asked the restaurant people where we could buy one already done up. They agreed to do it for us; we could pick it up the next day. At the local telecoms office, we sent a general information fax to our son Larry in Seattle. He passed these periodic updates to other members of our family.

When we got back to the pier, a strong wind was whipping up a steep chop in the strait. The dinghy ride out to *Tainui* was bumpy and wet. *Tainui* was diving into the troughs and bucking on her anchor chain. We climbed aboard and searched the chart for an alternative anchorage. We noticed a tiny inlet on the Raha side of the strait called Lohia Bay about three miles farther south. It looked well protected, but had a very narrow entrance. We motored to it and found that the entrance was more than wide enough for *Tainui* and anchored in the bay at a depth of 45 feet. The bay was beautiful and well protected, more like a lagoon than a bay. It had a sandy beach and was surrounded by jungle foliage. An old steel hulk lay rusting away on the shore. We were blissfully alone; there were no signs of human habitation. We sat on deck and watched the sun go down to the tinkling of ice cubes in our drinks. As night fell, the jungle came alive with a cacophony of insect and bird sounds. Compared to our quiet nights in the Pacific Northwest, we were amazed at how noisy the jungle was at night.

Deriska called us on the radio in the morning and told us that they would arrive in Raha around noon, and we briefed them about the facilities in the town. We motored *Tainui* back to town, met them at the pier, and toured the town with them. We shopped at the produce market and picked up our chicken from the Hawaiian Restaurant. Everywhere we went, local people crowded around to see the two very blonde youngsters from *Deriska*. With a little coaching from their parents, they handled it calmly when children reached out to touch their skin and their hair. (We had this same experience in Malaysia when our two blonde-headed boys were young.) Back at our boats, the strait was choppy again, so *Deriska* followed *Tainui* back to Lohia Bay, and we enjoyed their company in the evening.

After breakfast the next morning, we slipped out of little Lohia Bay and headed down the Butung Strait for the town of Bau Bau, near the southeastern corner of Butung Island. There was no wind, so we motored the entire steaming-hot 40 miles. En route we had to go through a narrow pass where Raja Muna Island came to within a few hundred yards of Butung Island. We had no current tables to tell us when it was safe to enter the pass, so we approached it cautiously. Narrow passages like this created strong tidal currents that could sweep a boat out of control. Fortunately the current was with us at only three knots, and we swished through the pass making five knots through the water and eight knots over the bottom.

As we approached the town of Bau Bau in the late afternoon, a trading vessel like the one I visited in Labuan Belanda was attempting to dock against the current at the city wharf. I watched to see how these engineless vessels could do this. Two crewmembers carried two anchors out ahead of the ship in their dugout canoe. They dropped their first anchor, and as the crew on the trading ship hauled the boat forward on that anchor, the men in the dugout paddled farther ahead, dropped their second anchor, and went back and pulled up the first one. As the crew of the ship pulled their vessel forward on that anchor, the men in the dugout paddled ahead again. They continued this leap-frogging with the two anchors until the ship reached shallow water, whereupon crewmembers on each side of the ship pushed the trading vessel to the dock with long poles.

We dropped our anchor off the waterfront, and while we were tidying up *Tainui*, two teen-aged boys paddled out to us in a dugout canoe. We invited them aboard, and they introduced themselves as Azwar and Arafat. Azwar spoke some English and asked to accompany us when we checked in. He said he liked helping visiting yachts and that it gave him a chance to practice his English. We hoped he wasn't going to be a nuisance or a phony like Dhani, but we didn't want to let that negative experience taint our subsequent relationships. I didn't need Azwar's help with the language, but because it would be useful to be shown where to go, we agreed to meet him on the wharf in the morning. That evening *Deriska* arrived and anchored near us.

At 4:30 a.m. a Muezzin, calling the faithful to prayer from a loudspeaker on the minaret of a mosque near the shore, woke us from a sound sleep. Before we could get back to sleep, we heard voices and thumping against our hull. I went up on deck to see what was going on and found that we were surrounded by dugout canoes. Some men had apparently been a little overzealous in satisfying their curiosity about *Tainui* and had banged their dugouts into us. I made a sweeping motion toward the dugouts with my hand and yelled to the nearest paddler, "What's happening?" He shouted back, "A big ship is coming. It will stand offshore and sell us fish." We gave up sleeping and got an early start on our day.

Instead of meeting us at the wharf as planned, Azwar paddled out an hour and a half early, saying that he wanted to practice his English before we went ashore. Hanook, from *Deriska*, joined us when we went ashore to check in. Azwar led us to the port office, where we checked in and were told that no more checking in was needed. Bau Bau was a small city—much larger than Raha. As we walked around town, several men came up to us and said they wanted to practice speaking English. (In Bau Bau, we found more enthusiasm for speaking English than anywhere else we visited in Indonesia.) We didn't see anything in the shops that interested us, so after buying a little fresh fruit at an outdoor market, Hanook and I returned to *Deriska* for a cold drink with Connie and his family.

Back aboard *Tainui*, Connie took a nap while Hanook and I took his dinghy up a river to take pictures of the town. Late that afternoon, Azwar, Arafat, and several other young men paddled out to *Tainui* and asked to come aboard. We had invited the family from *Deriska* for drinks at 5:00, so I told them this was not a good time for a visit and invited them to come back some other time. They ignored me and climbed aboard anyway. When I ordered them off our boat, some of them made insulting remarks before leaving begrudgingly. After they left, we had a pleasant visit with the family from *Deriska*. It was a farewell party. They were leaving in the morning and we were not likely to see them again, because we were taking different routes through Indonesia. They were taking the usual tourist route through Bali and Komodo. When we were living in Malaysia, we had had a wonderful visit to Bali, staying in the home of an Indonesian family. Bali's tourist industry had not yet exploded and we wanted to remember it the way it was. In addition, we had no enthusiasm for experiencing Komodo's main attraction, which was throwing a goat off a cliff and watching it be ripped apart and devoured by giant monitor lizards, nicknamed Komodo dragons. Instead, we planned to take advantage of my language ability and follow a less-traveled route via Sulawesi and Borneo.

An English teacher named Rothman, who enjoyed greeting yachts, met us at the town dock in the morning. He was accompanied by Pesali, one of his students. Rothman had been vouched for by several of our friends who had passed through Bau Bau before us, so we invited him and Pesali to *Tainui* for cold drinks and a visit. In return, he invited us to his house the next morning to meet his family and take baths.

The blaring loudspeaker from the minaret roused us before dawn again. After breakfast, we set out in our dinghy to find Rothman's house. Pesali met us at a bridge and guided us the rest of the way. The tide was out and the water in the river was low, which made it difficult to motor the dinghy up the river. We hit bottom several times and sometimes had to use our oars to pole our way to deeper water. Pesali helped us pole the dinghy up to the landing near Rothman's house. The river's banks were high and disgusting. In the city the banks were cement, but out by Rothman's landing they were mud and sloped steeply up from the river to a height of over 20 feet at low tide. The banks were the disposal site for all manner of garbage and, worse yet, for human waste from rickety little straight-through outhouses. The detritus remained in the mud until the next high tide carried it away. The stench was overpowering. From the flimsy little boat landing at the bottom of the bank, we scrambled up through the mud (and we tried not to think of what else). Rothman's new, nearly completed house was a crudely built wooden structure with just shutters at the window openings. It was surrounded by foul-smelling open storm drains and was pervaded by the riverbank's aroma. At that point we understood the peculiar name of the town. The Indonesian word *bau* meant "smell." Indonesians formed the plural of a word by doubling it; hence Bau Bau meant "smells" or "smelly."

Rothman was proud of his new house. The floors were dirt and the walls a single layer of rough wood, but it was larger than most of the houses in the area—a suburb of the city jammed chock-a-block with run-down wooden houses. Rothman appeared to be about 50 years old. He was still teaching English in a high school. At his invitation, we took a typical Asian bath, and then he introduced us to his grown daughter who lived nearby. The four of us adults sat in the four wooden armchairs that were the only furnishings in the living room, while Pesali squatted Asian-style on the floor.

From Rothman's house, we walked to town, took some pictures, left our laundry at a hotel, and bought some produce at the market. Azwar approached us at the market and tried to get us to pay him for a guided tour of Bau Bau. We were wary of Azwar after the incident with him and his friends at the boat and turned him down. He refused to take no for an answer and followed us, continuing to insist that we hire him. I finally had to sternly order him to leave us alone. When we returned to Rothman's landing, the tide had come in and the river was deep enough for the outboard.

We arose at 5:00 the next morning to keep an early appointment with Rothman. When we arrived at the dock, it was totally occupied by a large fishing boat. I got permission to tie our dinghy alongside, and we climbed over the big vessel to the wharf. We took a *becha* (pedal-driven trishaw) to the bridge where Pesali was waiting for us and walked to Rothman's house, relieved that we did not have to climb the riverbank again. Rothman helped us shop for some items that would have been difficult for us to find. It was hard to tell what one might find in a shop in Southeast Asia by just looking at it. One of our favorite examples was a shop in Thailand that sold fish and pianos. Rothman's local knowledge was a great help. He was a kind and helpful gentleman, and Pesali was a polite young man who often accompanied us and was never any way inappropriate. At the market we arranged for another live chicken to be killed, plucked, and dressed for us, and then went back to Rothman's house and bathed again. These baths were much appreciated after a hot, sweaty day of shopping.

Pesali accompanied us back to *Tainui* that afternoon. He was fascinated by the furnishings on *Tainui,* and especially by the pictures of our family. After a brief visit and cold drinks aboard *Tainui*, Pesali went ashore with me and took me to a shop where I filled four jerry jugs with diesel fuel. We brought them back to the wharf in a *becha* and ferried them out to *Tainui* in the dinghy. Pesali helped me hoist them aboard and tie them down. A deluge struck just as we finished. After the rain, I took Pesali back to Rothman's house, where I gave gifts to Rothman and Pesali in thanks for their hospitality and help, and we said good-bye. As I walked back along the riverbank, I noticed that the offensive odor was dramatically reduced—the recent downpour had "flushed the toilet." Before returning to *Tainui*, I recovered our laundry, bought some drinking water, and checked out of Bau Bau at the port office.

Thanks to the waterfront mosque, we got an early start in the morning. From Bau Bau we planned to work our way along the southern shores of Sulawesi and Borneo and up the west coast of Borneo to a good jumping-off place for Singapore, somewhere near the equator. We would pick our stopping places as we went along. There was no wind in the Butung Strait, so we motored for the first six hours. We had used the motor only briefly at anchor, so the long engine run helped to charge the batteries and bring the refrigerator temperature down. Bau Bau was at the lower end of the Butung Strait, so we were soon in the open sea between the strait and the southeast coast of Sulawesi. The island of Sulawesi was composed of three giant fingers of land. One circled up to the northeast and the other two pointed south. After we reached the island, it took us two days and nights to cross the Bone Bay, which separated the two southern fingers. The wind was so weak that we made only two knots under sail, so we alternated between two hours of motoring at five knots and two hours of sailing at two knots, day and night for two days.

Before we reached the far shore of Bone Bay, we had to pass through the Salyar Strait, a narrow waterway between two islands. We reached it at night, but conditions were calm, our radar was giving us a clear picture of the pass, and we would have good maneuverability under motor, so we entered the strait in the dark. Before we had gone very far, the alternator's warning buzzer sounded, indicating that it was no longer charging our batteries. Fortunately, our little diesel engine did not require electricity. (If it had, the engine would have quit and we would have been drifting in the dark at the mercy of the current in a narrow strait with rocky shores—a potentially dangerous situation.) We motored on through the strait and pulled in to Birangkeke Bay on Sulawesi. I let *Tainui* drift in the protected water of the bay while I checked out the alternator. The slotted steel strap that adjusted the tension on the alternator's drive belt had broken. Fortunately, I was able to overlap the two pieces enough to clamp them together as a temporary repair.

In the morning I found that our ham radio would receive but wouldn't transmit. I made sure that the batteries were fully charged, then checked the ground wire and the voltage reaching the radio, and found nothing wrong. These were the only faults I could have corrected, so I concluded that the transmitter probably could not be repaired until we reached Singapore.

Before leaving Birangkeke Bay, we searched our chart for a place where we might be able to get our alternator strap welded. The chart lacked detail, but there was a village called Bulukumba a little farther along the Sulawesi shore. The name of the village interested me. A *bulu kumba* was a decorative feather covering on an elephant's head, so there probably had been elephants in the area. I wondered if any were still there. No village was visible from the sea when we approached the area where the chart showed Bulukumba. There was no sheltered anchorage, so we approached the beach cautiously, keeping watch on the depth sounder. I could tell from the tide line on the beach that it was low tide, so I ran *Tainui* toward shore to a depth of 13 feet and anchored off the mouth of a small stream, which I suspected led to the village. Even at the 13-foot depth we were 200 yards offshore. We had arrived at 8:00 a.m. and were tired from my late-night alternator repairs, so we took naps before trying to find the village.

After our rest, Connie chose not to go out in the midday heat, and I rowed ashore with the alternator strap and a broken part from our anchor windlass. I beached the dinghy, pulled it up above the high-tide line, and tied it to a tree. From the beach, I walked a mile beside the stream in the sweltering heat before I came to the village. Bulukumba was a small village with dirt streets and rustic wooden houses and shops, most of which had thatched roofs. There was little sign of life in the early afternoon heat, but I noticed a group of men sitting and talking in a small gazebo-like structure with a thatched roof and walked over and introduced myself to them. After I satisfied their curiosity about who I was and how I got there, I asked if there was a welder in their village. They shook their heads, but after some consultation they told me that there was one in the next village. It was too far to walk, but one of the men offered to take the parts on his motorbike and bring them back when they were fixed. They were vague about how long I might have to wait, but there was no alternative, so I sent the man off with the parts. The other men invited me to sit and wait with them in their little meeting place. They asked many questions about our trip, and I asked them if there were any elephants in the area. They told me that there had once been many elephants, but only a few were left and they were seldom seen. I played chess with one of the men to pass the time. While we were playing, a policeman came by and informed me that foreign yachts were required to register at the police office. He gave me a ride on the back of his motorbike and returned me after I had checked in.

The courier returned after three hours with both parts neatly welded. I paid for the welding and tipped the motorbike driver, even though he insisted that I didn't owe him anything. This kind of experience was one of the benefits of traveling in remote places where no English was spoken. Untouched by commercial tourism, these people were genuinely kind and helpful with no ulterior motives.

Connie went ashore with me the next morning to see the village. At the beach a man introduced himself and offered to give us water for our boat. I thanked him and told him I would bring some jugs ashore later in the day. He also showed us where we could hire a trishaw to avoid the hot mile-long walk to town. An elderly gentleman peddled us to town in a bicycle-powered rickshaw with a convertible roof that shaded us from the sun. In the village, we bought watermelon, papaya, and bottled drinking water in the market. Then we sat in a little open-air café and ate ice cream cones and drank diet Cokes with ice (after we were assured that the ice was made from boiled water). When a young Indonesian couple at another table heard me ordering in Indonesian, they struck up a conversation with us. We shared a lot of information about ourselves and our families. We enjoyed this window into the lives and culture of this isolated village couple.

Back at the beach, the tide had gone out, and our dinghy was high and dry a long way from the water. Two young boys saw me struggling to drag it across the sand and ran out and helped me haul it to the water's edge. A strong onshore wind had come up, and surf was breaking on the beach, so the boys waded out into the water and pushed the dinghy through the breakers. We had a wet ride back to where *Tainui* lay bucking on her anchor chain. I inserted a short length of nylon line across a loop of chain to act as a snubber. The stretchy nylon absorbed the shock, which stopped *Tainui* from bucking. In the afternoon, when the wind calmed down and the tide came in, I went back to shore and got some jerry jugs of water from the friendly man on the beach. We would use this water only for washing up.

The next morning, I went back to the village, checked out with the police, and got my clearance papers. It was almost noon by the time I got back to *Tainui* and got the anchor up. We left Bulukumba with a fine sailing wind in calm seas. We were about to cross the 400-mile-wide Makasar Strait, which separates Sulawesi from Borneo. The wind switched to dead astern, but the sea was still calm, so we sailed downwind wing-and wing smoothly and comfortably. *Tainui* was a beautiful sight with her big white sails billowing out on both sides in the bright sun. An Indonesian ship hailed us on our VHF radio as it passed by. I was surprised that they hailed an American-flag vessel, since they did not speak English—maybe our reputation had preceded us. They told us they were going to Makasar, the original name for an ancient city that the Indonesians had renamed Ujung Pandang, meaning "Beautiful Point." We told them that we were headed for Kalimantan. Our smooth sailing continued until 3:00 the next morning when it was "all hands on deck" to tame our flapping sails in a sudden blast of wind.

The next day pleasant sailing conditions returned, and we had another100-mile day. The night wind backed around to the stern again, but by this time the wind had built up the waves, causing *Tainui* to roll uncomfortably. I got up at 3:00 a.m., shortened the sail, and put *Tainui* on a broad reach. This took us a little off course, but gave us a faster and more comfortable ride. We were a little nervous when we reached the Laurel Reefs in the early morning before daylight. Our chart of the area was out-of-date, but it showed a deepwater pass. I trusted that the pass wouldn't have changed position, and our GPS guided us through it without incident.

An electrical storm passed over us in the morning. When it was right overhead, lightning struck all around us. I went below and disconnected all of our electronics as fast as I could, but I feared that a direct hit would still inflict considerable damage on us. The lightning passed harmlessly, but the wind and rain continued. We tried to catch rainwater off of the mainsail, but the wind blew it away before it reached the bucket. The wind changed directions so often that day that it was impossible to keep up with the sail changes, so we took down the sails and motored while we waited for the wind to settle down. While we were motoring, we caught a two-foot barracuda. After I killed it and cut it up, the rain obligingly washed the blood and scales off of the deck.

We lost two fishing lures on this trip. When one of them broke while we were eating in the cockpit, we heard a bang like a gun going off. It must have been a big fish. We were using a heavy line, and the lure was attached to it with a length of steel trace. The fishing may have been good because the ocean was full of flying fish. Dozens of them sailed off the wave tops; one of them narrowly missed Connie's head and landed flopping on the deck.

Another gale accompanied by heavy rain hit us at 5:00 the next morning. We quickly took the mainsail down and rolled up the jib until only a scrap of sailcloth was showing. We were both tired and went back to bed for a while, but took turns looking out every 15 minutes. We got up again at 10:00. The rain stopped at noon, and the wind quit altogether two hours later. We motored to charge up the batteries and the refrigerator and make a few miles, but after a half an hour of motoring, a clattering sound came from the engine compartment, and black smoke poured out of the exhaust. I shut the engine down and let *Tainui* drift while I checked the engine compartment. I discovered that the exhaust elbow had sprung a leak. I would need to find another welder to repair it. Meanwhile, we would have to rely on sail power until the exhaust elbow was repaired.

For the second time in a few days, we searched the chart for a village that might have a welder. We found a village called Batakan on the southeastern coast of Borneo behind a promontory called Point Selatin. A slight breeze sprang up, but it was coming directly from the point. We had to tack slowly back and forth against the light wind all night to reach the point. After we rounded the point, the wind picked up and we sailed a little faster toward what we hoped was the shore near Batakan. The water was incredibly shallow as we approached the beach. We sailed toward shore until the water was only eight feet deep and anchored there. We were still two and a half miles from shore! There was a fishing canoe nearby, so I put the dinghy in the water, motored out to it, and asked the fisherman if there was a welder in Batakan. He told me that they did have a welder. Next I asked if I could anchor farther in toward the beach, and he advised me not to go any closer to shore. By then it was late in the afternoon and very windy, so I decided to wait until morning to look for the village.

It was still windy in the morning, the sea was rough, and surf was breaking on the shore. I didn't relish the two-and-a-half-mile dinghy ride in these conditions, so I hailed two men in a passing outboard-powered fishing canoe and negotiated a ride. I offered 10,000 rupiah each way (US$10 round-trip). They were glad to oblige; this was two days' pay for them. Their names were Ilme and Saharun, and they quickly began to call themselves my "good friends." They took me up a river to a rotting little wooden dock that was missing so many boards it looked more like a ladder held up by short sticks than a pier. The dock was the landing for a school near town. Ilme and Saharun waited at their boat, and I walked up a dirt road to the town. A young man named Novi immediately attached himself to me, insisting that I come to his house so he could practice his English. When I refused, he aggressively urged me to hire him as a tour guide for the village. I got him to show me the way to the welder's house and firmly impressed upon him that I no longer needed his services.

The welder worked in an open shed behind his house. It did not take him long to fill in the small hole. Connie had asked me to bring back some groceries, but they were in short supply in Batakan. Ilme and Saharun were waiting for me back at the school landing, and they took me back to *Tainui* in their sturdy craft.

We were back at *Tainui* by noon, and Ilme and Saharun, my new friends, came aboard and stayed until after 5:00. Typical boat people, they kibitzed while I installed the repaired exhaust elbow. When the engine was running, they offered to guide me to a better anchorage in the lee of a small island. We towed their boat behind *Tainui*, and they stayed aboard and directed me. The motor ran cool until I turned on the refrigerator compressor, whereupon it heated up. After the men left to go fishing, four monkeys came out of the jungle and walked on the beach. Several fishing boats came in at dusk and cooked dinner on open charcoal fires in the backs of their boats. After their dinners, they put back out to sea.

The village was a quaint and picturesque model of a rural Indonesian village, and I wanted Connie to see it. We wanted to visit the village in the relative cool of the morning, so I decided to move *Tainui* to the river mouth to shorten our dinghy ride to the village. Before we left the anchorage, I took the thermostat out of the engine to keep it from overheating. In the process, one of the thermostat's two mounting bolts broke off. (Unfortunately, this kind of secondary problem occurred frequently in my repairs at sea.) I drilled a hole into the piece of the bolt that broke off in the engine block and tapped threads into it for a smaller bolt. This was a temporary fix and added one more task to our list of repairs to make in Singapore. As soon as we anchored, three men on a fishing boat shouted, "Give us some shirts." I called back, "No," but they paddled over to us and begged some more. The river mouth was full of local boats, and we were uneasy about leaving our boat unattended there, so I offered the men a deal. I had Connie dig up three of my old T-shirts, and I told them, "I will give you these shirts if you will watch our boat while we are gone." They agreed. We didn't know if we could trust them, but hoped that they would feel some sense of obligation to keep their promise.

My engine work and change of anchorages took so long that we left for the village much later than we had planned. It was blazing hot, and the tide was out when we dinghied up the river. When it became too shallow to motor, I rowed. When it became too shallow to row, I took the bowline and waded ahead in the mud and pulled Connie in the dinghy. These efforts attracted a considerable audience along the shore. People laughed when we got stuck in the mud. Somehow, local motorboats were speeding up the river past us. When I saw one pulled up on the beach, I discovered that they were designed especially for shallow water. They were long and narrow with a shallow draft. A metal plate under their propellers protected the propellers from the bottom. They roared up the river with their props half in the water, throwing up a rooster tail of mud. I talked one of them into taking my bowline and towing us to the school landing. I had to get up on the dock and give Connie my hand to persuade her to put her feet on the decaying structure.

The vendors in the markets were already packing up their wares for their afternoon siesta when we reached the village. We managed to talk them out of only a few oranges and string beans. I saw Novi approaching and told Connie, "Oh, oh, here comes yesterday's nuisance." He pushed us to let him guide us to some supposedly "must see" sights around the village, but we begged off. We strolled down the main street and took pictures of the fine old Indonesian-style houses. One of the houses was decorated for a special occasion. A passerby told us the family was having a *bersanding*. In this part of the wedding ceremony, the bride and groom, dressed in ornate festive costumes, were seated on display on throne like chairs for an entire afternoon. They were supposed to look straight ahead and not smile as guests passed by and admired them. We had attended some *bersandings* in Malaysia.

When the people in the house saw us coming, some of them ran out to meet us and insisted that we come into their house. We politely declined, not wanting to interfere with their family's celebration, but they claimed that it was good luck to have Western people participate in a wedding and practically dragged us into the house. They seated us at a table and fed us curry and rice. We ate with our fingers, and when we needed to wash our hands, they led us to a sink. On the way, we passed the *bersanding* couple, who tried hard to pretend that they didn't notice us. Next the family insisted that we have our picture taken with the bride and groom, which they said would bring especially good luck to the couple. After the photo shoot, everyone shook hands with us and thanked us as we took our departure. It was a surprise bonus opportunity for us. They couldn't have known that I spoke Indonesian when they first invited us, and I wondered what kind of experience it would have been for a couple of tourists who couldn't communicate with them.

We walked down to the beach where we met a group of students from a university at Banjar Masin, a major city 25 miles up the river. They were camping out on a school holiday. They had come in private cars, and some of them were playing guitars and singing. They were friendly and chatted with us in English. Their English was better than my Indonesian.

We walked back along the beach to the river mouth, where there was a tiny village, sat down in a small open-air shop that had a few tables, and asked for a cold drink. They served us red Kool Aid with ice. We were already famous in the village from our struggle with our dinghy, and many people gathered around us. One of the men took me up the river to our dinghy in one of those shallow-draft motorboats, while Connie waited in the village. Novi showed up at the river mouth when I got back and asked to come out with us to see *Tainui*. He said a friend would come and get him after a short visit. We were hot and tired and didn't like him, but not wanting to be rude, we consented. As we were getting under way with him in our dinghy, we saw five men get into his friend's boat. We told Novi that we didn't want that many people, but he was unable to stop them, so they all came. We entertained them for an hour, and they left willingly when we told them that we were tired and needed to rest.

After they left, we motored *Tainui* back to the protected anchorage behind the island. As soon as we were anchored, Ilme and Saharun motored over, tied alongside, climbed aboard, and stayed for the afternoon. They went back aboard their boat and cooked their dinner around 6:00. We never got our afternoon rest. As Connie was cooking dinner, three men jumped aboard. They smiled and asked to see our boat. They said they had come in a small boat from a larger vessel anchored farther out. I reprimanded them sternly for boarding a vessel without permission, and they apologized but stayed until I asked them to leave so we could have dinner. They said that it wouldn't bother them if we ate, but I convinced them that, according to our customs, it would be rude for them to stay. They climbed back aboard their boat, but sat there tied to *Tainui* and watched us. They didn't leave until it got dark. That night Connie's log read: "At that point I finally lost it—I couldn't take it anymore and went all to pieces. We had no privacy. Boats were tied to both sides of us and people peered into our portholes."

We had mentioned to some of the men that we were considering going up the river to Banjar Masin for supplies and boat work. In the morning they were all eager to accompany us, and Ilme invited us to visit his home there, an invitation that we would have gladly accepted, but the pests that had attached themselves to our boat the night before wanted to accompany us as well. We had had enough of this crowd and decided to sail on. Our next planned stop was the city of Pontianak 530 miles away, which we had chosen as our point of departure for Singapore. We estimated that we had enough food, water, and fuel to go all the way, but there were one or two possible intermediate stops if we needed them.

The trip to Pontianak started out beautifully and wound up a maintenance marathon. A fast beam reach in a southerly 15-knot wind gave us 127 miles in our first 24 hours. During the first night, we saw what looked like a city on the horizon. It turned out to be an approaching luxury cruise ship. It occurred to us that it was, in fact, a floating city of 5,000 people. Ablaze with lights, it was a mini Las Vegas—a city that never slept—with 24-hour restaurants, bars, cabarets, and casinos. Our second day was much slower. *Tainui* crept along in light air, making between two and three knots. We were making so little progress we decided to anchor for the night and sleep. We headed for a charted anchorage protected by a point called Tanjong Putting. We arrived after dark and felt our way toward shore with our radar. Our depth sounder had quit, so we anchored in an area where a local fishing boat was anchored. Except for the fishing boat, we saw no signs of life. We talked to a fisherman on the radio in the morning and learned that there was, in fact, no village in that area.

As we sailed slowly along on a flat sea during the day, I fixed the depth sounder. It was simply a matter of cleaning a corroded connection. Corrosion in our electrical circuits was a common problem in the tropical marine environment. We spent the night dodging fishing boats. Many of them were anchored. The sea was only 30 to 40 feet deep, so boats could drop anchor at sea rather than seek an anchorage in a bay or near the shore. Dodging them required our full attention. They did not follow standard lighting rules. We could not tell by their lights whether they were anchored or under way. If a boat was under way, we could not tell which way it was going, which made it difficult to stay clear of any nets or long lines it might be towing. I would not risk fouling our prop on their gear, so no matter how little wind we had, we kept the engine off and sailed slowly through the fishing fleet. It was a long, tedious, sleepless night.

In the morning we rounded the southwest point of Borneo and started up its west coast in the Karimata Strait. We had decent sailing weather, but mechanical problems continued to plague us. We accidentally left the refrigerator relay on for 24 hours, which drained one of our battery banks. This required extra motoring. There were no fishing boats to dodge that day, but an elbow in our engine's water-muffler system rusted through and a stream of water poured into the boat. I installed a replacement elbow, but there was still a small leak. It was difficult for me to find the problem, because I was working at night with a flashlight strapped to my head like a miner's light. I quit for the night and got some sleep. We didn't have enough battery power to turn on our masthead running lights that night, so we used the fluorescent reading light in our dodger. Considering the irregular lighting we had been seeing, we felt we fit right in with the local boats. We continued to sail slowly to the north through the night.

In the morning, I found two cracks in the water-muffler assembly and wrapped them with a special heat-resistant shrink tape. Even if this leaked, I hoped it would slow the flow enough that we could use our engine. I started the engine and, incredibly, I found another leak. A hose clamp in the muffler system had corroded and fallen off. I replaced it with a stainless-steel clamp, and after an hour of battery charging a thorough inspection revealed no more leaks.

While I was playing plumber, Connie was playing captain, skillfully beating into a north-by-northeast wind. This wind lasted through the night, but it was another busy night. We passed through a narrow strait, called the Grieg Passage, that was clogged with fishing boats. By dawn we had safely cleared the strait, but the engine overheated. We were feeling the effects of sleep deprivation from two busy nights, so we had breakfast and got some sleep.

Somewhat refreshed from my nap, I tackled the engine-overheating problem. The engine overheated when we were under way and ran the refrigerator compressor. We were able to run the refrigerator compressor only when the engine was in neutral. I took the entire cooling system apart and found nothing amiss. I cleaned each part and put it all back together, but it still overheated when it was under a heavy load. We were becalmed in the afternoon, and I had to let *Tainui* drift. We couldn't run the engine any more than necessary until I resolved its overheating problem. We were only 60 miles from the mouth of the river that led up to Pontianak, and when a light following wind came up, we hoped we could sail to the river. However, the wind soon quit, and I tried to motor closer to shore to anchor for the night, but one of the engine's cylinders heated up and started smoking. We were in only 33 feet of water so we anchored where we were and went to sleep. I wasn't sure when we would be able to charge our batteries with the engine, so instead of running our masthead anchor light, we used the more efficient fluorescent dodger lamp again and kept a closer lookout that night.

In the morning, I tried again but could find nothing wrong with the engine cooling system. I sat down and thought about it. All of these problems had occurred after the exhaust elbow was welded at Batakan. I had assumed that it had been properly fixed and had not looked at it closely. So I took it off, thoroughly inspected it, and found that one of its internal passages was completely blocked. It looked as if some kind of soft sludge had been baked hard by the heat of welding. I dug out the material and cleaned every other part of the exhaust elbow. When I put it back on, voila—the cooling system functioned perfectly. We motored all day and anchored for the night 12 miles from the mouth of the river that would take us to Pontianak.

As we approached the river mouth in the morning, a full-sized freighter was anchored well offshore waiting for high tide. The chart of the area showed a shallow bar at the river mouth that had to be negotiated through a well-marked, narrow channel. We took a chance on *Tainui*'s shallow four-and-a-half-foot draft and successfully motored through at low tide. Then we gave our engine a good workout by motoring 12 miles up the winding river to the city of Pontianak. En route, we crossed the equator three times. If we had celebrated each crossing in the traditional fashion, we would have been tipsy by the time we got there.

The city was much larger than we expected, between 200,000 and 300,000 people. It had a large harbor, because it was situated in an area where the river became a mile wide. The harbor was full of rusting ships from many Southeast Asian countries. Their crewmembers looked ragged and poor when they passed us in their shore boats. We were uneasy with the situation. We had been warned that yachts were not safe from theft in the big cities in Indonesia, partly due to these transient, underpaid workers. That warning was one of the reasons we gave up the opportunity to see the ancient cities of Makasar and Banjar

Masin. We motored around the harbor looking for a place to anchor and finally picked a spot off a small city park. Connie stayed aboard, and I went ashore to check in and inquire about security. Neither of us was comfortable with this arrangement, but we had heard that most of the thefts occurred on unoccupied yachts, so we were even more uncomfortable with both of us going ashore and leaving *Tainui* unattended.

The immigration and customs offices were on the same pier as the harbor police office, which made checking in quick and easy. The harbor police chief told me that it would indeed be unsafe to anchor out and insisted that I bring *Tainui* in to the police dock, where his officers could keep an eye on her. We were, of course, greatly relieved at his offer and immediately brought *Tainui* in and tied her to the police dock.

With *Tainui* secure at the police dock, we went ashore and explored our new neighborhood. A modest store that claimed to be a supermarket and some fresh fruit stalls were located conveniently nearby. The Kartika Hotel was also located near the police dock. Connie was more than ready to eat out after cooking so many meals aboard, so we ate lunch in the hotel's dining room. The food was uninspiring, but the dining room was clean and had a view of the river—we could see *Tainui* safely tied to the police dock as we ate.

Our first night at the pier was a restless one because I needed to adjust the mooring lines with the rise and fall of the tide. At marinas we tied to floating docks, which went up and down with the tide, but the police dock was on pilings. It was high tide when we went to bed that night, so I got up several times to let out our mooring lines as the tide fell. However, it went down very slowly and did not start up after six hours as tides usually did, but continued its slow drop. In the morning, the harbormaster explained to me that Pontianak was one of the few places in the world that had 12-hour tides. There was only one high tide and one low tide every 24 hours instead of two a day as was the case in almost all of the rest of the world. Had I known, I could have gotten up half as often to attend to our mooring lines. To make our lives easier, the harbormaster took it upon himself to persuade the police to let me tie up to one of their boats, so I wouldn't have to adjust my mooring lines with the tide. This thoughtful act was typical of our continuing relationship with the harbormaster.

Lack of privacy was a constant problem at the pier. We were a novelty because very few foreign yachts passed that way. It had been five years since the last one had visited Pontianak. Another part of the problem was the foot traffic from the ferries. Our dock was shaped like a T. The police dock was on the left part of it, and the ferry docked at the other end. The city of Pontianak was divided by the river, and there was no bridge, so the ferries took cars, trucks, motorcycles, bicycles, and hordes of foot passengers back and forth across the river. The ferries ran frequently, and embarking and disembarking passengers couldn't resist walking to our end of the pier to see the little blue and white sailboat with the American flag. Sometimes men brazenly jumped aboard uninvited to get a closer look. One time when I was in town and Connie was taking a nap below, a man came aboard and climbed down into the cabin. At first she thought it was I and turned to say hello. When she saw the stranger, she got up shouting and trying to shoo him out. He said he had just come to ask for a drink of water, but she was having none of it. She kept yelling at him until he climbed out. He tried sitting on the deck, but she followed him out and chased him away. After that scare, I put a sign in the window that said in Indonesian, "Do not climb aboard this boat without the captain's permission." Somewhat to our surprise, there were no more uninvited boardings.

One day we took a bus across the river to Pontianak's big tourist attraction. The city sat squarely on the equator, and its one claim to fame was its equator tower. The white tile floor in the room at the base of the tower had a row of black tiles running down the middle of it that were supposed to be right on the equator. A large metal sign overhead bore the inscription:

Longitude: 109 deg. 19 min. east

Latitude: 00 deg. 00 min.

People came from far around to walk back and forth across the line and to have their pictures taken under the sign. Some straddled the line, and some had members of their party stand in different hemispheres. Couples, often honeymooners, were particularly fond of holding hands across the line.

At the police dock, I noticed that an elderly Chinese man, dressed in baggy shorts and a dirty T-shirt, frequently sat on a mooring bitt near our boat. One afternoon I sat down beside him and introduced myself, and we had a pleasant conversation. He was interested in our boat and our journey, and I was surprised to learn that, in spite of his unimpressive appearance, he was the captain of *Telok Bone*, a tugboat that shared our pier. He took us on a tour of his tugboat and introduced us to his crew. Although he had shared with me that he had a wife and family ashore, the crew included a young woman half his age who shared his sleeping quarters on the tug. At his invitation, thereafter we took our showers on the tug and filled our water tanks from the much larger tanks on the tug.

The use of the showers was a relief because we had been taking showers by special arrangement in the harbormaster's building after hours, when the building was dark and unoccupied. One day the captain took me along on the tug when he went out to assist an incoming ship.

Before leaving Pontianak, we took *Tainui* upriver to a pier where we were told there was a welder. We tied to the outside of another vessel, and before we could leave *Tainui*, we were beset with unwanted visitors. We posted our "no boarding" sign, went ashore, and found the welder. The welder brought his gear aboard *Tainui* and repaired the cracked connections in the water box of the engine's muffler system, welded a lifeline stanchion that had come loose from the deck, and removed the broken-off thermostat bolt and replaced it with a bolt of the original size. I was pleased with his work.

With all necessary repairs completed, we prepared to depart for Singapore. I motored *Tainui* upriver to a fuel dock to top off our diesel supply. The dock was crowded with lighters (heavily built open wooden boats that ferried cargo to shore from anchored ships) and other workboats, so we tied up to one of the workboats. I carried my jerry jugs across the cluttered and sloping decks of several vessels to reach the end of the fuel hose. It took me three trips to lug the full jugs back to *Tainui*, cautiously stepping from vessel to vessel. Back at the police dock, we provisioned at the nearby markets. Once again we disappeared while the butcher killed and dressed a chicken for us. For the second time in Indonesia we ate dinner at a Hawaiian Restaurant, and again there was nothing Hawaiian about the food; it was standard Chinese fare.

The next morning we cleared out with customs and immigration, stowed provisions, and secured our gear for sea. We treated ourselves to a departure lunch at the Kartika Hotel and then got *Tainui* under way down the river. The tide was coming in and the wind was against us, so it took us four hours to motor to the river mouth. The wind and the waves were coming straight at us as we sailed out to sea, and we tacked back and forth against the wind throughout the night. In the morning, *Tainui*'s previous night's track on the GPS display screen showed that we had made almost no forward progress. Each time we tacked, the wind and waves had pushed *Tainui*'s bow back so that we had been tacking back and forth sideways. We realized with regret that it would have been far better for us to have anchored at the river mouth, gotten a good night's sleep, and set off rested in the morning when there was usually less wind.

The wind calmed down and shifted enough in the morning that we could make progress in our intended direction. At noon, however, a series of severe squalls hit us with gusts in excess of 40 knots, and we quickly rolled up the jib and hove to on a close-hauled mainsail. After three hours, the wind slackened slightly, and we got under way again under a tiny scrap of jib and a double-reefed mainsail. The waves had grown to 10 to 12 feet high, and occasional strong gusts still hit us, but we clawed our way slowly ahead. However, within an hour we heard a sharp report, like the crack of a rifle shot, coming from high up on the mast. We looked up and saw that the roller-furling mechanism was swaying wildly back and forth. The forestay—the steel cable that ran from the top of the mast to the tip of the bowsprit—had broken inside the hollow furling gear. The mechanism was held up by the rope halyard that had hauled the furling gear to the top of mast, but without a tight forestay inside of it, the furler was swaying, which was putting excessive strain on the connectors that held its hollow four-foot sections together. If a connector pulled out or the rope halyard broke, the mast would come down.

I needed to get the strain off the furling gear as quickly as possible. I tried to roll up the jib from the cockpit, but it didn't respond when I pulled on its furling line, so I started the engine. Connie steered us to windward, which spilled the wind from the sails, and I went forward into the very lively bow pulpit and rolled up the jib by hand. Next, I dropped the mainsail and secured it to the boom. Removing the sails took considerable pressure off the mast. Finally, I made a temporary forestay by attaching a spare halyard from the top of the mast to the tip of the bowsprit and cranking it as tightly as I could with the mainsail halyard winch. I hoped that the mast was now secure enough to stay up while we motored back to Pontianak.

We were 43 miles from the river mouth and another 12 miles up the river from the city. Initially, I decided that the sea conditions were too rough to motor. We couldn't heave to without a mainsail, so we lay a-hull to wait for calmer weather. However, I didn't like the way the mast whipped back and forth while *Tainui* rolled in the troughs of the big waves. We studied our charts for nearby shelter and found an island 15 miles away that had a small bay on its leeward side that might provide a sheltered anchorage, and we motored off in that direction. A cable on the self-steering mechanism soon broke, so we took turns hand-steering. It was pitch-black and raining when we reached the island and cautiously entered a little bay. The radar screen was filled with bright green targets, which made us think that a fishing fleet must have been taking shelter there. I had Connie steer *Tainui* into the bay, while I stood in the bow pulpit with a powerful spotlight. Unfortunately, the beam couldn't penetrate very far in the heavy rain. I had to shout "Stop! Reverse!" when my light picked up two pilings a few feet ahead. Connie shut down the throttle, shifted into reverse, and brought the throttle back up as quickly as she could and *Tainui* came to a stop with her bow pulpit a few inches from one of the pilings. The pilings were part of a large wooden fish trap. We backed away and maneuvered around until I couldn't see any other obstacles, and then we dropped anchor. When we backed down on the anchor chain to set the anchor, our stern came to within a few feet of another fish trap. I couldn't tell if there were any other traps within the swinging range of our anchor chain, but I decided that if there were, we probably wouldn't bump into them hard enough to do any damage, so we settled down for the night.

We rocked a bit in the bay, but it was much calmer than the open ocean had been. We slept nervously that night, half expecting to bump into a piling, or worse yet, hear the mast come crashing down. An amazing sight greeted us at dawn. We were in the middle of a little bay that was filled with fish traps. It was a veritable maze. We couldn't see how we had managed to get so far into the bay without hitting at least one of them. I repaired the broken cable on the self-steering system, and we left the bay and set off on the long motor trip to Pontianak. As often happened, the wind and the sea calmed down in the morning, so we made good progress. The mast looked fairly stable when we rocked, which made us optimistic about its chances of surviving the trip. But within an hour another small breakdown occurred. We heard a rattling sound in the engine compartment and heard the alternator's warning buzzer. The slotted strap that tensioned the alternator belt had broken again, so we had to motor on without the alternator, which meant that we could no longer charge our batteries.

We got through the tricky river bar at dusk, anchored by the pilot station just inside the mouth of the river, and had a wonderfully peaceful night. In the morning, after a drenching deluge delayed our departure for an hour, we motored back to the city with no further problems. We tied up to the same small boat on the inside of the police dock that we had tied to before, and the harbor officials welcomed us back like old friends. I checked in with the officials who had just checked us out. Our Indonesian cruising permit had expired, but it was not a problem—the need for boat repairs qualified us for an extension.

Replacing the forestay and reinstalling the roller-furling gear required the services of a good machine shop. We asked around and were directed to a large shop in an open-air space under a high-rise office building. Piles of scrap metal and odd bits and pieces were scattered everywhere, but among that clutter we saw that the shop had every conceivable machine tool. The first thing we had the workers do was weld our broken alternator strap so that we could recharge our batteries. After that was accomplished, we discussed the repair of our broken forestay and damaged roller-furling gear. They were eager to help, but cautioned that they could not guarantee the straightening of our roller-furling parts, because the bent aluminum pieces might break when they attempted to straighten them.

The next day I began the forestay repair in earnest. The first thing we needed to do was to take down the furling gear, which consisted of 12 four-foot hollow aluminum extrusions. Several men volunteered to help me get it down, but to alleviate confusion, I hired one of them, Usman, and sent the others away. After we removed the sections that we could reach from the deck, the only way to get the higher ones down was to lower the mechanism by slackening the halyard that held them up. Without the bar-tight forestay inside of it, the mechanism sagged so much that several of the aluminum connectors between the extrusions were bent. In addition, the extrusions were fastened to the connectors by stainless-steel screws, which, being harder than aluminum, enlarged their holes in many of the extrusions.

I took the damaged pieces to the machine shop, and the manager cautioned me again about the danger of bending the aluminum. I told him to do what he could; if any were damaged beyond use, I would either have the machine shop manufacture substitutes, or I would order spare parts and wait for them to be delivered. Despite their warnings, the shop did manage to straighten the bent parts without breaking any of them. I think their disclaimer was mostly to cover themselves in case they broke any of the parts.

Finding and fitting a new forestay was not such a difficult problem. When I replaced our original backstay with an insulated one that served as the antenna for our ham radio, I stored the old one for a spare. Because the backstay was longer than the forestay, there was plenty of material out of which to make a new forestay. The locals watched with great interest as I climbed the mast steps and attached the new forestay to its fitting at the top of the mast.

All that was left to do was to slide the extrusions back up the forestay, fastening them together as we went, and then to secure the bottom of the new forestay to the bowsprit. But problems occurred in connecting them. Several times I had to run extrusions back to the machine shop and have them repair damaged screw holes in them. Some of the holes had become so large that they required bigger screws. There were no stainless steel screws in Pontianak, so I had to accept plain steel ones, which I knew would rust. When we got to Singapore, I planned to replace them with stainless steel screws. After two long workdays, I was able to wind the furling line around the drum on the bottom of the mechanism and roll and unroll the jib from the cockpit. We had had the full use of the big machine shop for a day and a half, and they charged me the grand total of US$20!

After one of our workdays, the captain of a government boat that shared our pier invited us to his home. We took the ferry across the river, and then Connie rode on the back of the captain's motorbike, and Usman took me on his. The captain and his family lived in a large, comfortable new house that was not quite finished. They fed us custard pie, hot tea, and fresh oranges. They were proud of their homegrown oranges, and we agreed that their tree-ripened fruit was tastier than the green-picked fruit that was trucked great distances to our supermarkets at home. The captain and his wife had six children living with them plus the captain's father.

Around 8:00 p.m. that same night, Usman and the captain took us by motorbike to Usman's home. It was a more modest house, but was clean and well furnished. Usman was much younger than the captain, and he and his wife had just two small children. They fed us tea and cookies, which were welcome, as we hadn't eaten dinner. Usman's wife was a schoolteacher, as was Connie. She spoke no English and Connie's Indonesian was limited, so I interpreted as they compared their teaching experiences. After the visit, the men took us back across the river in a motorized canoe and let us off in town near the police dock. On our walk back to *Tainui*, Connie and I stopped at an open-air shop and bought a couple of take-out *murtabaks* (a kind of East Indian meat-and-potato turnover) to make up for our missed dinner.

Usman was a mixed blessing. At noon on his first day, I suggested he go out and get some lunch, but he just came below and sat. I thought maybe we were expected to feed our help, so I took him out to lunch. Back on the job, he begged Connie for food throughout the afternoon and she gave him bread, an orange, a Coke, and coffee. I told him to report to work at 8 o'clock the next morning, but he showed up at 6:00 and shouted down the companionway. We were still in bed, and I told him to go away and come back in an hour. Having seen his home the night before, Connie decided that he wasn't poor and discouraged him from begging for food thereafter. At the end of the project I paid him our agreed-upon 40,000 rupiah, which was US$20. Considering the machine shop bill, he was probably grossly over-paid by local standards. On the other hand, by American standards I thought I had practically stolen the repair job.

We wanted to get under way again as soon as possible because Larry and Joyce and family had already made arrangements to meet us in Singapore and sail with us to Malaysia. The date of their arrival was fast approaching, and *Tainui* could barely make the passage in time for us to meet them there. In addition, our Indonesian cruising permit had run out, and we did not want to overstay it any longer than necessary. Therefore, as soon as the repairs were completed, we quickly stocked up at the supermarket, filled our water tanks and showered at the tugboat, checked out once again with the authorities, ate lunch at a Chinese restaurant on the waterfront (the view was better than the food), and motored off down the river, crossing the equator three more times as we went.

Near the mouth of the river, we were again hit with the headwind and steep choppy waves that had confronted us on our last departure attempt. Not wanting to repeat the mistake we had made last time, we decided to anchor for the night in the shelter of a small island whose Indonesian name translated as "Pig Island." (We didn't see any pigs on the beach.) As we maneuvered *Tainui* into position to drop the anchor, the engine revved up to a high pitch. I looked in the engine compartment and found that the rubber vibration-dampening coupling that connected the engine to the propeller shaft had split in two. This had happened once before, when we were en route to Mexico. It meant that we would have to return again to Pontianak and order a replacement coupling. We were wondering if Pontianak were actually cursed, since "Pontianak" was the name for a ghost in a local folk legend.

I made contact with the harbor police on the radio, and after a lot of consultation on their end, they said that they would send a boat down the river the next morning to tow us back to Pontianak. I especially appreciated my language ability in that situation. It would have been difficult to find an English speaker in that isolated spot, and we could have been stuck there for a long time.

The police boat arrived at about 10:00 the next morning. It was Sunday and the captain was making it a family outing. His wife and children were aboard dressed in their "Sunday best," if there was such a thing in a Muslim country. They towed us back to the police dock and tied us to their vessel. Somewhat embarrassed, I checked back in with the officials. They weren't concerned about our expired permit and joked with us about how hard we were to get rid of. By then we were well acquainted, and I think they enjoyed the novelty of having an American yacht in the harbor.

By then, we did not have time to wait for a part to be delivered, make repairs, and then sail to Singapore in time to keep our appointment with Larry and his family, so we telephoned them and told them we would fly to Singapore and tour Malaysia by rental car. The rental car option would actually be a better use of our limited time with Larry's family. I also arranged to have Larry bring the replacement rubber coupling to us at Singapore.

In order to ensure that *Tainui* was safe while we were away, I paid the harbor police US$100 to have two policemen sleep aboard her. Checking out was more complicated this time. The immigration officer took advantage of the fact that we were at his mercy regarding permission for us to reenter his country. He virtually demanded that we bring him a gift from Singapore. When I asked for a suggestion, he kept saying something that sounded like "Lebbees." This turned out to be "Levi's." I got his measurements and promised to come through. Those Levi's and the audiotape and packet of M&Ms that an official in Tonga extracted from us were the only instances of baksheesh on our entire trip.

I also had to deal with the immigration officer regarding our ham radio. It had quit transmitting, and I wanted to take it to Singapore to be repaired. However, Indonesia had strict rules about importing such powerful communications devices, for fear that they might be used by dissident revolutionary factions. He studied my radio carefully and noted its make, model, and serial number, which he would check again when I brought it back. This seemed routine at the time, but turned out to be a problem later.

We arrived in Singapore a few days before Larry and his family and took our radio to one of Singapore's sophisticated electronics repair shops. When our son and his family arrived, we toured Malaysia by rental car, revisiting the three communities we had lived in from 1968 to 1972, even locating each of the houses we had lived in.

When we returned to Singapore, we were told that our old Kenwood ham radio was unrepairable, so we bought a new, more modern Icom transceiver. This caused an interesting sequence of events when we got back to Pontianak. The immigration officer discovered that this was not the radio I had taken out. His starting position was that he would not allow me to bring the radio into Indonesia. I argued that a radio was a radio. We had always had one. What difference did it make which one I had now? His response was the Indonesian version of, "Da rules is da rules!" At this point the immigration officer remembered his request for a gift. Upon receiving an expensive new pair of Levi's, he softened up a bit. I mentioned that in similar situations the goods in question were sometimes kept in a sealed locker on board the boat until the vessel departed. He accepted that plan and wrapped the radio in heavy paper, wound lots of duct tape around it, and stamped the tape several times with his official seal. He warned me not to break those seals until I was out of Indonesian waters. I think he had been setting me up for a bribe, until he realized that he already had one.

Tainui was safe from thievery and vandalism while we were gone—the profusion of cigarette butts on her decks was ample evidence that the police night watchmen had slept there. However, the cabin was full of cockroaches and mold. We immediately scrubbed out the entire interior and washed all of our dishes, pots, pans, and utensils.

Back at the police dock, the harbormaster asked me how my radio repairs had come out. He was a kindly older gentleman who had taken a keen interest in us and gone out of his way to look out for our well being. I told him that the problem with sealing the radio was that I would have to try to install it at sea, where I could not get technical help if I ran into problems. Sitting behind his big desk in his impressive office, he made a sweeping gesture toward the window overlooking the harbor and said, "My friend, you see all this harbor area? Here, I am the king. I make the rules. I am granting you permission to install your radio, and if anyone objects, you send them to me."

I installed the radio, but I couldn't get it to respond to the automatic tuner that was located in the lazarette and connected to the backstay-antenna. Shortly after the harbormaster heard that I had a problem, two radio technicians from the Indonesian Navy showed up and went to work on my automatic tuner and antenna system. I was a little nervous when I saw them taking out things until bits and pieces were scattered all over the boat. At the end of the day, however, they had it working and told me that if I had any more problems to notify the harbormaster and they would come back.

After the technicians left, I installed the coupling that Larry had brought to Singapore and changed the engine oil in preparation for our departure. However, at that time Connie came down with severe diarrhea. For two days we tried the Lomotil in our medicine chest, but it didn't help. I then took Connie to a local clinic. No one spoke English at the clinic, not even the doctor, so I interpreted for the examination. He gave Connie a shot and a bunch of pills. Back at the boat, we became concerned about the fact that Connie was allergic to sulfa medications, and the doctor had not asked her about allergies. I took the pills back to the clinic and found that some of them were, in fact, sulfa. I gave the sulfa pills back and kept the rest.

The shot produced immediate results and the remaining medication sustained them. We were relieved that we had taken care of this before we were out at sea. When Connie appeared to be fully recovered, we repeated our usual departure procedure: groceries at the supermarket, fresh fruit and vegetables from the open-air produce stands, and another chicken—selected live and dressed in our absence. When I checked out again with the officials, the immigration officer asked, "Are you really going to leave this time?" I joked, "If we have to come back again, I will become a Muslim, buy a house, take three more wives, and settle down." I was relieved that they laughed at my joke—just in case we came back. Once again we wound our way down the river under motor, crossing the equator three more times. Our initial ocean crossing and our three-round trips up and down this river added up to 19 equator crossings, more than most sailors log in a lifetime. On November 29, 1992, we sailed out of the river mouth, crossed the shallow bar, and set out across the South China Sea for Singapore, hoping that this time it would be for real.

On the way to Australia we picked up a passenger. (above)
A pleasant day at sea as we start up the Great Barrier Reef in Australia.
(below)

Connie and Vern at the Townsville Motorboat Club awaiting the arrival of friends, Steve and Linda Gallon. (above)
The Gallons relaxing on a pleasant afternoon sail aboard *Tainui (below)*

Our passage to Cairns with the Gallons runs into rough weather. (above)
A hard landing in Indonesia. *Tainui* up on the reef at Tanimbar. (below)

A shop in the town of Ambon, Indonesia. (above)
Connie shopping for carvings at the home of a carver near Ambon,
Indonesia. (below)

Vern on the wooden trading vessel in Labauan Belanda sharing a chart
with the crew. (above)
The infamous riverbank in front of Mr. Rahman's house in Bau Bau,
Indonesia. (below)

Vern, Rahman and Pesali in Rahman's new house. (above)
Vern joins Ilme and Saharun in their canoe as they tie alongside *Tainui*.
(below)

CHAPTER FOURTEEN

SINGAPORE AND MALAYSIA

The passage to Singapore would be our last open ocean crossing. Singapore was only 330 nautical miles (363 statute miles) across the South China Sea as the crow flies, which, at our 100-nautical mile-a-day average, should take about three and a half days. But *Tainui* was no crow on this trip. It turned into a nine-day saga of gales, contrary currents, and mechanical failures.

As soon as we entered the South China Sea, a headwind forced us to beat slowly to windward, well south of our intended track, and our GPS showed that we were being pushed even farther south by a one-and-a-half-knot current. As a result, our first 24 hours at sea we traveled a scant 48 miles through the water, and worse yet, we made good only 30 miles toward Singapore—a very disappointing beginning.

On our second day, the wind backed enough after breakfast that we were able to point our bow toward Singapore. *Tainui* performed well to windward under her jib, staysail, and main, but our progress through the water continued to be much better than our progress toward Singapore, because the current was still pushing us 10 degrees south of our course. At dusk a sudden 45-knot gale swept into us. Connie grabbed the wheel and started the engine while I spilled the wind out of the sails by releasing their sheets and letting them flap in the wind. I furled the jib from the cockpit, went forward and pulled down the staysail, secured it on deck, and then put a double reef in the main. Back in the cockpit, I pulled the mainsail in tight, and Connie turned *Tainui* into the wind and killed the engine, leaving us hove to in the gale. The storm raged on through the night, but in spite of the wind screaming in the rigging and the waves roaring by, we were relatively comfortable "parked" in the sea.

It was 13 hours before we were able to sail again, and while we were hove to, we drifted even farther south in the current. When we started sailing again, we beat into a 20-knot northwest wind only a little south of our desired course. However, we were sailing toward Penjantan Island. If we could hold our course, we could beat our way north of the island, but if we fell off the wind and passed to the south of it, we would fall so far down wind from Singapore that it could take us days of tacking back and forth to get there. But passing to the north of it would make Penjantan Island a lee shore, which was risky. If the wind shifted against us, we might not be able to clear the island, and if the wind quit, the current would push us toward shore. Our situation was further complicated by the fact that we reached the Island in the middle of the night. I continued on our course north of the island keeping a close watch on the radar. If the wind headed us, I planned to jibe downwind and sail or motor back around the island and pass to the south of it. If the wind died, I planned to motor off shore. This decision was a departure from my usual conservative seamanship and mistrust of the engine. In retrospect I was surprised I considered it. Our frustration at being set so far south had gotten the better of me.

And indeed, while we were sailing along the north coast of the island, the wind dropped to seven knots, *Tainui* slowed to a crawl, and the current set us toward the island. The radar showed that we went from three miles offshore to one mile off in 30 minutes. I jibed *Tainui,* and we were able to sail slowly back downwind, but we were heading back toward Borneo and we would have to sail further south to clear Penjantan Island.

In order to speed up our progress, I started the engine and began to motor, but the engine overheated. This could have been a disaster if the wind had shifted and blown toward the island. With a 20-knot wind and the current against us, it might not have been possible for us to beat our way off the lee shore without an engine. By then it was 3:00 a.m., but I was so anxious to get the engine working that I worked on it by flashlight. I found nothing wrong with its cooling system but, in case the blockage was in the hoses that cooled the refrigerator condenser en route to the engine, I bypassed the refrigeration system, and the engine passed a short test.

In the morning, the wind freshened and we backtracked until we were able to pass to the south of Penjantan Island. By the time we cleared the island, we were almost directly downwind from Singapore. Our course to Singapore was northwest, but we could only sail due west against the wind, waves, and current. This was very frustrating. If this wind held, we could either continue west and make landfall in a group of Indonesian islands off the east coast of Sumatra, or spend days tacking back and forth to Singapore. We talked it over and decided that it would be easier on us and on the boat to go for the islands off Sumatra. We planned to land somewhere near the southern end of the narrow Riau Strait, which led north between two of these islands to Singapore. We would then, motor willing, motor up the strait to the Singapore Channel.

The wind gradually increased during the day and reached gale force again during the night. We did not heave to this time but sailed on. However, *Tainui* continued to make little progress against the wind and the waves. As we slammed along, I started the engine to charge the batteries, and it overheated again. I dismantled the entire engine-cooling system once again and still did not find the problem.

Connie and I were busy all the next day making sail changes in response to a series of squalls and calms. When I reconnected the refrigerator water hoses and ran the engine, the situation looked hopeful for a while, but the engine overheated after 40 minutes. The engine was critical, not only to charge the batteries for our lights and electronics, but because we would need it to get to Singapore. We needed the engine to motor up the Riau Strait and then to thread our way through the ship traffic when we crossed the Strait of Singapore—one of the world's busiest shipping waterways.

Our problems multiplied the next day. Our staysail, which was lashed on deck, blew overboard during the night and was shredded from being dragged under the hull. In addition, the engine overheated again. For the third time, I tore it apart, found nothing wrong, put it back together, and started it. For no apparent reason, this time it ran cool for an hour. I continued to use it conservatively because I had no idea how long it would last. About then, Connie reported that our double berth in the bow was wet. I had sealed the hatch above it with tape and covered the bed with plastic, but some water had gotten in and soaked one side of it. That night we had squalls with 20-knot gusts and heavy rain, and the ship traffic increased to the point that we often had four ships in sight at one time. The visibility was so poor that we were both up much of the night, looking out, monitoring the radar, and contacting approaching ships on the radio.

On the morning of our fifth day out we were 40 miles from the Riau Strait and another 60 from Singapore. I was reluctant to run the engine, so I tried to make it under sail, but our progress was frustratingly slow.

It was a day of passing showers, with wind during the rains and calms in between. Connie took a rain shower on deck and felt much refreshed after being cooped up in the hot, humid cabin below while we were hove to, and I got my shower accidentally. The drum that held the jib-furling line broke, and the line fouled under the drum. I spent an hour in the bow pulpit untangling the line and manually rolling up the jib. Before I finished, I was drenched by a heavy downpour and decided that that was shower enough.

We were feeling the effects of sleep deprivation, so we hoped to anchor at the entrance to the Riau Strait in time to get a good night's sleep. Unfortunately, once again the wind turned directly against us. We tacked into the night, but our GPS showed that we were tacking back and forth, making almost no forward progress. Finally, in desperation, at 2:00 a.m. I took a chance on the motor. I started the engine, and when I went back to the stern pulpit and set up the electric autopilot, I found that the GPS antenna's base was broken. After I got *Tainui* motoring along under the autopilot, I jury-rigged a new support for the GPS that I hoped would last until we got to Singapore. It seemed that either the curse of the ghost of Pontianak was still with us or the boat was falling apart. This was one of our most frustrating and tedious nights at sea. With the wind and seas against us, even motoring was painfully slow. We traded watches every hour because we couldn't stay awake any longer than that, and we needed to watch for traffic and monitor the engine heat. Miraculously, the engine ran at its normal temperature the whole way. I had no rational explanation for that—maybe we had sailed beyond the range of Pontianak's evil spirit.

We finally reached an anchorage at Matang Island, about 10 miles south of the Riau Strait, at 11:00 a.m. We took a nap, woke up, ate lunch, and took another nap. We woke up again at 9:00 p.m., saw that it was dark, and went back to sleep. Connie slept on the dry side of the V-berth and I slept on the settee; it didn't matter where we slept that night—we didn't wake up again until 7:30 in the morning.

Feeling much better, we had breakfast at anchor and started motoring up the Riau Strait—happy to be finished with the South China Sea. At 4:00 in the afternoon we spotted a quiet anchorage off our port side, behind a small island that was across the channel from an Indonesian Navy base. If we continued we would reach the Strait of Singapore in the dark, so we made a short day of it and anchored behind the little island. It was a great relief to have time to relax. After dinner, we fixed a drink and sat on the stern deck listening to classical music on our stereo as the sun went down behind the Navy base. Not fully recovered from the crossing, we turned in early for another good night's sleep.

The final day of this passage dawned sunny and calm. We motored up the Riau Strait and reached the Strait of Singapore around noon. This strait, between Singapore and Indonesia, was the northernmost deepwater passage between the Pacific Ocean and the Indian Ocean and Suez Canal. The nearest possibility to the south was the Torres Strait between Australia and New Guinea, but it was not suitable for huge ships. The only other possibility was a much longer trip south of Australia in the frequently stormy Southern Ocean. Singapore's prominence as a world shipping and commercial center is due to this propitious geographical location.

In the strait, long lines of ships were passing before us in both directions divided by a separation zone that kept the two lanes of ships a safe distance apart. With our engine purring as if it had never had a problem, we easily threaded our way through one line of ships and caught our breath in the relative safety of the separation zone. But when we continued across the strait, we soon found ourselves on a collision course with a supertanker. We were both under motor and I wasn't sure who technically had the right-of-way, so I followed the sailors' adage "Give way to weight" and went around behind it.

When we were safely out of the shipping lanes, we motored around the eastern tip of Singapore Island, turned northwest, and traveled up the Johore Strait—a narrow channel between Singapore and the southern tip of Malaysia—toward the town of Changi. We radioed the Changi Sailing Club for instructions with no response, but our friend Pat Henry on *Southern Cross* answered and directed us to the yacht club's mooring area for visiting yachts. These moorings were at Loyang, about a mile past the sailing club—all the closer mooring buoys were reserved for club members. After we paid our mooring fee at the sailing club, Pat served us coffee and cake aboard *Southern Cross*.

Pat's passage from Indonesia to Singapore had been much more difficult than ours. She had sailed nonstop from Bali—a longer passage than our trip from Pontianak—and she had done it alone. Sleep was nearly impossible due to the ship traffic in the South China Sea and the Singapore Strait. She suffered physically and mentally from sleep deprivation. In her book By the Grace of the Sea she writes, "My arms and legs were filled with sand and my head stuffed with steel wool. By morning, I would have gone 168 hours without any real sleep....Nausea, exhaustion and tears weighted me to the cockpit seat." After hearing her story, Connie and I were too embarrassed to complain about what we thought had been a rough crossing for us.

With a couple of good night's sleep behind us, the rigors of the crossing faded, and we were ready to explore Singapore. Checking in was an all-day process that took us from one end of the island to the other. The port authority was at the Tanjong Pagar Complex, which was near the sailing club, but the customs and immigration offices were in the World Trade Center building, downtown on the opposite side of the island. It took two busses and the MRT (a rapid transit system identical to the BART in the San Francisco Bay Area) to get there. The process took almost all day, but it gave us a good view of the city. The MRT was partly underground and partly elevated. On the elevated sections we had a panoramic view of Singapore. Its most striking feature was the hundreds of high-rise apartment buildings that stretched from horizon to horizon. They had replaced the villages that were there when we lived in Malaysia. Eighty percent of Singapore's 3 million citizens lived in them. In spite of the fact that 2.5 million people were packed into a sea of high-rise apartments, the city was impeccably clean. Singapore's antilittering laws were strictly enforced and conscientiously obeyed.

We were in Singapore 10 weeks. Immigration would grant us only a two-weeks' stay at a time, so we wasted a long hot day returning to the immigration office every two weeks. After six weeks, we had to justify our need for further extensions by providing evidence that we were not able to leave because we were waiting for boat parts, repairs to be completed, etc. As time went on, the authorities became harder and harder to convince.

Our first order of business in Singapore was to catch up on our delayed maintenance. Singapore was the best place for boat supplies that we had found since San Diego. We sent to Australia for a new staysail to replace the one that was shredded when it was washed overboard one night and dragged under *Tainui*. We had a rigging shop in Changi Village make up all new standing rigging for our mast. The old steel cables were showing wear, especially near the fittings on their ends. A telltale sign of the wear was little curled-up broken steel strands that sailors called "meat hooks," for reasons which we discovered after puncturing our fingers.

Changi was a long way from the city, but we got a great deal of help from Helen at the Eng Seng Hardware Store in Changi Village. She was a mechanical engineer with an encyclopedic knowledge of hardware items and where to find them. She was also a great help in sending equipment to be repaired. She found us a new alternator that was compatible with our engine's electrical system, and when our starter began working intermittently, Helen sent it out and had a new solenoid installed. She also helped us get our electric autopilot repaired and sold us a new stereo system at a discount price. From time to time Helen treated a group of us cruisers to dinner at her favorite restaurant—Chinese, of course—in downtown Singapore.

One day I had trouble starting the engine. After cranking the engine with the starter for a long time, I was shocked to see water coming out of the engine's air intake. It hadn't occurred to me to shut off the seacock to the cooling system. As the starter turned the engine turned over, the water pump pulled in water, and with no engine exhaust to force the water out, the engine was flooded. At first I thought that I would have to tear the engine apart and dry it out. Fortunately I consulted with Geoff from *Kanaka* before doing that. Geoff was a diesel mechanic from England. Under his guidance, I closed the water intake and cranked the engine until the water stopped coming out. Geoff guessed that the engine didn't start because of a faulty fuel pump, so I replaced the fuel pump, opened the engine seacock, and tried the starter. The engine started up normally, and all I had to do was run it for a few hours to dry it out. If it hadn't been for Geoff, I would have spent days tearing it down and putting it back together, one hopes, correctly.

We also had a few exciting moments on board when our alternator caught fire while we were running the engine. The fire extinguisher would suppress it momentarily, but it would flare up again. It continued to burn after I shut down the engine and died only after I turned off the main battery switch.

Singapore had an amazing array of electronics dealerships and outlet stores. While exploring them I found a Kenwood dealer. I was not aware that there was a Kenwood dealer in Singapore when I tried to have my old Kenwood ham radio repaired on my previous visit. One of the Kenwood technicians told me that my old ham radio could have been easily repaired. I went back to the Icom dealer who had told me the Kenwood was unrepairable (in order to sell me a new Icom?). To my surprise, he still had my old radio and returned it to me. The Kenwood dealership fixed it for US$68—I had paid US$850 for the Icom. I continued to use the Icom as our main radio, but I kept the Kenwood as a spare.

And we finally got both of our cameras fixed. We were able to take our Sony video camera to a huge Sony complex and our Minolta still camera to a Minolta technician. Everything we needed was in Singapore, but we spent a lot of time locating things and traveling all over Singapore to get them. Singapore no longer had duty-free prices, but it had the most complete selection of electronic equipment imaginable.

For the first time on our sailing trip we did not go home for the holidays. We had decided to make our future visits when it was summertime in the United States, because the Christmas season had been a hectic time for visiting our family. With parents working, children's school activities, and the Christmas shopping rush, we felt we were an added burden. We hoped we could have more relaxed visits in the summer, when our families were less busy and the weather was better. We missed our family as we celebrated our Christmases with boating friends far away from home in un-Christmas-like weather, but our summertime home visits did work out much better than the holiday ones had.

Christmas Eve in Singapore, Lita, who was alone on her yacht *Vauve Maria,* invited us to a potluck dinner aboard her vessel, along with Pat Henry from *Southern Cross*, Tita from *Afradite*, and Ragnar from *Ocean Quest*. The good food, wine, and interesting international fellowship helped ease the pain of being so far from home on Christmas Eve.

On Christmas morning we opened a package of mail from home and read aloud our Christmas cards and letters. *Tainui* was decorated with ornaments, garlands, and a tiny plastic Christmas tree, all of which we had bought at a Chinese shop, and the "Hallelujah Chorus" played in the background. Reading the cards and letters made us feel a little less lonely, and the decorations helped too, but we still missed our family. Jeff and Lisa, friends from our New Zealand days, arrived on *Inter-Mission* on Christmas Day and joined us for dinner at the posh Meridien Hotel. The meal was advertised as a "Traditional Christmas Turkey Dinner." To us Americans it was a Christmas dinner with a Chinese accent. However, the hotel decorations gave us as much of a Christmas atmosphere as was possible in a tropical garden setting, and an evening of festive fun and entertainment followed the dinner.

Our son Larry stopped off to see us in Singapore on his way to a business meeting in the Sultanate of Brunei on the island of Borneo. He came out to *Tainui* for lunch, and we had dinner in town at Lau Pa Sat (Helen Eng's favorite restaurant). It was located in a modern eating hall— a kind of luxury food court with an international gourmet cuisine.

We got a late start on the morning that we left for Malaysia, because it took us two hours to clean our anchor chain. A luxurious profusion of marine growth had accumulated during *Tainui's* 10 weeks in Singapore's warm, nutrient-rich water. Connie operated the anchor winch on the foredeck and cranked up a few feet of chain at a time, while I sat in the dinghy under the bow and chipped away with a screwdriver and scrubbed with a stiff brush. By the time I finished, my knuckles were bloody from encounters with razor-sharp barnacles and other crusty creatures.

The ideal way to reach the west coast of Malaysia would have been to travel through the narrow, calm Johore Strait between the north shore of Singapore the southern tip of the Malay Peninsula. Unfortunately, that strait was blocked in the middle by a causeway. Therefore, our course to the west coast of Malaysia took us through the congested waters south of Singapore. As soon as we rounded Changi Point at the east end of the island and turned west, we entered Singapore's eastern ship anchorage. Eighty full-sized ships and dozens of smaller vessels were anchored there, and several others were under way. There was a good sailing wind, but we motored through the anchorage in order to have good maneuverability among the moving vessels. After a 20-mile trip through that anchorage, we anchored for the night in a little channel between two small islands just south of Sentosa Island, the site of a luxury resort. We were just south of downtown Singapore, halfway across the island, and the western ship anchorage was still ahead of us.

Our anchorage was calm until after dinner, when *Tainui* dragged her anchor in a strong tidal current. We motored around trying to find a better spot, but couldn't find a place where the water was shallow enough to anchor, so we wound up back where we had first anchored. The current was so strong that *Tainui* swerved back and forth all night, and the current made so much noise against the bow that we abandoned the V-berth. We took turns keeping an anchor watch all night.

We reluctantly dragged ourselves out of bed in the morning and got away at 8:00. The western ship anchorage was the same size as the eastern one and just as busy. We motor-sailed through this one, keeping a sharp lookout to see which ships were anchored and which were moving. We passed a few small islands with "tank farms" on them. Pipes ran out from the tanks to the ends of long piers where supertankers off-loaded oil to them. Some of the islands had oil refineries on them. When we cleared the last of the anchored ships, we shut off the engine and sailed along in blissful silence on a beam reach. Late in the day the wind headed us so, we motored across the western entrance of the Johore Strait and made our first stop in Malaysia, off the shore of Pulau Kukup. We were much relieved to be clear of the ship traffic of Singapore and in the peace and quiet of rural Malaysia. We had also achieved a major objective of our trip—we had sailed back to Malaysia—a country that we had fallen in love with during the four years that I worked there as a Peace Corps officer.

Soon after we anchored, a small fishing boat came alongside and the fisherman asked us in English where we were from and then begged for a Pepsi. All we had was diet Coke; he turned up his nose at that and went on his way. A little later, a large wooden sailing vessel sailed into the anchorage. It looked like a Mediterranean dhow with a huge lateen mainsail made of green silk, and it towed a dugout canoe for a shore boat. The sailing vessel had a pirate-ship look, and we were uneasy as it bore directly down on us. At the last minute, it turned upwind, dropped its big sail, and anchored nearby. The crew peacefully cooked dinner in the open-air galley on their stern. Maybe they came so close to us because we had anchored in their favorite spot.

Our first full day in Malaysia we had perfect sailing as we cruised north along the west coast of that country in the Strait of Malacca. The wind direction fluctuated, but most of the time we were on a fast and comfortable broad reach. We made an excellent 58 miles in the daylight hours and anchored behind a point of land called Tanjong Johore at dusk. It had been an excellent problem-free run for *Tainui*—a welcome change from our troubles in the South China Sea. We were also happy to be back in coastal waters, during which we could anchor and sleep most nights without keeping watch.

We celebrated our trouble-free day with a gin and tonic before dinner. Just as we finished our drinks, a heavy squall swept into our anchorage. There was no one else around, so we quickly stripped and showered in the rain. (Many European cruising couples routinely skipped the part about "there was no one else around.") Whenever we washed our hair in the rain, there was a risk that the rain would quit just in time to leave us stumbling around with our eyes closed trying to find some rinse water, but this time the rain lasted long enough. While Connie baked a pizza casserole, I checked in to the Indian Ocean Ham Net. We heard Jeff and Lisa on *Inter-Mission* report in 270 miles from the Maldives on their way across the Indian Ocean.

The next day we made a short fifty-fifty motoring and sailing trip to Water Island near the old Dutch settlement of Malacca. We arrived in the late afternoon and took the dinghy ashore to see if we could have dinner at a new resort on the island. Signs posted on the beach warned that the island was for resort guests only, but undaunted, we walked up to the office and were eagerly invited to eat dinner. Judging by the lack of other diners, they would have been glad to serve anyone who came along. The fare was expensive—especially the drinks. We declined the wine at US$12 a glass. The high cost of alcoholic beverages may have been due to the fact that the hotel was operated by Malays, who are all Muslim and forbidden to drink alcohol. Most of Malaysia's hotels and restaurants were owned by Chinese and East Indians who had no such restriction. The menu offered Western-style food, but we ordered less expensive Malay dinners, which were excellent. After dinner we strolled in the cool of the evening on the resort's large and beautifully landscaped grounds. Back aboard *Tainui* the wind blew into our anchorage, and the wave action shook us out of our double-berth in the bow. Oh well, at least we didn't have to keep a night watch.

Two days later we arrived at Port Kelang after an overnight stop at Port Dixon. Kelang was the commercial harbor for the capital city of Kuala Lumpur, 20 miles inland. (*kuala* means "river mouth," and Kuala Lumpur literally means "muddy river mouth"). We tied up to the visitors' dock at the Royal Selangor Yacht Club and checked in at the office. Selangor is the name of the Malaysian state that Kuala Lumpur is in. (There are 13 Malaysian states, represented by 13 red and white stripes on their flag!) The yacht-club staff gave us a warm welcome and assigned us to a mooring buoy. The club provided free water taxis called "jingos" to take us to and from the club. That system prevented a dinghy pileup at their dock. The jingos ran every hour on weekdays and every half hour on weekends. We were happy to leave our dinghy aboard. That evening we caught the 6:00 jingo and had dinner at the yacht club, where we shared a table with a friendly mixed-race Chinese and Caucasian couple. Everyone at the club treated us cordially.

In the morning, after we checked in with the authorities, we walked around Port Kelang, which was a busy industrial shipping harbor. We stopped at a shipping company and inquired about the feasibility of shipping *Tainui* back to the United States on the deck of a cargo ship, in case we decided to end our voyage in Southeast Asia. It was possible, but expensive, and some yachts had been damaged, looted, and even washed overboard. Our other options were to sail her back ourselves, hire a delivery crew, or sell her in Southeast Asia.

At the yacht club, we were befriended by Eric, a Chinese businessman whom we had talked to on a ham net. He drove us to Petaling Jaya, a posh suburb of Kuala Lumpur, for dinner at an open-air stall in a large market. After dinner Eric took us to see the Selangor State Mosque. Unlike the ultramodern National Mosque in Kuala Lumpur, it was in traditional Moorish style, with four tall, graceful minarets surrounding a high dome, and the entire mosque was covered with blue tiles. Flood-lit because it was the beginning of Hari Raya (the fasting month of Ramadan), it was a beautiful sight in the twilight.

Before we left Port Kelang, I spent an afternoon working on our starter motor. Even with the new solenoid that Helen Eng had acquired for us in Singapore, it was responding intermittently, which made it hard for me to isolate the problem. Fortunately, that was our only maintenance problem since leaving Singapore. By the time I finished working it, it was too late to check out and leave that day, so we spent another night. At that time, I was acting as net controller for an informal morning radio net for cruisers in Singapore and Malaysia. I convened the net and invited those who were on-line to check in. Cruisers used the net to share information and to make contacts with their friends. After the net the next morning I went ashore and finished checking out with the authorities in time to catch the 10:00 jingo back to *Tainui*. Connie had everything stowed and ready for sea, and with no anchor chain to clean and winch up, we were off of our mooring buoy and under way in a few minutes.

On most days we used the land-and-sea breezes to sail up the Malaysian coast in the Strait of Malacca. The exceptions were the occasional calm or stormy days. We started off from Port Kelang with a steady land breeze that put us on a beam reach until about noon, when the wind became light and variable. (The land breeze provided the smoothest sailing because, with the wind coming from the shore, there was not enough fetch for the waves to build up.) The wind quit altogether after lunch, so we motored for a while to charge our batteries and refrigerator. The starter didn't work that time, so I had to hand-crank the motor. As we motored along, I cleaned up a poor ground connection that I thought might have been the problem. When the sea breeze filled in we sailed again in the afternoon. In that part of the strait, we had to thread our way through dozens of fishnets held in place by poles and fish traps attached to pilings. At one point, when I wanted to motor around a fishnet, the starter didn't respond, and I didn't have time to go below and hand-crank the engine. Fortunately, *Tainui* drifted over the net without snagging anything. If there was enough wind, we sailed when we were near fishnets; motoring over nets was risky because the nets could get caught in the prop.

The sea breeze lasted well into the evening, so we kept sailing until 10:00. There was no harbor nearby, so we just sailed toward shore until we reached a depth of 25 feet and dropped anchor in the strait near Kuala Bernam. There was no shelter and, although the sea breeze had died, it had built up some waves in the afternoon. The night was rolly for a while, but the sea soon flattened out.

We woke up early and ate a leisurely breakfast at anchor out in the strait. By the time I finished running the morning radio net and cranked up the anchor, the land breeze had built up to a good sailing wind. It was only 40 miles to our next destination, the Royal Perak Yacht Club, in Lumut (*perak* means "silver" and is the name of the Malaysian state north of Selangor). Once again we sailed steadily until midday, when the land had heated up enough to stop the land breeze. This time the starter took pity on my cranking arm and started the engine at the touch of the button. Two hours later we were sailing in the sea breeze.

The town of Lumut, our destination, was on the mainland side of a narrow channel between Pangkor Island and the mainland, near the mouth of the Dindings River. The wind swirled in the channel and there was a strong current, so we took down the sails and motored through the channel to the river mouth and upriver the short distance to the Royal Perak Yacht Club. The yacht clubs in Selangor and Perak were "Royal" because those states had sultans, and the sultans were patrons of the clubs. A dozen yachts were anchored off the beach in front of the club when we arrived, including *Viki*. Our friends Chuck and Dottie, who had arrived a few weeks before us, took us to dinner at the club, and after dinner we continued our reunion over coffee and dessert aboard their *Viki*.

Contrary to its ostentatious name, the Royal Perak Yacht Club was not very impressive. It was an older one-story wooden building, amid some palm trees, just above the high-water mark. It looked more like an extra-long private dwelling than a yacht club. It was run by a Chinese family who lived in the back. The wife cooked dinner at the club on request. We cruisers felt comfortable in its casual, relaxed atmosphere. Connie and I had read about this club years before in one of Lynn and Larry Pardee's *Seraphin* books and had put it on our "must stop" list. Unfortunately, a developer had recently petitioned the government for permission to tear it down and build a modern resort and marina in its place. The club's board of directors had appealed to their sultan protector, but they were not optimistic about the outcome. They speculated that the sultan himself was in on the deal. (According to our well-traveled yachting friends, this was part of a worldwide trend. Cheap yacht clubs were being replaced by expensive marinas, and free anchorages by pricey mooring buoys—especially in Europe.)

There were two small towns in the area, and checking in involved both of them. Immigration was at Sitiawan, the larger of the two, about eight miles up the river from the yacht club. We took a taxi to Sitiawan and got our passports stamped by immigration. Then we ate lunch at Kentucky Fried Chicken, shopped in the produce market, and took a bus back to the yacht club. Customs was on the ferry terminal in Lumut, within walking distance of the yacht club. The ferries connected the mainland with the fishing village and resorts on Pangkor Island. After being cleared by customs at the ferry dock, we extended Connie's vacation from cooking by eating dinner with Chuck and Dottie at an open-front Malay eating shop in Lumut.

The next morning we left our heavy washing at a laundry in downtown Lumut and washed our lighter things in an open tub beside the yacht club. We spent the rest of the day lounging around the club and getting acquainted with some of the people from the other yachts anchored there. One of them was a young woman named Sherie who was trying to convert a wooden Vietnamese refugee boat into a cruising yacht. She said that it was the only way she could afford to fulfill her dream of cruising in her own yacht. I wished her well, but her project looked hopeless to me. The refugee boat was a crudely built powerboat that was totally unequipped for sailing.

One morning, as I was walking to town to pick up a few groceries, I passed a recently opened five-star hotel. I wondered how it could succeed in rustic little Lumut and strolled in to check it out. The lobby was huge and expensively done up with high ceilings, potted palms, and a tile floor. Labor and local materials were cheap in Malaysia, so such luxurious construction was not uncommon, even in ordinary buildings. I inquired about room prices and found that they were not bad—about US$50 a night. On my way out, the hotel chef came out of the kitchen and introduced himself. He was a middle-aged German dressed in the typical chef's starched white coat and high hat. He recited his impressive *haute cuisine* credentials and encouraged me to come to dinner in the hotel dining room. Back at the yacht club, Connie and I rounded up Rob and Sandy from *Sarcoma*, and we all dined in style in the hotel's sparsely populated restaurant. Before we finished eating, Herr Chef came to our table, greeted me as an old friend, and introduced himself to the others in our party.

While we were in Lumut, Connie and I revisited Pangkor Island, where we had once gone on a family vacation when we were living in Malaysia. We left *Tainui* at the yacht club and took the ferry across to the fishing village. On that earlier trip, we had taken the ferry to the best resort on the island—Peace Corps staff were well paid. But this time we got off at the fishing village and asked a taxi driver to find us accommodations for no more than 50 ringgets (about US$16) per day. He took us up a long, sandy, one-lane road to the Nipa Bay Hotel. It was in poor repair and the rooms were crude, but we gave it a go—the price was right and Nipa Bay had a lovely beach.

Our room had an Asian-style toilet—a hole in the concrete floor, with blocks for your feet. It flushed from a hose attached to a tank on the wall. The bed had no sheets, and the hotel had no towels. The paint on the walls did not reach the floor, there were no baseboards, and the linoleum on the cement floor did not reach the walls. I had to kill a few large spiders before we could sleep.

The condition of the hotel was typical of enterprises run by Malays. Most business in Malaysia were run by Chinese, who made up 40 percent of the population. Malays generally came from rural backgrounds and did not take as naturally to business as the Chinese did, so the government subsidized projects like the Nipa Bay Hotel to help them get started in business. They still had a long way to go before they could compete with the Chinese, and unfortunately the subsidies made it possible for them to stay in business without learning to compete.

Nipa Bay had a gracefully curved sandy beach with lots of palm trees, and there was a little rock island about 200 yards from shore. We had the beach to ourselves when we went for a swim in the afternoon. The next morning, we were joined on the beach by a British couple. He was a doctor and she was a lawyer. The lawyer and I half waded and half swam out to the little island. Connie, who was not a strong swimmer, remained on the beach and the doctor, thought the swim was a waste of energy, sat under a palm tree and read a book.

After lunch we took a taxi back to the fishing village and spent a lazy afternoon strolling around and munching on Malaysian delicacies from the food carts and stalls. Malaysia and Singapore were the only places in Southeast Asia where it was safe to drink water out of a tap, and that meant the local food was safe as well. (There were 500 Peace Corps volunteers in Malaysia when we were there, and the health conditions were so good that we eliminated our Peace Corps doctor's position.) It was a nostalgic afternoon for us because the village had been unchanged by time—it was exactly as it was when we were there 23 years before. We went back to the Nipa Bay Hotel for the night and returned to Lumut the next day.

A few days later we heard that an interesting religious festival was about to begin on Pangkor Island. We had some time to kill while we were waiting for a mail packet from home, so we sailed *Tainui* over to check it out. *Timshell*, with a couple from New Zealand and their 12-

year-old daughter and 10-year-old son aboard, sailed along with us. We anchored in Siapu Bay and that evening we saw a crowd of colorfully dressed people onshore—some on the beach and some standing knee-deep in the water, and we went ashore with the family from *Timshell* for a closer look. Hindu priests were putting people in trances. They waded into the water, looked into the eyes of the celebrants (mostly East Indian with a few Chinese), and chanted. People went into trances very quickly and began dancing around with glassy eyes. The priests did not object to our watching; in fact they told us that this was just a preliminary exercise and invited us to come back in the morning to see the real thing. The six of us walked to a small hotel in the fishing village for dinner.

The scene on the beach the next morning was colorful and exotic, but gruesome. This time the trances were in preparation for all manner of body piercing in the celebrants, who were about to walk in a five-mile parade. Thin metal skewers six to eight inches long were stuck vertically down through the tongues of several women. Some of the men had pushed four-foot-long steel rods as big around as my little finger through their cheeks. Tridents were screwed on to the ends of the rods and the men supported the rods with their teeth. A few Chinese men had several large hooks inserted in the skin on their backs with cords attached to them and held by other men who walked behind them. The majority of the men carried a device called a kavadi. It was a framework that rested on their shoulders and supported what looked like half of an over-sized bicycle-wheel rim with many holes in it. One end of some long thin skewers about the size of metal coat hangers were threaded down through the holes in the rim and stuck under the skin on the chests and abdomens of the celebrants. Ostrich feathers were attached to the other ends of the skewers. In addition to the ostrich feathers, the *kavadis* were decorated with ribbons and flowers. The *kavadi* carriers were an impressive sight, marching in the parade, with their flowers and ostrich plumes bobbing high above them.

This was not an unfamiliar sight to us. We had witnessed two much larger celebrations of a similar ceremony called Thaipusan when we were living in Malaysia. We learned that people carried *kavadis* or endured the other piercing in order to pay back one of the Hindu gods for a vow that they had made. They had essentially made a deal with the god that, if certain requests were granted, they would participate in this spectacle. Typical vows to the deity were that, if their wife recovered from cancer, their child passed his or her exams, or they got a good job, they would carry *kavadi*. Unfortunately, they sometimes promised the god that one of their children would fulfill the vow for them. As before, on this occasion we saw no blood and no expressions of pain on any of the celebrants.

We walked along in the hot sun with the wild and weird parade as it made its way from the beach to a Hindu temple five miles away. The experience was a sensory overload. Along with the colorful *kavadis*, the celebrants wore silky saffron or crimson garments, and the women marching with them wore bright colored silken saris. For the entire way, the concelebrants kept up a beating of small drums, clapping of hands, and chanting, and the priests swung burning incense back and forth. When we reached the fishing village, the six of us stopped in an outdoor café on a street corner and sipped fresh cool limeade as we watched the parade pass by.

We reached the Hindu temple in time to see many of the celebrants arrive. The scene at the temple was even more frenetic than the parade had been. The temple courtyard was wall-to-wall people. Vendors at a dozen small tables sold all manner of brightly colored Indian confections. People were throwing fake paper money and written prayers onto a large bonfire that was burning between two six-foot-tall, one-foot-thick smoking joss sticks. The smoke from the fire was supposed to take their petitions and gifts up to heaven. Inside the temple, priests were taking out the piercing devices and clapping their hands in the faces of the celebrants to snap them out of their trances. Again, we saw no blood. When a priest clapped his hands in the face of one young man, he blinked his eyes and we heard him ask the priest, in English, "How did I do? Did I fall down? Did I make it all the way?" Apparently he had no recall of the experience.

I was fortunate enough to take an excellent videotape of the event. My closing scene was of a rooster perched on a corner of the tiled roof of the temple, looking down on the incredulous scene below with a cocked head.

Back at Lumut our mail had arrived, so we planned to leave the next morning. I checked out with the officials in Sitiawan and Lumut, and Connie sent a copy of the latest issue of her *"Tainui* Travel Log" to her brother-in-law, Dave Weed, who would duplicate it and send it to our mailing list.

The sailors at the Royal Perak Yacht Club made a practice of throwing farewell parties that lasted late into the night for the crews of departing vessels. Because such a party would prevent us from getting a good night's sleep on the eve of our departure, we slipped out of Lumut late that afternoon and motor-sailed 15 miles to uninhabited little Pulau Tulang. At anchor, we finished tidying up the boat for going to sea and had a relaxing dinner and evening. When it was dark we were amazed at the number of lighted fishing boats on the horizon. There appeared to be hundreds of them; it looked like a freeway at rush hour. We went to bed early and had a restful night's sleep.

It was still dark when we got up, so we waited until daylight before getting under way. With no wind, we motored all day weaving our way through the fishing boats and the lines and nets they were tending. We had never seen so many fishing boats—we had 70 of them in sight at one time. Whenever there was a bit of a breeze, we would put up some sails and motor-sail, which gave us a smoother and a slightly faster ride, but the wind would soon quit and we would take down the flapping sails. Later in the day, to our great relief, we motored clear of the entire fishing fleet. That afternoon we encountered an unusual school of fish. There were dozens of them. They scooted across the water on their tails, sometimes for several hundred yards. They looked more like a low flying flock of birds than a school of fish. We sat on deck and enjoyed that spectacle for an hour while the autopilot steered *Tainui*.

After the long day of motoring we anchored in the evening at Pulau Kendi—a beautiful, uninhabited, jungle-covered island. Pulau Kendi was only 15 miles south of Penang, where I had been stationed by the Peace Corps for the year 1969. Penang was a large island, 46 miles around, with the major city of Georgetown situated on its east coast directly across a 5-mile-wide channel from the city of Butterworth on the mainland. We were torn between a desire to stop at Penang, which was one of our favorite places, and the need to get *Tainui* to Phuket, Thailand, and haul her out for a bottom cleaning. She had not been hauled out since Brisbane, Australia. We had a peaceful night to think about it, with no wind and a flat sea.

We awoke to another windless day—no land breeze, no sea breeze, no breeze at all. Once again we had to dodge dozens of boats trailing fishing lines and nets. Once, a fishing boat roared over to us and guided us around its net, which was a good thing, because we hadn't seen its series of tiny white floats. Another time, we ran over a crab-pot's float and its line wrapped around our prop. I tried to unwrap it by reversing the engine, with no luck. I hated to cut the line because some local fisherman would then be unable to find his crab pot. While I was mulling this over, a fishing boat came along side and offered to help. There were two men aboard, an old man and a teenager. I asked the kid if he could dive. At first he said no. However, when I got out my snorkeling mask and a knife, he changed his mind, borrowed my mask and jumped in and untangled the line from our prop. I thanked him, and they went on their way.

As we motored away, our engine overheated. The sea at that time was full of jellyfish, so I guessed that one of them had been sucked into the engine's water intake. I shut down the engine to relieve the suction, let *Tainui* drift for a few minutes, and restarted it. That did the job. We reluctantly bypassed Penang and headed for Langkawi. As we were motoring off the west coast of Penang, a 25-foot wooden fishing boat with a low deck and a high central pilothouse roared alongside us. The man at the wheel began to pantomime drinking by putting his fist up to his mouth with his thumb extended. I shouted over the noise of our engines, "What do you want?" in English and Malay, but he did not answer. I called out, "Do you want a drink of water?" and he became angry, shook his fist, and shouting something unintelligible to me—probably curse words. I suspected that he wanted liquor, but I refused to offer him any. His crewman, seated on a pile of nets on the forward cargo hatch, waved his hands back and forth, palms down, in an apologetic manner as if to show that he was not a party to his captain's behavior. The captain turned his boat away for a few yards and then spun around and rammed *Tainui* at full throttle. Its high bow stem struck the side rail of our stern pulpit where our dinghy's outboard motor was clamped onto it. The blow dented the stern pulpit's steel railing and slightly damaged the outboard. The fishing boat bounced off and sped away.

Twenty-five miles north of Penang we anchored in the afternoon beside Pulau Song Song. It had been a tense day, and we needed an early break. The water in the anchorage was exceptionally clear. At 15 feet we could see our anchor in the sand, schools of colorful fish, and sea cucumbers crawling on the bottom. During the night, the wind blew us in toward the shore so I slept near the companionway stairs and kept an anchor watch. We were so close to the shore that, if the anchor dragged, we would be on the beach in a few minutes.

At 6:00 a.m. a rainsquall with a strong offshore wind pushed us away from the shore. We rode out the squall at anchor and then set out for the island group of Langkawi, which is situated 35 miles off the mainland near the Thai border. The squall left no wind behind so we motored all that day, glad that this time there were no fishing boats, floats, or traps to dodge. We arrived at Kuah, the principal town in Lankawi, at 4:00 p.m. Even though there had been no ocean crossing, we felt a sense of relief at making port after a trip that had had some tense moments. As soon as we were anchored, our friends Jeff and Heather had us aboard

Kanaka along with another Brit, Hugh from *Blue Idol*, for a kind of happy hour *cum* catching-up-on-each-other's-news session.

Checking in at Lankawi was not a pleasant experience. There was no dinghy landing. We had to tie up to a police boat, scramble across its deck, and climb up some old tires that were hanging off the pier. The tide was so low that I had to pull Connie from the tires up onto some steps that were above her head. And then the immigration officer scolded us. We had broken two rules. We had checked in to customs <u>before</u> immigration, and I had listed Penang as our next port-of-call when I left Lumut, but had not checked in there. There was no penalty for these infractions—just a sarcastic reading-out by a surly official who made us feel like arrogant Americans who thought we were above the rules. I apologized in my best Malay, but that didn't soften the official's foul mood.

That evening, we were the guests of honor at a cocktail party on *Paragon* that the two men aboard her had organized to introduce us to the other sailors in the harbor—a thoughtful gesture.

Kuah was a disappointment. There was no yacht club or marina where we could dock, take showers and have convenient access to shore, so we anchored out and rigged a shower aboard *Tainui*. The only freshwater for yachts was at a pier across the harbor and required a M $15 (US$6) service fee. We tried to catch rainwater, more because of the nuisance than the cost. The town did not have any supermarkets—just a series of small specialty shops, which made shopping time consuming and required a lot of hard hot walking. The best of these shops was the Cold Storage; it sold frozen meat, which was excellent for starting a voyage.

After a week of shopping and socializing, we left Kuah to explore other parts of the Langkawi Island group. We began with a short sail to Tanjong Sawi ("Rice Paddy Point"), where three new resorts had been built along the beach, and we anchored near the Holiday Villa resort. We arrived in a rainstorm and put up our rain catcher. We caught 10 gallons of water, which was a welcome addition to our water supply now that we were showering aboard. In the evening we had dinner at the Holiday Villa resort. The restaurant had been open for only a week, and the service was laughably uncoordinated—I wasn't served my dinner until Connie had finished eating hers—but the food was good. We combed the beach and swam for another day at Tanjong Sawi and then sailed to Dayang Bunting Island, which had a large freshwater lake a short walk into the jungle from where we anchored. We hiked to the lake and swam in its refreshingly cool freshwater along with a few other yachties and some local people. That evening, back on board *Tainui*, we watched two monkeys come out of the jungle and play on the beach. The evening was calm, but in the night, williwaws rushed down the steep slopes of the island, rocking *Tainui* and shaking her rigging.

From there we sailed back to Kuah to prepare for our passage to Thailand. The town was eerily quiet during the daytime, because it was the month of Hari Raya (Ramadan), when Muslims could not eat or drink until dark. Once it was too dark to tell a white thread from a black thread, they could feast until morning. Before we could leave, we had to send our starter and our alternator for repairs, which took three days. When they were ready, the immigration and customs offices were closed for the last three days of Hari Raya, which were legal holidays. Sometimes things moved slowly in Southeast Asia.

While we were waiting to leave, another sailor and I helped Phil motor his 50-foot trimaran, *Wikiwin*, across the bay to get water. Both of these older men had young live-in women aboard—a Philippina lived with Phil and a Thai woman accompanied the other sailor. Later, we found this arrangement to be especially common in Thailand.

When the holidays ended, we stocked up on fresh bread, vegetables, fruit, and meat and checked out of Malaysia. We started the trip to Thailand with a short afternoon run back to Tanjong Sawi, which was just a few miles south of the Malaysian-Thailand border. We had dinner again at the Holiday Villa Resort. The waitresses remembered us from our previous visit, and this time they got it right—the service and the food were excellent. After dinner, we went back to *Tainui* and rested up for the trip to Thailand.

CHAPTER FIFTEEN

THAILAND AND MALAYSIA

On April 1, 1993, we left Langkawi, Malaysia, and sailed northward through a series of islands along the west coast of Thailand. Each morning, we picked out our next likely anchorage from the relevant nautical chart. For our first anchorage in Thailand, we chose the mouth of a river in the national park on Ko (Thai for "island") Tarutao. We motored the entire 22 miles on a windless day. Our engine was getting a good workout in the Straits of Malacca; many times we motored all day, and most of the time it ran well. We arrived early in the afternoon, anchored off the beach near the mouth of the river, went ashore, and walked around the park. There was an open-air co-op café, and a few rustic cabins were scattered about among the trees, but there was no park headquarters. We had a cold drink in the café and chatted with a couple of backpackers—a girl from America and a man from Italy. We swam in the warm water off the beach for a while before returning to *Tainui*.

The anchorage was moderately rolling, but would have been comfortable enough for us to sleep, except that Connie got a malaria pill stuck in her throat and didn't get it down until 4:00 a.m.; until then neither of us slept. (In Indonesia and Thailand we took a Larium pill once a week as a prophylactic against malaria.)

We awoke to an early morning rainsquall with strong wind. Ko Phetra, our next stop, was only 25 miles away, so we delayed our departure until the storm passed, and then we left in a dead calm. We motored for two hours until the land breeze came up and then we sailed on a fast beam reach until we hit the usual noon calm. By then we were used to this land-and-sea-breeze phenomenon and drifted through a leisurely lunch and a short nap until the sea breeze came up and blew us the remainder of the way to Ko Phetra. The island had sheer rock-wall cliffs hundreds of feet high. A few fishing shacks were squeezed between the tide line and the base of the cliffs. They were temporary shelters for fishermen who spent days at a time on the island during fishing season. Some of the men came out to *Tainui* in a long-tail canoe. Long-tail canoes have motors the size of small car engines mounted on a swivel on their sterns, with long prop shafts coming out the backs of them and steering handles projecting from their fronts. The props at the end of the long shafts were only half submerged and threw up impressive "rooster tails." The fishermen offered to sell us cuttlefish and small crabs, which we declined. We couldn't talk to them because they spoke only Thai—a language that was completely unintelligible to us, spoken or written. Connie and I showered aboard, watched the sun go down with a gin and tonic after dinner, and got a good night's sleep.

On the chart, Ko Hngai, a short distance away, looked like it might have a village, so we decided to check it out. The wind was on the nose so we motored over to the island and arrived at 2:30 p.m. There was, in fact, a resort onshore and it was teeming with people. We beached the dinghy and walked up to the resort. A tour group had arrived, and Thai people were swarming into the restaurant. The tour guide spoke English and said that he had reserved the place for dinner for his group, but that we could eat there also if we wished. We went in and were shown to a table and given a menu that was, to our great relief, in Thai and English. We ordered chicken curry and tom yum—a spicy-hot fish soup that was very tasty except for the cuttlefish, which had no flavor and was the texture of rubber bands. It took an hour for us to get our food even though people who came in after us were served before us. It looked like an obvious preference for local people. Fair enough.

We set out after breakfast for Ko Phi Phi Don—a popular resort island just a day's sail from our destination of Phuket. We motored all the way again and got in to Phi Phi Don at 4:00 in the afternoon. We went ashore and milled around with the holiday crowd in the village. It was a tourist beach scene with little souvenir shops, snack shops, and restaurants along the sand paths. There were no roads and no motor vehicles in the village. We ate at a typical beach restaurant with a thatched roof and waist-high woven-mat walls.

The day's sail to Phuket turned out to be another motorboat trip. On the way, the engine overheated and made a clanking sound. I planned to change the oil in Phuket and I hadn't added oil so I wouldn't have so much to drain. Unfortunately, I had overdone it and the engine was out of oil. The engine was so hot that I had to handle the oil filler cap with a handful of rags. The rags must have interfered with my sense of feel when I screwed the cap back on, because when I pulled back the companionway stairs and checked the engine a little later, the filler cap had come off and oil was spraying all over the engine and dripped off of the companionway stairs onto the cabin sole carpet. I added more oil and we motored on, mess and all. There was no hope of saving the carpet, so we added that to our Phuket shopping list.

We arrived at Ao ("Bay") Chalong, in the late afternoon. There were 50 cruising boats there, all anchored far offshore. The beach sloped so gradually out into the water that there was no anchoring depth near shore. At low tide, 200 yards of mud separated the water from the beach, and dinghies could not get back and forth to the shore from their boats. The usual landing place for dinghies was on the beach in front of the picturesque Latitude 8 Restaurant, distinguished by its lighthouse tower. Latitude 8, with showers and fax services, was a popular hangout for cruisers. The building faced the sea with an open-air front that could be shuttered in inclement weather. We could watch our boats and see arriving and departing vessels from our seats. The restaurant even provided loaner binoculars to give us a better look.

The island of Phuket is about 25 miles long. It is surrounded by many small islands, which made it feel more like a mainland than an island. Its major city was also named Phuket. Ao Chalong was at the southern tip of the island. We took a half-hour bus ride into the city center to check in the morning after we arrived. We then hired a taxi-like minivan to take us to the Office of Immigration, but couldn't check in because government offices were closed for a Thai holiday. We went back to town and ate at the Kanda Bakery restaurant, happy to be in an air-conditioned room. It was extremely hot and the buses had not been air-conditioned. The food at the bakery was good, but expensive by local standards. Even so, the bakery, with its casual coffee shop atmosphere, was a favorite meeting place for cruisers. We often ran into friends there. A fax from our daughter, Kathleen, was waiting for us when we got back to Latitude 8, where we ate dinner before returning to *Tainui*.

We checked in the following day. It required another bus ride to town and a suffocating minivan ride to immigration, followed by a hot minibus ride back to the Kanda Bakery for lunch. After lunch, we rode back to Ao Chalong in a very crowded bus during the hottest time of the day. We arrived feeling sticky and much in need of a shower. However, we were stranded at the Latitude 8 Restaurant for three hours because the tide had gone out, leaving 200 yards of mud between our dinghy and the water. While we were killing time at the restaurant, we met Pat and Jim, from *Beau Jeu*, a Canadian couple who had been cruising for nine years. That meeting began a close long-term relationship.

We negotiated with the Phuket Marine Company to rebuild *Tainui*'s aging teak steering pedestal. It had been crudely constructed and was coming apart. They offered to build an attractive teak replacement for US$500, which we felt was a bargain. Phuket Marine was operated by two engineers, Willy, a German, and Jimmy, an American. Jimmy and his Thai wife also owned Latitude 8. At that time we had no idea how intimately involved we would eventually become with Phuket Marine. The work on the pedestal was done by local craftsmen under Jimmy and Willy's supervision. They did a beautiful job, but due to other commitments and the slow pace of their work, it took "forever." They started on April 15 and finished on May 12. Although much of the work was done in their shop, it required disconnecting the steering wheel, so we were stuck at Ao Chalong for the whole time—frustrated that we couldn't sail out into the surrounding islands.

On my birthday we rented a car and spent two nights in a cabin at the rustic Thai-style Kamala Beach Resort. On the way back we stopped at the Boat Lagoon Marina, which was being built about five miles north of Phuket City and made arrangements to have *Tainui* hauled out and stored ashore while we were visiting the United States. We had decided to spend the Thai rainy season (our summer) at home and return during our winter, which was the dry season in Thailand. There was no hurricane season in Thailand, but we were planning a six-month home visit and preferred to have *Tainui* safely out of the water when we were away that long. She couldn't sink, and she wouldn't grow a "garden" on her bottom. The Boat Lagoon was also to become more of a part of our lives than we expected.

Finally, standing at the wheel behind our freshly varnished teak pedestal, I steered *Tainui* out of Ao Chalong to explore Ao Phang Nga. Most Westerners referred to it as Phang Nga Bay. *Tainui* started the trip a little reluctantly. First the engine overheated—by now a chronic problem. When I opened the valve in the hull that let the seawater into the engine cooling-system, only a trickle came through. I couldn't clear it from the inside, so I let *Tainui* drift and jumped into the warm water, put on a mask, and dove underneath the hull for a look. The inlet's opening was almost completely blocked by barnacles. I surfaced, Connie handed me a scraper, and I went back down and cleaned it out. Shortly after we satisfied ourselves that the overheating problem had been solved, we lost all of our electric power. This was also a recurrent problem. I cleaned the main ground connection, as I usually did in this situation, and while I was at it, I cleaned every other electrical connection I could find. After that, all of our electronic equipment lit up more brightly than ever.

We stopped for the night at Ao Po on Phuket Island, a good jumping-off point for Ao Phang Nga. The long tricky channel to the anchorage at Ao Po was marked only by a series of sticks. With the aid of these sticks and one of our many detailed charts, we twisted our way into the anchorage. Ao Po was well sheltered, but a thunder-and-lightning storm with strong wind gusts forced us to keep an anchor watch all night. We wended our way back out the channel in the morning and motored into nearby Ao Phang Nga. The bay was a deep cut into the Thai mainland north of Phuket Island. It was a popular sailing ground for cruising yachts and private charters. Several dozen limestone islands of all sizes were scattered throughout the bay. The wind and sea had eroded them into strange shapes. At a distance, they looked like a menagerie of strange animals floating in the misty haze. Up close many of the smaller ones looked like giant mushrooms because the sea had undercut them near their waterlines. Some of those "mushrooms" where so eroded that they looked as if they would soon be cut clear through and topple into the sea. The larger islands had sheer limestone cliffs hundreds of feet high, and some of the large islands had hollow interiors, which the Thais called *hongs*, meaning "rooms." One of the James Bond movies was shot in this bay on an island that is still called "James Bond Island."

Our first anchorage was, in fact, called Ko Hong ("Room Island"). Anchoring depth near these islands was difficult to find. Their steep cliffs dropped straight down into the sea, making the water very deep close to shore. After searching around, we found a place to anchor on a ledge about a hundred yards off Ko Hong and took our dinghy into its "room." The entrance was a narrow waterway between high cliffs, with a huge limestone pillar in the center of it. Once inside, the pillar shut off all view of the sea outside. We landed our dinghy on a small patch of sandy beach and "hung out in the *Hong*" for a while. It was warm and still with an echo like the inside of a cave.

The islands in Ao Phang Nga were fairly close together, so we usually slept in and got a late start for our next anchorage. We left Ko Hong mid-morning for Ko Rai only eight miles away. The wind in Ao Phang Nga was not good for sailing. It was mostly calm and the infrequent winds were light and variable. We couldn't find a good anchorage depth at Ko Rai but had plenty of time to sail on to Ko Du Noi, or so we thought. We wound up racing to our anchorage, trying to stay ahead of some approaching ominous black rain clouds. We finished anchoring at 4:00 in the afternoon, just before the storm hit. It came on with severe wind gusts followed by driving rain and thunder and lightning. Happily, the electrical activity passed far enough away that it did not threaten *Tainui*. We were relieved that the storm was out of the area by early evening so that we did not have to keep another anchor watch that night.

Our last night in Ao Phang Nga, we anchored off a small island, that showed a *hong* on our chart. We circled it in our dinghy and found a low tunnel that led into its interior "room." We ducked our heads and cautiously motored in. It was a small dark room with sides too steep to land the dinghy. We feared that the entrance tunnel would fill with water at high tide and, not sure whether the tide was rising or falling, we left after a few minutes.

The next day we left Phang Nga Bay for the Laem Phrao Marina on the north end of Phuket Island to secure *Tainui* while we left for Lumut, Malaysia, to join our friends, Chuck and Dottie, from *Viki*, on a trip to Lake Toba in Sumatra. Phang Nga Bay's fluky winds held up and we coasted along slowly with all of our sails up most of the way. It was a relief to have the motor off, but the wind eventually died and we had to motor the last bit to the marina. The marina, run by a Dutch engineer, offered mooring buoys, a yacht charter service, yacht repairs, and a restaurant. We stayed three days, meeting other sailors and eating in the marina's dining room. We left *Tainui* on a mooring buoy in plain view of the marina office, where she could be easily watched.

We flew to the island of Penang and took a taxi to the ferry terminal. The ferry took us to Butterworth on the mainland. We had made this crossing on the ferry dozens of time when I was stationed in Penang for a year as the Peace Corps representative for North Malay. A beautiful modern bridge had subsequently replaced the car ferry service, but there was still a passenger ferry. In Butterworth we walked to the "outstation" taxi stand—a parking lot full of taxis each with the name of a different Malaysian town painted on its doors. They left whenever they had their full four passengers. We found an old diesel Mercedes taxi with "Lumut" on the door and waited, but there was not much interest in Lumut that day. The fare was inexpensive, so Connie and I hired the whole taxi, which made the ride more comfortable. At the Royal Perak Yacht Club in Lumut, we spent two nights on *Viki* with Chuck and Dottie while we made final arrangements for our Sumatra trip.

We had a wonderful 10-day trip to Sumatra. We crossed the 75-mile wide Strait of Malacca on a large catamaran ferry from Penang, Malaysia, to Medang, Sumatra. It was a night passage and we sailors noticed that the stars appeared to cross back and forth across the bow as much as 10 degrees on either side. If it were light enough to see our wake, it would have looked like a sine wave on an oscilloscope.

When one of the officers learned that we were sailors, he invited us to visit the bridge. The vessel was steered electronically by an autopilot with a little steering wheel no larger than a CD disk. The captain explained that the autopilot was reacting sluggishly, causing the ferry to swing from side to side. (By the time of our return trip, the autopilot had been replaced, and the ferry steered a straight course.) The entire crew operated the ferry from the wheelhouse. The engineer operated the two big diesel engines by an instrument panel in the wheelhouse and monitored the engine room with two closed-circuit television screens. He only went below if there was a problem.

Lake Toba was the 60-mile-long crater of an extinct volcano. It was high enough in elevation to have a pleasantly cool climate. We took a ferry to the Hotel Carolina, which was on a large island in the lake. A room on the beach cost us US$12 per night, and dinners at the hotel were about US$3.50. Chuck and I rented motorbikes, and we toured some villages and cultural shows with Connie and Dottie riding behind us. The island had large rice fields that were surrounded by high hills. It took Chuck and I all day to ride our motorbikes solo all the way around the island. Our wives elected not to join us on that adventure.

From Lake Toba we took a bus to an orangutan rehabilitation center. We spent two nights at a nearby hotel at the confluence of two swift rivers. The rivers were beautiful, but were so noisy that it was hard to sleep at night. Sick orangutans were treated in hospital cages at the center and then released into the wild and fed at a jungle platform until they became independent. The four of us got into an overloaded dugout canoe that our guide pulled across the river along a cable to the trail that led to the feeding platform. We hiked a mile into the jungle and watched two men feed some of the released orangutans. The big animals came crashing through the jungle swinging from tree to tree and dropped onto the platform to be fed. The men fed them milk in a cup and gave them bunches of bananas, which they carried away. The men did it all while looking away because they considered it dangerous to make eye contact with the large beasts. One large orangutan swung playfully out over the spectators, which was entertaining until he urinated on the crowd. Fortunately we were standing far enough back to be out of the "line of fire."

After the return ferry crossing, we spent two days enjoying Penang before returning to Thailand. We loved Penang, but it felt oppressively hot after the mountain air of Lake Toba. An air-conditioned hotel room was a must. A Thai Air flight to Laem Phrao and a cab ride to the marina brought us quickly back to *Tainui*. When Connie unpacked she found that her camera was missing—probably stolen at the hotel in Penang. All was well with the boat.

Tainui was due to be hauled out for a variety of maintenance chores, including cleaning and renewing her anti-fouling bottom paint, but it was early June and the rainy season was already bringing wind and torrential rain. I did not want to work outside in these conditions, and it would be impossible to keep the steel from rusting while preparing to paint it in wet weather. Because the monsoon season would last for six more months, I deferred the work until the dry season. We sailed back to the Boat Lagoon Marina, hauled *Tainui* out, left her there, and flew home for the summer.

We came back from our home visit to a drier Phuket and went to work on *Tainui*. We spent the first six weeks touching up paint on the topsides, revarnishing the interior, and resealing the portholes. Then all that was left to do was to clean the bottom and put on two coats of anti-fouling paint before we "splashed down" and went sailing again. When I cleaned off the old bottom paint, I was surprised to find some small rust spots. It was common to touch up rust spots on the inside of the hull and on the topsides, but I had never seen any rust on the outside of the hull below the waterline. As I tried to grind out these spots, they got larger instead of smaller until, to my shock, they went clear through the hull! They had started on the inside and rusted all the way through. I found eight such places.

The entire inside of *Tainui*'s hull had been sprayed with a two-inch-thick coating of polyurethane foam to stop condensation, reduce sound, and insulate against heat or cold. Saltwater had seeped between the foam and the hull under the galley sink, the head, and the anchor-chain locker and the steel rusted away hidden from view by the foam. This was a devastating blow to Connie and me. We didn't know how much more rust there might be and whether or not *Tainui* was even salvageable. (I later learned that steel boat builders had stopped the practice of foaming below the waterline),

Willy and Jimmy, who had moved their Phuket Marine operation to the Boat Lagoon, advised us to take some time out to calm down and think it over before we did anything rash like holding a "fire sale" to salvage *Tainui*'s equipment. We took their advice and checked into the fancy Marina Hotel on the beach for two days to celebrate Connie's birthday and examine our alternatives. It was a dispirited birthday celebration. We then consulted with Jimmy and Willy about repairs by their company, and they quoted us a firm US$10,000 to repair the hull, providing we did as much of the work ourselves as we could. We decided to spend the money to protect our investment.

We moved into a small hotel in downtown Phuket City for the duration of the repairs. Its official English name was the Crystal Guest House, but to get a taxi driver to take us there, we had to say it in the local version of English, i.e., the "Kisten Get How." We got a small clean room with a TV that "spoke" only Thai, for a discount rate of US$360 per month, provided that they cleaned it and changed the linens only once a week. We actually preferred that schedule for the sake of our privacy, but the maids couldn't break their daily cleaning habit for long and soon serviced the room daily as a "favor," even though we protested that we really preferred the privacy of once-a-week cleaning.

The first thing we needed to do on *Tainui* was to expose all of the steel below her waterline. We began by moving everything out of our lockers. We carried armload after armload of gear to a storage facility about 50 yards away until we had filled two large storage rooms. The next step was to remove the plywood locker bottoms and all other equipment that obscured any part of the lower portion of the hull. That task included pulling out the water tanks, the galley stove, the shower pan, the head, and the chain locker—a hot, heavy, and time-consuming job. The foam then had to be scraped off the steel below the waterline. The scraping was done by hand in tightly cramped and stiflingly hot quarters. I hired a small young Thai man to help me do that part of the job. He was a good worker when he showed up sober. I had to send him home "sick" a few days when he was drunk. Between us, we were able to expose all of the affected steel, but it was a long, hot, dirty job and took more than a week.

After the steel was exposed, Jimmy and Willy came aboard and helped me mark out the areas that needed to be replaced. Then their welding crew went to work replating much of *Tainui*'s bottom. It was quicker and cheaper to replace a whole plate than to make small patches. I was fascinated by how quickly a torch could cut out sections of steel and how "invisible" the seams were when new sections were welded in and the bead of weld was ground flush.

Tainui's large keel was filled with cement and iron punchings for ballast, so I couldn't inspect the inside of it. Because the keel was open on the top, if it leaked water would come up into the boat. I solved that problem by having the workers weld a watertight steel plate over the top of the keel. That way, if the keel ever leaked, the water couldn't get up into the boat. Since the keel was already underwater, water in the keel wouldn't affect *Tainui's* buoyancy. This plate had other advantages. It stiffened *Tainui's* hull and *Tainui* could no longer be sunk from striking her keel on a rock or reef. If the keel ever rusted through, the next time *Tainui* was hauled out we would see water running out and drain it and repair the hole.

After the welding was finished, I had the entire exposed part of the interior of the hull painted with glossy white two-part epoxy paint to make rust easier to spot. I then put the locker bottoms and all of the other equipment back in easily removable sections so that I could inspect every part of the hull periodically.

At first Connie rode the bus with me each morning from the hotel to the boatyard and helped clear out the boat. We ate lunch on outdoor tables at a little mom-and-pop Thai eatery at the boatyard, visiting with friends who were also working on their boats. The food was cheap and acceptable, but simple and repetitious. During the repairs, we enjoyed the company of our Canadian friends Pat and Jim, who were similarly immersed in a lengthy and frustrating paint job on their vessel, *Beau Jeu*. They helped keep our spirits up during the rust crisis on *Tainui*, and we celebrated Christmas with them and several other cruisers at a festive party in a classy restaurant in Phuket town.

Later on, when there wasn't much she could do at the boatyard, Connie stayed in town. Those were boring days for her. She ran errands for me, tracking down parts and hardware bits; otherwise, she read, shopped, ate lunch out, and killed time as best she could. We took Sundays off and rode a bus to a big beautiful beach in front of some five-star hotels. We rented lounge chairs with beach umbrellas and swam, read, did the Sunday crossword, dozed, and watched the crowd of rich tourists, including many fashionable women sunbathers who only wore half of a bathing suit (that half was as skimpy as possible). This would have caused a religious calamity in Muslim Malaysia, but Thailand had a more casual attitude toward things sexual.

Our repairs were not completed by the time of the next rainy season, so we left *Tainui* on the hard and went home again for six months. Before we left, we found that our engine's cooling water jacket had rusted through and needed to be replaced. This was not surprising, since it was 15 years old and seawater-cooled engines generally lasted only 10 years. By a happy coincidence, the Phuket branch of the Moorings International Yacht Charter Service was in the process of replacing its Volvo engines with new Yanmars. I bought the best of their used Volvos and left instructions for it to be installed while we were gone, along with the completion of several other unfinished odds and ends. We hoped *Tainui* would be ready to sail when we got back, but we had been in Third World countries long enough that we didn't count on it. It had been a long hard job, but we were satisfied that *Tainui's* hull was in better shape than it was when she was built.

We arrived back in Phuket on December 9, 1994, and checked into the Country Lodge Hotel near the Boat Lagoon Marina. It was a much nicer hotel than the little Crystal Guest House in downtown Phuket and only a little more expensive. We had a larger room, and the hotel had a nice dining room. Our first morning, we ate breakfast at the hotel and walked to the boatyard to see if our repairs had been completed. Not surprisingly, we found that the engine installation and much of the other work that had been promised had not been completed. They had had six months to do it, but put other jobs first. A customer on hand was served before one who was far away and easily forgotten. Connie was depressed by the filthy condition of *Tainui*. There were greasy fingerprints all over the new white paint and unexplained rust spots everywhere. We even considered trying to sell *Tainui* as she was and walk away from the project.

After our disappointing morning at the boatyard, we hitchhiked to town. I got a haircut at my regular barbershop, and we had our favorite lunch at the Kanda Bakery: chicken cashew on rice served in a half-pineapple shell. The next day we took some dishes, utensils, and a hot pot from *Tainui* back to the hotel so we could make some of our own meals. We conferred with Willy and Jimmy and felt a little better after they promised to give our job a high priority and honor their US$10,000 quotation. This did not include the engine replacement, which was on a separate contract.

Phuket Marine started on the odd jobs quickly but it took a lot of prodding to get the local diesel mechanic to keep working on the motor installation. During this time we ate frequently with Pat and Jim and spent two weekends anchored out with them aboard *Beau Jeu*. The boatyard finally lowered *Tainui* into the water on December 28, after 18 months on the hard. The engine started up and we powered over to one of the marina's slips. It was a wonderful feeling to be at the wheel and feel *Tainui* moving through the water again.

It took two weeks at the slip to get *Tainui* ready to cruise again. I finished hooking up the refrigerator compressor and was pleased that all it needed was to be refilled with freon. Our marine head leaked, so I sent a fax to Larry requesting him to airmail us a new part. And when we tried to use our propane stove the odor of propane filled the cabin.

Fortunately we had not tried to light it. Some of the pipes to the burners had rusted through. A Chinese tinsmith agreed to custom-make new ones. Happily, all of our electronic equipment came back to life without any problems. We decided to sail away without a stove or functioning head—which would require a little creativity.

We were such long-standing residents at the marina that we had a lot of good-byes to say. Some of our friends came to the dock, untied our lines, and helped us out of our slip. Others waved from the decks of their vessels or sounded their horns as we motored away. We were immediately confronted with the challenge of staying in the narrow winding channel that led to deep water. When we first came in, the boatyard launch had met us and led us, but that was a year and a half before. We were on our own on the way out. To make matters worse, to keep *Tainui* in the channel, we had to fight a brisk crosswind. I felt a little rusty after so long away from the helm and had some anxious moments when I misjudged how slowly *Tainui* turned on her long full keel. When we finally escaped into open water and *Tainui* responded to her sails, after a long and depressing year and a half, Connie and I once again felt the thrill of being underway at sea on our own vessel. We sailed around the south end of Phuket Island and up its west coast to Kata Beach where we joined some friends who were anchored there.

We spent two happy weeks at Kata Beach, socializing, relaxing, swimming, eating at the Dive Shop Restaurant, and waiting for the parts for our stove and head. We watched the Australian Open tennis Tournament's championship match and the American Super Bowl on TV at a Scandinavian restaurant. We were feeling a lot better about *Tainui* and had lost interest in a cheap sale—she was in excellent condition and we were no longer ready to part with her. We contacted a delivery skipper and arranged for him to bring *Tainui* back to Oregon. He agreed to meet us in Penang in two months. He would then sail with us to Singapore, where a friend would join him for the delivery and Connie and I would fly home.

When we were ready to leave, I rented a motorbike and rode to town and checked us out for Langkawi, Malaysia. That night the wind blew 40 knots. It was still blowing hard in the morning, but we departed from Kata Beach anyway and sailed south down the coast in a strong gusty offshore wind. We were headed for the Ban Nit Marina in Ao Chalong to take on water. Ban Nit was on the opposite shore of the bay from Latitude 8 and when we entered Ao Chalong Ban Nit was directly to windward of us, so we took down our sails and motored very slowly across the bay into a fierce headwind. We took a mooring buoy at

Ban Nit in the afternoon and hoped that we could have dinner at its restaurant. However, we could not get our dinghy across the reef until high tide, which was not until 8:00 that night. By the time we got to the restaurant, the cooks said they were out of food, but they took pity on us and rustled up some fried rice.

The strong wind continued the next day. Pat and Jim, who had already left on their way to Langkawi, reported on the nightly ham net that they were crashing through big seas at speeds of eight and nine knots in fierce east winds, so we waited for better weather. That night we were repeatedly awakened by our mooring buoy banging into our hull with the changes in the wind and tide. At 2:00 in the morning, Connie got up with me, and we silenced the buoy by hauling it aboard and lashing it to the bow pulpit. The wind died down two days later, but by then we had used up some of our fresh provisions. I rented one of the marina's motorbikes, made the long trip around Ao Chalong to the town of Chalong, and brought back fresh vegetables and a newspaper.

The wind was calm at Ban Nit the next morning, so we cast off from our mooring buoy and sailed smoothly out of Ao Chalong. Outside of the bay, there was only 15 knots of wind blowing, but the sea was full of steep, choppy waves left over from the five days of gales. We sailed on, hoping the sea would calm down in the deeper water off shore, but the farther out to sea we went, the worse it got. Welcome back to the ocean! We discussed turning back but hated to delay our departure any longer. We hoped that when we cleared the southern point of Phuket Island and turned toward Phi Phi Don, we would have smoother sailing. Even though it was a wet, tough slog to the turning point, the ride was, in fact, a little less violent after we turned. About halfway to Phi Phi Don the wind began to decrease, and it quit altogether as we approached the island in the late afternoon. We arrived under motor and anchored off of the island's touristy little beach town. We went ashore for the evening, strolled through the shops, ate pizza in an Italian restaurant, and bought a few extra groceries before returning to *Tainui*.

The bay at Phi Phi Don was not completely sheltered from the sea, and small rollers washed through the anchorage all night. Connie moved to the settee in the aft of the cabin and I hung on spread-eagled in the double berth in the bow. On the morning local radio net there was an urgent call for the catamaran *Bijou*, which was anchored near us. *Bijou* didn't respond, and we couldn't raise them on the VHF radio, so we swung by on our way out, roused them, and told them that the local radio net had an urgent message for them. Back at sea we had beautiful sailing most of the day. However, typical of this trip, the wind picked up in the afternoon, with the strongest gusts at anchoring time. Worse yet, when we turned in toward our intended anchorage at Ko Ngai, we had to motor directly into the wind. Steep four-foot waves stalled *Tainui* to a crawl. At times we wondered whether we were moving at all. The sky became darker and more threatening as we fought our way in, and it took us three hours to smash our way through the last three miles.

We were nervous about making our way around to the lee side of the island to anchor, with a storm approaching, and considered running back out to sea and riding out the storm farther from land. But the lure of a night's sleep won us over, and we gingerly "felt" our way around the island with the radar. The rainsquall hit us while we were anchoring. Connie was behind the wheel, out of the shelter of the dodger, and I was working in the bow pulpit. Anchoring usually took only a few minutes, but this time, when we wanted to finish it quickly and get out of the drenching rain, was an unpleasant exception. Twice, the anchor scraped along rocks and failed to set. Each time, I cranked up the anchor—a slow process with our hand-cranked anchor winch—and we moved and tried again. Before we made another attempt, I took extra time to rig a trip line from the crown of the anchor so that I could pull it up backwards if it got stuck under a rock. The anchor held on our third try, but by then we were both soaked.

The rainstorm soon passed by, and sheltered from the waves in the lee of the island, we had a peaceful evening. Our dinner was a return to yachting fare—a can of Dinty Moore stew and a cabbage salad. With no wind, the cabin was warm and stuffy, so we needed to open the hatch over our bed. Our dinghy was lashed upside down over the hatch, so we untied it, slid it aside, and opened the hatch. However, during the night, williwaws came blasting down from a rocky cliff. When one of the gusts hit us, we were awakened by a loud splash. I stuck my head out the hatch and saw that the dinghy had been blown off the deck. Fortunately, it landed right side up and its bowline was tied to a deck cleat, so I let it trail behind and went back to bed. However, it soon woke me up again when another gust banged it into the hull. I got up and tied it to the stern rail with a longer line and it drifted far behind us.

The water was clear enough that we could see the anchor on the bottom in the morning, which was a good thing because it was caught under a rock. I had made the trip line so long that, when the tide went down, it had also wound around some other rocks. Connie took the helm, and I stood on the bow and unwound the trip line by shouting directions: "Forward!" "Starboard!" "Reverse!" " Port!" I had to shout as loud as I could for her to hear me over the sound of the engine. After the trip line was unwound, I pulled the anchor out from under the rock with it and then winched the anchor up by its chain. Fouling the anchor in clear water was a lucky coincidence—we seldom saw our anchor on the bottom. Freeing this mess would have been impossible in murky water and that anchor might still be there.

Again the wind was lighter in the morning. We shook out the two reefs we had put in the sails during the strong afternoon winds the day before, unrolled the big jib, and ghosted along at two to three knots. We were not in a hurry, and I didn't need to run the engine because I had run the refrigerator compressor while we were motoring into our anchorage, so we relaxed and enjoyed the peaceful ride while we could. During these quiet times, we read, listened to the stereo, searched for news on the short-wave radio, or did small maintenance tasks. The afternoon wind blew offshore and pushed us farther out into the Strait of Malacca. As a result, once again we had to motor three and a half miles against the wind to reach our anchorage, this time at Ko Phetra. Approaching the anchorage was frustrating. Our faces were stung from the spray and burned by the wind, and what would normally have been a half-hour run stretched into one, two, and then three hours. We were both worn out from the strain by the time we reached the shelter.

While I was lowering the anchor, three boys in a longtail tied alongside and jumped aboard uninvited. They backed off when Connie yelled, "No! No!" at them. When I finished anchoring, I tried a more friendly approach, but communication was difficult because I did not speak Thai. They did manage to communicate that there was a sandy bottom before they gave up and left, but I had already heard the chain dragging across some rocks.

We had done so much motoring to get into our anchorages that our little refrigerator had frozen a tray of ice cubes. It had no freezer section, but we had a vertical ice tray that we forced against the cold plate. Not wanting to waste the ice, I made gin and tonics before dinner. The performance of the refrigerator was a major influence on when we made drinks. One would have to be very thirsty to tolerate drinks without ice in the tropics. That night we got a much-needed full night's sleep. It had been over a week since we had slept undisturbed. On previous nights, williwaws had shaken us awake, *Tainui* had drifted crossways into the troughs and almost rolled us out of bed, the dinghy had blown overboard and the chain had growled on rocks. Most of these nuisances required our getting out of bed and making adjustments.

The next day started out with the best sailing of the trip. We made five or six knots almost all day on a broad reach. The wind did pick up again in the late afternoon as we headed into Ko Tarutao near the Thai-Malaysian border. The island had very high cliffs, and as we cruised along the shore looking for an anchorage, gusting east winds and williwaws roared down the steep slopes, making steering difficult for our wind vane. We sailed past a small village with fishing boats and long-tail canoes crowding the beach and anchored off an isolated white-sand beach. It was a good thing we had slept well the previous night, because the prevailing wind and the williwaws both increased throughout the night, howling in our rigging and shaking *Tainui*. In addition, the anchor chain banged as *Tainui* bucked against big waves that rolled through our anchorage. The only good thing about the night was that we were only a short day's sail from Langkawi, Malaysia, where we planned to spend several weeks.

Conditions were no better in the morning, so we got up at 6:30, ate a quick bowl of cereal, and got away from Ko Tarutao as quickly as possible. We were much relieved to get out of the range of the williwaws but, although Langkawi was not far, getting there was no fun. The wind was gusting at 20-to-25 knots through the gap between Ko Tarutao and Langkawi.

We sailed with a little bit of jib and could beat our southeasterly course against the east wind, but the wind vane struggled to handle the weather helm. *Tainui* rounded up into the wind every time a big gust of wind hit her. I tried hand steering, but I was also unable to fight off the weather helm. Eventually, in an especially strong gust *Tainui* not only turned into the wind, her bow crossed the wind, which back-winded the jib and heeled *Tainui* far over. The wind then pushed her bow downwind until she had made a "U" turn. In a mad scramble, I freed up the jib, and Connie started the engine, and powered *Tainui* back on course. At that point we gave up sailing, took down the sails, and motored on. Without sails, there was no weather helm and the electric autopilot steered us well.

A short bumpy ride took us across the Malaysian-Thai border to the main island in the Langkawi group, where we anchored next to Jim and Pat on *Beau Jeu*. They welcomed us aboard *Beau Jeu* with a cocktail hour, and we all went ashore and ate dinner at the Last Resort Restaurant— the "first resort" for those of us coming from the north. The wind blew all night, but we slept surprisingly well, maybe because of a couple of drinks, a big dinner, and a relaxing evening with friends, or maybe we were just tired enough from our trip to sleep through almost anything.

Jim and Pat sailed away in the morning. They were on their way to Thailand to compete in the Andaman Sea Race between Phuket and the

Andaman Islands in the Indian Ocean. After seeing them off, we took a taxi 12 miles to Kuah, and checked in with the officials. Since our last visit, the town had opened a new building on the jetty that housed all the offices needed for checking in. The process was impressively efficient and inexpensive. While we were in town we picked up a letter from my mom and a package of mail from Larry at general delivery in the post office and a fax that the Sea Speed marine store was holding for us. Sea Speed provided a variety of services to yachts, including faxes and duty-free boat supplies. The fax was from Vera, the mother of our son-in-law, Mark Zorn. When we had heard that Vera and her friend Barbara were on a trip through Southeast Asia, we had suggested that they visit us in Langkawi. Vera's fax confirmed that they planned to arrive in Kuah in three days. We shopped for groceries and took a taxi back to *Tainui*.

We were glad to be back in Malaysia. We felt more comfortable, relaxed, and secure in Malaysia than in any of the other Third World countries we visited. It seemed natural that we would feel that way because we had lived there and spoke the language, but many of our cruising friends who had not been there before said that they felt the same way. I think there were many reasons for this. English was widely spoken. Government officials were courteous and efficient with no hint of baksheesh or bribery. There was less poverty than in most Third World countries; in fact, we thought the term "Second World country" should have been created for Malaysia. The government was democratic, moderately Muslim—even restricting Islamic fundamentalist expressions. The people were friendly, the country was beautiful, and quality goods and services were inexpensive. And, oh yes, you could drink the water! This made it possible to safely enjoy the wonderful variety of exotic and tasty eating opportunities from Malaysia's three major ethnic communities: Malay, Indian, and Chinese. Malaysia was an ideal tourist destination for Americans, but most Americans were not aware of it.

We were anchored in a crescent-shaped bay at a quiet spot called Pantai Kok. There were never more than four or five yachts anchored there during our stay. *Pantai* is the Malay word for "beach," and our anchorage was aptly named. There was at least a mile of smooth sand beach at Pantai Kok. There were two upscale resorts a mile up the beach from us, but the eating establishments at Pantai Kok were informal. On our second night, we went ashore for dinner at the Jungle Bar on the beach. The tables were on the sand in an area enclosed by a waist-high fence made of woven palm leaves. The main kitchen was a shack-like outbuilding and chickens were grilling on an outdoor barbecue made of half of an oil drum. We were welcomed in the bar by a mixture of local people and sailors. The crowd was in a party spirit that looked like it was going to last late into the night, so we excused ourselves early, went back to *Tainui*, and caught up on our sleep.

We spent two days getting *Tainui* in shipshape for our visitors and then sailed to Kuah to meet them. We put Tainui in a slip on the jetty to provide easy access to her for our visitors. We arrived on Saturday and our guests were due to arrive on Sunday, but when we checked in at Sea Speed, we found that Vera had faxed us a change of plans—they were already in Kuah at the Gates Hotel near the jetty.

We rushed to the hotel, but they were not in their room. The desk clerk said that they had registered and gone out. We went to the jetty and ate lunch at its huge new Colonel Sanders restaurant, and then came back and sat in the hotel lobby watching for Vera and Barbara. After sitting for an hour, Connie had an inspiration. "Let's check out the hotel pool," she said. Sure enough, we found them, relaxing by the pool in lounge chairs, sipping cold drinks in the shade of a palm tree. They were very relieved to see us. They had been desperately trying to locate *Tainui* and were afraid that they might have missed us. At their invitation, we rushed back to *Tainui*, got our swimming suits, and swam and lounged around the pool with them. At dinnertime we took a taxi to town and ate at an open-air restaurant.

The next evening the women asked us to find them a more interesting eating adventure, so we took them to the waterfront and bought food from night hawkers' carts that were lit with kerosene or propane lamps. Vera told us, "Barbara and I make a practice of seeking out this kind of experience when we travel." However, they were not quite so sure about a sailing experience. With some trepidation they agreed to let us sail them to one of the resorts near Pantai Kok. They showed up at *Tainui* the next morning at 9:30 ready to go. Fortunately, the weather was calm, and there was just enough wind for gentle sailing. They were curious and interested and asked good questions about everything we did. Vera was ecstatic. She stood on the side deck holding on to the shrouds and had Barbara take her picture as she shouted, "Look at me. I'm sailing! I'm sailing!" After three and a half hours of smooth sailing, we anchored in Barau Bay, just north of Pantai Kok, in front of the Barau Bay Hotel. It took two trips in the dinghy to take our guests and their luggage to shore. Hotel porters came to the beach and lugged their bags to the hotel. Vera and Barbara took a cabin at the resort for two nights, and we remained anchored offshore. During their stay we enjoyed their pool, ate at the Last Resort Restaurant with them and, at their request, took a taxi to town on their last night and ate from the night hawkers' carts one more time. The next morning, we had breakfast with them at the hotel's huge breakfast buffet before they left for the airport. It had been a fun visit for us. They were good sports, and we enjoyed introducing them to Malaysia and exposing them to a bit of the sailing life.

After Vera and Barbara left, we went back to Pantai Kok for two pleasant weeks of relaxation, socializing, and minor boat maintenance. On the work side, we did painting and varnishing and some outboard-motor maintenance. On the fun side, we swam most afternoons and ate many evening meals at small restaurants on or near the beach, often in the company of other cruisers. We especially enjoyed our friendship with South Africans Paul and Debbie and their terrier, Cindy, on *Bijou*. We had not formally met them but, as we pulled out of the anchorage at Phi Phi Don, we had shouted to them that they had a message from the local radio net. At Pantai Kok we visited back and forth between each other's boats for drinks and meals and twice shared a rental car to Kuah to shop for boat supplies. Kuah was so spread out that it was difficult to shop on foot and it was hard to bring supplies back by bus—especially heavy things like storage batteries.

After our pleasant stay at Pantai Kok, we sailed in company with *Bijou* to Pulau Dayang Bunting, the island with the freshwater lake. It's Malay name, "Pregnant Lady Island," referred to a legend that the island was haunted by the ghost of a distraught pregnant woman, who had hurled herself off a cliff into the lake when spurned by her lover. We anchored *Tainui* and *Bijou* off the beach of the haunted island, took our dinghies ashore, and hiked to the lake. The swimming dock was crowded with a tour group of Chinese young people. They were not from China, but were Malaysian Chinese—Malaysia was 40 per cent Chinese. That evening we said goodbye to Paul and Debbie with drinks aboard *Tainui*. They departed for Singapore the next morning.

Our anchorage at Pulau Dayang Bunting had been exposed and rolly that first night. In the morning, as we looked for an alternative, we spied the tops of the masts of some sailboats sticking up from a narrow channel between a small island and the shore of Pulau Dayang Bunting. The spot looked better protected, so I cranked up the anchor and we motored over and joined them. *Green Dolphin* was among the three boats anchored there. We had met Don and Linda in Tonga and had been with them again in Fiji, where I sold them our old working jib when I got our new roller-furling sail.

The jungle on the high hills of Pulau Dayang Bunting opened up to a small clearing on the beach near us. Some interesting animals came out of the jungle onto that beach. Every time I saw one, I called *Green Dolphin*. When a group of six gray monkeys poked around on the beach at low tide eating something they were picking up from the rocks I called *Green Dolphin* and told Linda, "There's a group of monkeys on the beach." Another time I called and said, "Look Linda, there's a wild boar on the beach!" When I saw a giant monitor lizard and called *Green Dolphin*, Linda replied in a tone of resignation, "Okay, Vern. What is it this time, an elephant?"

We enjoyed visiting back and forth with the other boats in the anchorage. Sometimes I swam from boat to boat for exercise. When I swam to *Green Dolphin* and started up the boarding ladder unannounced, I was confronted with a hissing, puffed-up cat. Don and Linda had aptly named their ship's cat, "Cat'n Bligh," Our last evening at the anchorage, a band of black-and-white monkeys came to the edge of the jungle swinging from tree to tree. They frolicked in the trees near the beach, plucking and eating leaves. I was disappointed to see that Don and Linda were also out in their cockpit watching them. I would have enjoyed calling and hearing Linda's reaction to yet another radio call.

We motored back to Kuah one windless morning, and I got my teeth cleaned and Connie had a tooth crowned by a woman dentist named— I'm not kidding—"Dr. Chew." At Sea Speed I picked up a propane cabin heater sent duty-free from West Marine in California. Our boat-delivery deal from Singapore to Oregon looked like a go, and the crew would need heat sailing back via Japan and the Aleutians. Also, in anticipation of that trip, I had our six-man life raft serviced.

We sailed back to Pantai Kok and hung out for another 11 happy days. We did a lot of odd jobs on the boat, getting her in perfect shape for her North Pacific crossing, but we kept our workdays short and swam in the afternoons and relaxed with friends in the evenings, often eating out. We met some interesting people aboard yachts at Pantai Kok during that period. Inos, from Australia, was sailing around the world on *Qually II*, alone, sort of. Her friend Paul, also a solo sailor, sailed alongside of her in his yacht *Sioux*. Henry, a lone elderly Swedish sailor on *Wasa* had sailed twice around the world in his 16 years of cruising. He usually picked up a crewmember for major crossings and had had a woman companion aboard for five years until she jumped ship for another man. Such is the life of a single sailor. When I asked him why he had a five-inch-diameter rope hanging over the side into the water, he said, "Let me show you." He threw his kitten off the opposite side of the boat, and she swam around to the rope and climbed back aboard, wet and probably feeling as wretched as she looked. He explained, "I'm training her in case she falls overboard when I'm not around." I sold my spare Kenwood ham transceiver radio to a hippie couple who were cruising on a shoestring in an old, partly unfinished wooden boat. We hated to leave idyllic little Pantai Kok, but it was time to head for Penang to do some more work on *Tainui* before our delivery skipper arrived. Our pleasant days at Pantai Kok and in the little anchorage by the jungle at Pulua Dayang Bunting were the kind of experiences that kept us (and others) cruising.

We checked out at Kuah and left for Penang after six pleasant weeks in Langkawi. We started with an easy 20-mile sail to Pulau Paya, which is a Malaysian national park. Anchoring was forbidden in order to prevent damage to the park's beautiful coral reef, but the park provided free mooring buoys. People came by the boatload from nearby resorts to snorkel or scuba dive on the reef. We checked in at the ranger station, signed their guest book, and examined the informative display of pictures and information about their living reef. We lowered our swim ladder into the water and swam off *Tainui* before dinner. A thunderstorm blew in during the evening, but only lasted until midnight.

We untied our mooring line after a late breakfast and set out under a cloudy sky on a short run to Song Song Island. We were then back in the land-and-sea-breeze pattern, and because of our late start, we had gone only six miles when the land breeze died. We motored the rest of the way and were anchored by the time the sea breeze filled in. In the early afternoon a huge band of black clouds that stretched from horizon to horizon bore down upon us. It came over us at 4:00 with 25 knots of wind, but its thunder, lightning, and rain passed in the distance. All we got was the wind and a few wisps of rain; it was gone by 6:00 in the evening.

The next day we sailed until noon and then motored in a flat calm all the way to Penang. This was our first chance to test our new motor in flat water without the effects of wind and current. The motor moved us at a speed of only four and a half knots at the same 2200 rpms that had given us six knots with the old motor. We thought we might need a different prop for this engine, but we learned later from the Volvo dealer in Penang that this Volvo was a "high rev" engine. The reduction gear in its transmission required 50 percent more revolutions to produce the same speed that the former engine did. Running at higher revs solved the problem, but we didn't like the increased noise of the speeded-up engine. Not running the engine at high enough revs undoubtedly partly accounted for our incredibly slow, upwind approaches to our anchorages on our trip from Thailand.

We motored under the new bridge that connected the island of Penang to the mainland and on to the junk harbor in the old section of the city of Georgetown. Anchoring there was a challenge. The wind was blowing one way, and the current was running in another. The anchorage was crowded, so I had to drop the anchor where *Tainui* would come to rest clear of other boats. On my first two tries, after we set the anchor and let *Tainui* swing, she settled down too close to other vessels. Twice I had to hand-crank the anchor, in the suffocating mid-afternoon heat and humidity, pick another spot, and drop it again. The place where we finally anchored successfully was of course, farther from the pier than any other boat in the crowded harbor. Fortunately, we didn't have to take the dinghy ashore. We could hail a wooden sampan called a "bumboat" and get a ride to shore for 1 Malaysian ringgit, about US60 cents.

As soon as we were satisfied that *Tainui* was securely anchored, we hailed a bumboat and an elderly Chinese gentleman powered his outboard-motor-driven sampan along side. We jumped down onto its bench seats, and he delivered us to the end of one of the long piers that extended out into the water from the city. The pier was a rickety wooden structure about two city blocks long, held above the water by slender wooden poles. It supported houses and small shops fronted by a plank walkway. Walking along the pier was like walking through a poor section of a China town with all of the sights, sounds, and smells of its family and business activities. We walked off the pier into the oldest section of Georgetown and were happy to find that, unlike most of the city, it had remained unchanged in the years since we had lived on the island in 1969.

We strolled up and down narrow, bustling Chulia and Campbell streets, soaking up the atmosphere. The streets were crowded with commercial vehicles and vendors on bicycles, and the crowded sidewalks were lined with open-fronted shops and restaurants. Bright red signs in Chinese characters were painted vertically on most shops, and there was a sprinkling of more conventional signs in Malay and English. Campbell Street was noted for East Indian jewelry shops, which were guarded by tall bearded and turbaned Sikhs with shotguns. Many of the shops carried such an unrelated selection of goods that it was impossible for us to shop without local knowledge. Indian food was our favorite cuisine when we lived in Malaysia, and our favorite Indian Muslim restaurants, Hameediah and the Taj Mahal, on Chulia Street were still in business. The scene brought back memories of grand meals and happy times with gatherings of Peace Corps staff and volunteers in these eating houses on old Chulia Street.

That evening we ate chicken curry at Dawood, another old favorite. At the restaurant, Connie flipped the new crown out of her tooth with a toothpick. Dr. Chew had set it in place to see how it fit, and then had been unable to get it out to glue it back in, so she decided that it must have been all right as it was. However, the tooth had become progressively more tender until Connie had not been able to chew on that side, and the crown finally came out. It was 7:00 in the evening and dentists' offices were all closed, but the staff at Dawood was very concerned and one of them began calling every dentist in the phone book. After about 10 calls he found a cooperative Chinese dentist who opened up his shop for us and glued the crown in properly.

After an interrupted night's sleep due to a windstorm that got us up several times to check our anchor and our position relative to other boats, we took a bumboat ashore in the morning to check in. It turned out to be our all-time worst checking-in experience. We were told that customs and immigration were in Butterworth on the mainland. We walked to the ferry dock—about eight blocks away. Although a new modern bridge had been built, there was still a passenger ferry for those of us without wheels. At the ferry terminal in Butterworth, we did not find any posted information about customs or immigration. We asked a man for directions, and he pointed hesitantly and said, "that way" with little conviction. We walked "that way" for several blocks and found nothing. When we inquired at a railroad office, we were told to walk over a long viaduct to the main shipping terminal. After a long hot walk on the concrete structure, we found a customs office. However, it was noon, and we were told that the man who could check us in would be at lunch until 2:45 p.m. because he had to pray after lunch. We gave up and trudged back to the ferry terminal and returned to Penang.

From the ferry terminal, we walked several blocks through the city to the Penang Yacht Club at the extreme northern end of the city and made arrangements to moor *Tainui* there while we made some final repairs. From there we walked to a new modern shopping center, bought groceries, and took a taxi back to the pier at the junk harbor. We arrived back at *Tainui* hot, sweaty, and weary of foot, having accomplished nothing toward checking in. Another storm passed through the anchorage that night and brought a lot of rain, but not much wind and only a little thunder and lightning.

The next day we tried again to check in. The people at the Penang Yacht Club had told us that we could check in at a kiosk across from the customs building in Georgetown, so we walked the 10 blocks to the kiosk. They could not help us, but directed us to a pier on the waterfront.

We walked six blocks to the pier and found many shops and businesses there, but no customs office. A man at the pier directed us to an office eight blocks farther along the waterfront. This turned out to be the right office, but the customs officer demanded two copies of our clearance paper from Langkawi. We had only one copy, and the customs office, of course, either had no copy machine or chose not to make it available if they had one. Back out into the blazing sun, we walked eight blocks to a shipping company that had sent some faxes for us, made a copy, and started back to the customs office. On the way back, Connie spotted a post office with chairs in its air-conditioned lobby and waited there while I returned to customs. Customs stamped our papers and then told me that we must still clear in with immigration in Butterworth. This was getting old! I collected Connie at the post office, and we walked to the ferry terminal and took the ferry to Butterworth again. This time we took one of the waiting trishaws to immigration to rest our weary feet. At immigration I was chewed out for not having a clearance paper from Langkawi, where Malaysian immigration had told me that no paper from immigration would be required in Penang. "In that case," the immigration officer said, "there is nothing I can do for you now. Just return when you are checking out and I will give you the paper you need for your next stop." Two days of frustration ended with another wasted trip to Butterworth.

The Penang Yacht Club charged US$16 per day, so we planned to stay in the free junk harbor until all of the supplies we had ordered for our maintenance jobs arrived. However, we left the junk harbor early because we couldn't stand the stench. The houses on the piers had no sewer connections. Their open-bottomed privies emptied directly below. When the tide was out, they emptied onto the mud. This massive toilet was "flushed" out through our anchorage by the tide twice a day. This was unappetizing enough, but while the tide was out in the heat of the day, the stench from under the piers was unbearable.

At the Penang Yacht Club, I installed our cabin heater, replaced a cracked Lexan companionway hatch board, and cleaned up a few rust spots. We cooled off after work each afternoon in the yacht club's swimming pool, usually in company with Al and Katherine, from *Ethereal,* who showed us movies aboard their boat and accompanied us on several eating expeditions in town.

Our unfortunate boat-delivery experience began in Penang. The delivery skipper met us in Penang and sailed with us to Singapore, where we finished outfitting and provisioning *Tainui* for the trip to Newport, Oregon. We flew home, and a second crewmember joined the delivery skipper in Singapore. They planned to cross the North Pacific from Japan. When they started across the South China Sea from Singapore, they made such slow progress the first few days they decided that they wouldn't be out of Japan before the approaching typhoon season. They cited the fact that on one particular day they had only made 50 miles to justify their decision and returned to Singapore and abandoned the delivery. Of the $6,000 we paid for the delivery, they returned their $1,000 fee; the rest had been spent on travel and provisioning. They agreed to leave *Tainui* at any port of my choosing, so I had them take her to Lumut, where it was inexpensive and safe.

This was, of course a major disappointment. We were in Salem buying a house when we got the bad news. I blamed myself for not insisting that they allow more time for the delivery. We had disagreed about the timing from the beginning. I should have insisted that they come earlier or not at all. I blamed them for not allowing any contingency time in their plan. They knew enough about sailing to know that it was foolish to depend on making *Tainui*'s average of 100 miles a day with no allowance for delays due to weather or repairs.

After settling Connie into our new house in Salem, I returned by myself to Malaysia where it took me three months to sell *Tainui*. These were lonely months for both of us. While I was there, I met a couple who had delivered a 50-foot steel boat from Singapore to Vancouver, B.C.—a similar route to the one attempted by our delivery crew. On their South China Sea crossing, they had actually had negative progress one day on a bigger and faster boat than *Tainui*. They had allowed six weeks of contingency time and used all of it. They told me that they had had lunch with our delivery crew in Singapore and were unimpressed. They said, "These guys didn't have a chance of making it on time. They had no clue about how long it would take them on the route they had chosen."

In spite of this unpleasantness, our trip ended well. I had the good fortune to sell *Tainui* for a reasonable price. The delivery debacle cost us $5,000 and a little frustration, but these things were puny in relationship to the total experience. We had lived our dream. We had been full time travelers for seven adventurous years in some of the world's most beautiful and exotic places. Our lives were changed forever by this experience. We had successfully met the challenges of the sea: weather, navigation, mechanical malfunctions, and sailing skills, which gave us a new sense of pride and self-sufficiency. We had also been profoundly altered by our experience of how little so many people in the world have compared to what we have. When we came home we had culture shock and embarrassment at the overabundance of material things that we Americans take so much for granted. And, finally, we enjoyed the wonderful fellowship, mutual caring, generosity, and helpfulness of cruising people among whom we made many lifelong friends.

To dream such a daring dream and live it to the fullest has to be one of life's richest and most fulfilling experiences.

A gathering at the Royal Perak Yacht Club in Lumut, Malaysia aboard *Kanaka.* From left to right: Dottie, Vern, Chuck, Geoff, and Heather. *(above)* Celebrant in the religious festival on Pangkor Island, Malaysia with hooks in his back. (below)

A celebrant with a "spear" through his cheeks. (above)
The boardwalk through the village on stilts at the junk anchorage in
Penang, Malaysia. (below)

Christmas eve in Singapore aboard *Vauve Maria*. Pat Henry, on the far right, is the author of <u>By the Grace of the Sea.</u> (above)
Tainui entering Phang Nga Bay in Phuket, Thailand. (below)

Vern in a *hong* in one of the islands in Phang Nga Bay. (above)
Tainui anchored near a sheer cliff in Thailand on our way back to
Malaysia. Watch out for williwaws! (below)

Tainui repainted after replating at the Boat Lagoon in Phuket, Thailand. (above)
Tainui goes back into the water after 18 months on the hard. (below)

CHAPTER SIXTEEN

CONNIE'S VIEWS

When people hear that my husband and I sailed a small boat halfway around the world, they often turn to me and ask, "What did you think about cruising? Were you ever afraid, bored, or wishing you were back home?" They also ask how I handled storms, how I spent my time, and what I did at night.

For the first four years I was really excited about the venture. I was anxious to see the world by boat. After our four-year experience with the Peace Corps in Malaysia, I didn't want to just fly into a foreign country, spend one or two weeks in a hotel, and briefly visit the tourist sights. I wanted to meet the people, visit their homes, learn about their culture, shop in their markets, attend their churches, and invite them into our little home. That part of cruising was the highlight for me. I was not disappointed in it.

The last three years were not as enjoyable, because the boat needed more and more repairs. We spent a great deal of our time in boatyards or sitting at a dock waiting for boat parts to arrive from the United States. However, even when *Tainui* was in a boatyard, we were in interesting countries, and we did spend quite a bit of time traveling by car and bus, getting to know local people, eating in their restaurants, visiting them in their homes, and swimming and snorkeling in the crystal clear water.

Yes, there were times when I was terrified. When Vern fell overboard it was my worst nightmare. My first impulse was to stop the boat, so I turned the motor off, but the boat kept sailing at 6 knots because the sails were still up. I was petrified and tried to think what to do next, when the boat heeled over with the rail in the water and I saw Vern roll himself onto the deck. I shook with fear for about an hour. I tried to get Vern to let me handle the boat while he changed his clothes, but he insisted on pulling down the sails and motoring into the port of Coos Bay, Oregon. He knew from the chart that it was a difficult entrance.

And there were other times when I was terrified as well. Our crossing from Fiji to New Zealand was very rough. We had eight days of gale-force winds. We were in contact with a New Zealand ham radio net, which was comforting. They knew we were out there and perhaps could send help. But when the weather forecast wasn't good, it would make me uneasy. But I sometimes wished we didn't know what to expect, so we could hope that the next day was going to be better.

I also took comfort in the fact that Vern was an excellent sailor and a superb mechanic, who could fix anything. On many occasions at sea something would break, he would tell me that we had a serious problem and his head would disappear into the engine compartment. But before long he would reemerge and tell me what he did to solve the problem. I never ceased to marvel at his ingenuity.

When the seas were rough, I took my watch as usual, but on one night during the Fiji-to-New Zealand crossing, when Vern called me at 2:00 a.m., I let him down. I went up the companionway steps, looked out, and immediately saw a wall of water at least 20 feet tall rising up behind the boat. I ran down the steps crying and screaming that I could not do it. I was petrified. I told Vern that I was through sailing and as soon as we got to New Zealand I wanted to sell the boat. Vern told me to go back to bed, that he would handle the boat until things calmed down, and that we would talk about selling it when we got to New Zealand. When daylight came and I was able to see how nicely the boat rode the huge swells, I relieved Vern and took an extra-long watch so he could sleep. I have always felt bad about letting him down, but he never complained about it and seemed grateful that I was able to handle things on almost every other occasion.

Another scary crossing was when we left Horn Island, at the top of Australia, to cross the Gulf of Carpentaria en route to the small town of Gove—a 400-mile crossing. When we were just 15 miles out we heard on the radio that there was an unusually strong high-pressure cell moving across southern Australia that would cause up to 30-knot winds in the Gulf of Carpentaria. We talked it over, decided to take a chance since we had weathered worse winds before, and sailed on. For two days we had excellent weather conditions of 15-knot winds and made 125 miles each day. However, the third day the storm hit. Since the water was quite shallow, the waves were close together and seemed to be coming from all directions. It was one of my worst experiences. I was really afraid. Again, I couldn't take my watch when the time came, so Vern stayed on. I told Vern, for the second time, that I was through sailing and when we got to shore I wanted to sell the boat and go home. Each time, after we got to port, I was so excited to be in a new place to explore that I changed my mind about selling the boat.

On these occasions it was so rough, cooking was impossible. Breakfast was just a bowl of cereal. We had to pour the milk on the cereal over the sink and try to get it to the table without spilling it or even stand over the sink to eat it. Lunch and dinner were just crackers, cheese, peanut butter, fresh fruit, and a can of pop. Sometimes this was our menu for several days. We had to eat sitting on the settee with the food wedged between us, so it wouldn't land on the sole.

On the other hand, I was bored when we were in a boatyard for weeks at a time. The worst boatyard experience for me was in New Zealand. We had to remove the teak decks from *Tainui,* because there was rust under the teak. It was an extremely dirty, dusty job. After the decks were stripped, the workmen had to sandblast all of the glue and paint from the deck and house before new paint and deck tread could be applied. We sealed the windows, hatches, and the doorway with heavy paper and duct tape, hoping to keep the sand out of the interior, but we were amazed at how much sand sifted in spite of our efforts. It took weeks of vacuuming before it felt clean to me again. It had seeped into all of our lockers, drawers, and bedding, even though we had rolled up our bedding and covered it with a tarp.

During this time we continued to sleep on the boat because there were no accommodations nearby. Each night we would unseal the front hatch over our bed, vacuum our bed with the boatyard shop vacuum before unrolling it, crawl in, and sleep till morning, when we would get up, roll up the bed again, and crawl out a hatch. We would seal the hatch again so the work could continue that day. The whole process took weeks. I insisted that, from then on, I would never sleep on a boat in a boatyard again. Even if we had to rent a car, after that, we always found accommodations off the boat when it was in a boatyard.

Another tiresome time was while *Tainui* was on the hard in a boatyard in Thailand for a year. We spent the first six months in a small hotel in downtown Phuket. The room consisted of a double bed, a dresser with a mirror, a tiny refrigerator, and a stand with a TV on it that only "spoke" Thai. It also had some built-in shelves and a tile bathroom with a toilet, a washbowl, and a cold shower without a curtain (which was typical of tiled bathrooms in the tropics). Because we were going to be there for several months, we were able to get the room for just US$12 a day.

To keep from being bored out of my mind, I worked out a daily schedule for myself. We rose at 7:00 a.m. Coffee was delivered to our room at 7:30 a.m. After a light breakfast of a pastry or a bowl of cold cereal, Vern left for the boatyard. I returned to the bed, since there were no chairs in the room, and read, wrote letters, or did a crossword puzzle. At 10:00 a.m. I left the hotel, so the maid could clean the room, and walked to the Kanda Bakery restaurant, where I had coffee and sometimes my favorite drink: a banana-pineapple crush. I often shopped at the bakery for our breakfast roll for the next morning. Sometimes Vern would give me a list of things he needed for the boat, like paint, bolts or screws, and I would look for them. He often gave me a sample to show the clerks, since I couldn't speak the language. I stopped at the post office each day to see if we had any mail and then returned in the late morning to the hotel. At noon I went to a restaurant across the street from our hotel for lunch. Sometimes Vern would join me there, but only if he needed the things I had bought. During the afternoon I again read and lazed around in the air-conditioned room, because it was too hot to walk outside by then. After Vern returned, about 5:30 p.m., we walked across the street to our favorite restaurant for dinner. We explored many restaurants that were in walking range, but preferred the one across the street. Sometimes after dinner we would take a long walk before retiring for the night.

One day, while we were staying at the hotel, I showed some material I had bought and a picture of a dress I had drawn to the girls at the hotel desk. They didn't speak a word of English, but they understood what I wanted. One of the girls motioned for me to wait and disappeared out a back door. A few minutes later she appeared at the front door on a motorbike and motioned for me to get on. I climbed on the back, and she sped off through the Phuket traffic for blocks and blocks. She finally stopped at a shop, and we went in. We showed the people in the shop the material and the picture, and they immediately measured me and then pointed at a calendar to a day one week away. I climbed back on the motorbike, and we sped back to the hotel. On the promised day the girls brought me the dress. Unfortunately, the skirt of the two-piece dress was too tight, so I had to show the girls at the desk that it wasn't right. So, off we went again on the motorbike, and I was able to show the dressmaker the problem. Again they measured my waist and exclaimed in the Thai language with hand motions that they would fix it. They pointed at the calendar again to a day a week later, and off we went. In the end they did a good job.

While we were in a port, there was always plenty to do. We spent time touring the country that we were in and socializing with other cruisers on our boat or on their boats. We often enjoyed eating out with them, attending picnics and potlucks ashore, going to local festivals and feasts, sharing cocktail parties, and swimming and snorkeling throughout the South Pacific. Then there were the usual "household" duties that had to be performed—meals to be planned and prepared, shopping to be done, and clothes to be washed. I started out washing all of our clothes by hand in buckets until we got to American Samoa, where there were regular American Laundromats. What a luxury! After that, I found laundries ashore and sent out our linens and heavy clothes, but continued to wash the lighter clothes on the boat. Shopping often took most of the day, because there were no supermarkets in the South Pacific and we were usually on foot. Meat was bought at an open market. Sometimes we would find it just spread out on banana leaves on the ground. Fresh vegetables and fruit were also displayed in that manner. Often we would have to walk several blocks to a bakery to buy our bread. If we wanted dry foods or canned foods, we had to walk to another store. Chickens were sometimes sold live. If we wanted a chicken to eat, we would point at a chicken and ask them to kill it and dress it for us while we wandered away until the duty was done. I often had to cut up a whole chicken. We seldom found them already cut up until we got to New Zealand and Australia. Sometimes I would make a pot of chicken curry during the evening hours when it was cooler and just warm it up the next day for our dinner. The night before we left a port I usually cooked up a pot of stew or curry, so all I had to do was warm it up at sea. This was a big help, because it was often too rough to cook the first day or so out. Ocean waves often were biggest in the shallower water near shore.

Even taking a shower could be a time-consuming experience. In most countries showers were provided onshore for boaters. In American Samoa the cruising boaters had erected their own crude shower on shore. They just ran a pipe vertically with a showerhead on it, and built a wooden platform to stand on with wooden walls and a door. There was no roof, so you could see heads protruding out the top and feet at the bottom. Throughout all of the South Pacific and Mexico we had only cold showers.

At sea we were both very active when we were awake. During the day we each took a nap, because of our lack of sleep during the nights. I handled the boat while Vern slept. If the weather was calm at sea and the boat was just sailing along steered by the wind-vane, I could spend quite a bit of time sitting in the cockpit reading, working a crossword puzzle, writing in the log, writing letters, etc.

At night while at sea, life was quite different. In the early evening we always checked into a net on the ham radio. On the long 33-day crossing from Mexico to the Marquesas, I enjoyed tuning into the net and charting our position and the positions of all the other boats that were making the same crossing on our South Pacific Ocean chart.

But for me nighttime was not always pleasant. Many nights were moonless and the sea was rough. When I was on watch and Vern was sleeping, I dreaded having to go on deck and look out. It was hard not to worry about what could be floating out there that we might hit. I always scanned the horizon looking for ships (which we were able to see because of their lights), checked the compass to see if we were on course, glanced at the sails and wind-vane to be sure they were working properly, and then ran back down below as quickly as possible to our cozy cabin, where I felt more secure. This routine was followed every 15 minutes. I was always happy when my watch was over and I could crawl into the bunk and sleep. The second night watch was the worst one for me. Vern would call me around 2:00 a.m. It was so hard to stay awake at that time of night.

However, on a clear, calm, moonless night, sitting in the cockpit was one of my fondest memories. The sky came clear down to the horizon and the stars were so bright and beautiful that it brought tears to my eyes. It was a very emotional experience.

On my watch I tried to handle the boat without waking Vern, but there were times when I had to ask for help. Vern was nice about being awakened, because he knew that I wouldn't wake him unless it was really necessary. On occasions when I saw a ship that appeared to be heading toward us, I followed it on the radar for a while. If it was apparent that it was on a collision course with us and was within four miles, I called Vern to help me decide what to do. We always had success calling the ship on the VHF radio. We made sure that they saw us on their radar and that they would alter their course.

I had an inventory of all of the canned and dried foods (beans, rice, pasta, etc.) aboard. I crossed out cans or dried foods from the list as they were used. This was helpful when it was time to provision for another crossing. Our long crossing across the Pacific was my biggest challenge. We knew it would take us at least a month, so I provisioned for three months in case we were becalmed, broken down, or lost. We bought fresh meat, vegetables, and fruit the last minute before we left a country, but the cans, dried food, paper products, etc., could be obtained earlier in the week. Most of the food was stored in lockers below the dinette seats. Two lockers held canned goods, one held dried foods, and the other locker held paper products and miscellaneous things like cooking oil, peanut butter, jams, etc. The fresh produce was stored in string hammocks that hung from hooks over our heads in the galley, in the dinette, and even above our bunk in the forepeak. We had a refrigerator under the chart table in the saloon area, where some of the produce and meat was kept. Every time we needed something from the refrigerator, we had to clear off the chart table and lift the lid. Since it was a top-loading refrigerator, we had to paw through the things on top to get to the things on the bottom, which was not always convenient, especially in rough seas.

Tainui had a four-burner propane stove with an oven. There was a railing around the stove and potholders called "fiddles" clamped to the railing. However, in rough weather I had to tie pots and pans to the railing with bungee cords. There were times when it was too rough to cook, and on those occasions I sometimes stood and held a coffee pot or a pan on the burner until the food was ready. I could only use one hand on the pan because I had to hold on to the boat with the other hand. We also had a gimbaled single kerosene burner fastened to a bulkhead that I used in heavy weather.

The most interesting cultural experiences we had were when we traveled through Indonesia. During our stay in Malaysia, when Vern was working for the U.S. Peace Corps, we had traveled by airplane and train in Indonesia to Bali and Java. Therefore, when we cruised there, we decided to take a different route. Vern spoke the Indonesian language fluently, which is the same language as Malay, so we decided to travel in the more remote areas. We stopped at several small islands, including Ambon, Tanimbar, and Batakan, and also along the shores of Sulawesi and Borneo. This turned out to be both the most exciting and frustrating part of our whole cruise, for me.

Some metal things broke that needed welding—like an exhaust elbow and the bracket for the alternator, which necessitated finding a village big enough to have a welder. We examined our charts two different times looking for places where we could drop an anchor, reach shore, and look for a welder. I was so thankful that Vern could speak Indonesian. I understand the language but never became fluent at speaking it. These villages were so remote that their inhabitants had never seen a foreign boat. We were surrounded by people everywhere we went and had many visitors coming out to our boat in their small rowboats and canoes. Some would remain on their boats, but others would crawl onto our boat without permission. The problem was that they didn't understand privacy. After they had sat and stared at us for four or five hours, we would ask them to leave because we were going to eat. They would make no move to leave, so finally Vern would just have to order them off the boat. The lack of privacy was really hard on me. They were all men, and I just couldn't handle having them staring at everything we did.

In Batakan we both went ashore to visit the village. In the village, we noticed a house elaborately decorated with palm branches, flowers, and crepe-paper streamers. Before we even got to the house, a crowd of people rushed to us. They grabbed us and pulled us toward the house. They explained that they were having a wedding and they wanted to take a picture of us with the bride. They ushered us to a table in the front yard, and as soon as we sat down, they put a plate of rice with a curried meat sauce on it in front of us. When we finished eating it, they escorted us inside the house to where the bride was sitting on a decorated "throne." We later learned that they believed having their picture taken with Western people brought good luck to the bride and groom. After they took the picture we were free to go.

When we finally got to the west coast of Borneo and sailed 12 miles up the Bandak River to the city of Pontianak, the police insisted that we tie up to the police dock for safety's sake. We appreciated the fact that we were safe there, but the lack of privacy became a real issue here also. People would line up on the dock and stare at our boat; watching every move we made. They would even step on our boat without asking. Vern put a sign written in Indonesian in our window asking them to please ask permission before climbing on our boat. That did help, but one time Vern was in town to buy boat parts and I was on the boat by myself. I decided to take a nap, and I had my back to the companionway entrance when I felt the boat rock. I assumed it was Vern returning. I turned to say something to him and discovered a strange man in the boat. I yelled, "Get off of our boat!" in English as well as Indonesian. He said he just wanted a drink of water. I kept yelling at him until he finally got off the boat. It really scared me. After that I was afraid to stay on the boat alone in Indonesia.

In spite of the lack of privacy, the Indonesian experience was a real highlight of our cruise. We found the people very friendly, and the wonderful experiences outweighed the bad ones.

I did wish at times that I was back home, but rarely. On some of our rough crossings I would wonder why I was doing this. But by the time we arrived in the country we were headed for, I was so excited that all of my homesick feelings were gone. There is nothing that compares with the relief and excitement of arriving at a new country after days or weeks at sea.

We flew home once a year, usually at Christmas time, and spent two months visiting our children and friends. That helped keep me from being homesick. The last two years of our cruise we went home during the summers, which meant that we spent Christmas aboard our boat. Those Christmases were hard for me. We ate our Christmas dinners in nice restaurants in Singapore and Thailand, but I missed our families.

The cruising experience has changed my outlook on life. It was hard to come home and see the greed and wasted wealth in our country after seeing the poverty and corruption that so many people in our world have to live with. I saw schools in Indonesia and the South Pacific that didn't have textbooks. Unfortunately, they weren't teaching in English so used American textbooks would not help them. I saw people living in shacks without running water, electricity, or any furniture. They slept on the floor. They literally had only a roof over their heads. (However, in the cities the Europeans lived in beautiful houses with all of the conveniences.) I saw corrupt government officials and police who required people to pay a bribe before they would help them in any way. Sometimes it was the last dollar they had. The list went on and on. I know that there isn't much I can do for those people, so the only way I can live happily as an American is to get involved in volunteer work with the underprivileged. This is what I have done, and it has helped.

Connie goes forward in her inflatable harness and tether. (above)
View of *Tainui's* galley and dinette looking toward the berth in the bow.
(below)

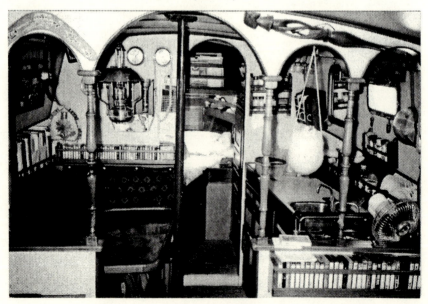

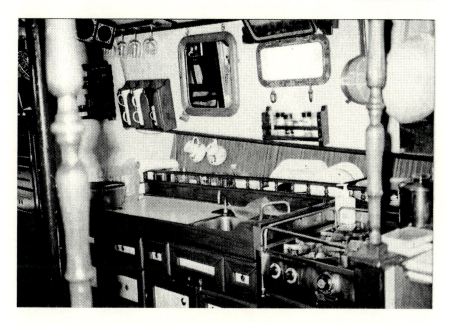

View *of Tainui's* galley.

GLOSSARY

<u>Boat Terms</u>

Line - a piece of rope used for a specific purpose on a boat. On a yacht, lines are never referred to as "ropes."

Halyard - a line run through a pulley up on the mast that is used to pull up the sail.

Sheet - a line run from the back end of a sail to the cockpit that lets out or pulls the sail in.

Whisker pole - a large diameter aluminum pole that hooks unto the mast and holds the jib out to catch the wind from behind for downwind sailing.

Beam - the width of a boat; also: crosswise to the boat. "Wind on the beam" means wind blowing directly into the side of the boat.

Companionway - the entrance to the cabin. Companionway doors open to the companionway stairs that lead from the cockpit down into the cabin.

Cockpit - a rectangular "foot well" just aft of the companionway doors that contains the steering wheel. The crew sits on the edges of the well for trimming the sheets or steering.

Dodger - a canvas or wooden cover attached to a windshield on the cabin top and extending back over the cockpit.

Helm - another term for the ship's wheel

Head - a marine toilet.

Cabin sole - the floor of the cabin.

Lazerette - A large storage hatch below the stern deck that is entered through a hatch near the stern of the vessel.

Hawse pipe - A deck opening near the bow of the boat where the anchor chain comes up out of the chain locker.

Jack lines - Bow to stern lines lying on each side deck to which the tether from our safety harness was clipped whenever we left the cockpit at sea.

VHF radio - a short distance (about 20 miles) radio used for ship to ship communication.

Sat Nav - an early satellite navigation device that gave the boat's position on an irregular basis.

GPS - a satellite navigation device that gives instant, continuous positions with excellent accuracy.

EPIRB (Emergency Position Indicating Radio Beacon) - a hand-held device that sends out a radio beacon to assist search and rescue efforts.

Snubber - a short, springy piece of nylon line hooked across a loop of anchor chain to act as a shock absorber when anchored in rough weather.

Berth - a bed on a boat.

Lee cloth - a canvas rigged from the outside side of a berth to a place overhead to keep a sleeper in the berth.

Forestay – a steel cable that runs from the top of the mast to the tip of the bowsprit and helps support the mast. Jibs or roller furling gear were attached to it and pulled up to the top of the mast.

Sailing Terms

Beat - Sailing on an angle as close to the wind as possible. On *Tainui*, about 50 degrees away from the wind. All sails are pulled in or "**close hauled**" for beating.

Close reach - Sailing a little further off the wind than beating. The sails are let out a little to catch more wind.

Beam reach - Sailing at 90 degrees to the wind. The sails are set at about 45 degrees off the centerline of the vessel. This is a very fast and comfortable point of sailing.

Broad reach - Sailing with the wind coming in at an angle from behind the beam. The sails are let further out. This is the fastest point of sailing for most vessels.

Run - Sailing downwind with the wind coming from directly behind the boat. The sails are pushed out as far as they will go. The wind tends to push the stern from side to side and the boat rolls a lot when sailing downwind.

Wing and wing - A downwind setting of the sails in which the boom holds the mainsail straight out on one side of the vessel and the whisker pole holds the jib straight out on the other side

Roller furling - A device on the forestay that acts like a roll-up window blind for the jib. This makes it possible to roll up or unroll the jib from the cockpit, making it unnecessary to go forward and pull up or take down the jib in the traditional fashion.

Tillermaster electric Autopilot - A device that attaches to the wheel and steers the boat by its internal compass. Used when motoring.

Autohelm wind vane - A device that steers by the wind. It has no compass, but steers by keeping the boat at a constant angle to the wind. Used when under sail.

Reef - Pull portions of the mainsail down and lash them unto the boom to make the mainsail smaller in strong winds.

Tack - Bring the bow across the wind when sailing to windward.

Jibe - Bring the stern across the wind when sailing down wind.

Broach - Slide sideways down the face of a steep wave out of control.

Weather helm - The tendency of a boat to turn into the wind in strong winds.

Raft-up – Tie two or more boats together side by side.

Heave to – Stop the boat at sea with the sails set to keep the bow pointed toward the wind.

TAINUI'S SAIL PLAN

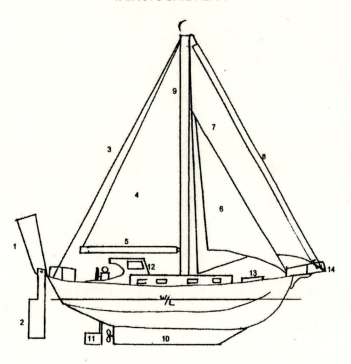

1. Self steering wind vane
2. Self steering rudder
3. Backstay
4. Mainsail
5. Boom
6. Staysail
7. Jib
8. Roller furling gear on forestay
9. Mast
10. Keel
11. Rudder
12. Dodger
13. Forward hatch
14. Bow pulpit
W/L Water Line

Printed in the United States
39967LVS00007B/73-84

9 781420 838183